# Teaching Postcolonial Environmental Literature and Media

# Teaching Postcolonial Environmental Literature and Media

Edited by
**Cajetan Iheka**

Modern Language Association of America
New York                    2022

To order MLA publications, visit mla.org/books. For wholesale and
international orders, see mla.org/Bookstore-Orders.

The MLA office is located on the island known as Mannahatta (Manhattan)
in Lenapehoking, the homeland of the Lenape people. The MLA pays respect
to the original stewards of this land and to the diverse and vibrant Native
communities that continue to thrive in New York City.

Options for Teaching 56
ISSN 1079-2562

Library of Congress Cataloging-in-Publication Data
Names: Iheka, Cajetan Nwabueze, editor.
Title: Teaching postcolonial environmental literature and media /
    edited by Cajetan Iheka.
Description: New York : Modern Language Association of America,
    2022. | Series: Options for teaching, 10792562 ; 56 | Includes
    bibliographical references.
Identifiers: LCCN 2021027824 (print) | LCCN 2021027825 (ebook) |
    ISBN 9781603295536 (hardcover) | ISBN 9781603295543 (paperback) |
    ISBN 9781603295550 (EPUB)
Subjects: LCSH: Ecocriticism—Study and teaching (Higher) |
    Environmental literature—Study and teaching (Higher) | Ecology in
    literature—Study and teaching (Higher) | Nature in literature—Study and
    teaching (Higher) | African literature—Study and teaching (Higher) |
    Latin American literature—Study and teaching (Higher) | East Asian
    literature—Study and teaching (Higher) | Caribbean literature (English)—
    Study and teaching (Higher) | LCGFT: Essays.
Classification: LCC PN98.E36 T43 2022 (print) | LCC PN98.E36 (ebook) |
    DDC 809/.93355—dc23
LC record available at https://lccn.loc.gov/2021027824
LC ebook record available at https://lccn.loc.gov/2021027825

*For Justina Iheka, with everlasting gratitude*

# Contents


Acknowledgments     xi
Foreword     xiii
    Graham Huggan

Introduction     1
    Cajetan Iheka


## Part I:   Background and Theoretical Foundations


Environmental Justice and Postcolonial Ecocriticism     23
    Byron Caminero-Santangelo

Indigenous Cosmologies     32
    Brendon Nicholls

The Queer Ecofeminist Politics of Flora Nwapa's *Efuru*     44
    Laura Wright

Finding Balance: Disability and the Ecocritical Lens     55
    Roanne L. Kantor

Place and Postcolonial Megacities: A Project-Based Approach     68
    Brady Smith


## Part II:   Global Ecologies and Uneven Flows


Decolonizing the Environmental Classroom: Increasing
    Student Agency through a Journal Assignment     81
    Margaret Anne Smith

Teaching Postcolonial Climate Fiction     92
    Nicole Cesare

Toward an Interdisciplinary Symbiosis in Environmental
    Literary Pedagogy     104
    Elaine Savory

## Part III:   Regional and Local Perspectives

Postcolonial Cartographies, Environmental Humanities,
and Sea Level Rise    119
Christina Gerhardt

Decolonial Possibilities in an Introductory Environmental
Humanities Classroom    129
Salma Monani

Ecocriticism and Environmental Justice in Anglophone
Caribbean Literature    141
Supriya M. Nair

Humane Education and Latin American / Latinx
Cultural Production    153
Stacy Hoult-Saros

Teaching East Asian Ecocriticisms    164
Simon C. Estok

## Part IV:   The Lives of Animals

Teaching Multispecies Entanglement    181
Jonathan Steinwand

The Lives of Animals in Postcolonial Cultural Production    198
Amit R. Baishya

Postcolonial Animal Studies: Animal and Animist Codes    210
Jason Price

## Part V:   Extractive Ecologies, Environmental Justice,
and Postcolonial Ecomedia

Examining Speculative Petrofiction through Journaling
and Blogging    227
Rhonda Knight and Mary Laffidy

The Colonial Relation between Digitization and Migration
in Mohsin Hamid's *Exit West*    240
Sofia Ahlberg

For a dEcolonization of the Caribbean: Edouard
  Duval-Carrié's *Imagined Landscapes*    251
  Charly Verstraet

The Visuality of Environmental Disasters    263
  Juan Meneses

*Colonize Mars*: Precolonial Pedagogies for Anticolonial Praxis    273
  Rachel Rochester

Postcolonial Environmental Fiction, Media, and Pedagogy
  in the North of the Global North    284
  Hanna Musiol

Anthropocene Storytelling: Ecological Writing and
  Pedagogies of Planetary Change    298
  Kirk B. Sides and Tjawangwa Dema


## Part VI:  Place-Based Approaches


Ecocriticism in Nigeria: Toward a Transformative Pedagogy    311
  Sule Emmanuel Egya

Postcolonial Environmental Justice and Ken Saro-Wiwa
  in Malaysia    323
  Shalini Nadaswaran

Narrative Close Reading and Land Education:
  "On the Wings of This Prayer" and *Medicine Walk*    333
  Kristin Lucas and Gyllian Phillips

Working with Environmental Justice Organizations
  in Postcolonial Environmental Literature Classes    346
  Sarah Dimick and Cheryl Johnson

Web Resources    357
Notes on Contributors    361

# Acknowledgments

This book was conceived when Gaurav Desai invited me to participate in a roundtable on teaching African environmental literature at the 2018 African Literature Association conference in Washington, DC. I thank Gaurav for the invitation and email exchange that followed and for introducing me to the MLA editor James Hatch. My praise is due to the book's contributors—the best cohort an editor can imagine—for responding to the call for papers and crafting the insightful essays in this volume. I remain in awe of their professionalism and ability to meet deadlines amidst life events and upheavals of a global pandemic. The COVID-19 pandemic did not stop Graham Huggan from writing a thought-provoking foreword reminding us of the important work before us as teachers and scholars in an era of increasing planetary crisis. He earned my lasting respect for this labor and for his groundbreaking contributions to the environmental humanities and to postcolonial studies. The manuscript benefited from the insightful feedback of two anonymous reviewers to whom I am immensely grateful.

I started this project as an employee of the University of Alabama (UA) and completed it on the faculty at Yale. I am grateful to colleagues at both institutions who have supported my endeavors. Lauren Cardon read an early draft of the introduction and offered useful feedback, while Jocelyn Hawley's excellent work as a research assistant at UA improved the manuscript a great deal. My thanks to them, and to Michael Warner and Paul Sabin for stimulating conversations on the environmental humanities at Yale.

My family deserves my appreciation for providing a supportive environment for completing this book: my darling Eve for indulging my escape into intellectual mode and Kamsi for his productive distractions and his insistence that I stop working at 5 p.m. Kenenna joined us midway into the project; his reassuring smile continues to motivate me. I am lucky that I can count on the support of my parents and siblings. My mother, the unsung hero of the family, traveled thousands of miles to help us care for Kenenna. This book would have taken longer to complete without her assistance. I will never be able to repay my debt to Justina Iheka and so dedicate this book to her as token of my everlasting love and gratitude.

# Foreword

Graham Huggan

"The trouble with the Engenglish is that their hiss hiss history happened overseas, so they dodo don't know what it means" are the comically stumbling words of the Indian film producer Whisky Sisodia in Salman Rushdie's now all-but-forgotten 1988 novel *The Satanic Verses* (343). I last taught the novel about twelve or thirteen years ago, shortly after arriving in the United Kingdom. If I were to teach it again now, most of my students wouldn't have been born when it first came out and when the various scandals surrounding it first rose to global prominence—scandals that turned Rushdie into, if not exactly a household name, then certainly the most famous writer-in-hiding of his times.

The times move on, not that we are particularly adept at learning our lessons from them. The postcolonial field—of all fields—should be attentive to history, not least its own, but that is not necessarily the case. As I have argued elsewhere, the field stands most to benefit today by showing greater attention to its own origins—to the anticolonial sentiments that gave rise to it in the first place, and to the contemporaneous liberation struggles to which it gave full-throated support (see Huggan, *Oxford Handbook* and Afterword). Again, though, these historical lessons have not always been learned, and the field's almost legendary self-reflexivity has not always extended to the battles it previously fought—including the fierce institutional battle to legitimize itself.

Today, all the talk is of decolonizing the curriculum, which is as necessary as it ever was but is certainly not a new debate, still less a revolutionary one. Similarly, animated debates about postcolonial pedagogy—"unlearning our privilege as our loss," as Gayatri Spivak puts it—can tend to overlook the fact that Spivak first said this more than thirty years ago (9). Many of the most energetic postcolonial debates at around that time were about pedagogy, following Aruna Srivastava's stern injunction that "postcolonialists must scrutinize the place that pedagogy . . . has in our theorizing of the postcolonial and that we must also write about it, talk about it, deprivatize the almost pathological isolation in which we teach" (13).

This is as true now as it was then, as are at least some of the circumstances surrounding it, such as what Afonso Dias Ramos has recently called "the ongoing row over cultural appropriation, identity politics, political correctness and free speech" (158). "Row" is right, and, as Dias Ramos asks, this and other examples enjoin us to think about how we might "develop periodic outrage into sustained political action," which is very much a question for our times (180; see also Huggan, Afterword). Take the empty moralism that has accompanied such recent media-orchestrated campaigns as Rhodes Must Fall and Why Is My Curriculum White? It's not that these campaigns are not worth pursuing—they definitely are—but they also demonstrate the stranglehold of the media over public discourse in our attention-seeking times. These times, as Richard King perhaps over-dramatically interprets them, are frequently seeing a coming together of "narcissism and allegiance" in which "smug self-righteousness . . . passes for real political engagement," and politics itself risks becoming a "matter not of reasoned argument but of identification," a conspicuous form of virtue signaling in which public opportunities are taken for personal self-display (190–91; see also Huggan, Afterword).

Two points follow from this, both of them as relevant to the environmental field as they are to its postcolonial counterpart, and both more relevant than ever in the wake of what Cajetan Iheka calls, in his excellent introduction to this volume, the ecocritical turn in postcolonial studies. The first is that both fields have been pedagogical from the start and have a great deal to learn from that history. The second is that practitioners in both fields have sometimes tended either to assume that teaching in itself constitutes a form of radical activism or to stray into unnecessary didacticism as a way of justifying this to themselves. Teaching *is* political, and rightly so, but whether teachers of postcolonial and environmental studies are activists seems, to me at least, to be a moot point. Too much has been said, perhaps, about such teachers' "accountability beyond the confines of the classroom" (Sugars 15), too little about the qualities of humility and uncertainty needed to teach effectively in fields whose historical and geographical reach were always likely to exceed their intellectual grasp. The two fields employ an even longer reach, of course, now that their global scope has been fully recognized, while there are additional difficulties attached to their increasing disciplinary range. Studying across the disciplines is hard enough; teaching across them is even more difficult, and both these processes run the risk of diluting hard-won disciplinary knowledge even when the challenges, and the undoubted benefits, of interdisciplinary teaching and learning are provisionally met.

Having said that, teaching is the most valuable thing we postcolonial/environmental scholars do, and certainly far more valuable than the vast majority of our scholarship, which may be democratically inclined but is not always democratically organized, even if its availability and affordability have generally improved since the inception of what most of us now take all too readily for granted, the digital age. The historical divide between cultural analysis and institutional practice may be narrowing for both fields, but there is still some way to go before what Iheka calls "ethico-justice work in the classroom" yields significant dividends in the wider public domain. What can be done is much more modest, it seems to me: a renewed commitment to inclusiveness and widening participation in our universities and schools and a renewed focus on student-centered learning that takes experiential knowledge seriously without using it to replace other forms of epistemic authority, for example, those associated with disciplinary expertise.

Most of us in the Global North are not particularly well equipped to practice a pedagogy of the oppressed when many of our students are just as privileged as we are. That doesn't mean that the moral imperatives of the postcolonial and environmental fields, which have always been closely aligned, are impossible to teach, or that as critical educators we are necessarily compromised in the exercise. What it does mean is that, together with our students, we should resist the temptation to occupy a moral high ground that is always more unstable than it seems. And what it also means is that we should recognize that the collective search for greater equality and justice—the search to which all education worth the name should commit itself—is always over the horizon, its ultimate goals reaching far beyond what we have the physical, mental, and moral capacity to accomplish by ourselves.

## Works Cited

Dias Ramos, Afonso. "From Cecil Rhodes to Emmett Till: Postcolonial Dilemmas in Visual Representation." Kim, pp. 157–87.

Huggan, Graham. Afterword. Kim, pp. 261–67.

———, editor. *The Oxford Handbook of Postcolonial Studies.* Oxford UP, 2013.

Kim, David D., editor. *Reframing Postcolonial Studies: Concepts—Methodologies—Scholarly Activisms.* Palgrave, 2021.

King, Richard. *On Offence: The Politics of Indignation.* Scribe Publications, 2013.

Rushdie, Salman. *The Satanic Verses.* Viking, 1988.

Spivak, Gayatri Chakravorty. *The Post-Colonial Critic: Interviews, Strategies, Dialogues.* Routledge, 1990.

Srivastava, Aruna. "Introductory Notes: Postcolonialism and Its Discontents." *Ariel,* vol. 26, no. 1, 1995, pp. 12–17.

Sugars, Cynthia, editor. *Home-Work: Postcolonialism, Pedagogy, and Canadian Literature.* U of Ottawa P, 2004.

**Cajetan Iheka**

---

# Introduction

Two developments in the second decade of the twenty-first century necessitate a volume on teaching postcolonial environmental literature and media. The first development is the ascendancy of postcolonial ecocriticism, a branch of ecocriticism that addresses the ecological implications of colonialism, neocolonialism, and globalization. The ecocritical turn in postcolonial studies is driven by the inextricability of colonial plundering from environmental conditions in the affected areas, a point that Bonnie Roos and Alex Hunt acknowledge when they assert that "any postcolonial critique must be thoroughly ecocritical at the same time" (3). This ecocritical turn is necessary because colonialism in Africa, Asia, the Caribbean, and other parts of the world entailed resource and mineral extraction, land theft, displacement, and other forms of environmental exploitation. Yet until recently the critical studies brought together under the rubric of postcolonialism did not pay enough attention to the environmental consequences of colonialism and to the threat they posed to Indigenous cosmologies, especially these cosmologies' valuation of human-nonhuman entanglements. Granted, there were some environmental inflections in earlier anticolonial and postcolonial theorizing, especially in the writings of Frantz Fanon and Edward Said, but such musings were marginal to the

1

authors' preoccupations (DeLoughrey and Handley; Wenzel, "Reading Fanon").

The growing body of scholarship devoted to the intersections of post-colonialism and environmentalism in recent years has tried to address this oversight. This corpus has also offered a corrective to mainstream ecocriticism, which, as Elizabeth DeLoughrey and George B. Handley write in *Postcolonial Ecologies: Literatures of the Environment*, "positioned Europe and the United States as the epistemological centers" even when literature from the "global South has contributed to an ecological imaginary and discourse of activism and sovereignty" (8). Ecocriticism in the United States until the 1990s prioritized nature writing and wilderness preservation, the deep ecological perspective characteristic of ecocriticism's first wave. As Ursula Heise explains it, "deep ecology foregrounds the value of nature in and of itself, the equal rights of other species, and the importance of small communities" (507). Deep ecologists found the writings of Henry David Thoreau, Aldo Leopold, and Gary Snyder particularly useful for their core themes—a conscious attachment to place and "a staunch rejection of anthropocentricism" (Hiltner 2).

The deep ecological perspective came under criticism from the environmental historian William Cronon, from feminists, and from scholars working in postcolonial studies for its ahistoricism and for what Lawrence Buell terms its "mystical-holistic dimension" (90). Cronon complicates the narrative of the pristine, untouched wilderness that is the touchstone of deep ecology. Tracing this narrative to the nineteenth century, Cronon recalls the fact that Native Americans have always depended on nature—supposedly pristine—for survival, while reminding readers that the removal of these Indigenous peoples into reservations was indissociable from the movement to set aside wilderness areas and national parks. Feminist thinkers also critique deep ecology's valorization of outdoor pursuits as manly activities and its ascription of femininity to the land. Postcolonial ecocritics have since joined Cronon and these feminist thinkers in emphasizing the social and cultural processes that enabled deep ecology. Whereas Cronon implicates deep ecology in the dispossession of Native Americans, and feminists deconstruct its masculinist foundation, postcolonial ecocritics demonstrate how first-wave ecocriticism was complicit in colonial violence.

In their introduction to *Postcolonial Ecocriticism: Literature, Animals, Environment*, Graham Huggan and Helen Tiffin write that postcolonial ecocriticism, as a manifestation of social ecology, investigates "the colonial/

imperial underpinnings of environmental practices" and "opens up for contemplation . . . how the real world might be transformed" (3, 13). In addition to *Postcolonial Ecocriticism* and *Postcolonial Ecologies*, other books have recently contributed to the field within both regional and global frames. Regional approaches include *Caribbean Literature and the Environment: Between Nature and Culture*, edited by DeLoughrey, Renée K. Gosson, and Handley; and Handley's *New World Poetics: Nature and the Adamic Imagination of Whitman, Neruda, and Walcott*, on Caribbean environmental imaginaries. Karen Thornber's *Ecoambiguity* focuses on East Asian environmental literature, while Byron Caminero-Santangelo's *Different Shades of Green* and Cajetan Iheka's *Naturalizing Africa: Ecological Violence, Agency, and Postcolonial Resistance in African Literature* exemplify an African regional frame. On a global scale, Rob Nixon's *Slow Violence and the Environmentalism of the Poor* stands out for its examination of literature from different parts of the world through the lens of environmental degradation and for its recalibration of environmental time and violence. *Ecocriticism of the Global South*, edited by Scott Slovic, Swarnalatha Rangarajan, and Vidya Sarveswaran, features the work of scholars mostly living and working in postcolonial environments across the world, thereby bringing their perspectives to international attention. Jennifer Wenzel builds on these works with *The Disposition of Nature*, in which she reorients understandings of world literature by investigating how literature and film, especially from Africa and South Asia, imagine the planet.

These studies have effectively enunciated how postcolonial writings have grappled with environmental disasters; however, none of them explores teaching postcolonial environmental texts, which brings me to the second factor that necessitates this collection. The advent of postcolonial ecocriticism coincided with the push for a diverse curriculum in English departments and the broader humanities across Europe and America. As scholarship in postcolonial ecocriticism drew renewed attention to the works of a broad range of writers, including Derek Walcott, Wangari Maathai, Ishimure Michiko, and Jamaica Kincaid, instructors were also seeking opportunities to broaden the range of works they were teaching in response to the demand for a diversified curriculum. Students were demanding not only geographic diversity but also thematic diversity that reflected their experiences and needs. The environmental crisis was a natural fit because of its pressing relevance and its global dimension—hence, there was a surge in courses devoted to ecology.

These eco-themed courses have been brought together under the rubric of environmental humanities, whose mission Greg Garrard describes as the "historicization of ecology and the ecologization of history" (*Oxford Handbook* 3). While the humanities in general have seen some pushback and even financial contraction because of their alleged inability to help solve the biggest challenges we face today, the environmental humanities continue to gain in popularity within the United States and abroad. Environmental humanities institutes are also proliferating across Europe, America, Asia, and Africa, funded by prestigious donor bodies such as the Mellon Foundation. The increasing popularity of the environmental humanities—evident in the increasing number of courses, centers, and institutes devoted to them, as well as funding opportunities for studies in the field—buttresses a recognition that they have a crucial role to play in addressing the problem of climate change (Emmett and Nye 2).

Robert S. Emmett and David E. Nye consider the environmental humanities "a global intellectual movement that reconceives the relationship between scientific and technical disciplines and the humanities, which are essential to understanding and resolving dilemmas that have been created by industrial society" (4). The interaction between the sciences and the humanities that takes place under the rubric of the environmental humanities recognizes that technical questions are embedded in sociocultural and historical contexts. As Serpil Oppermann and Serenella Iovino explain it, "environmental problems are not the concerns of Earth scientists only. They are also social and cultural, philosophical and political, as their insidious signals of precariousness and risks have long extended into the social sphere" (2).

Environmental humanists recognize the classroom as a site for engaging the social dimensions of environmental sciences and technologies. DeLoughrey and Handley, for example, underscore the value of the inexact interpretations of the humanities at a time when many conclusions of indisputable science have turned out to be incorrect. For these authors, we "need to put more faith in the performance of such inexact sciences as listening, interpretation, reading, and ethics" as we work to confront the global climate challenges of the twenty-first century (34–35). The classroom is suited for the critical reading and writing that DeLoughrey and Handley endorse. Stephen Siperstein, Shane Hall, and Stephanie LeMenager, the editors of *Teaching Climate Change in the Humanities*, observe that "teaching climate change in the humanities, with attention to representations and mediations, histories and ethics, material artifacts and cultural forms, can push us through despair, perhaps, and toward the social practice of caring . . . [and] compel us to place questions of justice and of collective survival at the forefront of our thinking" (8–9).

Postcolonial texts from across the world often aid ethico-justice work in the classroom. These texts have become popular for many reasons, including the fact that they originate from sites of egregious ecological disasters and injustices. One can think of the Bhopal gas leak at the Union Carbide plant in India in December 1984, represented in narratives such as Indra Sinha's *Animal's People*, or of the ecological degradation from oil pollution in the Niger Delta that led to the martyrdom of the environmental activist and writer Ken Saro-Wiwa. Saro-Wiwa was hanged in November 1995 by Nigeria's military government for his sustained activism against the exploitation of the Ogonis and their land by Shell's oil-exploration activities. Tanure Ojaide's poetry and Helon Habila's *Oil on Water* are some examples of Niger Delta petroliterature. Taken together, the growing interest in postcolonial ecologies and the demand for a diversified curriculum addressing social concerns, including the climate crisis, make this book a crucial contribution to the environmental humanities.

## Postcolonial Scopes

Postcolonialism "bears witness to the unequal and uneven forces of cultural representation involved in the contest for political and social authority within the modern world order" (Bhabha 245). This contest took place in the environment of the colonized, whose values and ways of being were denigrated in order to uphold the superiority of the colonizer. The denigrated values include the environmental cosmologies of various Indigenous communities in Africa, in the Americas, and elsewhere. Many of these communities uphold relationality as an epistemology and social praxis, recognizing the imbrication of humans with various aspects of the environment. Juan Carlos Galeano's documentary film *El rio* captures one such entanglement—the relationship between Indigenous people inhabiting the Peruvian Amazon and their land. Across Africa, there is a widespread recognition of interdependence between humans and nonhumans as well as attribution of sacred status to nonhumans, a practice that Harry Garuba dubs "animist materialism" (268).

However, colonial modernity worked hard to discredit these knowledge systems as indicators of primitivity. Promoting what Val Plumwood calls "hyperseparation" between humans and nonhumans as a sign of modernity and enlightenment (49) and what Cheryll Glotfelty terms the "dualisms prevalent in Western thought" (xxiv), colonial systems institutionalized an anthropocentric bias as the basis of what it means to be human, eliding humble forms of human subjectivity more cognizant of ecological entanglement. The humans in these colonized spaces were not spared, as they too were summarily dismissed as nonhuman animals or reduced to inferior humans in need of civilizing through the colonial project. Ironically, in the context of the climate crisis precipitated by unsustainable levels of consumption, many now recommend turning to Indigenous cosmologies for an alternative conception of nature, one that is antithetical to the notion of human superiority. The resurgence of interest in these cosmologies is registered in literary and media texts informed by site-specific land ethics. Scholarship on ecological entanglement oriented around Indigenous cosmologies has also gained a foothold, reflecting renewed interest in animism and the study of what Marisol de la Cadena calls "earth beings."

In a move that shifts the center away from the West to foreground the pluriverse of worldviews, this scholarship performs the "epistemic disobedience" that Walter Mignolo ascribes to decolonial thought (2). This disobedience constitutes a refusal to respect hierarchical valuation of knowledge in the current world order, one that places Western thought and the human at the top of the epistemic ladder. Eliminating this epistemic hierarchy, so that humans are seen to exist alongside other beings in the ecosystem, and foregrounding other modes of knowing, decolonial scholars push against the colonizing tendencies of Western Man with his pretensions to superiority and technological advancement. For decolonial thinkers, "master paradigms are just . . . options dressed with universal clothes" (1). Decolonial ideas, as they coalesce in Mignolo's writings and those of Sabelo Ndlovu-Gatsheni and Aníbal Quijano, have become attractive to postcolonial ecocritics who see their potential for transforming mainstream environmental thought by removing its Western bias. Many of this book's contributors deploy aspects of decolonial thought, including its critique of what Sylvia Wynter terms the "coloniality of being" and its election of a liberating impulse oriented around "a freedom to choose between various cultural orientations," in their teaching epistemologies (Quijano 32).

The inequality characterizing the valuation of various cultural orientations around the globe has material consequences. In Latin America, for instance, the displacement of Indigenous worldviews was accompanied by land dispossession as well as toxic infringement of human and nonhuman bodies (Ybarra; Wald et al.). Many of the writers brought together in *The Latin American Ecocultural Reader* concentrate on the material, environmental implications of colonialism and neocolonialism in the region (French and Heffes). Fanon, among others, eloquently critiques the plundering of African colonies by European powers. Under the watch of Kind Leopold II of Belgium, for instance, the extraction of rubber from forests in colonial Congo led to the maiming and killing of millions of locals, and deforestation and the loss of wildlife to the ivory and animal-skin trade left African spaces impoverished not only economically but also in terms of biodiversity (Bales 12–46).

Unfortunately, the official end of colonialism did not fulfill the promise of independence as envisaged by the nationalists. Fanon's admonition that the national bourgeoisie is inept, only interested in replacing the colonizer as exploiter, should guide our understanding of postindependence realities and the disillusionment that followed the process of failed decolonization. Formerly colonized countries of the Global South, including those in Africa, Asia, Latin America, and the Caribbean, remain trapped in underdevelopment. Some aspects of these countries' lagging development are traceable back to slavery, the rest to colonialism and more contemporary forms of neocolonial relations that leave these countries vulnerable to the imperial designs of the United States and European countries, as well as to those of multinational and transnational organizations such as the World Bank and the International Monetary Fund.

The Global South has been racked with environmental consequences of development and modernity, like the Minamata disaster in Japan, in which mercury was released for years into the groundwater by the Chisso Corporation, and the pollution caused by oil spills in the Niger Delta. Some of these spaces have seen the displacement of Indigenous communities and ways of knowing to make way for development. Postcolonial literary and media productions have grappled with forms of what Nixon terms "slow violence," including the environmental injustices committed against migrant farmworkers in Helena Maria Viramontes's *Under the Feet of Jesus*, land dispossession due to colonialism in Ngũgĩ wa Thiong'o's *Weep Not Child*, deforestation and privatization of the commons in Wangari Maathai's *Unbowed*, ecological fallout of modernization in Ishimure Michiko's *Lake of Heaven* and Indra Sinha's *Animal's People*, and touristic exploitation of Caribbean landscapes in Derek Walcott's *Omeros* and Jamaica Kincaid's *A Small Place*. To think of these texts as grappling with exploitation does not render the inhabitants of these spaces passive victims. Many of these artifacts, including documentary films such as Stephanie Black's *Life and Debt*, on the consequences of neoliberalism in Jamaica, and Franck Bieleu's *The Big Banana*, on large-scale agriculture in Cameroon, depict the resistance of the local people to exploitation, what Ramachandra Guha and Joan Martinez Alier describe as the "environmentalism of the poor" (18).

If Britain, France, and Portugal were at the forefront of colonialism until World War II, the ascendance of the United States as a global hegemon following the war has significantly altered the economic cartography of the world. The successive waves of independence across the world, beginning with India in 1947 and through the 1960s and 1970s across Africa, allowed renewed exploitation that coalesced under the guise of globalization since the 1980s. Globalization's proponents have celebrated the flow of goods and culture, as well as the liberalization of trade, across national territories. The gains touted by the proponents of globalization have, however, skipped many parts of the Global South that remain steeped in poverty and rife with social conflict. The Africanist anthropologist James Ferguson has written of the "hopping" of global finance, which skips most parts of Africa while shuttling between enclaves of wealth on the continent and centers of finance in Europe and America (38). Ferguson may be speaking of Africa, but his thesis is applicable to other parts of the world, like the Jamaica that Black's film represents, where only a tiny elite and their Western collaborators reap the benefits of global trade. Sinha's *Animal's People* suggests that the Indian context is not especially different. In his novel, the masses are left to endure poverty and the psychological, social, and health implications of toxic contamination while local politicians conspire with the culpable multinational corporation to downplay the impact of the chemical disaster, benefitting from what Naomi Klein terms "disaster capitalism." In all these countries, the elite class receives monetary compensation for betraying their people while their Western backers, often located in the United States, maximize profit without suffering the consequences of their actions in far-flung places.

The United States' imperial power certainly reaches across the world, but the damage it has inflicted began within the country's borders, in its history of decimating and displacing the original inhabitants of the land and of subjugating African Americans since their forced migration as enslaved people, and it continues in its treatment of recent immigrants. In *The Environmental Justice Reader: Politics, Poetics, and Pedagogy*, Joni

Adamson, Mei Mei Evans, and Rachel Stein detail the environmental injustices ensuing from the "disproportionate incidence of environmental contamination in communities of the poor and/or communities of color" in the United States (4). Scholars have also documented the "historical marginalization of Latinx communities" in the United States and their "experience of being exploited alongside the land through the processes of colonization and present-day coloniality and ongoing neoliberal abstraction" (Wald et al. 3). The United States may be a colonizing force in the world, but within its borders are communities still grappling with the *longue durée* of colonial dispossession and exploitation. These communities have much in common with formerly colonized peoples of the Global South, yet there is little attempt to bring them together in the environmental humanities. The authors in the present volume take seriously Nixon's recommendation that we study American minority literatures together with conventionally understood postcolonial literature in ecocriticism (256).

Consequently, this volume embraces an expanded sense of the postcolonial, which also reaches out to colonized spaces in the Global North, especially in North America where there are well-demonstrated cases of the colonization and displacement of, and commission of slow violence against, Indigenous communities. The volume is equally inspired by recent scholarship that has sought to interpret Native American, Latin American and Latinx, and African American literatures from a postcolonial perspective (Cheyfitz; Singh and Schmidt). Well-documented cases of environmental racism, like siting toxic waste nearby or in impoverished communities of color and the recent lead poisoning of the water in Flint, a predominantly black community in Michigan, show that micronations within powerful countries are not altogether immune to the exploitative practices that constitute daily life in the postcolony. This volume adopts a broad definition of *postcolonial* that accommodates not only areas of the Global South usually associated with the term but also Global North locales subject to environmental degradation resulting from their country's previous or ongoing colonial transgressions. Despite the shortcomings of the term *postcolonialism*, it is useful for its critical edge and its ability to account for the multivalent dimensions of colonialism's afterlives (McClintock). Contributors to this volume recognize the power differentials that continue to haunt formerly colonized places and their tethering to "Empire," Michael Hardt and Antonio Negri's term for the governmental and nongovernmental organizations that control global capital and structure the world order.

Considering disjunctures between centers of global capital and the postcolonial cartographies being mapped in this book, we must qualify the idea that humans have become significant geological actors. Paul J. Crutzen and Eugene F. Stoermer coined the term *Anthropocene* to name a geological epoch that began after the eighteenth century wherein humans have significantly altered climatic conditions through industrialization and massive burning of fossil fuel. For Dipesh Chakrabarty, with the onslaught of the Anthropocene, human history has become inseparable from natural history (201). While the concept is useful for comprehending the causes of the climate crisis, it does not rigorously differentiate between the humans—mostly in the Global North—whose consumption patterns are primarily responsible for the problem and those in the Global South, many of whom are already suffering the impacts of the Anthropocene: drought, famine, and rising sea levels, to mention just a few. A postcolonial perspective on the Anthropocene demands a consideration of the disproportionate distribution of ecological risks, to the detriment of developing countries and minority communities in the advanced countries of the western hemisphere. Our classrooms need to reflect that disparity as a crucial matter of intellectual and pedagogical action.

By foregrounding pedagogical practices and by including understudied environmental media, *Teaching Postcolonial Environmental Literature and Media* sets itself apart from other studies that have engaged the broader postcolonial landscape. The present volume will address the geographic and thematic limits of existing scholarship by reflecting recent ecocritical trends and their implications for pedagogical scholarship and practices. While some of this existing scholarship is tilted in favor of certain regions or topics, this volume aims for a more comprehensive coverage. It builds on the MLA volume *Teaching North American Environmental Literature*, edited by Laird Christensen, Mark C. Long, and Fred Waage; Greg Garrard's *Teaching Ecocriticism and Green Cultural Studies*; and *Teaching Climate Change in the Humanities*. While the MLA volume's multicultural approach to American literature is exemplary, the absence of postcolonial texts warrants the publication of a collection with non-Western inflections. Although the more recent *Teaching Ecocriticism* and *Teaching Climate Change* include a few chapters with postcolonial inclinations, there remains a pressing need for a volume devoted especially to looking at literary and other cultural media through a postcolonial lens. This book also expands the perspective of media studies focused on the environment, which hardly engage with postcolonial sites and do not concern themselves with teaching-related questions. In this respect, the present volume builds on Sean Cubitt's *EcoMedia* and Stephen Rust, Salma Monani, and Cubitt's *Ecomedia: Key Issues*.

*Teaching Postcolonial Environmental Literature and Media* addresses the identified gaps in the scholarship while providing scholars and teachers, many of whom have no significant experience of postcolonial cultures, with resources to make their teaching effective and inspiring. The inclusion in this book of media other than literature is a nod to the proliferation of films, music, photography, and other artistic productions on the environment and the use of these materials in courses in the humanities and social sciences. The collection of essays will appeal to teachers incorporating literary writings and other media not only into literature courses but also into courses in philosophy, Africana studies, Asian studies, sociology, and history, as well as courses that fulfill general-education requirements.

## Organization of the Book

*Teaching Postcolonial Environmental Literature and Media* comes at an important time, when we are grappling not only with the environmental crisis but also with the crisis in the humanities, and when administrators, faculty members, and parents are paying fresh attention to teaching effectiveness and high-impact learning. The essays that follow keep these issues in mind as they reflect on pedagogical challenges and tools, such as introductory materials, theoretical resources, contextual scaffolding, classroom activities, and student assessment. Their authors, who range from more experienced instructors to recent entrants into the profession, are all armed with the most innovative theoretical toolkit for recalibrating teaching and learning to meet the demands of the present and future.

The volume is divided into six parts. In the first, "Background and Theoretical Foundations," Byron Caminero-Santangelo, Brendon Nicholls, Laura Wright, Roanne L. Kantor, and Brady Smith ground postcolonial ecocriticism in the historical and theoretical issues animating the field. Caminero-Santangelo historicizes and theorizes the environmental justice approach and its usefulness for teaching postcolonial environmental texts. Positing the indispensability of environmental justice to postcolonial ecocriticism, Caminero-Santangelo demonstrates the link between the activism at the heart of environmental justice and the consciousness-raising for social transformation that grounds postcolonial texts. Postcolonial ecocriticism often ties environmental justice concerns to Indigenous cosmologies. This move is partly precipitated by the climate crisis and the turn to Indigenous knowledge by artists intent on showcasing alternative conceptions of land and broader ecosystems and away from the mercantile and commodifying impulses of the dominant capitalist regime. Brendon Nicholls addresses Indigenous cosmologies, using cultural production informed by Maori worldviews to explicate their relational philosophy, visions of sustainability, and pedagogical import.

Like Nicholls, Wright explores the subject of human-nonhuman entanglement but with attentiveness to gender and sexuality. Wright demonstrates how postcolonial texts such as Flora Nwapa's *Efuru* (1966), the first novel published by a Nigerian woman, can be productively taught at the intersection of queer theory, ecofeminism, and postcolonialism while signaling that her pedagogical goals include helping students "understand that sexualities—as well as environmental histories and ecological tragedies—vary from culture to culture and are impacted by the colonial politics that have shaped both landscapes and peoples." In her essay, Kantor eloquently brings together two areas that ought to be studied jointly more often, especially in the context of teaching: disability and ecocriticism. Centered around a course called Disability and World Literature, which she has taught at Brandeis, Harvard, and Stanford, Kantor's essay shows the connection between ecological risk and disability in the Global South. Focusing especially on Sinha's *Animal's People* and Rohinton Mistry's *A Fine Balance*, Kantor reveals the complex relations among geopolitics, health, and the environment while raising pedagogical questions that should concern would-be teachers of these texts about the connections between disability and the environment.

Concluding the first section, Brady Smith's contribution asks what it means to teach place in the context of megacities, shifting place-based thinking away from the rural. Sketching some ways of using Nnedi Okorafor's *Lagoon* to teach place and postcolonial megacities, Smith illuminates the value of project-based learning for postcolonial urban epistemologies. His essay demonstrates that urban settings can be significant sites for environmental justice activism and can help transform student understanding of nature and place.

The global dimensions of the topics and texts examined in the first section become the major organizing logic for the essays in part 2, "Global Ecologies and Uneven Flows." This section proceeds from the understanding that the planetary dimension of climate change requires transnational and transregional responses. Another motivating factor is that many environmental humanities courses are organized around the global category. Given that the broad classification of courses often falls within the neoliberal logic underpinning university governance, how can we appropriate the global, in our pedagogical practice, without being caught in the market-economy trap? Many of the contributors to this section address this challenge while explaining their choices of texts and methodologies, along with the pedagogical pitfalls and successes of these choices.

Addressing a theoretical issue—decolonizing the classroom—and drawing its pedagogical materials from across the globe, Margaret Anne Smith's essay bridges the first and second sections. Her work takes up the teaching methods, including principles of active and experiential learning, as well as the assessment methods that are activated in teaching ecological literacy with texts by Indigenous, African American, and Caribbean writers. The provocative questions animating Smith's essay include, "How . . . can students best decide for themselves how to learn and how to demonstrate their learning to themselves and to me—the one assigned the nebulous task of grading them? How can I structure a course to optimize student discovery and simultaneously 'get out of the way' so that students are establishing and meeting their own learning criteria instead of mine?"

Equally foregrounding student learning, Nicole Cesare elucidates the process of creating and teaching an upper-level undergraduate course titled Global South Climate Fiction. Cesare argues that this fiction, which is set in places where climate change has already arrived—reshaping coastlines, destabilizing ecosystems, and uprooting human and nonhuman communities—gives students the opportunity to gain and create knowledge from an engagement with the political and aesthetic functions of literature. Elaine Savory discusses another idea of the global, embodied by a lecture course anchored in literary studies with guest lecturers from various disciplines with a shared interest in environmental studies, including chemistry, biology, design, religious studies, and history. Her essay describes the pedagogical payoff of this form of team teaching, including the enhanced educational experience yielded by the symbiotic multidisciplinary-interdisciplinary approach, in which insights from respective fields enrich course content and maximize student learning. The essay also provides a model for bridging the humanities-STEM divide in the classroom.

While a universal approach to environmental texts is indeed appropriate for tackling large-scale problems such as climate change, there is also value in underscoring regional perspectives. DeLoughrey and Handley's admonition that postcolonial ecocriticism should find ways "to speak in ethical terms about the global and the local without reducing difference" is a guiding principle of the third cluster, which brings together essays on texts from conventionally understood postcolonial regions and essays on literature from marginal communities in the Americas (25). Christina Gerhardt opens part 3 of the volume, "Regional and Local Perspectives," with a discussion of her course Postcolonial Cartographies, Environmental Humanities, and Sea Level Rise, which educates students on the effects of climate change on low-lying islands in the Pacific, including the Hawaiian Islands, and their inhabitants' struggle to address the problem. Gerhardt's essay—like her class—is designed around mapping: it compares precolonial, colonial, and postcolonial maps of the Pacific, considers countermapping strategies, and explores the significance of the different modes of cartography for transforming students' environmental knowledge and inspiring their participation in the quest for environmental justice. The transformative ambition and concern for justice motivating Gerhardt's class and essay are also central to Salma Monani's essay, which focuses on a module introducing students to Indigenous decolonial concerns. Describing her teaching approaches and text selection, Monani concludes that the module is useful for challenging students' resistance to the value of stories in environmental decision-making and exposing students to the ethics and consequences of settlers' colonial activities.

Supriya M. Nair's essay contends that the Caribbean is a particularly significant region for environmental pedagogies. Providing a historical background that locates issues of land, settlement, colonialism, and sovereignty at the heart of the region and its literature, Nair discusses the thematic preoccupations of important Caribbean writers and texts, her approach to selecting and teaching them, and her writing assignments. Stacy Hoult-Saros's essay focuses on the use of Latin American and Latinx cultural productions to underscore humane education, as theorized in Zoe Weil's *The World Becomes What We Teach*. Hoult-Saros emphasizes the importance of humane education for understanding and addressing environmental issues and argues that cultural artifacts from poetry to film to self-portraits can motivate students to develop a deeper knowledge of the colonial legacy shaping nature-culture interactions in Latin America.

Simon C. Estok's essay on the unique colonial and postcolonial coloration of nature-culture interactions in East Asia concludes this section. Estok ponders the heterogeneity of the region and the linguistic challenges that have rendered many of its important texts inaccessible to anglophone readers. According to Estok, the central issue animating environmental writing from the region is the rapid transformation of the environment due to industrialization and modernization. He concludes that in courses devoted to East Asian ecocriticism, "it is not only heterogeneous development patterns, histories, religions, relations of people with each other and the land, and language, but also diet, sexuality, and indigeneity that need to be on the radar in the classroom."

While the socioenvironmental inclination of postcolonial ecocriticism means that its scholarship has primarily focused on the human condition, interest is increasing in animals, their victimhood in a late-capitalist dispensation of commodifying bodies, and their status in Indigenous cosmologies that offer alternative modalities of human-animal relationships (see Woodward; Huggan and Tiffin; Iheka). The essays in part 4, "The Lives of Animals," probe facets of postcolonial zoocriticism, "concerned not just with animal representation but also with animal rights" (Huggan and Tiffin 18); the politics of framing animals in relation to humans; and conservation ethics. The essays in this section, by Jonathan Steinwand, Amit R. Baishya, and Jason Price, examine the conjunctions of the human and animal; the relations among anthropocentricism, anthropomorphism, and zoomorphism; and the pedagogical challenges of teaching about animals through a postcolonial lens in Western settings. These essays are offered with the conviction "that the ecocritical classroom can be an ideal place to discuss—and work towards—the return of the animal" as well as the ability of animals to flourish alongside humans (Welling and Kapel 104).

The first two essays in part 5, "Extractive Ecologies, Environmental Justice, and Postcolonial Ecomedia," examine the textual forms responding to the dirty extractive processes involved in the quest for minerals and fossil fuel in the Global South. In the first, Rhonda Knight and Mary Laffidy reflect on student writing in the petrofiction unit of a class on postcolonial speculative literature. Knight and Laffidy's instructor-student collaboration offers a unique opportunity to examine student writing and digital enunciations for their value for ecoliteracy and cultivating global citizens. Sofia Ahlberg's essay details the use of Mohsin Hamid's *Exit West* to teach the theme of energy extraction and consumption. Ahlberg discusses her use of literary didactics to challenge teachers in training to trace the energy costs of their media use as a consciousness-raising strategy. Ahlberg's class, offered in the English department at Sweden's Uppsala University, addresses the unequal distribution of toxic wastes from digital processes and the fact that postcolonial sites ultimately bear the cost of these processes.

The literary bias in the study of postcolonial environmental humanities does not correlate with teaching environments, where films, photography, paintings, and other visual media are routinely incorporated into the curriculum. Attending to what W. J. T. Mitchell terms the "pictorial turn" (9), Charly Verstraet focuses on how to use art to teach environmental themes, and Juan Meneses addresses the teaching of the continuities between image and text as well as the challenges of addressing visuality in the environmental classroom. Rachel Rochester discusses the intricate process of creating her digital platform *Colonize Mars*—part adventure novel, part nonfiction, and part video game—as well as its success as a tool for teaching postcolonial environmental humanities, while Hanna Musiol outlines transdisciplinary mixed-media courses, developed at the Norwegian University of Science and Technology. Musiol articulates the benefits and challenges of a unique pedagogical approach that traverses learning spaces and disciplines by bringing together literary texts, art installations, and visiting speakers including artists and local refugee academics. She highlights the innovative use of postcolonial texts for decolonizing the curriculum and the Norwegian space. This section of the volume closes with an essay by the literary scholar Kirk B. Sides and the poet Tjawangwa Dema on their collaborative academic-creative writing workshops on planetary change, which draw from a range of media, including poetry, film, and video. Exploring what they term "Anthropocene storytelling," Sides and Dema probe planetary problems from scholarly and creative perspectives, identifying intellectual promiscuity, transdisciplinarity, and multimodality as the pedagogical principles of their collaborative endeavor.

Teaching does not happen in a vacuum but is shaped by locational and institutional factors. As Garrard puts it in the introduction to *Teaching Ecocriticism*, "literatures . . . look quite different when the environs of the classroom are allowed to register within it" (5). The essays in the final section, "Place-Based Approaches," are concerned with the dynamics of teaching environmental works in specific places. From Sule Emmanuel Egya's discussion of a transformative pedagogy connecting ecowritings to the world through excursions and other experiential activities in Nigeria to Shalini Nadaswaran's essay on teaching the work of the Nigerian ecomartyr Ken Saro-Wiwa in Malaysia, the contributors balance the imperatives of their content with the exigencies of their locational contexts. Critics often lament the neglect of literariness and form when ecocritics read texts as transparent social documents, which makes Kristin Lucas and Gyllian Phillips's focus on close reading as a method for teaching land narratives at Canada's Nipissing University a welcome addition to this section.

In "Teaching the Postcolonial/Ecocritical Dialogue," an essay in *Teaching Ecocriticism and Green Cultural Studies,* Erin James grapples with the "pedagogical challenge of asking students to engage with potentially unfamiliar terrains, languages, and customs" of postcolonial spaces. How, she asks, "do you ask students in Nevada to approach the Sundarbans in Ghosh's novel?" (64–65). An experiential-learning approach that uses resources from the institution's locality can help bridge the gap between contexts of postcolonial literature and pedagogical venues in the West. Sarah Dimick and Cheryl Johnson, in their essay in this volume, emphasize the value of such experiential learning in a Northwestern University literature course on environmental justice. Connecting industrial toxicity in the Global South to toxicity in the South Side of Chicago, Dimick and Johnson argue that courses that include visits to local sites allow students to reflect on their positionality and the ethics of toxic tourism. In their contribution, Dimick, the instructor of the course, and Johnson, the executive director of People for Community Recovery, make a case for the pedagogical value of partnerships between postcolonial-literature classes and local environmental justice organizations.

*Teaching Postcolonial Environmental Literature and Media* concludes with a list of web resources that will help instructors refine and sharpen their pedagogies and deepen students' engagement with ecological complexities in the classroom and beyond. As an example of Timothy Morton's "hyperobjects," which defy easy narrativization and comprehension, the climate crisis demands the kind of multimedia and multisensory interventions that this volume advocates. Positive learning outcomes depend on teachers bringing the multimodality already characterizing students' social habits and networks into the formal curriculum. At the very least, courses that incorporate a range of media can offer the kind of "visual field trips" that enable students to "appreciate the setting" of postcolonial texts (James 69). This book is offered with the conviction that courses in the environmental humanities are crucial avenues for cultivating the critical thinking, reading, and writing skills undergirding humanistic disciplines alongside the ethical values necessary for admirable ecological citizenship in a time of climate change. This ethics-informed citizenship demands an engagement with the local alongside an awareness of and sensitivity to other parts of the world, especially those in the postcolonial regions discussed in the following pages.

## Works Cited

Adamson, Joni, et al. "Introduction: Environmental Justice Politics, Poetics, and Pedagogy." *The Environmental Justice Reader: Politics, Poetics, and Pedagogy*, edited by Adamson et al., U of Arizona P, 2002, pp. 3–14.

Bales, Kevin. *Blood and Earth: Modern Slavery, Ecocide, and the Secret to Saving the World*. Spiegel and Grau, 2016.

Bhabha, Homi. *The Location of Culture*. Routledge, 1994.

*The Big Banana*. Directed by Frank Bieleu, ArtMattan, 2011.

Buell, Lawrence. "Ecocriticism: Some Emerging Trends." *Qui Parle: Critical Humanities and Social Sciences*, vol. 19, no. 2, 2011, pp. 87–115.

Caminero-Santangelo, Byron. *Different Shades of Green: African Literature, Environmental Justice, and Political Ecology*. U of Virginia P, 2014.

Chakrabarty, Dipesh. "The Climate of History: Four Theses." *Critical Inquiry*, vol. 35, no. 2, 2009, pp. 197–222.

Cheyfitz, Eric. "The (Post)colonial Predicament of Native American Studies." *Interventions*, vol. 4, 2002, pp. 405–27.

Christensen, Laird, et al., editors. *Teaching North American Environmental Literature*. Modern Language Association of America, 2008.

Cronon, William. "The Trouble with Wilderness; or, Going Back to the Wrong Nature." *Environmental History*, vol. 1, no. 1, 1996, pp. 7–28.

Crutzen, Paul J., and Eugene F. Stoermer. "The 'Anthropocene.'" *Global Change Newsletter*, no. 41, 2000, pp. 17–18.

Cubitt, Sean. *EcoMedia*. Rodopi, 2005.

de la Cadena, Marisol. *Earth Beings: Ecologies of Practice across Andean Worlds*. Duke UP, 2015.

DeLoughrey, Elizabeth, and George B. Handley. "Toward an Aesthetics of the Earth." *Postcolonial Ecologies: Literatures of the Environment*, edited by DeLoughrey and Handley, Oxford UP, 2011, pp. 3–42.

DeLoughrey, Elizabeth, et al., editors. *Caribbean Literature and the Environment: Between Nature and Culture*. U of Virginia P, 2005.

Emmett, Robert S., and David E. Nye. *The Environmental Humanities: A Critical Introduction*. MIT Press, 2017.

Fanon, Frantz. *The Wretched of the Earth*. Grove Press, 1963.

Ferguson, James. *Global Shadows: Africa in the Neoliberal World Order*. Duke UP, 2006.

French, Jennifer, and Gisela Heffes, editors. *The Latin American Ecocultural Reader*. Northwestern UP, 2020.

Garrard, Greg. Introduction. Garrard, *Teaching Ecocriticism*, pp. 1–10.

———. Introduction. *The Oxford Handbook of Ecocriticism*, edited by Garrard, Oxford UP, 2014, pp. 1–24.

———, editor. *Teaching Ecocriticism and Green Cultural Studies*. Palgrave Macmillan, 2012.

Garuba, Harry. "Explorations in Animist Materialism: Notes on Reading/ Writing African Literature, Culture, and Society." *Public Culture*, vol. 15, no. 2, Spring 2003, pp. 261–85.

Glotfelty, Cheryll. "Literary Studies in an Age of Environmental Crisis." Introduction. *The Ecocriticism Reader*, edited by Glotfelty and Harold Fromm, U of Georgia P, 1996, pp. xv–xxxvii.

Guha, Ramachandra, and Joan Martinez Alier. *Varieties of Environmentalism: Essays North and South.* Routledge, 1997.

Habila, Helon. *Oil on Water: A Novel.* W. W. Norton, 2010.

Handley, George B. *New World Poetics: Nature and the Adamic Imagination of Whitman, Neruda, and Walcott.* U of Georgia P, 2007.

Hardt, Michael, and Antonio Negri. *Empire.* Harvard UP, 2000.

Heise, Ursula K. "The Hitchhiker's Guide to Ecocriticism." *PMLA*, vol. 121, no. 2, Mar. 2006, pp. 503–16.

Hiltner, Ken. "First-Wave Introduction." *Ecocriticism: The Essential Reader*, edited by Hiltner, Routledge, 2015, pp. 1–2.

Huggan, Graham, and Helen Tiffin. *Postcolonial Ecocriticism: Literature, Animals, Environment.* Routledge, 2010.

Iheka, Cajetan. *Naturalizing Africa: Ecological Violence, Agency, and Postcolonial Resistance in African Literature.* Cambridge UP, 2018.

Ishimure Michiko. *Lake of Heaven.* Translated by Bruce Allen, Lexington Books, 2008.

James, Erin. "Teaching the Postcolonial/Ecocritical Dialogue." Garrard, *Teaching Ecocriticism*, pp. 60–71.

Kincaid, Jamaica. *A Small Place.* Farrar, Straus and Giroux, 1988.

Klein, Naomi. *The Shock Doctrine: The Rise of Disaster Capitalism.* 2007. Penguin Books, 2014.

*Life and Debt.* Directed by Stephanie Black, New Yorker Films, 2001.

Maathai, Wangari. *Unbowed: A Memoir.* Knopf, 2006.

McClintock, Anne. "The Angel of History: Pitfalls of the Term 'Post-Colonialism.'" *Social Text*, nos. 31–32, 1992, pp. 84–98.

Mignolo, Walter. "Coloniality of Power and De-colonial Thinking." *Globalization and the Decolonial Option*, edited by Mignolo and Arturo Escobar, Routledge, 2010, pp. 1–21.

Mistry, Rohinton. *A Fine Balance.* Knopf, 1996.

Mitchell, W. J. T. *Picture Theory.* U of Chicago P, 1994.

Morton, Timothy. *Hyperobjects: Philosophy and Ecology after the End of the World.* U of Minnesota P, 2013.

Ndlovu-Gatsheni, Sabelo J. "Decoloniality as the Future of Africa." *History Compass*, vol. 13, no. 10, 2015, pp. 485–96.

Ngũgĩ wa Thiong'o. *Weep Not Child.* Heinemann, 1964.

Nixon, Rob. *Slow Violence and the Environmentalism of the Poor.* Harvard UP, 2011.

Okorafor, Nnedi. *Lagoon.* Saga Press, 2014.

Oppermann, Serpil, and Serenella Iovino. "The Environmental Humanities and the Challenges of the Anthropocene." *Environmental Humanities: Voices from the Anthropocene*, edited by Oppermann and Iovino, Rowman and Littlefield, 2016, pp. 1–21.

Plumwood, Val. *Feminism and the Mastery of Nature*. Routledge, 2002.

Quijano, Aníbal. "Coloniality and Modernity/Rationality." *Globalization and the Decolonial Option*, edited by Walter D. Mignolo and Arturo Escobar, Routledge, 2010, pp. 22–32.

*El rio*. Directed by Juan Carlos Galeano, Galeano Films, 2017.

Roos, Bonnie, and Alex Hunt. "Narratives of Survival, Sustainability, and Justice." *Postcolonial Green: Environmental Politics and World Narratives*, edited by Roos and Hunt, U of Virginia P, 2010, pp. 1–13.

Rust, Stephen, et al., editors. *Ecomedia: Key Issues*. Earthscan/Routledge, 2016.

Singh, Amritjit, and Peter Schmidt, editors. *Postcolonial Theory and the United States: Race, Ethnicity, and Literature*. UP of Mississippi, 2000.

Sinha, Indra. *Animal's People*. Simon and Schuster, 2007.

Siperstein, Stephen, et al. Introduction. *Teaching Climate Change in the Humanities*, edited by Siperstein et al., Routledge, 2017, pp. 1–13.

Slovic, Scott, et al., editors. *Ecocriticism of the Global South*. Lexington Books, 2015.

Thornber, Karen. *Ecoambiguity: Environmental Crises and East Asian Literatures*. U of Michigan P, 2012.

Viramontes, Helena Maria. *Under the Feet of Jesus*. Plume, 1995.

Walcott, Derek. *Omeros*. Farrar, Straus and Giroux, 1990.

Wald, Sarah D., et al. "Introduction: Why Latinx Environmentalisms?" *Latinx Environmentalisms: Place, Justice, and the Decolonial*, Temple UP, 2019, pp. 1–31.

Weil, Zoe. *The World Becomes What We Teach: Educating a Generation of Solutionaries*. Lantern Books, 2016.

Welling, Bart H., and Scottie Kapel. "The Return of the Animal: Presenting and Representing Non-human Beings Response-ably in the (Post-)Humanities Classroom." Garrard, *Teaching Ecocriticism*, pp. 104–16.

Wenzel, Jennifer. *The Disposition of Nature: Environmental Crisis and World Literature*. Fordham UP, 2019.

———. "Reading Fanon Reading Nature." *What Postcolonial Theory Doesn't Say*, edited by Anna Bernard et al., Routledge, 2015, pp. 185–201.

Woodward, Wendy. *The Animal Gaze: Animal Subjectivities in Southern African Narratives*. Wits UP, 2008.

Wynter, Sylvia. "Unsettling the Coloniality of Being/Power/Truth/Freedom: Towards the Human, after Man, Its Overrepresentation—An Argument." *New Centennial Review*, vol. 3, no. 3, Fall 2003, pp. 257–337.

Ybarra, Priscilla Solis. *Writing the Goodlife: Mexican American Literature and the Environment*. U of Arizona P, 2016.

# Part I

## Background and Theoretical Foundations

**Byron Caminero-Santangelo**

---

# Environmental Justice
# and Postcolonial Ecocriticism

It is impossible to imagine pedagogy informed by postcolonial ecocriticism that does not take account of environmental justice activism and its history, just as it is impossible to imagine teaching informed by postcolonialism more generally that does not include consideration of anticolonial struggle and its history. Indeed, without a consideration of environmental justice as a political project, postcolonial ecocriticism risks falling into academic abstraction divorced from the material conditions that have shaped its underlying principles and purpose, including the concerns and struggles of those who have been on the losing end of colonial modernity. Just as important, to foreground the relation between postcolonial ecocriticism and the environmental justice struggle necessitates drawing attention to the unique contributions that postcolonial ecocriticism could make to transformative ways of imagining the world and to possibilities for action.

The term *environmental justice* can be traced back to movements in the United States in the 1980s in which activists fought against the injustices of the uneven distribution of environmental risk and damage as it correlated with race and histories of dispossession and disenfranchisement. Such activism includes the protests against the dumping of PCB-contaminated soil in landfills in Warren County, North Carolina, whose residents were over-whelmingly African American and poor, and the struggle against mining interests by the Sokaogon Ojibwe Nation in Wisconsin. These grassroots movements contrasted with earlier forms of environmentalism, drawing attention to the voices and agency of those who had been silenced and ignored by mainstream environmentalists. In the process, they challenged the articulation of identities that suppressed social difference and injustice, the supposedly unified "we" of a singular nation or of a species. They focused on "sacrifice zones," where the unjust siting of polluting industry and of toxic dumping devastates the health and livelihoods of low-income and minority communities (see Lerner), and they eschewed discourses of wilderness and the white, privileged interests underlying those discourses. Ultimately, they drew attention to a particular imbrication of the social and the ecological, in which processes of mutual shaping between the two are mediated by social conflict and in which environmental projects are always interwoven with politics. If these grassroots movements initially tried to work within official legal and policy channels, as had mainstream environmentalists, they quickly became aware of the extreme difficulty, if not impossibility, of achieving their goals through the existing channels of government and industry; they challenged how business was done, underlying assumptions about development and knowledge, and the possibility of separating the struggle against environmental degradation from foundational social relationships and injustice. They represented a threat to business as usual in industry, government, and mainstream environmentalism, as well as to the comforting myths of white privilege.

"Environmental justice," often qualified by "global," is now used to designate a wide range of movements around the world, although those movements are also referred to under the umbrella "environmentalism of the poor." However, it would be a mistake to view environmental justice movements in the Global South, such as the fight against commercial deforestation by the Green Belt Movement in Kenya and by the Chipko movement in India, as necessarily stemming from the environmental justice activism in the United States (Martinez-Alier). Even if they shared the concerns and underlying philosophical orientation of American environmental justice, these movements are neither belated nor peripheral. They have also tended to diverge from or expand on the environmental justice movement in the United States in some important ways. For example, they have foregrounded the role that transnational relations play in environmental injustice and the necessity for transnational solutions. In addition, they have emphasized that the transnational landscapes of injustice have been shaped not only by colonialism but also by current neocolonial and neoliberal global relations. At least initially, they challenged the national framing of injustice and a focus on the nation as the organizing geographic boundary of concern in ways that environmental justice movements in the United States often did not (Walker; Williams and Mawdsley).

Despite points of divergence among environmental justice movements, from early on they developed as a global network. In 1991 the first National People of Color Environmental Leadership Summit was held in Washington, DC, where seventeen guiding principles of environmental justice were developed to guide the coalition of movements represented at the summit. The preamble included a commitment "to secure our political, economic, and cultural liberation that has been denied for over 500 years of colonization and oppression, resulting in the poisoning of our communities and land and the genocide of our peoples" (Bullard 299). Although there was significant representation from other nations, most of the participants in that first summit were from the United States. However, the following year a broader coalition of activists joined together at the United Nations Conference on the Environment and Development in Brazil "to ensure that the intended outcome of . . . negotiations—an action agenda for global cooperation on 'sustainable development'—would not reproduce the eco-neoliberal version of the idea of sustainability, that is, sustaining business-as-usual by setting aside the global commons to serve free-flowing capital circuits to keep intact northern standards of living" (Di Chiro 102). Since then, global coalition building has expanded exponentially and has brought attention to a wide range of concerns that include not only toxic contamination and waste dumping but also risk and injustices associated with dams, tourism development, biodiversity conservation, deforestation, and global heating.

In general, environmental justice activists point to how the association of institutionally sanctioned expertise with objectivity, the view from nowhere, all too easily becomes a means of denigrating other forms of knowledge and other voices and, therefore, of enabling injustice and silencing dissent. These activists may need to draw on the language of science, policy, and the law, but they also give equal or greater priority to other idioms, including "the respect for sacredness, the urgency of livelihood, the dignity of human life, the demand for environmental security, the need for food security, the defense of cultural identity . . . and of indigenous territorial rights" (Martinez-Alier 150). Challenging neoliberal rhetoric, they represent in vivid terms "the human and ecological costs" paid by marginalized communities and peoples in order to maintain the lifestyles of the wealthy and privileged (Nixon 26).

However, while it is important to formulate environmental justice as a global movement or type of environmentalism, it is equally important to emphasize that coalitions are intersectional and to foreground the particularity of circumstances, challenges, and movements—especially given activists' focus on grassroots organization and resistance to universalizing discourse. In turn, pedagogical commitment to the project of environmental justice requires emphasizing such particularity through and in texts, even as connections are made among a wide variety of conditions and movements. This dual focus can help highlight a generative tension for environmental justice activism in which movements are defined by their efforts to give voice to the silenced or marginal perspectives of particular communities, to resist universalizing discourse, and to address specific conflicts, inequalities, and ecological change *in place*, even as they must negotiate relations and structures operating at wider scales (Caminero-Santangelo 32, 183–84; Harvey 400).

Postcolonial ecocriticism has been heavily influenced by and overlaps with global environmental justice activism, as well as with political ecology, which studies the struggle for environmental justice in the Global South from the perspective of the social sciences (Bryant; Peet et al.). Postcolonial ecocritical pedagogy necessarily entails familiarizing students with the histories of specific movements and the global struggle for environmental justice, and it is driven by a commitment to making visible the links between social injustice and environmental degradation and to exploring possibilities for transforming consciousness and for imagining agency. Politically, this pedagogy is dedicated to the need for material, collective efforts to combat environmental injustices, and it strives to connect aesthetics with the transformation of consciousness leading to the possibility of action.

Yet, despite its close alignments with both environmental justice activism and political ecology, postcolonial ecocriticism should not be conflated with either. As practiced in the classroom, this pedagogy does not focus on using texts to identify and advocate for a particular course of action or the best set of principles or to build organizing capacity or develop leadership; nor does it focus on the empirical truth of textual representation and claim making. It does draw "out the advocacy function that

is often embedded within postcolonial . . . and environmental literature"
(Huggan and Tiffin 14), placing a particular emphasis on the transformation of consciousness. However, its critical focus is on the aesthetic and
rhetorical aspects of texts and their political significance or usefulness
(12–16). Postcolonial ecocriticism pays close attention to the role of the
imagination and textual choices in the perception and representation of
the world (e.g., to how artist-activists pursue their roles as witnesses). Postcolonial ecocritical pedagogy aims to develop students' ability to examine
such issues as colonial and anticolonial discursive constructions of the
human and nonhuman or less than human (Wenzel); the use of genre, especially in relation to traditions of anticolonial and environmental advocacy; and the potential for a transformation of consciousness leading to
new possibilities in the struggle for socioecological justice.

To tie the concerns and principles discussed above more firmly and
clearly to classroom practice, I turn to my teaching of writings by two
author-activists connected with the struggle for environmental justice in
Nigeria's Niger Delta: Ken Saro-Wiwa's manifesto *Genocide in Nigeria* and
prison "diary" *A Month and a Day* and Helon Habila's novel *Oil on Water*.

Saro-Wiwa's activist texts provide a good basis for discussing the history of environmental devastation and injustice in the delta and of the
struggle for environmental justice in the 1990s. They introduce students
to the cycles of destruction and violence created by oil extraction, to their
links with the neocolonial development of Nigeria, to the way transnational
relations and neoliberalism contributed to these cycles, and to the development and trajectory of the Movement for the Survival of the Ogoni
People (MOSOP), which Saro-Wiwa helped found and lead. Having students brainstorm about the similarities and differences between this and
other examples of environmental injustice we have read about (or I have
summarized) enables them to get a sense both of the specificity of the conditions in the delta and of connections with the concerns and strategies of
environmental justice activism understood as a global coalition of movements. However, the emphasis ultimately is on Saro-Wiwa's aesthetic and
rhetorical choices—the kinds of stories he tells, the textual strategies he
uses, and the way these stories and strategies serve (or fail to serve) his purposes. For example, I have students consider why he chose to use the term
*genocide*, how it might be useful given its implications, and what draw-
backs it might have (Caminero-Santangelo 142). I also have them consider
what function a prison diary might serve: what it suggests about the conditions faced by MOSOP, how it might be understood as a form of resistance,

how it could help make an appeal to Nigerian and non-Nigerian audiences, and so on (144).

I spend a good bit of time having students consider the elements and significance of the pastoral story Saro-Wiwa tells of a singular Ogoni identity dating back to before the advent of British colonialism and serving as a basis for unity and for the hope of environmental justice. In many ways, this story is foundational to the appeal he makes and to his strategy for mobilization (Caminero-Santangelo 138–39, 142–43, 147–51). The projection of an ethnic "genius" or spirit was a means to overcome divisions among the Ogoni and to enable a sense of agency. It also suggested that MOSOP's success would result in a truly decolonized Ogoni federal state free from the neocolonial injustice and violence plaguing the rest of Nigeria. Finally, the claim that a transhistorical Ogoni sensibility included care for the land based on ecologically sensitive animism suggested that the success of MOSOP would *necessarily* result in ecosystem restoration. Students are often quick to identify this story of Ogoni identity as trafficking in an eco-indigene trope, which projects images of indigenous societies harmoniously dwelling with nature and embodying an impeccable environmental ethic, and to link it with other examples of the trope in literary and activist writing. They also want to know more about the truth of Saro-Wiwa's representations. This is the provenance of political ecology, and I draw on scholarship that calls into question the notion of a unified Ogoni identity predating the activism of MOSOP and that argues that it papered over divisions that would lead to problems after Saro-Wiwa's execution (Watts, "Petro-violence" and "Violent Environments").

However, equally important is a consideration of how the trope of Ogoni identity works in relation to Saro-Wiwa's larger narratives and his various purposes, including its implications for reinforcing or challenging problematic assumptions. For example, I ask students what the relation might be between Saro-Wiwa's use of the trope and Western audiences' expectations and assumptions, how his use of it matches up with colonial and anticolonial narratives, and what alternative narratives of resistant identity it occludes or forecloses. The focus here is not on which story of identity should be pursued or which course of action is best but on how the stories are constructed and on their rhetorical function. This aspect of the pedagogical work is not concerned with the truth of the representations but with the possible connections among stories, critical (aesthetic) analysis of them, and environmental injustice. I have found that making this approach to texts an explicit topic of discussion is especially important when one is teaching environmental studies students, many of whom are inclined to read activist writing as transparent documents or to engage in uncritical celebration.

I have often paired Saro-Wiwa's writing with Habila's novel, although I have also, because of time constraints, used excerpts from that writing and an overview of the conditions Saro-Wiwa describes. *Oil on Water* tells the story of a young reporter, Rufus, who seeks a British woman kidnapped by militants amid the oil wars in the delta in the decades following the execution of Saro-Wiwa. During this period, the delta spiraled into violence: armed rebel groups and gangs proliferated and turned to kidnapping oil workers, sabotaging installations, and fighting for oil companies' protection money, and the Nigerian government continued to protect the interests of the oil industry using all the means of coercion at its disposal. Meanwhile, the industry's negligence only made the environmental devastation worse, destroying the possibilities for traditional livelihoods and the very ground on which communities lived.

I ask students how the novel might be understood as matching up with Saro-Wiwa's project, and how it might be connected to environmental justice advocacy more generally, while also encouraging them to be attentive to the ways that the fictional form enables different possibilities for consciousness-raising. As they closely examine Rufus's representations of violence, dying landscapes, social breakdown, and the responsibility of the "slick alliance" between the Nigerian government and the oil industry (Watts, "Petro-violence" 208), students can identify how Rufus echoes the efforts of Saro-Wiwa (and of environmental artist-activists in general) to bear witness. In turn, they become aware of how Rufus mocks what Saro-Wiwa called "Shell speak," a form of neocolonial development discourse that depicts Shell and the oil industry as bringing economic progress and as having at heart the best interests of the people and the land. I draw attention to a scene in which Rufus directly challenges this discourse in an interaction with a petroleum engineer named James Floode, in the privileged space of an oil-industry enclave. I ask students what role dialogue plays in the scene, what it might achieve that other forms of representation do not, and how it draws the reader in and serves the ends of persuasion and consciousness-raising. I also ask students to consider how Rufus's bearing witness to recent conditions in the delta through various narrative techniques (including dialogue) might be read as engaging in the project of environmental justice advocacy precisely by pointing to the limitations of Saro-Wiwa's narratives and by trying to imagine new ways forward. For example, having the students do a kind of discourse analysis of Rufus's interactions with "rebels" and "criminals" leads to productive discussion about how Habila calls into question Saro-Wiwa's narrative of Ogoni identity as a basis for successful resistance, justice through financial compensation, and healing.

To help students consider the advocacy role of the novel, I also push them to formulate what new possibilities for imagining identity, resistance, and survival are offered up by *Oil on Water*, especially through its narrative arc and its generic form (a quest narrative). For example, the novel steadily places greater emphasis on cultural practices that encourage an ethic of ecological care and a sense of community that move away from forms of bounded ethnic identity, ideas about ownership of the land, and neocolonial assumptions about the instrumentality of the nonhuman that the novel depicts as an integral part of the crisis in the delta. Asking students to consider the relation between the novel and environmental justice activism enables them to consider the political role literary representation might play by generating new narratives of identity and resistance, imagining new bases for hope and healing, and addressing the setbacks, challenges, and conundrums of resistance and the movement toward justice.

At the same time, postcolonial ecocritical pedagogy necessitates an awareness that neither the text nor the critical work being done in the classroom can be conflated with environmental justice activism or political ecology. Even if students recognize implicitly that politically engaged fiction such as *Oil on Water* does not necessarily make a case for a particular course of action or focus on establishing the empirical truth of its representations, bringing this issue and its significance out into the open helps them consider the project that the classroom community is collectively pursuing. *Oil on Water* is a useful text in this regard because Habila is suspicious of authoritative truth tellers, including intellectuals and activists. I draw attention to Habila's use of the quest narrative in order to ask students if Rufus is successful in his search for "the big story" that will explain what is happening in the delta and why the story he tells shifts bewilderingly in time and space, frustrating our desire for a linear timeline or coherent map. Admittedly, this discussion of form can lead to a kind of postmodern valorization of individual truth and suspicion of politics; however, it can also help students consider how skepticism about a single story and attention to how stories work to construct the world might be meaningful for struggles toward environmental justice. Postcolonial ecocritical pedagogy comes into full play in such moments, as explicit attention to the commitments and concerns of environmental justice activism and advocacy is connected to a careful attention to language and form.

## Works Cited

Bryant, Raymond. "Power, Knowledge, and Political Ecology in the Third World." *Progress in Physical Geography*, vol. 22, 1998, pp. 79–94.

Bullard, Robert D. Appendix A. *The Quest for Environmental Justice: Human Rights and the Politics of Pollution*, edited by Bullard, Counterpoint, 2005, pp. 299–301.

Caminero-Santangelo, Byron. *Different Shades of Green: African Literature, Environmental Justice, and Political Ecology*. U of Virginia P, 2014.

Di Chiro, Giovanna. "Environmental Justice." *Keywords for Environmental Studies*, edited by Joni Adamson et al., New York UP, 2016, pp. 100–05.

Habila, Helon. *Oil on Water*. W. W. Norton, 2010.

Harvey, David. *Justice, Nature and the Geography of Difference*. Blackwell Publishers, 1996.

Huggan, Graham, and Helen Tiffin. *Postcolonial Ecocriticism: Literature, Animals, Environment*. Routledge, 2015.

Lerner, Steve. *Sacrifice Zones: The Front Line of Toxic Chemical Exposure in the United States*. MIT Press, 2010.

Martinez-Alier, Joan. *The Environmentalism of the Poor: A Study of Ecological Conflicts and Valuation*. Edward Elgar, 2002.

Nixon, Rob. *Slow Violence and the Environmentalism of the Poor*. Harvard UP, 2011.

Peet, Richard, et al., editors. *Global Political Ecology*. Routledge, 2011.

Saro-Wiwa, Ken. *Genocide in Nigeria: The Ogoni Tragedy*. Saros International, 1992.

———. *A Month and a Day: A Detention Diary*. Ayebia, 1995.

Walker, Gordon. *Environmental Justice: Concepts, Evidence and Politics*. Routledge, 2012.

Watts, Michael. "Petro-violence: Community, Extraction, and Political Ecology of a Mythic Commodity." *Violent Environments*, edited by Nancy Lee Peluso and Watts, Cornell UP, 2001, pp. 189–212.

———. "Violent Environments: Petroleum Conflict and the Political Ecology of Rule in the Niger Delta, Nigeria." *Liberation Ecologies: Environment, Development, Social Movements*, edited by Richard Peet and Watts, Routledge, 2004, pp. 273–98.

Wenzel, Jennifer. "Turning Over a New Leaf: Fanonian Humanism and Environmental Justice." *The Routledge Companion to the Environmental Humanities*, edited by Ursula K. Heise et al., 2017, pp. 165–73.

Williams, Glyn, and Emma Mawdsley. "Postcolonial Environmental Justice: Government and Governance in India." *Geoforum*, vol. 37, no. 5, 2006, pp. 660–70.

**Brendon Nicholls**

---

# Indigenous Cosmologies

Indigenous communities worldwide face losing their land and marine resources. And yet violence—from the intrusion of capital markets to media representations to state suppression to land theft and despoliation—typically meets with resilience and inventiveness. Indigenous cosmologies and land claims theorize environmental and communal futures, notwithstanding the steady encroachment of neoliberal capital and its socioeconomic ills. For instance, animist belief reveals an "attitude of philosophical accommodation" (Soyinka 54), as when the postindependence elites of Nigeria esteemed Sango (the Yoruba god of lightning) as "a mythological figure whose incipient scientific consciousness was demonstrated in his ability to harness the electrical charges of lightning to serve his own sometimes undisclosed purposes" (Garuba 262). Animism is materialist because "animist thought spiritualizes the object world, thereby giving the spirit a local habitation" (267). Once such conceptual modes are turned toward political struggle, human-nonhuman coalitions become possible. In Latin America, Marisol de la Cadena asserts, "earth practices are relations for which the dominant ontological distinction between humans and nature does not work" (341). As indigenous political movements disrupt the operations of neoliberal capital, they occasionally muster nonhuman political allies: "when mountains—say Quilish or Ausangate—break into political stages, they do so also as earth-beings" (342). Amerindian perspectives contain the power to radically remake our founding assumptions about the separability of human and animal beings. Eduardo Viveiros de Castro has argued that in indigenous cosmologies, animal perspectives may themselves be enmeshed in human-like understandings: "jaguars see blood as manioc beer, vultures see worms as grilled fish" (57). In this sense, the promise of indigenous thought is that it may become a "basis for our own thinking . . . the products of people(s) who ought to be acknowledged as having a status equal to that of practitioners of modern science" (Skafish 12).

As a form of ecologically inclined theory grounded in relation and observation, indigenous perspectives should be engaged seriously on their own terms. The pedagogical import and the lasting value of indigenous cosmologies is that they often collapse the foundations of Western epistemes. A case in point might be the humanities themselves, where the primacy of the human cleaves us from the world of things and the intermediary worlds of other species. If the academy's knowledges share in a distribution of our world and its wreckage, then the axiomatic challenge of the indigenous is to remodel the anthropocentric biases of the academy and reorient our ecological dispositions. In what follows, I elucidate an instance of indigenous cosmology with the aid of Witi Ihimaera's 1987 novel *The Whale Rider* before advancing some general principles for teaching indigenous thought. I go on to place Disney's *Moana*, a film many students will know, in conversation with Ihimaera's novel and with George Grey's Maui tales, gathered from Māori storytellers in 1855.

The power of indigenous cosmology as a strategy of resistance and imagining is that it disrupts the foundational orders of law (only certain living humans may assert rights) and science (only certain organic bodies are deemed alive or sentient, only certain communities of knowledge are deemed intellectually specialized). Indigenous critique exceeds the axioms of the conceptual systems that it seeks to contest. There are dangers in thinking through the intersection of the indigenous with environmental politics. First, indigenous communities have suffered from representational bestialization—being seen as closer to natural (often animal) states and to "the earth." For this very reason, they have become placeholders for Westerners' cherished fantasies of their own primordial past: "The primitive, one might conclude, is a simulacrum of the self that the modern industrialized and globalized subject would like to imagine that he or she might once have been" (Nicholls, "Indigeneity" 208). Second, indigenous stories are susceptible to appropriation for their marketability (witness *Pocahontas* or *Moana*), much like animal stories (witness *The Lion King* or *Finding Nemo*), or susceptible to facile reapplication in environmental discourse. While our students may be most familiar with and endeared to such films, indigenous stories may fuel the very modes of capitalist encroachment that some indigenous communities seek to contest, permitting colonial modes such as racism and speciesism to reemerge in our present. Even in environmentalist discourse, the indigene may become the model for retrograde zoographic motifs. As Mette Bryld and Nina Lykke caution, like "another double, the 'noble savage' of early modern ethnography, the dolphin and the whale will allegedly guide us to insight into the 'true and sacred' pleasures of a simple life in harmony with the natural environment" (2–3). Bryld and Lykke's point is that early colonial stereotypes of the indigene may furnish oversimplistic templates for environmental politics in our present. Third, indigenous claims to political sovereignty and historical priority tip too readily into media associations with primordial protohumanity and cultural exceptionalism. Finally, in environmental discourses, indigenous communities may be subject to ideational overvaluation, such as in the notorious 1971 Keep America Beautiful advertisements in the United States of America, in which the "crying Indian" was played by Espera Oscar de Corti (aka Iron Eyes Cody), an Italian American actor.

## Indigenous Politics and the Environment

One strategy for resisting these pitfalls is to historicize indigenous epistemologies, which locate indigenous environmentalist interventions within the accruals of long memory and land activism. To demonstrate how history interfaces with indigenous cosmologies, I analyze a text of the Māori cultural renaissance in Aotearoa (New Zealand): Ihimaera's *The Whale Rider*. The novel emerges from the larger political activist movement to reclaim former lands and revitalize indigenous culture. To understand how Ihimaera engages the long history of land disputes in Aotearoa, we need to go back to one of the founding legal documents of settlement. In the second article of the Treaty of Waitangi (1840), the British guaranteed Māori land custodianship and use: "Her Majesty the Queen of England confirms and guarantees to the Chiefs and Tribes of New Zealand and to the respective families and individuals thereof the full exclusive and undisturbed possession of their Lands and Estates Forests Fisheries and other properties which they may collectively or individually possess . . ." (New Zealand Ministry for Culture and Heritage). This guarantee was soon flouted. By 1880, for example, the New Zealand government had alienated Māori land at Bastion Point for the purpose of defense. These lands were then returned to Auckland City Council, not to the Māori communities who had a claim on them. In the 1970s, the council proposed to sell off the land to housing corporations, sparking a land occupation by Māori activists from 1977 to 1978. As part of the occupation, Māori activists farmed the land at Bastion Point and built a meeting house and dwellings on it, reasserting both land custodianship and use, as well as cultural sovereignty. It was only through the violent intervention of the police and the military that the peaceful Bastion Point occupation ended. The Bastion Point occupation occurred just two years after the 1975 Land March "from Te Hapua (in the far north of the North Island) to Wellington, the seat of government, in protest at the continuing expropriation of Māori land" (Keown 140). The 1970s were also marked by the establishment of the Waitangi Tribunal in 1975 to hear Māori land claims (139) and the decade-long occupation of the Raglan golf course from 1968 to 1978. That land had been appropriated in 1941 to build an emergency airstrip. After the war, the airstrip was converted into a golf course instead of being returned to Māori custodianship. Neither the Raglan golf course nor Bastion Point had "legally been purchased" (142).

Such land occupations were more than the political assertion of Māori land rights. They also staked wider Māori cultural claims to full and equal status in Aotearoa. An efflorescence of Māori cultural production—novels, poems, and films—resulted from the land occupations and from educational initiatives to create Māori language nests. Since land and its use were so central to the Māori renaissance, the environment emerged as an abiding concern within this formation. *The Whale Rider* contains a character, Koro Apirana, who is involved in organized governance (the Māori Council) and in Māori renaissance activism—the Land March; the Bastion Point occupation; the establishment of language nests, or *Kōhanga Reo* (Ihimaera 30); and land disputes (88). However, like other Māori renaissance writing, *The Whale Rider* remakes the past for new purposes. The whale rider is a founding ancestor (Paikea) who is accompanied by "the song in the sea" as he creates the environment by throwing spears to land, which turn into pigeons or eels (4). The last spear lands but is withheld for the future moment in which it is needed. Ihimaera innovates a braided narrative form in which origin, the hemispheric travels of whales, and the development of a girl, Kahu, are interwoven until Paikea's prophecy is fulfilled. The braiding of the narrative follows the incantation at the end of many of the chapters: "*Hui ē, haumi ē, tāiki ē*" ("Join everything together [let everything gather or meet], bind it together, let it be done"; italics in source).[1] The narrative wills its own completion, and it is embodied in Kahu, whose hair is in braids (71). In this arrangement, we see corresponding nonlikenesses working in parallel: Paikea's creative acts in chapter 1 are followed by a second chapter and another beginning on the "cetacean crib" off the Valdes Peninsula in Patagonia (8). Chapter 3 begins the novel again: "I suppose that if this story has a beginning it is with Kahu" (10). This is a deeply resonant third beginning, since chapter 1 began with Kahu—Paikea's other name is Kahuti-te-Rangi. The novel begins with three narrative strands but submits the moment of creation and the prophecy of Paikea's return to a corresponding nonlikeness: Kahu is a girl who both ruptures the mythological origins of the known world and breaks the line of male descent. Her rupture of origin and destination allows for cultural creativity. Kahu exhibits what Elizabeth DeLoughrey, writing on Patricia Grace's *Potiki*, terms "the necessity to transgress prohibition to initiate cultural regeneration" (66).

These chapters braid three narrative origins. Braiding allows a temporal interplay between the origins of the Whāngārā Marae (the sacred meeting place of the Ngāti Porou confederation) and the present, mediated by the life cycle of cetacean companions. Ihimaera views the "power of speech with whales, the power of *interlock*" (Ihimaera 31) as deriving from the undifferentiated human-environmental states of the actors in the Rangi and Papa creation myth, in which one of the "God children" (Lord Tangaroa) has dominion over the seas and appoints guardians (of the oceans, of the tides, and of their denizens) to assist him. Two guardians of the land intercede on behalf of lake-bound whales and sharks, who are freed to roam the seas. Initially territorial, these large creatures breach boundaries to become marine inhabitants. By contrast, Koro Apirana claims the contemporary separation of environment and humanity as proof that we have grown away from our "godliness" (31). The principal actors in the creation myth are not quite men but do have human characteristics. Ihimaera's criticism of ungodly men in his own time is that masculinity requires something more than itself to achieve its highest possible state. It is for this reason that Koro refers to "our ancestor, the whale" (40), which is "consistent with the Pacific ethic of genealogical connection among living beings" (Steinwand 186). To reestablish the link with this cetacean ancestor, *The Whale Rider* allows the masculine politics of the Māori renaissance to strain against the entwining of male and female genealogies: Kahu has the blood of the female ancestor, Muriwai, and the male ancestor, Porourangi, in her. Ihimaera "lifts the Muriwai story from the set of traditions surrounding the naming of Whakatāne, or 'Act-like-a-male.' Kahu is not only a descendent of Muriwai on her father's side, but also through her mother" (Dodd 18). As the narrative develops, Kahu's circumstance increasingly coincides with feats (Ihimaera 27) and prophetic fulfillments (71–72) that her grandfather, Koro Apirana, expects a boy to achieve.

The novel is broken into six sections—a prologue, Spring, Summer, Autumn, Winter, and an epilogue. The human narrative, marked mainly by Kahu's age, jumps around in time, so that the human characters are shown to live in the seasons but also in a way that is out of time. Nevertheless, *The Whale Rider* offers environmentalism (by way of the obligation to Lord Tangaroa) as a unifying cause between Māori and Pākehā (83). It submits the bicultural Māori-Pākehā nation to the broader hemispheric consciousness of its marine bioregion, prompted by whale journeys from Easter Island (20), from the Tuamoto Archipelago and its Muruora Atoll to legendary Hawaiki (44) to the Antarctic (77) to Whāngārā (79). Threats such as the French and American testing of nuclear weapons in Polynesia exceed borders. The nation's political territory becomes, precisely, fluid the moment global pressures are articulated in transspecies dialogue and subsumed in environmental consciousness. Ihimaera's concept of "interlock" unifies human and cetacean worlds by means of braided species histories and shared ecological interests.

And yet the novel is in no easy sense global or transnational in outlook. When two hundred whales beach themselves at Gisborne, international charities such as "Greenpeace, Project Jonah, and Friends of the Earth" fail to save any of them (84). By contrast, when Kahu mounts the beached bull whale in a reembodiment of Paikea, the whale rider, she successfully leads his herd back out to sea (104–07). In Kahu's empathic fright at a film featuring a whale hunt (33–35), we see a literary precedent for Cajetan Iheka's useful recommendation that we need to "bridge the distance between these [human and animal] bodies and to imagine the impact of such punishment upon our human bodies by way of appreciating the abuse often suffered by nonhuman life forms" (50).

The very success and marketability of *The Whale Rider*, especially its film version, led to the consumerist co-option of environmentalist narratives. As Graham Huggan and Helen Tiffin contend, *The Whale Rider* exemplifies "the shift from the culturalist perspective of the Māori Renaissance to a brazenly consumerist ethos in which the international branding of Māori culture has been adjusted, not least by Māori themselves, to the changing national cause" (63). Notwithstanding its entanglements and complicities, Ihimaera's novel applies itself to four discursive sites. First, whales and whaling were a key commercial basis for empire (Huggan viii). In this sense, the novel contests the longer historical placement of Aotearoa and its cetacean sea life in the globalizing movement of empire and capital. Second, whales embody environmentalist melancholia—they are "a multipurpose catalyst for human-centered contemplations of loss and guilt as well as an opportunity for recovery and redemption" (xvi). Ihimaera's intervention, coming just a decade after the global Save the Whales campaign, converts the environmental melancholia of the stranded whale into the cosmological recovery of human and cetacean kinship, with indigenous endurance and futurity in mind. The marine environment is not something to be acted upon, Ihimaera suggests, but something to communicate with. Third, the 1986 global moratorium on commercial whaling has often affected indigenous whaling practices (xii–xiii). Writing a year later, Ihimaera acknowledges but also eschews such Māori practices (32, 40). Fourth, *The Whale Rider* advances protocols and rites of ecologically inclined action—including shrines and offerings to Tangaroa to protect fishing grounds, the blessings of new nets and lines, and never overfishing. In this way, the community never outcompetes its cetacean ancestor and retains the possibility of linking to its past.

## Pedagogical Principles

Teaching environmental literatures and film requires us to provoke a new kind of consciousness in our students. This is the goal of all education—to formulate and work with what is new. Part of what needs to be new in an age of environmental crisis is the idea of the human itself and the modes of self-interest in which it operates. In a previous MLA volume I asserted that the differential pedagogy of the multicultural postcolonial classroom "demands of us—as teachers, students, readers—acts of provisional self-placement in relation to unanticipated auditors" ("Reading Ngugi" 134). In the environmentalist classroom, indigenous thought encourages us to consider animals, plants, inanimate objects, and the dead among our listeners and interlocutors. We might provoke our students to acknowledge that they are no longer the primary agents of their own knowledges or futures. This move does not seek to disempower students but rather to attune them to the idea that the future, environmentally speaking, will increasingly determine their own possibilities, mitigated only by new bases for worldly dialogue. I advance below some general principles for teaching indigenous cosmologies, with the aid of a film (*Moana*), Ihimaera's novel, and Grey's Maui tales. This is equivalent to placing a commodified indigenous story (*Moana*) in relation to activist renaissance and indigenous theory (Ihimaera) as it encounters colonial epistemes (Grey).

Principle one in teaching indigenous cosmologies is to mark the violence that makes indigenous stories visible. In *Moana*, students might easily identify Disney's distortion of Maui's feats by contrasting the story with Grey's assembled tales of the demigod, which were gathered while Polynesia was still colonized.[2] For instance, the mythical Maui is the first human to die when he crawls into his grandmother Hine-Nui-Te-Pō's vagina in a bid for immortality and is squeezed to death (Tamaira and Fonoti 305; Grey 44). Maui dies in myth and so people consequently die in the world. In the film, Moana's grandmother dies (though she returns as a stingray) while Maui lives. Human death preexists the Disney hero, changing his mythical function in the cosmos. Secondly, the singular, mythical Hine-Nui-Te-Pō is reconstructed in the film as the plural Te Fiti, whose "heartless" aspect is her frightful avatar Te Kā. Disney Maui's bid for immortality is in stealing her heart, a *pounamu* (a round nephrite jade spiral carving), whose return resolves the plot. Disney Maui's magic is returned to him, but at the cost of human mortality. Disney Maui lives while people die.

Principle two is to ask in whose service the violation of indigenous stories takes place. What forms of power does representational violence permit? In *Moana*, as in *The Whale Rider*, there is a seemingly female-centered story. Moana the headstrong girl transgresses her father's demand that she stay in the reef. She disobeys so that she may reach her potential and become an individuated heroine. But the original myth's injunction against sexual violence (Maui's fatal penetration of Hine-Nui-Te-Pō's vagina) is set aside as Disney Maui lives on. The powerful cartoon Maui and the slight-bodied heroine Moana dramatize dysphoric and disproportionate gender power without Hine-Nui-Te-Pō's representational checks and balances. Moreover, Moana's empowerment as next in line to the chiefdom is historically inaccurate. The genealogy of her character owes more to a Disney princess than to a Polynesian chieftainess (see Robinson). Moana's troublesome feminism is resolved as conventional gender inequality and representational violence.

Principle three is to understand the institutions of indigenous storytelling. For Grey's original interlocutors, the story of Maui is inseparable from the social occasions of its telling. Storytelling always presumes community. Like other heroic narratives, Maui's is "about the generations of the ancestors of the Maori. . . . [W]e repeat them in our prayers, and whenever we relate the deeds of the ancestors from whom each family is descended, and upon other similar occasions" (Grey 44). In *The Whale Rider*, "*hui ē, haumi ē, tāiki ē*" includes the idea of a community gathering in seriousness (*hui*) to arrive at a common purpose or decision proclaimed in the choral acclamation (*tāiki ē*, or "let it be done"). Despite the Disney corporation's laudable and groundbreaking attempts to tell a sensitive story by paying consultants in the Oceanic Story Trust (Tamaira and Fonoti 314), it has, quite simply, managed relations with indigenous communities to better assemble a profitable cinematic audience. In the classroom, students might be challenged to find strategies for dissociating themselves from the film's commercial communities and then taking the more difficult second step of reflecting on what form a decolonized political coalition with indigenous communities might take in the global present. As the Oceanic Story Trust member Dionne Fonoti says, by way of a Samoan proverb, "Fesili Mulimai ia Muamai" ("The last to arrive should ask the first to arrive"; Tamaira and Fonoti 317).[3] I reinvoke this proverb to suggest that non-indigenous students or academics who arrive belatedly upon the scene of indigenous custom and perspective should learn from its inaugurators and practitioners before configuring their solidarity or activism.

Principle four is to understand that the vast marketability of indigenous stories risks the expropriation of indigenous intellectual property. Disney Maui's theft of the *pounamu* on screen is closer to home than audiences might at first imagine. *Moana* grossed $643 million worldwide and netted a profit of $121 million ("Moana"; Fleming). Notwithstanding *Moana*'s cast, the majority of whom were of Polynesian descent, students might ask exactly how much of the production budget or the gross profit contributed to community development in Oceania, especially investments of funds outside the continental United States. At stake is the extent to which indigenous intellectual property rights are respected and recompensed. In asking such questions, students may formulate an ethics of indigenous and environmental imaging and render transparent the circulation of narrative as a commodity in the global marketplace.

Principle five is to establish how indigenous ecological consciousness might provoke wider ecological consciousness. Reflecting on Ihimaera's entangling and braiding together of cetacean and human genealogies, we might ask students to contemplate or imagine into being their own non-human genealogies. We might set students the task of construing a basis for dialogue with extrahuman actors in these genealogies. Further, we might challenge students to set out how the fluid political territory and the so-called hemispheric consciousness arising out of intertwined environmental destinies could take form in our own historical moment.

Principle six is to decide how to transform the institutions in which we participate, in line with our revised understandings of fluid political territory and the urgent need to revise human self-interest. In short, students might consider the logical implications of a revised humanity for the institutions in which they participate: for instance, the classroom or the university, students' faiths and histories, their constitution, the economy. We might ask students what animal, floral, territorial, oceanic, and atmospheric participation and partnership in such institutions would look like and which new protocols and practices would be required to make such participation materially possible.

There are no easy answers to exercises of this kind—their point is that they require students to work with forms of consciousness, modes of telling, and participatory communities that are centuries old and that see environmental possibilities and dangers very differently from how our students might in the contemporary moment. One of the most powerful features of indigenous origin myths (such as the stories of Maui or Lord Tangaroa) is that they contain first principles. If an environmental politics requires us to remake ourselves, indigenous cosmologies offer alternative first principles in the project of becoming more than simply human for our planet. We might ask students to contemplate the mechanics and devices of unmarketable environmental stories, whose telling and comprehension are difficult, and to devise safeguards against obvious representational complicities. To conclude, we would be asking students to reconceive their roles as cultural and economic consumers and inviting them to augment their status as environmental actors.

## Notes

1. *Tāiki ē* signifies choral participation and general acclamation or agreement. The *hui* is a communal meeting that often works toward a decision or resolution. The incantation "*Hui ē, haumi ē, tāiki ē*" is thus also an expression of

accomplished collective purpose in an institution (*hui*) designed for decision-making through consensus.

2. I do not claim authenticity for Grey. My method here submits Disney's representationally violent text to Grey's representationally violated text—but with the proviso that Grey's text is produced closely with Māori interlocutors and is closer in historical time both to the event of colonization and to precolonial understandings. Representational violence is inescapable—it has always already happened—but alerting students to its different moments and textures may prove productively unsentimental.

3. Tamaira and Fonoti are positive about *Moana*'s power to transform global understanding through the film's wide distribution of collaboratively produced indigenous narratives. In defense of her participation in *Moana*'s Oceanic Story Trust, Fonoti cites the Samoan proverb in response to indigenous critiques of the film on social media. I reintroduce the proverb not only as a guideline for the university classroom but also as a respectful and open-handed performative marker of Fonoti's possible indigenous intellectual disagreement with my own reading of the film.

## Works Cited

Bryld, Mette, and Nina Lykke. *Cosmodolphins: Feminist Cultural Studies of Technology, Animals and the Sacred*. Zed Books, 2000.

de la Cadena, Marisol. "Indigenous Cosmopolitics in the Andes: Conceptual Reflections beyond 'Politics.'" *Cultural Anthropology*, vol. 25, no. 2, 2010, pp. 334–70.

DeLoughrey, Elizabeth. "The Spiral Temporality of Patricia Grace's *Potiki*." *Ariel: A Review of International English Literature*, vol. 30, no. 1, 1999, pp. 59–83.

Dodd, Kevin V. "Whale Rider: The Re-enactment of Myth and the Empowerment of Women." *Journal of Religion and Film*, vol. 16, no. 2, 2012, pp. 1–26.

Fleming, Mike, Jr. "No. 12 'Moana' Box Office Profits—2016 Most Valuable Movie Blockbuster Tournament." *Deadline Hollywood News*, 24 Mar. 2017, deadline.com/2017/03/moana-box-office-profit-2016-1202050505/.

Garuba, Harry. "Explorations in Animist Materialism: Notes on Reading/Writing African Literature, Culture and Society." *Public Culture*, vol. 15, no. 2, 2003, pp. 261–85.

Grey, George. *Polynesian Mythology and Ancient Traditional History of the Maori As Told by Their Priests and Chiefs*. 1855. Edited by W. W. Bird, Whitcombe and Tombs, 1961.

Huggan, Graham. *Colonialism, Culture, Whales: The Cetacean Quartet*. Bloomsbury, 2018.

Huggan, Graham, and Helen Tiffin. *Postcolonial Ecocriticism: Literature, Animals, Environment*. Routledge, 2010.

Iheka, Cajetan. *Naturalizing Africa: Ecological Violence, Agency, and Postcolonial Resistance in African Literature*. Cambridge UP, 2018.

Ihimaera, Witi. *The Whale Rider.* Harcourt, 1987.

Keown, Michelle. *Pacific Islands Writing: The Postcolonial Literatures of Aotearoa / New Zealand and Oceania.* Oxford UP, 2007.

"Moana." *Box Office Mojo,* boxofficemojo.com/release/rl4249847297. Accessed 18 Aug. 2020.

*Moana.* Directed by Ron Clements and John Musker, Walt Disney Pictures, 2016.

New Zealand Ministry for Culture and Heritage. *Treaty of Waitangi.* 1840. *New Zealand History,* 18 June 2020, nzhistory.govt.nz/politics/treaty/read -the-treaty/english-text.

Nicholls, Brendon. "Indigeneity, Visuality and Postcolonial Theory: The Case of the San." *Indigeneity: Culture and Interpretation,* edited by Ganesh Devy et al., Orient Blackswan, 2009, pp. 203–11.

———. "Reading Ngugi on Four Continents: Relational Aesthetics and the Global Multicultural Classroom." *Approaches to Teaching the Works of Ngũgĩ wa Thiong'o,* edited by Oliver Lovesey, Modern Language Association of America, 2012, pp. 129–35.

Robinson, Joanna. "Earning Trust: How Pacific Islanders Helped Disney's *Moana* Find Its Way." *Vanity Fair,* 16 Nov. 2016, www.vanityfair.com /hollywood/2016/11/moana-oceanic-trust-disney-controversy-pacific -islanders-polynesia.

Skafish, Peter. Introduction. *Cannibal Metaphysics: For a Post-structural Anthropology,* by Eduardo Viveiros de Castro, edited and translated by Skafish, Univocal, 2009, pp. 9–33.

Soyinka, Wole. *Myth, Literature and the African World.* Cambridge UP, 1976.

Steinwand, Jonathan. "What the Whales Would Tell Us: Cetacean Communication in Novels by Witi Ihimaera, Linda Hogan, Zakes Mda, and Amitav Ghosh." *Postcolonial Ecologies: Literatures of the Environment,* edited by Elizabeth DeLoughrey and George B. Handley, Oxford UP, 2011, pp. 182–99.

Tamaira, A Mārata Ketekiri, and Dionne Fonoti. "Beyond Paradise? Retelling Pacific Stories in Disney's *Moana.*" *The Contemporary Pacific,* vol. 30, no. 2, 2018, pp. 297–327.

Viveiros de Castro, Eduardo. *Cannibal Metaphysics: For a Post-structural Anthropology.* Edited and translated by Peter Skafish, Univocal, 2009.

**Laura Wright**

---

# The Queer Ecofeminist Politics
# of Flora Nwapa's *Efuru*

In ecocritical postcolonial works of literature, the potential fluidity of sexual orientation and identity can present a provocation to the rigidly di-
chotomous structuring by colonial forces—of nature as inferior to "civilization," women as inferior to men, and animals as inferior to humans. An
ecofeminist framework helps students engage with such texts and recognize the ways that they queer our understandings of indigenous and postcolonial sexualities as well as our embedded assumptions about pre- and
postcolonial interactions with the natural world and its nonhuman species. I use Flora Nwapa's foundational novel *Efuru*—the first English-
language novel published by a Nigerian woman—to teach the intersections of queer theory, ecofeminism, and postcolonialism. While the work
does not engage explicitly with queer identity, its presentation of its protagonist as a childless Igbo woman who worships the environmentally conscious goddess Uhamiri of Oguta Lake provides a lens for teaching alternative African sexualities, such as the socially sanctioned practice of Igbo
women living with other women as "female husbands." In discussing *Efuru*,
I trace the ways two other works of postcolonial literature, the New Zealand
author Keri Hulme's novel *The Bone People* and the South African author
J. M. Coetzee's novel *Disgrace*, link sexuality to various postcolonial en-

vironments, because I want students to understand that sexualities—as well as environmental histories and ecological tragedies—vary from culture to culture and are affected by the colonial politics that have shaped landscapes and peoples. Further, I want to situate *Efuru* as both part of and distinct from a wider tradition of postcolonial environmental narratives in which characters eschew gender norms and expectations, norms and expectations that are dictated within indigenous cultures and imposed on them by the mandates of Western imperialism.

In this essay, I discuss the novels that I teach and a project that I assign in an upper-level postcolonial literature course taken predominantly by English majors—but also, as an elective, by international studies majors—at a regional comprehensive university in the rural southern United States. I focus on *Efuru* because, of the works that I teach, Nwapa's novel most clearly demonstrates the way that women's freedoms were curbed by colonization. The novel is set in the 1940s, between the Igbo Women's War of 1929, during which thousands of women successfully protested the colonial imposition of taxes on married Igbo women—an event that demonstrated the ways that Igbo women's precolonial rights were infringed on by colonialism—and the discovery of oil in Nigeria in 1956, which led to the environmental degradation of the Niger Delta. Written in the 1960s, during the second wave of Western feminism, the novel also tacitly engages with the tensions between Western feminism and Igbo womanhood. As a member of Nigeria's upper-class Christian elite, Nwapa struggled with the "mixed blessings of Westernization" (Jell-Bahlsen 285), and Efuru's attempt to understand why Igbo women would worship a goddess who gives them no children even as she gives them wealth and beauty juxtaposes communal Igbo conceptions of womanhood and individualistic, capitalistic Western ones.

We begin our discussion of alternative sexualities and environmentalisms by exploring the opening of *The God of Small Things*, by the Indian novelist Arundhati Roy, in which the narrator claims that the story at the heart of the novel could have begun "thousands of years ago . . . in the days when the Love Laws were made. The laws that lay down who should be loved, and how. And how much" (33). The narrative is set in Kerala, India, and focuses on the breaking of "Love Laws" dictated by the caste system. Roy's explicit mention of love laws helps foreground works by Nwapa, Hulme, and Coetzee, particularly because her novel also engages with the environmental degradation of the Meenachil River caused by the damming projects and introduction of pesticides that took place during the so-called Green Revolution. I ask my students what love laws exist or have existed in the United States, and we discuss those that have made certain relationships illegal at certain times—interracial and same-sex marriage, for example—and what the fact that some of these relationships are now legal tells us about the fluidity of boundaries, the policing of desire, and the very meaning of what is "natural." I use Kate Soper's article "Unnatural Times? The Social Imaginary and the Future of Nature" to help students understand the ways that the designation "unnatural" has historically bolstered "spurious claims that were being made about the supposed 'perversity' of homosexuality, or about the 'naturally' ordained character of divisions and differences (relating to class, gender, ethnicity) that in reality owed more to social construction than to biological determination" (224). We explore the ways that our understandings of the "natural" world are mediated through culture and colonial history.

For their final essay, I ask students to write a researched comparative analysis of a love law from one of the novels we have read in class and a love law that is familiar to them from their own culture. The laws that they discuss may be legally enforced or socially sanctioned. I ask that students reflect on the role that various love laws play in the works we studied during the semester, noting polygamy in Igbo culture, arranged marriage in Victorian England, and caste-appropriate relationships in India. I remind them that what is considered appropriate behavior for women and men depends on context, and that the rules governing this behavior hinge on all sorts of variables—like location and time period. What may be unacceptable in one place may be perfectly fine in another. The tragedies that befall the characters in Roy's work are clearly a result of "civilization's fear of nature, men's fear of women, power's fear of powerlessness" (292), a causality that ecofeminism makes explicit.

In teaching ecofeminism, I use Greta Gaard's essay "Ecofeminism Revisited," which traces ecofeminism from its origins in the 1980s through its mischaracterization as essentialist and the subsequent "antifeminist backlash" that led to its rebranding—as, for example, "feminist environmentalism"—in the 1990s (26). According to Gaard,

> Ecofeminism emerged from the intersections of feminist research and the various movements for social justice and environmental health, explorations that uncovered the linked oppressions of gender, ecology, race, species, and nation [and] exposed the historical and cross-cultural persecution of women as legitimized by the various male-dominated institutions of religion, culture, and medical science . . . , linking the

physical health of women and the environment with the recuperation
of a woman-centered language and thought. (27)

Effectively, an ecofeminist framework recognizes that the oppression of
the environment, of women, of colonized people, and of nonhuman animals are all linked through patriarchal ordering that establishes the binary
oppositions of black and white, nature and culture, woman and man, colonized and colonizer, homosexual and heterosexual, and animal and
human that privilege whiteness, culture, masculinity, colonization, heterosexuality, and humanity over their supposed opposites. The ecofeminist
position maintains that because all oppressions are linked, it is necessary
to elevate what is associated with but not essential to the feminine: nature,
women, the colonized, and animals, for example.

But such a position could still be guilty of sustaining the binary
thought responsible for ecofeminism's original disenfranchisement, which
is why, particularly in a postcolonial context, Homi K. Bhabha's work helps
students move beyond the Western authorized narratives of imperial nation formation that perpetuate a history dependent on a belief in a superior self and an inferior other. I share with my students Bhabha's characterization of liminality in his 1990 work *Nation and Narration*. "[T]he
boundary that marks the nation's selfhood," Bhabha writes, "interrupts
the self-generating time of national production with a space of representation that threatens the binary division with its difference," and "it is from
the liminal movement of the culture of the nation—at once opened up
and held together—that minority discourse emerges" (299, 305). Understanding the notion of the liminal helps students engage with the taboo
space between oppositions, allowing them to recognize alternative sexualities within postcolonial narratives as disruptive of dualistic thought. According to Bhabha, "nationness" is a continuing hybrid story constructed
over time by people who have different amounts of power. The people who
are marginalized have more power to participate or compete in the telling
of this story than one might at first think, and it is from within the space
of the liminal—the queer space of identification—that their stories can take
shape.

## Queering the Postcolonial Environment

Before discussing *Efuru*, I want to touch briefly on Hulme's and Coetzee's
novels, since I teach them in conjunction with Nwapa's work. Hulme's *The*

*Bone People* challenges and queers New Zealand's sense of itself as a bicultural nation, addresses environmental devastation through interpersonal transformation, and offers a picture of a society whose members refuse to fit into neat binaries of Pakeha[1]/Maori, man/woman, and straight/gay. The main characters form a composite family: the Maori man Joe, the white European child Simon, and the hybrid woman Kerewin, who claims that, despite her "racial" status as one-eighth Maori, she feels *all* Maori (Hulme 62). Kerewin identifies as asexual, a "neuter human" (96), and Joe's bisexuality eschews rigid enforcement of Maori masculinity and challenges the notion that homosexuality was a European import that did not exist in Maori societies before colonization (Thomas). Simon's silent inability—or unwillingness—to speak and his androgyny destabilize the narrative of encounter authorized by the white men who colonized New Zealand. We discuss the ways that Kerewin, a virgin, complicates our conceptions of the ecofeminist "earth mother" archetype, even as she and the other characters' ultimate stewardship of the land—in particular the 796 acres given to Joe by the Maori elder Tiaki—offers a potential first step in the process of reviving long-sleeping Maori gods and potentially healing a country fractured by its colonial legacy. We discuss how the ancient Maori term *takatāpui*, meaning "intimate companion of the same sex," was driven out of usage for hundreds of years by British colonization, reflecting the way the colonizers' Victorian ideology pathologized nonheteronormative sexualities and led to a denial of those orientations within the indigenous populations of Aotearoa (Thomas).

Hulme's novel offers a new mythology to heal a bicultural (Pakeha/Maori) nation, one based on an embrace of hybrid cultural identities, alternative sexualities, and ecofeminist stewardship of the postcolonial land. From here, by way of our analyses of the ecofeminist character Lucy Lurie in Coetzee's *Disgrace*, we examine the ways that denial of African queer precolonial identities has worked to undermine land reclamation and sexual orientation in postapartheid South Africa. Despite the fact that South Africa's 1996 constitution guaranteed rights to LGBTQ individuals, arguments against homosexuality in the country as well as elsewhere in Africa—as in New Zealand—stem from the belief that homosexuality was a colonial import, unknown in traditional African societies before colonization. Activists counter this argument by "citing African words for homosexuality" and arguing that "it was homophobia rather than homosexuality that the colonizers brought" ("Drag Queens"). Pushback against notions of nonheteronormative African sexualities focuses on the ways that colonization across the continent emasculated black African men. The rape at the heart of *Disgrace* is perpetrated by three black men against the protagonist David Lurie's white, environmentalist, vegetarian, lesbian daughter, Lucy, a woman whose sexuality David seems unable to comprehend, noting that "perhaps she simply prefers female company. Perhaps that's what lesbians are: women who have no need of men" (102). According to Brenna M. Munro, "Lucy's rapists . . . summon up the terrifyingly high rates of sexual assault in post-apartheid South Africa, a nightmare incarnation of heterosexuality that is often interpreted as both symptom and sign of the failure to build the hoped-for new nation" (415). Lucy's rape can also be placed in the context of the South African practice of "corrective rape," the "rape of gay men and lesbians to 'cure' them of their sexual orientation" (Carter), a postcolonial, postapartheid intervention dependent on the denial of precolonial African queer identities. But Lucy refuses to leave her farm or tell the police what happened to her, saying to her father, "[I]sn't there another way of looking at it, David? What if . . . what if *that* is the price one has to pay for staying on? They see me as owing something. They see themselves as debt collectors" (Coetzee 155). The debt that Lucy feels she and other white South Africans owe is the land itself.

## *Efuru*'s Homosocial Ecofeminism

My students unpack the complexities and historical circumstances that foreground *Disgrace*'s problematizing of Lucy's rape and her response to it as well as the environmental displacement of black South Africans that underscores these experiences. If Lucy's reaction is troubling, it is also, I argue, an ecofeminist recognition of the various racial, sexual, and environmental oppressions that have shaped South Africa's history, before and after apartheid. Our discussions of *Disgrace* and *The Bone People*—works set after colonization has ended in South Africa and New Zealand—help provide a framework for reading the ways that colonization affected indigenous conceptions of sexuality and land stewardship. When we turn to Nwapa's novel *Efuru*, a work that is set in 1940s Nigeria, during that country's colonization by England, students can see the way precolonial Igbo sexualities and environmental practices remain within the narrative, even as they are challenged by European norms and laws.

*Efuru* is foundational not only because it was the first novel published in English by a Nigerian woman but also because it focuses on the women's culture of communal Igbo society, a culture largely ignored by Nwapa's male contemporaries, particularly Chinua Achebe. In *Efuru*, Nwapa explores the personal lives of women in the town of Oguta, eschewing the nationalist mythmaking undertaken by Nigerian male authors of the time and providing instead, as Elleke Boehmer notes, a "female" version of reality (7). Efuru, we learn early on, is a "remarkable woman" (Nwapa 7)—in that she is remarked upon by those around her because of her beauty, her ability to make money, and her generosity. Women in Igbo society gain status through, and are expected to have, children, but Efuru's only daughter dies early in the novel, and Efuru does not conceive again. After her daughter's death, Efuru is called to become a follower of Uhamiri, the goddess of Oguta Lake, a deity that gives women wealth and beauty but denies them children.[2] Further, the men in Efuru's life treat her terribly and eventually vanish, leaving Efuru in the company of the other village women under the protection of what Ifi Amadiume refers to as a "matriarchal umbrella" ("Bodies" 43), a homosocial community in Igbo society in which women support other women throughout their adult lives. Along with this matriarchal support system and Efuru's childlessness, her relationship with her second husband's second wife, Nkoyeni, and the conservationist dictates of Uhamiri all help Efuru navigate an environmentally significant homosocial space within a changing colonial Nigeria.

The goddess Uhamiri appears to Efuru in her dreams, calling her to become an adherent. According to Sabine Jell-Bahlsen, the goddess of Oguta Lake "is the mythical mother of the Oru people. Their farming cycle and the timing of their cultural activities revolve around the flooding and receding of the lake and its adjacent rivers" (254). I have written elsewhere that Nwapa's interpretation of Efuru's worship of Uhamiri as a deity that denies her adherents children, along with the goddess's conservationist dictates of avoiding fishing on Orie day[3] and respect for the power and importance of water, allows Efuru to function as a "postcolonial, ecofeminist prototype, a woman situated at the historical moment when Igbo women's matrilineal power was in decline [as a result of colonization] and environmental devastation, particularly as a result of the discovery of oil in Nigeria, was just beyond the horizon" (Wright 135). In defense of Uhamiri's environmental mandates, Omirima, the village gossip, chides Efuru's mother-in-law for letting Efuru's maid, Ogea, fish on Orie day: "You allow Ogea to fish today being Orie day. The day our Uhamiri says that we should keep holy. . . . That is why there are no fish in the lake. . . . The children of these days have polluted the lake" (Nwapa 195).

When teaching about environment and sexuality in *Efuru*, one must engage with the "bath," or female circumcision, that Efuru undergoes early in the novel. While many students have strong feelings about the way this procedure curtails women's sexuality in patriarchal societies, in *Efuru* the ceremony is performed by a woman in the presence of other women, and the novel barely discusses the actual surgery beyond brief admonishments from village women that Efuru should have had her bath before marrying her husband, Adizua, and the reminder that "the pain disappears like hunger" (14). More attention is placed on the feasting in which Efuru engages afterward, as she grows plump and "more beautiful every day" (17). We discuss the ways that circumcision is treated as a love law and rite of passage that allows women to become full members of their society. Darja Marinsek notes that Nwapa gives us a depiction "of the complexity of the issue at hand, mostly by constant interweaving of apologetic passages, explaining the African view of circumcision, by the choice of vocabulary . . . [and] by the ideological stance of the narration itself" (136). To understand the way that the bath—as well as other Igbo sexual practices—functions in the world of Nwapa's novel, we must recognize how our Western perspectives shape our understanding of African sexualities. In Igbo culture, which is communal and polygamous, men marry more than one woman. Efuru's status as "barren" puts her at odds with the expectations of the women in the novel; it is the female characters who criticize Efuru for not having children and who encourage her to find another wife for her second husband, Gilbert, whom she marries after being abandoned by Adizua. Omirima says of Efuru, "[S]he is good but she is childless. She is beautiful but we cannot eat beauty. She is wealthy but riches cannot go on errands for us" (Nwapa 163). Efuru can and does, however, find a second wife for her husband to marry, and the second wife, Nkoyeni, who refers to Efuru as "mother," is able to have a baby.

So what are we to make of Efuru, a childless Igbo woman who worships Uhamiri, a goddess of ambivalence (Krishnan 2), offering a kind of Igbo female autonomy by capitalist means, an environmentally conscious hybrid deity with both precolonial and postcolonial attributes? According to Madhu Krishnan, Uhamiri—one of many water goddesses known collectively as Mami Wata—is "contradictory, both known as a nineteenth-century invention and signifying . . . a pantheon of water goddesses, long pre-dating colonial intervention" (2). It is in this space of ambivalence, the space of the liminal, I tell my students, that we should consider the alternatives that Igbo culture—including Uhamiri, a deity that champions conservation and a kind of alternative sexuality—gives to women like Efuru, particularly with regard to their status as mothers and wives, categories that would seem immutable. In her foundational *Male Daughters, Female Husbands: Gender and Sex in an African Society*, Ifi Amadiume explains the Igbo practice of "woman-marriage," whereby certain women were allowed to marry other women (99); according to Andrew Apter, Amadiume locates the practice "within a flexible gender ideology associated with significant female autonomy and empowerment" (48). Kenneth Chukwuemeka Nwoko explains that "in some cases, it was the barren wife in a marriage that took a younger wife for herself," and he argues that even though "it would appear that the invention of the woman to woman marriage was to ensure the continuity of patriarchy as a social system . . . , it stripped the latter of its purity" (76, 79). Further, the practice of women marrying other women in Igbo society was about ensuring the benefits of continued lineage and had nothing to do with sexual attraction between women, even as the practice has been treated as erotic by outsiders (Apter 41).

While Efuru's choice of Nkoyeni as a second wife for her husband is not characterized in the novel as a marriage between two women, it is possible to read the power Efuru wields in making this choice and her continued prominence in her society despite her status as barren as reflecting the ways that Igbo "women, perhaps most importantly, could become mothers through the taking of wives and custodial arrangements, separating the discourse of maternity from that of fertility" (Krishnan 4). At the end of the novel, Efuru has left her husband and returned to the home of her dead father, adamantly refusing her friend Difu's entreaties to return to Gilbert. In the tradition of the African dilemma tale, the novel ends with a question. After returning to her father's house, "Efuru slept soundly that night. She dreamt of the woman of the lake, her beauty, her long hair and her riches. She had lived for ages at the bottom of the lake. She was as old as the lake itself. She was happy, she was wealthy. She was beautiful. She gave women beauty and wealth but she had no child. Why then did the women worship her?" (Nwapa 221). I ask my students to answer this question. I contend that Efuru worships Uhamiri because the love laws that shape Igbo culture are flexible enough to allow her to do so, just as those of other African societies and of the Maori of New Zealand historically allowed less rigid orientations than the European model that was imposed on them. These discussions, and my students' engagement

with these various texts, allow us to examine what *natural* means in relation to sexuality and the environment, and they help us to better understand the importance of recognizing that the exploitation of environmental
resources during the colonial period is linked to the suppression of sexual
and gender relations and to queer and trouble the imperial narratives that
tell us otherwise.

## Notes

1. *Pakeha* means white New Zealander.

2. Unlike her portrayal in Nwapa's novel, the lake goddess did not traditionally require celibacy or childlessness of her adherents. Jell-Bahlsen reads Nwapa's
characterization of Uhamiri as a goddess who supports her adherents "beyond—
not instead of—childbearing" (256).

3. The Igbo week is made of up four market days: Eke, Orie, Afo, and Nkwo.

## Works Cited

Amadiume, Ifi. "Bodies, Choices, Globalizing Neocolonial Enchantments:
   African Matriarchs and Mammy Water." *Meridians*, vol. 2, no. 2, 2002,
   pp. 41–66.

———. *Male Daughters, Female Husbands: Gender and Sex in an African
   Society.* Zed Books, 1987.

Apter, Andrew. "Queer Crossings: Kinship, Marriage, and Sexuality in Igboland
   and Carriacou." *Journal of West African History,* vol. 3, no, 1, 2017,
   pp. 39–66.

Bhabha, Homi K. *The Location of Culture.* Routledge, 2004.

Boehmer, Elleke. "Stories of Women and Mothers: Gender and Nationalism in
   the Early Fiction of Flora Nwapa." *Motherlands: Black Women's Writing from
   Africa, the Caribbean, and South Asia,* edited by Susheila Nasta, Women's
   Press, 1991, pp. 3–23.

Carter, Clare. "The Brutality of 'Corrective Rape.'" *The New York Times,* 27
   July 2013, archive.nytimes.com/www.nytimes.com/interactive/2013/07
   /26/opinion/26corrective-rape.html.

Coetzee, J. M. *Disgrace.* Penguin, 1999.

"Drag Queens Outrage Africa." *Independent,* 21 Nov. 1999, www.independent
   .co.uk/news/world/africa/drag-queens-outrage-africa-739037.html.

Gaard, Greta. "Ecofeminism Revisited: Rejecting Essentialism and Re-placing
   Species in a Material Feminist Environmentalism." *Feminist Formations,*
   vol. 23, no. 3, 2011, pp. 26–53.

Hulme, Keri. *The Bone People.* Penguin, 1984.

Jell-Bahlsen, Sabine. *The Water Goddess in Igbo Cosmology: Ogbuide of Oguta
   Lake.* Africa World Press, 2008.

Krishnan, Madhu. "Mami Wata and the Occluded Feminine in Anglophone
   Nigerian-Igbo Literature." *Research in African Literatures,* vol. 43, no. 1,
   2012, pp. 1–18.

Marinsek, Darja. "Female Genital Mutilation in African and African American Women's Literature." *Acta Neophilologica*, vol. 40, nos. 1–2, 2007, pp. 129–46.

Munro, Brenna M. "Queer Family Romance: Writing the 'New' South Africa in the 1990s." *GLQ*, vol. 15, no. 3, 2009, pp. 397–439.

Nwapa, Flora. *Efuru*. 1966. Waveland Press, 2013.

Nwoko, Kenneth Chukwuemeka. "Female Husbands in Igbo Land: Southeast Nigeria." *Journal of Pan African Studies*, vol. 5, no. 1, 2012, pp. 69–82.

Roy, Arundhati. *The God of Small Things*. 1997. Random House, 2008.

Soper, Kate. "Unnatural Times? The Social Imaginary and the Future of Nature." *The Sociological Review*, vol. 57, no. 2, 2009, pp. 222–35.

Thomas, Melody. "Early Maori View on Sexual Fluidity Far More Liberal than Previously Believed." *Stuff*, 6 July 2018, www.stuff.co.nz/life-style/love-sex/105284489/early-mori-view-on-sexual-fluidity-far-more-liberal-than-previously-believed.

Wright, Laura. *Wilderness into Civilized Shapes: Reading the Postcolonial Environment*. U of Georgia P, 2010.

**Roanne L. Kantor**

# Finding Balance:
# Disability and the Ecocritical Lens

This essay emerges out of my experiences developing a class on narratives of disability from the Global South, versions of which I have taught at Brandeis, Harvard, and Stanford. The Global South contains the vast majority of the world's disability burden (Soldatic and Grech). But you wouldn't know it from the way the academic field is constituted, focusing primarily on political and literary developments in Europe and North America and on the majority-white populations in those areas (Bell). The distribution of disability is akin to the distribution of English speaking around the globe. If scholarly areas were to reflect the real distribution of either category, both fields would focus primarily on the Global South (Elam). Like the global spread of English speaking, disability in the Global South is indissolubly intertwined with histories of colonial violence and its current extensions in global capital.

Disability in the Global North is usually studied through frameworks developed in conversation with the social model, which holds that disability is a socially constructed condition derived from the marginalization of people with embodied differences, or impairments (Shakespeare). In this model, impairment happens offstage, such that its causes cannot be politicized or legally redressed (Soldatic and Grech). The model also assumes that impairment happens naturally as part of prenatal development, the normal aging process (an idea critiqued by Michael Davidson), or the "contingency" of random accidents, what insurers sometimes call, in a rare flourish of poetry, "acts of God" (Quayson, *Aesthetic Nervousness*).

None of that is true on a global scale. Instead, building on the work of scholars like Davidson, Ato Quayson, Karen Soldatic and Shaun Grech, and Michele Friedner and Tyler Zoanni, my class is premised on the idea that a significant proportion of disability in the Global South originates from the uneven distribution of the risk of bodily harm around the globe. Environmental degradation is a major source of such risk, leading intuitively to ecocritical approaches in the classroom. The reverse is also true: any course on postcolonial ecocriticism should include some treatment of disability.

With that in mind, I examine here the way that two South Asian anglophone texts, Indra Sinha's *Animal's People* and Rohinton Mistry's *A Fine Balance*, can be taught through a framework that weaves together disability, medical humanities, and ecocriticism. I aim to show how these fields interact in contexts of the Global South in quite different ways than they do in contexts of the Global North. Both novels concern large-scale disasters related to environmental policy, disasters that have a quite literal disabling effect on the main characters of each text. Both also reveal the role of medical practitioners and discourses in alternately creating and accommodating disability.

Sinha's novel concerns the health effects and legal ramifications of the 1984 Bhopal disaster. As a result of gas exposure, the novel's protagonist, Animal, exhibits a dramatic, painful spinal curvature that forces him to walk on all fours, while several other main characters experience physical and respiratory impairments. Mistry's novel follows the ill effects of purportedly environmentalist slum clearance and population control efforts of the 1975 Emergency. The plot is set in motion as one of the main characters, Dina, finding herself unable to work because of failing eyesight, opens an illegal sewing shop in her home. It is capped off when the tailors she employs, Om and Narayan, are intentionally maimed under the auspices of a government-sponsored sterilization campaign. Despite these similarities, only *Animal's People* is usually read through the frameworks of disability or environmental policy. And yet the same ambiguities and complexities that have usually prevented *A Fine Balance* from being read with these frameworks also make it a more valuable tool for revealing the complex relations between geopolitics, health, and the environment.

## Beyond Compare

The class I teach attracts a mix of literature majors seeking distribution electives, health and policy students looking to fulfill their English prerequisite for medical school, and, increasingly, students who self-identify as disabled. This broad mix of preparation and investment is probably characteristic of courses taught in interdisciplinary fields like disability studies, ecocriticism, and, to a lesser extent, postcolonial studies. For this reason, though the class is taught from my field of literary studies, I try to incorporate a variety of disciplinary perspectives—literature, anthropology, and policy—as well as a variety of locations and embodied perspectives—gender, caste, age, class, and sexuality—from the Global South.

This kind of comparativism carries risks (Melas). From a field like postcolonial studies that has launched so many critiques of Enlightenment-era universalism, scholars caution us against assuming that even our categories of disability are shared or that identifying as disabled is politically desirable among groups impaired by structural violence (Soldatic and Grech; Friedner and Zoanni). Shital Pravinchandra likewise warns that the threat of shared ecological disaster may override our attention to the continued global unevenness of exposure to risk. Yet the two novels themselves agree that comparison is part of what makes disaster thinkable (Donig). This happens both synchronically across forms of marginalization—Mistry's comparison of gender, caste, class, and disability—or diachronically across various disasters—Sinha's statement that his allegorical city of Khaufpur stands not only for Bhopal but for "every place in which people have been poisoned and then abandoned" (Donig 529).

The composition of my classrooms has also prompted this comparative approach. Scholarship on pedagogy for global literature and postcolonial ecocriticism tends to assume that our courses address student populations with no relation to the geographies and identities covered in course materials (James; Raja et al.). This has never been the case in my classes. Instead, up to thirty percent of students in this course identify as disabled. Even more are attracted to the course because they have a close family member with a disability—as I do myself. Students of color make up thirty to eighty percent of enrollees, a high proportion of them underrepresented minorities. Some of these students came to the United States from countries of the Global South—either as children or to attend college—and a much larger group have strong family ties outside the United States (up to fifty percent).

In my experience, these students are much more likely than white peers to self-select into a course about literature billed as "postcolonial" or "global." They consistently report the perception that these global stories relate clearly to their identities, and the class gives them space to both substantiate and challenge that perception. I make it clear at the beginning of term that students are invited, but never expected, to draw on their identity experience in class. This is perhaps especially important for students who are in the process of identifying as disabled, since they perceive, sometimes quite rightly, that revealing that status can be stigmatizing in academic and professional contexts. Whether or not your own classes reflect these demographics, I believe it is imperative to reject the pedagogical stance of orienting toward the notional white, American-born student with no preexisting knowledge, the student around whose experience such "global" or "postcolonial" classes are often imagined to revolve (Raja et al.). Instead, collectively, students in this course hold a vast body of situated knowledge about the contexts and problems we will discuss.

However, I also build in more formal ways to expand students' contextual and literary knowledge. I begin the first class with a group exercise aimed at teaching the basics of close reading. This is followed by a close reading essay, modeled for students by readings from Quayson and Davidson. In this way, students get early feedback about how well they engage with the formal qualities of the text. In the second essay, focused on context, students practice drawing on secondary literature from allied disciplines (using required or suggested texts from the syllabus in addition to their own research) while addressing a fundamentally literary research question. These skills come together in the longer final essay about a text and question of their choice—when class size permits, this is accompanied by a final presentation about their topic. For many premed students, this is the longest writing assignment of their college career.

In order to expand students' contextual knowledge, I often teach literary texts comparatively alongside ethnography about the places and events described in those texts. This is not just for students for whom these regions are unfamiliar; it is just as important for students with some background in the world areas we study. Ethnography is sometimes illuminating for students who overestimate the applicability of their particular (often privileged) experience to vast and socially complex regions. But just as often the secondary reading can be affirming in an academic context, articulating things they already know, sometimes inchoately, about cultures in which they participate. For a long time, anthropology has been the whipping boy, the bad other of postcolonial literature (Said; Quayson,

*Calibrations*; Huggan). This coheres especially in the idea that an anthropological reading of literature flattens its aesthetic qualities, treating it only as a repository of social-scientific fact. And indeed, the risk of a content-only approach to literature needs to be actively managed among the many students who come to this class from outside the literature major. Some of that management happens naturally as literature majors model formal analysis for other students during class discussion.

I also turn to anthropology because we scholars of literature would do well to remember that anthropologists are often pretty skilled readers too. Like us, they are attentive to metaphor and style and tone, things we sometimes assume belong to our own private domain (Visweswaran; Narayan; Kantor). These allied scholars also show us the way that narrative and poetic forms create meaning for real people who resemble the characters we read about. To teach *Animal's People*, I draw on Kim Fortun's *Advocacy after Bhopal* for an analysis of poetry as a tool of resistance and Anand Taneja's *Jinnealogy* for an excavation of ecocritical thought in Urdu and Persian verse. Likewise, I draw on Taneja's attention to literature as an alternative to insufficient state archives for the 1975 Emergency. Both Taneja and Emma Tarlo, in "Body and Space in a Time of Crisis," attend to the way various forms of writing act alternately as tools of oppression and forms of resistance against the structural violence of the Emergency, making them useful complements to *A Fine Balance*.

## Family Resemblances

With all these caveats about comparison in mind, I offer in this essay a relatively simple juxtaposition of two novels written about and within the span of a quarter century, focusing on people of the same age and gender in the same general region of the same country (the neighboring states of Maharashtra and Madhya Pradesh in India). Unfortunately, because both novels are so long—*Animal's People* is nearly four hundred pages and *A Fine Balance* is just over six hundred—there's not usually time to put both of them on the same syllabus. This is in part why I pose the following as a polemic between them, when in any other context either one would be a valuable addition to a syllabus on disability and ecocriticism.

The main characters' life stage makes these books good for undergraduates to think with. Though large political events overshadow the texts, much of their actual plots involve romantic and sexual developments among characters the same age as the typical student. They offer, in other words, highly relatable content that works like a charm to get students talking. These plot intrigues also open space to discuss the formation of nonnormative, "cripped" families in each text and the intersections of disability and sexuality (Wilkerson; Kafer; Parvulescu). Not all these intersections are positive. Both books represent boorishly sexist behavior by young men who inhabit marginalized identities. They therefore confront students with their desire that disabled and otherwise marginalized characters be portrayed as innocent so that they can identify with them emotionally and politically (Ticktin). These scenes also present an opportunity to unpack how one's positionality in a marginalized identity does not automatically create solidarity with other marginalized groups.

This attention to romance and family formation also plays a role in a striking difference between the two novels: their narrative structures. That is, both books are devastatingly sad in terms of the political realities they explore. But *Animal's People* is still a comedy as Shakespeare understood it, in that all the main characters survive and marry each other at the end. *A Fine Balance* is a tragedy for the same reason: one of the main characters dies, and the tentative "cripped" family of mutual interdependence is left in tatters, dispersed into atomized situations in which each of the main characters' labor power is coerced into furthering able-bodied, normative structures of exploitation. Students respond differently and somewhat unpredictably to these narrative forms. Some are galvanized by a tragic story told tragically, while others feel overwhelmed. Some students are tickled by a cynical, humorous approach, while others are put off (Fisher). Instructors can help students sort out the possible meaning of the form in these postcolonial narratives with reference to the scholarship of yet another anthropologist, David Scott (developing ideas from Hayden White).

### *Animal's People*: Ruffling a Smooth Reception

Between the two novels, *Animal's People* is much more appealing for reading in a postcolonial framework, especially one with an ecocritical focus. There's a remarkable consistency in what scholars have written about this book. Because Sinha's protagonist is brash and untrustworthy, and because Sinha frames the narrative as a way of "talking back" to the Global North, scholars have consistently overimbued the story with that resistant energy (Taylor; O'Loughlin; Johnston). In fact, despite moments of brilliance, the book is formally quite baggy. The ending is strikingly conventional. It's also noticeably didactic: there's almost no ambiguity about good and bad, and the path toward environmental and social justice is clear and uncomplicated.

Some of these elements arise from Sinha's positionality—not only a novelist but a longtime advocate. Sinha is one of the many middle-class Indian advocates that Fortun studies in *Advocacy after Bhopal*, appearing briefly in that monograph as the English translator of poetry written by Union Carbide's victims.

It is in part because of this intertextual relationship that I use Fortun's research to illuminate the essential role of poetry in Sinha's novel. Fortun is a skilled interpreter of poetry herself. In *Advocacy after Bhopal*, Fortun includes several selections of poetry by disaster victims and their advocates. She also draws comparisons between the Bhopal disaster and previous, smaller scale ecological disasters Union Carbide caused among marginalized communities in the United States. These include powerful readings of Muriel Rukeyser's *The Book of the Dead*, the response of another artist-cum-advocate in the wake of the 1930–1935 Hawks Nest Tunnel Disaster in West Virginia. Of course, Rukeyser's poetry would fit ideally on a syllabus with *Animal's People*.

More extensively, Fortun's focus on poetry as a tool of advocacy reminds us to pay attention to the poetic traditions on which Sinha draws in his novel and their relation to an ecocritical reading. This relation emerges most potently in the inclusion of a *marsiya*, an epic poetic representation of the battle of Karbala that helps organize the climactic action of the novel. The battle of Karbala (in present-day Iraq) in 680 CE was the scene of the martyrdom of Hussain and his followers, who fought heroically in the face of impossible odds and whose ritualized mourning forms the center of the Shia holiday of Muharram.

Monolingual postcolonial scholars have overlooked the centrality of the Karbala motif in *Animal's People*. This is the tradition that Syed Akbar Hyder has described as the archetype of resistance in South Asia. Sinha uses scenes from the observance of Muharram, including snippets of translated *marsiyas*, to reinforce the novel's political resistance. The ethical power of Hussain's martyrdom no doubt informs what the Khaufpuri movement's leader, Zafar, calls "the power of zero" (Sinha 229), a concept that has generated much of the critical energy on the novel (Taylor). Sinha uses Karbala to crystalize the stakes of the Khaufpuri's struggle in the novel's climactic hunger strike, during which Zafar and his followers refuse even water—an echo of the way Hussain's forces were prevented from accessing water during the battle.

Sinha's association of Karbala with the hunger strike and his association of both with hellish heat and thirst also make available an ecocritical reading. As Taneja has argued, Urdu literary and religious writings are a source of cultural memory through which everyday South Asians can articulate ecocritical stances in the present. We see something similar in the short story "Yazid" by the mid-century Urdu writer Saadat Hasan Manto, who uses the name of the villain of Karbala, Yazid, to add moral weight and historical dimension to a story about water management across the newly divided Punjab. An ecology-focused course might include a unit on postcolonial water rights and forms of political resistance that reads *Animal's People* and "Yazid" in concert with Mohsin Hamid's *How to Get Filthy Rich in Rising Asia* and Arundhati Roy's essays about the environmentalist movement Narmanda Bachao Andolan.

Finally, Fortun's book helps unlock the thorny ethical problems of advocacy. Scholars have argued that Elli is a stand-in for the NGO-ization of the postcolonial novel (O'Loughlin). I want to push this one step further by suggesting that Elli seems patterned heavily on Fortun. This includes everything from her physical description—blue eyes, a long nose, and close-set eyes—to her backstory—the experience of growing up in an American landscape depredated by multinational corporations, one that makes both Fortun and Elli sensitive to Bhopal's plight.

Over the years that I have taught *Animal's People*, students have become more and more suspicious of Elli's role in the novel. While this shift has many causes, not least among them is a projection of anxiety about their own role as future global-health workers. Including a reading of Fortun helps students draw together Elli and Zafar, another middle-class, outsider advocate whose marriage to a disaster survivor, like Elli's, helps legitimate him as a Khaufpuri. Like the discussions about intersecting privileges that respond to the novel's sexism, this line of inquiry helps students nuance their approach to difference, bringing their knowledge of white-nonwhite binaries in the United States into conversation with other social hierarchies in South Asia.

While scholars often laud the novel for its unresolvable politics, the book is simplistic at the level of plot, protagonist and antagonist, and hero and villain. The villainy in *Animal's People* is straightforward. The agent of evil, the Kampani (Dow Chemical / Union Carbide), has a single motivating force: greed. Moreover, because of the nature of the disaster, total harmony exists between the social justice narrative (recognition and compensation for disaster victims) and the environmental narrative (protection for the environment). This appealing simplicity is precisely why undergraduates tend to like the novel so much!

While Rob Nixon has used *Animal's People* as an example of how the world's poor fight back against "slow violence," the story Sinha presents is not complicated or hard to trace in the way Nixon's book suggests. Yes, Sinha's novel is a powerful way to force students in an American classroom to sit with their status as what Bruce Robbins calls "the beneficiary" of uneven global distribution. But the book also suggests that the solution to the problem of catastrophic environmental degradation is morally simple, black and white, even if it remains bureaucratically complex. One of the hard lessons of ecocriticism is that this is rarely the case.

## *A Fine Balance*: Creating New Resonances

Mistry's book is structurally similar to Sinha's—a book about disability and environmental rhetoric in central India that was short-listed for the Booker Prize. Yet, while scholars have read Mistry's novel in terms of disability (see Yorke) or the environment (see Donish), certainly no one has tied these two threads together. This is in part because the novel does not make itself readily available to trendy readings of its own moment, but mostly it's because the novel is simply a more complex, more deftly and consistently controlled, more traditionally literary text than *Animal's People*. And it is in part because *A Fine Balance* presents a view of agency that is much more complex than the one in *Animal's People*.

*A Fine Balance* concerns the suspension of democratic rule in India during the Emergency, from 1975 to 1977. Involving many loosely connected threads, the plot coalesces around environmentalist projects, slum clearance and forced sterilization, that ultimately lead to the disabling of two of the main characters, Om and Narayan. In addition to their employer-cum-roommate, Dina, various characters Om and Narayan meet in the slum are disabled, either impaired while working their risky jobs or intentionally maimed by a "beggarmaster" to be more competitive as beggars. While some of these representations are problematic, Mistry's novel is admirable for the way it consistently links impairment to economic precarity and environmental risk.

What makes *A Fine Balance* difficult for students? First, there's a mismatch between the social justice narrative and the ecological one. Both beautification and population control are avowedly environmentalist goals. Controlling population, in particular, is something that many students come into the class feeling is an unambiguous ethical good. Although theories of the so-called population bomb of the 1970s have since been modified or discredited, we are still inundated with rhetoric about the planet's limited resources and the individual choices we can make to shepherd them responsibly. What Mistry's novel illustrates, however, is that implementation of notionally ecoconscious programs and the ideologies of people who enforce them are violently opposed to the social justice narrative of the book. I use Tarlo to underscore Mistry's point that seemingly neutral policies like population control can be used to further oppress minority populations.

Second, medicine and doctors operate quite differently in *A Fine Balance* than they do in *Animal's People*. While much of the early plot of *Animal's People* revolves around other characters' suspicions about Elli, she ultimately proves herself to be a staunch and unambiguous ally to the people of Khaufpur. In *A Fine Balance*, medical professionals are not all intentionally evil, although it is through their actions that certain bodies become "operable." Here I use Tarlo's concept (further elaborated by Lawrence Cohen), which Tarlo develops to describe victims of slum clearance and forced sterilization. Tarlo argues that certain identity characteristics like gender or religion make citizens vulnerable to medicalized victimization, subject to rather than the subject of medical care. This is a relatively new but deeply necessary concept for students in my classroom: that medicine has a dark history of harming certain bodies in the pursuit of higher, seemingly ethical goals (Owens). Like other difficult conversations described in this essay, the conversation about the potential of medicine to do harm needs time and space to bloom in students' minds. That's why I recommend teaching this course in a seminar format, rather than a lecture class, whenever possible.

This discussion about the operation of medicine in the novel, however, risks driving us away from Mistry's literariness, when it is aesthetic choices that most clearly distinguish his engagement with ecocriticism from Sinha's. In contrast to the violence in *Animal's People*, which results from the simple desires and unified actions of the Kampani, violence in *A Fine Balance* emerges from the actions of many different agents with very different motivations. These motivations may be venal or noble, and they are often justified in the characters' own minds. While Sinha presents us with a strongly marked first-person voice and perspective in *Animal's People*, Mistry offers an omniscient narrative in which we are invited into the perspectives of several different characters and asked to witness how they make sense of their actions according to variously situated ethics.

Scholars of environmentalist movements in South Asia have long emphasized similar ethical complexities in ecological activism in the Global South. They remark, for example, on the uneasy harmony between far-left and far-right positions in everything from animal rights to pollution (Dave; Doron and Jeffrey; Govindrajan). They have likewise illuminated the conflict between advocacy for the rights of historically marginalized groups and the standard environmentalist dogma on issues like land protection (Vaidya). The conflicts also point us toward the deeper disjunctures between the central tenets of postcolonial scholarship and the philosophical underpinnings of the ecocritical turn (Pravinchandra). The way Mistry's novel surfaces these complexities makes his writing a rich impetus for discussions about ecology in the Global South.

Still, as I wrote toward the beginning of this essay, the polemic between these two novels is born primarily of the limited number of weeks in an academic term. Both do an admirable job of weaving together strands of ecocritical, medical humanist, and disability frameworks. Both focus on characters and problems that are productively relatable to American undergraduates while also exposing them to histories and experiences that may be—but are not always—radically unfamiliar. Topics like ecocriticism and disability emerge into literary study already framed by their social justice dimension (Wiegman). The aim of this essay has been to help teachers find the balance between addressing that dimension in the classroom and honoring literature's unique qualities as an aesthetic object—not least considering the way its aesthetics may contribute to its orientation to justice (Scott; Levine; James; Aubry).

## Works Cited

Aubry, Timothy. *Guilty Aesthetic Pleasures*. Harvard UP, 2018.

Bell, Christopher M., editor. *Blackness and Disability: Critical Examinations and Cultural Interventions*. Michigan State UP, 2011.

Cohen, Lawrence. "Where It Hurts: Indian Material for an Ethics of Organ Transplantation." *Zygon*, vol. 38, no. 3, 2003, pp. 663–88, doi:10.1111/1467-9744.00527.

Dave, Naisargi N. "Witness: Humans, Animals, and the Politics of Becoming." *Cultural Anthropology*, vol. 29, no. 3, 2014, pp. 433–56, doi:10.14506 /ca29.3.01.

Davidson, Michael. *Concerto for the Left Hand: Disability and the Defamiliar Body*. U of Michigan P, 2008.

Donig, Deb. "Seeing Double in Indra Sinha's *Animal's People*: Local Toxins, Global Toxicity and the Universal Bhopal." *Journal of Postcolonial Writing*, vol. 54, no. 4, 2018, pp. 528–41, doi:10.1080/17449855.2017.1402808.

Donish, G. P. "Environmental Concern in Rohinton Mistry's *A Fine Balance*." *Language in India*, vol. 18, no. 6, 2018, pp. 45–48.

Doron, Assa, and Robin Jeffrey. *Waste of a Nation: Garbage and Growth in India*. Harvard UP, 2018.

Elam, J. Daniel. "The Form of Global Anglophone Literature Is Grenfell Tower." *Post45*, 2 Feb. 2019, post45.research.yale.edu/2019/02/the-form-of-global-anglophone-literature-is-grenfell-tower/.

Fisher, Susan. "Teaching Rohinton Mistry's *A Fine Balance*: Two Cheers for Universalism?" *Canadian Literature*, vol. 190, Autumn 2006, pp. 180–87.

Fortun, Kim. *Advocacy after Bhopal: Environmentalism, Disaster, New Global Orders*. U of Chicago P, 2001.

Friedner, Michele, and Tyler Zoanni. "Disability from the South: Toward a Lexicon." *Somatosphere*, 17 Dec. 2018, somatosphere.net/2018/disability-from-the-south-toward-a-lexicon.html/.

Govindrajan, Radhika. *Animal Intimacies: Interspecies Relatedness in India's Central Himalayas*. U of Chicago P, 2018.

Huggan, Graham. *Interdisciplinary Measures: Literature and the Future of Postcolonial Studies*. Liverpool UP, 2008.

Hyder, Syed Akbar. *Reliving Karbala: Martyrdom in South Asian Memory*. Oxford UP, 2006.

James, Erin. "Teaching the Postcolonial/Ecocritical Dialogue." *Teaching Ecocriticism and Green Cultural Studies*, edited by Greg Garrard, Springer, 2016, pp. 60–74.

Johnston, Justin Omar. "'A Nother World' in Indra Sinha's *Animal's People*." *Twentieth-Century Literature*, vol. 62, no. 2, 2016, pp. 119–44, doi:10.1215/0041462X-3616552.

Kafer, Alison. *Feminist, Queer, Crip*. Indiana UP, 2013.

Kantor, Roanne L. "Common Ground: Filth as an Idiom of Critique in Two South Asian Communities." *Comparative Studies of South Asia, Africa and the Middle East*, vol. 36, no. 1, 2016, pp. 134–51, doi:10.1215/1089201x-3482171.

Levine, Caroline. *Forms: Whole, Rhythm, Hierarchy, Network*. Princeton UP, 2015.

Melas, Natalie. *All the Difference in the World: Postcoloniality and the Ends of Comparison*. Stanford UP, 2007.

Mistry, Rohinton. *A Fine Balance*. Alfred A. Knopf, 1996.

Narayan, Kirin. *Alive in the Writing: Crafting Ethnography in the Company of Chekhov*. U of Chicago P, 2012.

Nixon, Rob. *Slow Violence and the Environmentalism of the Poor*. Harvard UP, 2013.

O'Loughlin, Liam. "Negotiating Solidarity: Indra Sinha's *Animal's People* and the 'NGO-ization' of Postcolonial Narrative." *Comparative American Studies: An International Journal*, vol. 12, nos. 1–2, 2014, pp. 101–13, doi:10.1179/1477570014Z.00000000073.

Owens, Deirdre Cooper. *Medical Bondage: Race, Gender, and the Origins of American Gynecology.* U of Georgia P, 2017.

Parvulescu, Anca. "Reproduction and Queer Theory: Between Lee Edelman's *No Future* and J. M. Coetzee's *Slow Man.*" *PMLA,* vol. 132, no. 1, Jan. 2017, pp. 86–100, doi:10.1632/pmla.2017.132.1.86.

Pravinchandra, Shital. "One Species, Same Difference? Postcolonial Critique and the Concept of Life." *New Literary History,* vol. 47, no. 1, 2016, pp. 27–48, doi:10.1353/nlh.2016.0002.

Quayson, Ato. *Aesthetic Nervousness: Disability and the Crisis of Representation.* Columbia UP, 2007.

———. *Calibrations: Reading for the Social.* U of Minnesota P, 2003.

Raja, Masood Ashraf, et al., editors. *Critical Pedagogy and Global Literature: Worldly Teaching.* Springer, 2013.

Robbins, Bruce. *The Beneficiary.* Duke UP, 2017.

Said, Edward W. "Representing the Colonized: Anthropology's Interlocutors." *Critical Inquiry,* vol. 15, no. 2, 1989, pp. 205–25.

Scott, David. *Conscripts of Modernity: The Tragedy of Colonial Enlightenment.* Duke UP, 2004.

Shakespeare, Tom. "Social Models of Disability and Other Life Strategies." *Scandinavian Journal of Disability Research,* vol. 6, no. 1, 2004, pp. 8–21, doi:10.1080/15017410409512636.

Sinha, Indra. *Animal's People.* Simon and Schuster, 2007.

Soldatic, Karen, and Shaun Grech. "Transnationalising Disability Studies: Rights, Justice and Impairment." *Disability Studies Quarterly,* vol. 34, no. 2, 2014, doi:10.18061/dsq.v34i2.4249.

Taneja, Anand Vivek. *Jinnealogy: Time, Islam, and Ecological Thought in the Medieval Ruins of Delhi.* Stanford UP, 2018.

Tarlo, Emma. "Body and Space in a Time of Crisis." *Violence and Subjectivity,* edited by Das Veena, U of California P, 2000, pp. 242–70.

Taylor, Jesse Oak. "Powers of Zero: Aggregation, Negation, and the Dimensions of Scale in Indra Sinha's *Animal's People.*" *Literature and Medicine,* vol. 31, no. 2, 2013, pp. 177–98, doi:10.1353/lm.2013.0014.

Ticktin, Miriam. "A World without Innocence." *American Ethnologist,* vol. 44, no. 4, 2017, pp. 577–90, doi:10.1111/amet.12558.

Vaidya, Anand. "Woh Jangal Hamara Hai." *India Seminar,* 2017, www.india-seminar.com/2017/690/690_anand_vaidya.htm.

Visweswaran, Kamala. *Fictions of Feminist Ethnography.* U of Minnesota P, 1994.

Wiegman, Robyn. *Object Lessons.* Duke UP, 2012.

Wilkerson, Abby. "Disability, Sex Radicalism, and Political Agency." *NWSA Journal,* vol. 14, no. 3, 2002, pp. 33–57.

Yorke, Stephanie. "Realism and the Immaterial Disabled Body in Rohinton Mistry's *Such a Long Journey* and *A Fine Balance.*" *South Asian Review,* vol. 32, no. 1, 2011, pp. 267–84, doi:10.1080/02759527.2011.11932823.

**Brady Smith**

# Place and Postcolonial Megacities: A Project-Based Approach

The concept of place in ecocriticism often evokes a specific set of literary locales—Wordsworth's Lake District, for instance, or Emerson's New England woods. However, teaching postcolonial ecocriticism means asking students to expand their sense of the genres and settings that make up literary accounts of place. What, for example, might be gained from teaching place in the context of postcolonial megacities? How might literary accounts of a city like Lagos, Nigeria, help students reconsider ideas about environments and environmentalism in a time of global climate change? This essay sketches some approaches to teaching place in Nnedi Okorafor's *Lagoon*, a novel that treats Lagos as a vibrant site of environmental activism, interspecies conviviality, and even interplanetary and interdimensional exchange. Though I include critical materials and organizing questions that can be used to guide student discussion of the text, my goal in this essay is to offer some thoughts on how a project-based approach to teaching the environmental humanities can help students reframe the way they think about environmentalism and the relation between urban environments and the phenomenology of place. While the ideas about nature and place that many students bring with them to the classroom are rooted in the wilderness imagination of the United States, I suggest an approach to teaching place and postcolonial megacities that helps students cultivate a sense of place more appropriate to our globally interconnected age.

One of the foundational precepts of project-based learning is that students learn best by doing. As opposed to direct instruction, in which a teacher lectures or leads discussion about a topic or a text, project-based learning involves students completing a project while developing the skills and achieving the goals that organize the course. A course or a unit using a project-based approach will certainly include minilessons oriented toward the development of certain skills or the exegesis of texts, but such lessons complement, not constitute, the learning activities that structure the course. Taking a project-based approach to teaching place and postcolonial megacities thus requires instructors to reimagine traditional approaches to teaching in the humanities classroom. Instead of asking how they can guide students through the assigned texts, teachers should instead ask how key examples of postcolonial urbanism might serve as the foundation for a multidisciplinary, project-based inquiry into the nature of place. How can working with texts about postcolonial megacities help students reorient their thinking about how humans make meaning out of the human and natural worlds? How can undertaking such work help students reimagine their sense of place in the context of the global climate crisis?

In building projects about place and postcolonial megacities, instructors have a wealth of compelling texts and sources from which to choose. Indeed, one of the most exciting aspects of teaching postcolonial ecocriticism is the way postcolonial fictions frequently turn the tropes of Anglo-Northern environmentalisms on their heads. Ngũgĩ wa Thiong'o's *Wizard of the Crow*, for example, cycles between visions of pastoral nostalgia and urban decay, charting a trajectory from colonial forms of environmental aesthetics to the urban forms of environmental justice politics around which the novel's plot revolves. Lauren Beukes's *Zoo City* represents a Johannesburg of the not-so-distant future in which a great many tropes of the Anglo-Northern environmental imagination are present but incorporated entirely into the metropolis that the characters call home. And Henrietta Rose-Innes's *Nineveh*, about an ill-fated housing development in Cape Town, asks readers to probe how place is made and mediated across different spatial and temporal scales. Each of these texts can be paired with canonical works of ecocriticism to help students grasp how they rework some of ecocriticism's foundational tropes—selections from *The Environmental Imagination*, Lawrence Buell's foundational study of the American environmental canon, make for interesting reading alongside these novels, as do many of the essays in Tom Lynch, Cheryll Glotfelty, and Karla Armbruster's *The Bioregional Imagination*. These novels also work well with canonical examples of postcolonial ecocriticism to spur creative thinking about how the urbanization of environmental imagination complicates even postcolonial thinking about nature and place. Rob Nixon's "Environmentalism and Postcolonialism" is a useful resource for students, as is the first chapter of Ursula Heise's *Sense of Place and Sense of Planet*, especially when paired with fundamental readings in the history and theory of the Anthropocene such as Donna Haraway's "Anthropocene, Capitalocene, Plantationocene, Chthulucene" or Dipesh Chakrabarty's "Anthropocene Time."

In teaching the environmental humanities, however, I have become intrigued by the way that project-based learning enables students to materialize critical concepts in engaging and unexpected ways. Any of the aforementioned novels are more than capable of sustaining project-based work, but in what follows I focus on outlining some project-based approaches to *Lagoon* because, in teaching it, I have seen that students find the text unexpected and therefore productive for rethinking the nature of place. Not only does it blend classic tropes of environmental literature with the particularities of its settings in ways that students find challenging to consider within conventional ecocritical frames, but it also represents a deeply heterogeneous kind of storytelling that allows students to develop projects in different forms.

*Lagoon* is, on one level, a city narrative and an alien invasion story, chronicling the arrival of aliens in Lagos through the intertwined narratives of Adaora, a local marine biologist; Agu, a Nigerian soldier; and Anthony Dey Craze, a Ghanaian rapper on tour in Lagos when the aliens first appear. However, what makes the novel especially interesting for teaching place and postcolonial ecocriticism is the way it draws on and reworks the long history of the locale in which it is set. The city takes its name from the Portuguese word for *lake*, but this rather unimaginative designation actually conceals a long history of interaction and exchange—in precolonial Nigeria, the waters around Lagos were trading centers for the peoples of the region, waters that eventually became a port of call for European slave traders. In the novel, the arrival of aliens represents not a radical break in human history but a redoubling of the activity that has defined the lagoon for centuries and that defines the present of the novel as well. Indeed, in *Lagoon*, Lagos is not only a place where aliens encounter people but one wherein both aliens and people encounter myriad forms of life. As the novel makes clear, the denizens of Lagos are never solely human—the creatures that emerge from the water join an already lively community of human and nonhuman beings. Okorafor's dedication reads, "To the diverse and dynamic peoples of Lagos, Nigeria—animals, plant, and spirit," and the novel that follows introduces readers to not only human characters but the wide range of animal, plant, and spiritual beings. Notable among them are the road spirit that underlies the dangerous Lagos-Benin expressway and Ijeli, an ancestral spirit who suddenly appears in the flesh as chaos spreads throughout the city.

Read as environmental literature, *Lagoon* invites students to radically reorient their conceptions of place. While the paradigm to which discussions of place often default is rural and entirely nature-focused, *Lagoon* thinks differently—place here is urban, hybrid, and inclusive of a vast array of beings and forces whose presence decenters human beings in relation to their worlds. The novel is certainly capable of sustaining seminar-style discussion and conventional essays. How, for instance, does *Lagoon*'s complex representation of human, animal, and material agencies complicate accounts of bioregionalism? How does the novel's interplanetary narrative rework our grasp of a transnational ethics of place? But students can just as easily explore such questions in the context of interdisciplinary projects as well. If instructors are uncomfortable diving into project-based learning all at once, *Lagoon* makes an abundance of creative assignments available. What might it mean to rewrite sections of *Lagoon* from the perspective of Chicago or New York City? What places might the aliens of *Lagoon* be drawn to if they set down in Miami, Cleveland, or Los Angeles?

In asking students to explore such questions creatively—and in using postcolonial texts to think place more generally—one has to be careful not to design the assignment in such a way that it reinscribes the Eurocentric forms of urbanism that *Lagoon* contests. The point is not to ask students to rewrite the text so that it recenters American or European cities but to use the frame that Okorafor develops to rethink place in a way that enables them to see their own environments anew. A range of artistic and multimedia assignments are possible as well, depending on instructor goals and resources. Okorafor is especially interested in the musical and cinematic culture of West Africa, both of which could be part of student work on the text. But Okorafor's representation of Lagos as a multispecies and multidimensional community opens up some especially interesting possibilities as well. There are some extraordinary passages that could make for compelling student artwork or creative retellings of the story—the scene in which Ijeli appears, for instance, could spur student representations of deep time in relation to their own locales.

None of the aforementioned assignments, however, represent project-based learning in a fully fleshed-out way. While project-based learning certainly emphasizes creative assignments, its defining feature is that the work of undertaking the project guides the overall unit or course. What if teachers are interested in using these texts to think about place and postcolonial megacities from a genuinely project-based perspective? How can one use project-based learning to help students reimagine the way they think about nature and the phenomenology of place? It helps, in this context, to shift one's focus away from particular texts to more capacious concepts or projects—to present, in other words, the reimagining of nature or place as not only the idea that students will study but the project on which they will work throughout a unit or a course. Consider, as an example, a project that might be called "Thinking Place in the Anthropocene." One might begin such a project by asking students to create a representation of what they think of when they imagine concepts like "nature" or "place." This first activity could be done in conjunction with some of the aforementioned foundational texts in ecocriticism to help students build a critical vocabulary for thinking about what they have just represented. For instance, while constructing their own sense of place, students might also read the chapter on place from Buell's *The Environmental Imagination* to begin to develop a conceptual understanding of place as it is discussed in the field. This work could be done privately, if class time were at a premium, or students could present their initial representations of place, and the concepts they use, to build a shared conceptual vocabulary for the rest of the course.

The first part of the project would therefore be oriented toward putting students' preexisting senses of place into conversation with a critical vocabulary derived from the world of ecocriticism. That done, instructors might then turn to the project itself—remaking, in whatever mode students wish, the concept of place in an age of climate change. In one version of this project, a teacher would focus exclusively on *Lagoon* and its attendant critical materials as the means through which students can reimagine their own senses of place. Scholarship by Robin Law, Matthew Gandy, and Kristin Mann on the history of Lagos can be a useful primer for students, while Erin James's "Bioregionalism, Postcolonial Literatures, and Ben Okri's *The Famished Road*" enables students to situate the concept of bioregionalism in a postcolonial frame. Alternatively, for advanced classes, students might be given a range of texts and critical materials to pursue—*Lagoon*, *Zoo City*, and *Nineveh*, for instance, alongside the aforementioned critical sources, relevant contextualizing materials (Besteman; Mbembe and Nuttall), and the Haraway and Chakrabarty essays mentioned above. In such a scenario, students would not be required to read everything a teacher makes available. Instead, students would work singly or in groups and would choose the texts and critical sources around which to build their work. And instead of having class conversations organized around specific texts and critical sources, class meetings could be centered more fully around the conceptual threads that tie students' separate project inquiries together.

Whether one organizes the project around one or multiple texts, however, these examples of direct instruction would occur alongside and in conversation with students' project work—the means through which students creatively engage with and rework the critical concepts presented in the course. Projects in such a context could take many different forms. For first- and second-year students, teachers might want to define project work in advance, offering, for instance, a long-form version of the speculative fiction writing assignment outlined above or the opportunity to design the cover art for a new edition of *Lagoon* meant to bring out the novel's unique approach to place. More advanced students might define projects on their own, taking their inquiries into whichever direction best suits their particular skills and interests—a collection of poems, a short story, a digital animation, a photography collection, or an interactive map, to name just a few possibilities. In either context, it is helpful to set up a series of benchmarks to guide students as they work. Students should submit project proposals as soon as possible to help them develop ideas and get feedback from peers. They might also write a short analytical paper to demonstrate conceptual understanding of the text with which they are working and a literature review to help them understand the critical sources that they are using to develop their projects. Additionally, teachers might want to include presentations of work in progress to ensure that projects are ongoing and actively in dialogue with those of their peers. Using office hours as an opportunity for one-on-one meetings wherein teachers and students share feedback and work through challenges can be helpful as well. Finally, in project-based learning it's important for students to have the opportunity to present their final work to an audience. In some instances, classmates might suffice, but college campuses are especially rich in public spaces in which students might present their learning to outside groups. It might seem unorthodox to have students setting up gallery spaces in dining halls or organizing symposiums in their dorms' communal spaces, but that's precisely the point. Teaching place by means of project-based learning not only multiplies the kinds of learning that students can do in remaking their sense of the environments in which they live; it expands the boundaries of the classroom as well.

So far, I've shown how project-based learning can reveal to students a wide range of new forms of thinking about postcolonialism and the politics of place. However, the foregoing discussion also raises a number of practical questions about logistics, supplies, and assessment. How can one teacher guide a classroom full of students who might be doing completely different things, many of which are beyond the teacher's areas of expertise? How can such an approach to teaching be supported by an English department or a program in environmental studies, neither of which usually maintains the kinds of spaces and resources necessary for this kind of multidisciplinary learning? How is anyone supposed to grade a design for cover art, or a soundtrack, or a virtual reality rendering of the world of *Lagoon*? It is actually not as complicated as it sounds, provided that one can arrange the right institutional support. A key point to keep in mind is that, from a project-based perspective, a teacher need not be an expert in everything that students in the classroom are doing to address the texts and questions the class puts into play. In my experience, it is often better if they are not. Indeed, the point of project-based learning is not that teachers need to master all the skills that students might use as they work their way through a concept or a text. Instead, project-based learning allows students to bring the artistic and conceptual skills they already have into conversation with the skills in critical reading and writing developed in a humanities classroom. The role of the teacher or teachers is to guide students as they marshal their expertise in, for instance, digital animation, music curation, or creative writing to make and remake the meaning of place. It is to ensure, in other words, that students are using what they know to engage productively with what they are learning in the classroom.

The issue of institutional support is somewhat more complicated. Project-based learning in a university setting requires considerable lead time to make sure that the necessary resources are available to students. If teachers have little time or simply lack the institutional infrastructure, assigning shorter creative projects of the kinds described above makes the most sense. Some students may be comfortable providing their own supplies—a course might have a moderate materials fee—while such work might also be supported by university departments if possible. But faculty members who want to run a full-fledged project-based course will likely need special institutional support—a teaching grant from a teaching and learning center, for instance, or the backing of an interdisciplinary humanities center that can connect the myriad resources that a project-based course might require. Teachers might also want to build something akin to lab requirements into the course, should the space and resources be available. Having a time and space in which students can work collaboratively on projects related to place not only provides structured time for students to advance their work but enables the kinds of serendipitous encounters among students that can take inquiry in unexpected new directions.

Finally, consider the issue of assessment. The perception among many teachers is that projects are often insufficiently substantive and therefore lack the academic rigor on which they pride themselves. As I have tried to demonstrate, however, a project-based approach is not necessarily an alternative to developing the critical reading and writing skills that most English professors are accustomed to teaching. Instead, project work lets students bring the skills they already have into conversation with the skills developed in the humanities classroom, heightening engagement with those skills and enabling them to make the humanities more meaningful to the work they do elsewhere. Assessment should therefore focus less on the projects themselves and more on how well students' project work brings the aforementioned skills in relation to one another. How well does a detailed, interactive map of the world of *Lagoon* represent the main preoccupations of the novel? How well does the project demonstrate a conceptually astute reimagining of place? An essential part of any project is a rubric that spells out the goals of the project and the methods of assessment so that students know what to do and what instructors will be looking for. The form of the project should be clear, as should the benchmarks students are expected to meet and the project-specific learning outcomes. The rubric also affords an opportunity for learning standards to be cocreated among students and faculty members to give students greater ownership over the learning process. An equally important part is what is sometimes called a "wrapper," which is akin to an artist's statement—an essay that defines the aims and goals of a project and explains how the student pursued those goals. Along with any essays that students have completed up to that point, it forms a key part of the written course components and provides students an opportunity to carefully consider how well their projects meet the overall aims. Teacher comments and critiques can then be framed in conversation with students' own reflections. Such an assignment also enables peer feedback, should teachers want to include it in a course, and makes possible self-assessment as well.

Why, in the end, should instructors consider adopting a project-based approach to teaching place and postcolonial megacities? What can students learn by being challenged to reimagine their environments in this way? I advocate project-based learning for a number of reasons. One reason is that, as much as I value the craft of writing, I am aware that the academic essay can for some students pose a barrier to meaningful engagement with the concepts driving our courses, and I look for opportunities to supplement essays with other kinds of assignments wherever I can. Another reason is that I appreciate the serendipity that students bring to my classroom, and I aim to teach in a way that cultivates and builds on it as much as possible. But perhaps the most important reason stems from the peculiar nature of place and the problems we face in imagining it in a time of climate crisis. As mentioned above, the term *place* names a bounded environment or locale—a particular geographic setting, however defined. But as all ecocritics know, place is not just a set of geographic features—place is also profoundly historical, which means that place is also made. Increasingly, it is also made in relation to a growing sense of climate catastrophe across a wide range of spatial and temporal scales. By asking students to use project work to explore the concept of place, the assignments outlined here allow students not only to acquaint themselves with alternative understandings of place but also to remake their own senses of place by means of the perspectives opened up by texts like *Lagoon* and the others mentioned above. Thinking about postcolonialism and the politics of place, in other words, enables not merely an encounter with literary alterity but also an opportunity for students to reimagine themselves and their worlds in radically different ways—to defamiliarize the concept of place in the name of making it anew.

## Works Cited

Besteman, Catherine Lowe. *Transforming Cape Town*. U of California P, 2008.
Beukes, Lauren. *Zoo City*. 2010. Little, Brown, 2016.
Buell, Lawrence. *The Environmental Imagination: Thoreau, Nature Writing, and the Formation of American Culture*. Belknap Press, 1995.

Chakrabarty, Dipesh. "Anthropocene Time." *History and Theory*, vol. 57, no. 1, 2018, pp. 5–32.

Gandy, Matthew. "Learning from Lagos." *New Left Review*, vol. 33, 2005, pp. 37–53.

Haraway, Donna. "Anthropocene, Capitalocene, Plantationocene, Chthulucene: Making Kin." *Environmental Humanities*, vol. 6, 2015, pp. 159–65.

Heise, Ursula. *Sense of Place and Sense of Planet: The Environmental Imagination of the Global.* Oxford UP, 2008.

James, Erin. "Bioregionalism, Postcolonial Literatures, and Ben Okri's *The Famished Road.*" Lynch et al., pp. 263–77.

Law, Robin. "Trade and Politics behind the Slave Coast: The Lagoon Traffic and the Rise of Lagos, 1500–1800." *The Journal of African History*, vol. 24, no. 3, 1983, pp. 321–48.

Lynch, Tom, et al. *The Bioregional Imagination: Literature, Ecology, and Place.* U of Georgia P, 2012.

Mann, Kristin. *Slavery and the Birth of an African City: Lagos, 1760–1900.* Indiana UP, 2007.

Mbembe, Achille, and Sarah Nuttall. "Writing the World from an African Metropolis." *Public Culture*, vol. 16, no. 3, 2004, pp. 347–72.

Ngũgĩ wa Thiong'o. *Wizard of the Crow.* Anchor, 2007.

Nixon, Rob. "Environmentalism and Postcolonialism." *Postcolonial Studies and Beyond*, edited by Ania Loomba et al., Duke UP, 2005, pp. 233–51.

Okorafor, Nnedi. *Lagoon.* Saga Press, 2014.

Rose-Innes, Henrietta. *Nineveh.* Unnamed Press, 2016.

# Part II

## Global Ecologies and Uneven Flows

**Margaret Anne Smith**

# Decolonizing the Environmental Classroom: Increasing Student Agency through a Journal Assignment

In *Teaching to Transgress*, bell hooks writes that she has "been most inspired by . . . teachers who have had the courage to transgress those boundaries that would confine each pupil to a rote, assembly-line approach to learning" (13). Like the teachers hooks describes, I seek to create a framework in which my students can discover their own power. How, I ask myself, can students best decide for themselves how to learn and how to demonstrate their learning to themselves and to me—the one assigned the nebulous task of grading them? How can I structure a course to optimize student discovery and simultaneously "get out of the way" so that students are establishing and meeting their own learning criteria instead of mine? (For I am the one who must meet institutional standards by establishing a conventional syllabus, a fair system of assessment, and a thirteen-week semester.) How can we best grow aware of power dynamics in the classroom and explore the inner workings of the power in texts and contexts in an environmental, postcolonial class in literature?

As we interrogate power, context, voice, and perspective through course material, Peter Mayo's question becomes even more key: Whose side are we on when we teach? (9). Noah De Lissovoy suggests that a decolonial approach to education implies a profound reordering: he calls for a "more sensitive orientation to relationships, both within the classroom and at the level of the imagination of global society" and proposes "a curriculum against domination" (281, 285). Students are increasingly aware of locations of power in their educational lives. Richard Paul and Linda Elder's definition of critical thinking as "self-directed, self-disciplined, self-monitored, and self-corrective" demonstrates quite clearly that—if the focus of twenty-first-century education is indeed critical thinking, as is so often stated by our institutions—the focus of our various educational enterprises has to be the students themselves (4). The results of the student projects from my recent course show that students learned to place themselves at the center of their learning—not in a self-absorbed way, but in a way that reflects the critical inquiry and self-reflection of the adult learner, a learner who takes risks, engages in challenging work, and claims power.

## Context

Initially, in an early iteration of the course, my reading list included conventional forms of nature writing in the North American tradition, beginning with Henry David Thoreau. However, as my own understanding of the field grew, I began to incorporate more postcolonial theory and texts by writers of color into the curriculum. Course themes now include concepts of human nature and identity in an environmental context; land and landscape; nature and wilderness; territoriality and notions of land ownership; and culture, economics, and privilege and how they determine our relationship with the earth and its resources. I begin with Walt Whitman's "Song of Myself," from *Leaves of Grass*, to help establish an understanding of the traditional approach to environmental literature or nature writing. Ironically (and usefully), Whitman's questions and use of grass as a unifying symbol immediately establish a basis of inquiry that does not privilege traditional power. In Whitman's poem, it is a child who asks, "What is the grass?" (section 6, line 98). The poet answers:

> I guess it is a uniform hieroglyphic,
> And it means . . .
> Growing among black folks as among white,
> Kanuck, Tuckahoe, Congressman, Cuff, I give them the same, I
>     receive them the same. (lines 106–09)

Despite the mention of the Kanuck and Tuckahoe peoples in these lines, this is a settler poem, mostly overlooking Native Americans, but it broadly includes black and white, elected representative and laborer. We pursue this symbol of grass throughout the texts we read in the course. It comes to represent the natural state of the land and is used as a trope by several authors we read for the interaction among government, science, and corporate agriculture; for the indigenous identity formed by family and landscape; and for questions of displacement, treaties, and land ownership.

Joy Kogawa's novel *Obasan* describes the narrator's elderly Japanese Canadian uncle watching prairie grasses. When her uncle is forcibly removed from his home on Canada's west coast during World War II and stripped of his livelihood as a fisherman, his property, and his rights, he and his family are relocated to Alberta, where they live and labor on a sugar-beet farm, spending winters in an uninsulated hut with a dirt floor. Later, the old fisherman revisits the prairie fields over and over, repeating of the blowing grasses, "*Umi no yo.* It is like the sea" (1, 247). His livelihood and dignity have been taken from him, but he retains his story and his way of seeing the world.

Jamaica Kincaid's essay "Alien Soil" explores the political and cultural implications of landscape and landscaping. Both the people and the plants in her birthplace of Antigua have been brought there by the English: her people as slaves, and the vegetation as tamed and cultivated features of country gardens in faraway England. The equivalency between humans and decorative plants creates an uneasy portrait of a place in which humans are forced to labor for the economic benefit of their enslavers, Europeans who impose ownership on people and impose a European aesthetic on the landscape itself. Humans and plants are objects, and nothing remains untouched by colonial and environmental conquest.

In "Big Grass," the Native American writer Louise Erdrich delights in the mysterious simplicity of the northern tallgrass prairie. She recalls her childhood expeditions hunting and gathering with her father, reflects on natural cycles of death and renewal (including the essential role of wildfire and the buffalo who belong on the prairie), and observes in detail the complex ecosystem of a field. She notes, "The green fringe gave me the comforting assurance that all else planted and tended and set down by humans was somehow temporary. Only grass is eternal. Grass is always waiting in the wings" (1044). She would be converted to a religion of grass: "Sleep the winter away and rise headlong each spring. Sink deep roots. Conserve water. Respect and nourish your neighbors and never let trees gain the upper hand. . . . Connect underground. Provide. Provide. Be lovely and do no harm" (1047). Her integration of human beings with other life-forms allows grass to be a role model for ethical behavior.

Thomas King, an Indigenous writer who moved to Canada from the United States, reflects on grass in "As Long as the Grass Is Green," an essay in *The Inconvenient Indian: A Curious Account of Native People in North America.* He explores the difference between indigenous and settler concepts of land and home. Land is a defining element of indigenous culture and is integrally linked to language, stories, histories, food, and survival. Land is home: it is shared and not owned. For settlers, and even more so for European and North American governments, land has been a commodity to be occupied, used, or sold. This difference in concepts of land is at the heart of centuries of displacement and conflict, which King examines through the history of treaties in North America. Over the course of his essay, King returns to the phrase "as long as the grass is green and the waters run," a trope in use since at least the eighth century, when Charlemagne employed it to indicate the perpetuity of a treaty and a promise. For King, like Erdrich, the grass represents the wild, the natural, and the eternal.

I conclude the course with Maya Angelou's "Still I Rise," a powerful and hopeful poetic anthem. Although our readings include reflections on the beauties of the natural world, they also deal with climate change, our conflicted relationship to the land, and the injustices of colonialism and land appropriation that determine who lives where and how, so by the end of the semester we need hope. Angelou's song of freedom uses tropes of the black body, the female body, and the land. She builds her anthem using images of unrestricted nature ("moons" and "suns," the "ocean," and "daybreak"; lines 9, 31, 34) and images of natural resources ("oil wells," "gold mines . . . in my own backyard," "diamond"; lines 7, 19, 27) that are all under her own control. In freedom from shame, enslavement, and oppression, she rises. Her body has been used like a resource, like the earth, and she is now its owner.

Students explore these and other literary texts, write literary analyses, and give presentations on assigned readings. Most of this work is traditional in format, and students tend to perform in typical ways. However, particularly because we discuss land ownership and the environmental impacts of colonialism, it is important to challenge practices of classroom "ownership" by giving students more autonomy over their own learning. Going beyond the traditional methods of assessment creates a situation of risk and uncertainty for students, since they will not be graded on the usual, more predictable assignments like tests, research papers, and a final exam; however, I am mindful of the risk we all face as a result of climate change and the increased anxiety students feel when we study this crisis; I know there is power in choosing our own responses to it and to our course material. We talk about this fear at length over the first few weeks of the class. As Stephen Siperstein, Shane Hall, and Stephanie LeMenager observe in *Teaching Climate Change in the Humanities*, "[P]recisely because despair undermines the self, or at least the comfortable habits through which we live our everyday lives, it is often a precondition for fresh thought, new habits, and rethinking the kinds of socio-ecological relationships that generate livable futures" (7). It is my hope that students can confront fear and find solutions—in terms of action, but also in terms of personal ways of coping with anxiety around climate change. A journal assignment challenges students to explore course material, observe and express their own responses to it, cultivate new ways of living in the world, challenge power, and experiment more intentionally with how they learn.

## Method

I create a diverse reading list and a schedule of readings, discussions, student presentations, guest lectures, and activities. I encourage students to choose their own topics for papers and presentations, offer open-response prompts for student conversation, and invite students to identify and respond to current events. I create an open-ended journal assignment with the following prompts and requirements:

> Make connections and integrate academic learning with life learning.
> Gain facility in integrative writing by making frequent entries.
> Expand our usual model of academic writing by including creative work.
> Demonstrate an increasing awareness and understanding of our place in the environment by reflecting on readings, class discussions, and presentations—but also on the world around us.
> Spend at least ten minutes outdoors each day being *reflective*. Write about this experience.

I explain that the journal has personal, environmental, and literary value: personal, because it helps students cultivate a habit of noticing and reflecting and because patterns in our observing and thinking are more apparent when we write them down; environmental, because it encourages students to notice, read about, and engage with place and with environmental issues locally, regionally, and globally; and literary, because it requires students to hone their skills at literary analysis, through their writing about authors' style and technique as well as their engagement with various ideas, concepts, philosophies, and ideologies.

Finally, I tell students that spending reflective time outdoors should not include doing routine things like taking the dog out, waiting at a bus stop, or mowing the lawn. Instead, students should spend time outside in an intentional way, paying close attention to the environment immediately around them, everything from birdsong to trucks driving by.

## Results

Student journals have generally demonstrated a high level of engagement and critical thinking. Several students initially imitated authors we read in the course, but they eventually found their own voices. They questioned concepts of land ownership, belonging, and home. Most experimented with various art forms—illustration, painting, and collages of photos, leaves, flowers, moss, and plastics. One journal was a seemingly casual yet carefully structured and illustrated exploration of the world around the student, and it discussed various natural elements (sea, wind, moon, snow). One student began by reflecting on her "not too great" relationship with nature, based on fear, and expressed a strong desire to realize the calming effects of being in nature and a wish to put herself less at the center of her world. Her final entry concluded that she spent more time outside than usual during the semester, and she became less afraid of nature and more aware of the damage we do to it.[1]

Many charted our changing seasons, from warm September days to December snowstorms, and considered how our relation to weather varies based on convenience and economic position. Some wrote about current events: government response to fires in California, a proposed carbon tax, statements about the environment by world leaders, debates around food sources, and use of natural resources. Some wrote about the privilege of those with the luxury of being able to spend leisure time outdoors and the realization that men are typically more likely to be safe outdoors than women. Many wrote about various forms of animal life, how we anthropomorphize them, how we domesticate them, and how we encroach on their territory. One student intended to write about a family road trip through beautiful countryside but ended up reflecting on her use of plastics while traveling. She concluded, "I have a responsibility I must honor, to the environment and my children." While most of this student's journal was illustrated by hand and filled with beautiful images, this entry was accompanied by plastics pasted onto two pages.

Most students—from their very first journal entry—were aware of their own learning process and deliberately set out to try new things, reflecting on the effect of attempting to experience nature in a new way. A botanist colleague took us on a guided walk through the nearby forest, and one student made astute observations of her peers:

> One thing I noticed on this walk was how little my classmates actually looked around. . . . They stood almost completely still as if they could understand the trees by being like them rather than by getting close to them. Most of them walked only forward and only when instructed to do so, inspected only those plants that they were handed by the teacher, touched and picked up only what they were told to. Though they were surrounded by wild, stimulating nature, my classmates seemed to me to be the least natural things there, simplistic robots following orders as if their programming didn't allow for listening and independent movement at the same time.
>
> Perhaps it is the way our society's school system demands the obedience of students that has dulled my classmates so? Is it the insistence of sitting motionless and absorbing every word our teachers utter as if we are merely sponges and they some sort of Messiah bringing us knowledge like life-giving water?

I had, in fact, been disappointed by the awkward silence of my students on this forest walk. This student's observations helped me realize that some students do not spend much time outdoors, that they are uneasy in the forest (I will need to address this unease in future classes), and that most of my arts students were perplexed by the botanist's scientific approach.

Other students reflected lucidly on the act of journaling:

> I'll admit that I tend to favor logic and the impersonal over anything involving emotion or the personal in my own writing. I'm decent at essays and have been writing almost exclusively those for a while. Unfortunately, this meant that the idea of a reflective exercise such as this

journal was approached with hesitation as it tends to require emotion to make the sort of meaning written about in these types of things. I suppose if you don't care about nature it's rather difficult to write about. . . .

The opportunity to create something outside of an essay on a subject barely cared about or a book no one really wanted to read is a luxury rarely afforded to university students, and I appreciate it. I find that creating comes from, is itself, and reflects, experience. Natural things adapt to their environments, and experience becomes the environment of creation. . . .

Despite initial reservations, I found this exercise conducive to growth and will consider extending it to other areas of my life as well as continuing to use it as a way to connect with nature and myself moving forward.

Others addressed contemporary busyness, the demands of student life, and our increasing inability to sit quietly:

As I am walking down the stairs out of our classroom to sit outside for ten minutes doing absolutely nothing, there is really only one thing on my mind, "How else could I be spending this time?" . . . Sitting here for just ten minutes just listening and observing nature disassociates me from the social aspect of my everyday life but connects me deeply with an unfamiliar feeling of nature. It is hard to sit here doing nothing; I have a strong urge to pull out my phone and browse the internet and text my friends. . . . The new expectations of communication and socialization are transforming everyone to be incapable of just enjoying moments with others and appreciating the natural beautiful world we live in. When it was finally time to go back into the classroom after ten minutes outdoors, I understood how even though I started thinking about all the things I could be using that time for, it led me to reflect on how people are too reliant on others today and could use this time to be alone.

This same student concluded at the end of the semester that the "course has been a revelation [of] how [being] disconnected [from] social interaction is not always a negative thing" and that

[c]onnecting with wilderness can open people's reflective opinions up to themselves more than anything else. For example, when reflecting on nature topics in the journal I find my mind can make connections with virtually anything regarding nature; I have found out a lot about myself on different controversial topics where previously I did not really take a stand on either side.

Another student set out with clear intentionality to foster self-awareness as well as a greater understanding of her position in nature. She writes after the first class:

> Today, as a break from class, we were asked to go outside and sit. No phones. No laptop. No talking. Only observing and opening our minds to nature. This is something that was very different for me. I never take the time to sit outside and enjoy what nature has to offer. To ease into the journals, I thought I would reflect on my first session outside.
>
> My classmates were scattered all over the quad. . . . I sat and really tried to open up to the world around me. I found this very difficult, as I am usually an indoor girl. So I sat there for a while, and I found myself bored. After boredom took hold, I realized I was not concentrating on the world around me; I was just waiting for time to be up so that I could go back inside. I decided to actually invest in the challenge and concentrate.
>
> . . . I have decided that 10 minutes isn't enough for me and most of my journals will be based around my sessions outside lasting 30–60 minutes, until it gets too cold to do so.
>
> I hope that this exercise will become an escape for me. I am hoping to reconnect with nature and spend more time engulfed in it since I can honestly say I spend most of my time inside.

By week 6, her boredom was gone:

> I think this was one of the first times I had actually been anticipating my time with nature. When I got home from class I was ready to spend some time outside. It became an escape for me, a time when I had no homework, housework, papers, and laundry, none of it. Just time for me, my thoughts, and nature.

Her final entry reflects on her learning over the course of the semester:

> I wanted to reflect on how my journaling and views on nature have been altered with this experience.
>
> To start, I was really proud of the fact that my sessions lasted as long as they did. . . . It became a weekly routine and before I realized, I was finding myself outside even when I was not journaling. Nature became an escape for me. . . . It became a time that I looked forward to and anticipated. I found when I came in I was feeling more refreshed and energized. I also think it had an effect on my overall mood for the week.

> All in all, this was a good experience and I think it also helped me process the course material better. . . . I found it was easier to make connections in the fresh air when I had nothing else on my mind.

Ultimately, the students' work surpassed my expectations, as did their expressions (collected through course evaluations) of enjoyment, enrichment, and freedom. While some expressed unease with the openness of the journal project, each student flourished. If ambiguity and a request for creativity initially made my students feel awkward, I am now more compelled to seek ways to encourage experimentation, individuality, and freedom. Finally, I know that lessons learned from course content are often temporary. My students developed habits, intentional practices, and awareness that might outlast the fleeting classroom lessons. Increased agency can help students overcome powerlessness and anxiety and give them hope. Education must create opportunities for students to transgress boundaries and transform the future. Particularly in courses in which we expect students to examine oppressive structures of colonialism and environmental resource extraction and consumption, it is fitting to free students to explore ways to increase their own autonomy through self-directed critical inquiry and reflection.

## Note

1. Anonymized quotations from student journals are from the course Special Topics: Environmental Literature, held in fall 2018 at the University of New Brunswick, Saint John. Quotations are used with permission of the authors and have been edited for length. I am grateful to have learned with and from these students.

## Works Cited

Angelou, Maya. "Still I Rise." *And Still I Rise: A Book of Poems*, Random House, 1978, pp. 61–63.
De Lissovoy, Noah. "Decolonial Pedagogy and the Ethics of the Global." *Discourse: Studies in the Cultural Politics of Education*, vol. 31, no. 3, July 2010, pp. 279–93. *ResearchGate*, doi:10.1080/01596301003786886.
Erdrich, Louise. "Big Grass." *The Norton Book of Nature Writing*, edited by Robert Finch and John Elder, W. W. Norton, 2002, pp. 1043–47.
hooks, bell. *Teaching to Transgress: Education as the Practice of Freedom.* Routledge, 1994.
Kincaid, Jamaica. "Alien Soil." *The Norton Book of Nature Writing*, edited by Robert Finch and John Elder, W. W. Norton, 2002, pp. 1015–22.

King, Thomas. "As Long as the Grass Is Green." *The Inconvenient Indian: A Curious Account of Native People in North America*, Doubleday Canada, 2012, pp. 215–47.

Kogawa, Joy. *Obasan*. Penguin, 1981.

Mayo, Peter. *Echoes from Freire for a Critically Engaged Pedagogy*. Bloomsbury, 2013. *ProQuest Ebook Central*, ebookcentral.proquest.com/lib/unb/detail .action?docID=1099523.

Paul, Richard, and Linda Elder. *The Miniature Guide to Critical Thinking: Concepts and Tools*. 4th ed., Foundation for Critical Thinking Press, 2007.

Siperstein, Stephen, et al., editors. *Teaching Climate Change in the Humanities*. Routledge, 2017.

Whitman, Walt. "Song of Myself." *Leaves of Grass*, edited by Sculley Bradley and Harold W. Blodgett, W. W. Norton, 1973, pp. 28–89.

**Nicole Cesare**

---

# Teaching Postcolonial Climate Fiction

Between 2015 and 2017, the following headlines appeared in *Wired*, *The Guardian*, *The Atlantic*, and the *Los Angeles Review of Books* respectively: "Cli-Fi—That's Climate Fiction—Is the New Sci-Fi" (Tonn); "Cli-Fi: A New Way to Talk about Climate Change" (Abraham); "Climate Fiction: Can Books Save the Planet?" (Ullrich); and "So Hot Right Now: Cli-Fi Comes to YA" (Robins). They announced the arrival of a new portmanteau designed to grab the reading public's attention. Climate fiction, according to these articles, was a newly identified set of novels focused on anthropogenic climate change, offering literary representations of possible futures. Ideally, the articles suggest, these books would stir readers into awareness, even action. While representational literature has long engaged environmental themes, reading literature specifically through the lens of climate change is a recent phenomenon. As such, it offers a unique opportunity to engage students on several levels. First, students born in the twenty-first century feel the urgency of climate change. They have seen its effects, at the very least through news reports about extreme weather events and rising sea levels. More than any previous generation, they have a stake in thinking through the manifestations and implications of climate change. Second, the novelty of the scholarly conversation allows students to be contributors to, rather than simply consumers of, knowledge. Unlike many other literary fields, whose contours are often stable—at least when taught at the undergraduate level—climate change fiction has few settled characteristics and has yet to be fully filtered through the rich strata of literary criticism. Inviting students into the conversation at this stage of its development allows them to envision themselves at the vanguard of a necessary project.

The articles mentioned above offer a fairly consistent list of titles and authors that meet their definition of cli-fi, including Margaret Atwood, J. G. Ballard, Jeff VanderMeer, Barbara Kingsolver, Paolo Bacigalupi, and Kim Stanley Robinson. Occasionally, they might list Black American authors like Octavia Butler or N. K. Jemisin, but the lists skew white and Western. During this same period (2015–17), academics also began adopting the language of climate fiction. An *MLA Bibliography* search for the term in May 2019 turned up twenty-seven results, most published in the five previous years.[1] Nine of these results came from a 2018 special issue of *Studies in the Novel* titled *The Rising Tide of Climate Change Fiction*. The articles in this collection also skew white and Western, although Adeline Johns-Putra's "The Rest Is Silence: Postmodern and Postcolonial Possibilities in Climate Change Fiction" looks at the work of the Korean American writer Chang-rae Lee and the Indigenous Australian writer Alexis Wright. The few monographs and anthologies in the broader MLA list also focus on North American and European texts. With some exceptions, then, the discourse of climate fiction in these early stages has tended to focus on Western writers and environments.

This, to borrow a term from perhaps the most visible thinker on the literature of climate change, is deranged.[2] A Euro-American focus on any global topic is limited, but on climate change it misses most of the picture. Anthropogenic climate change and its accompanying environmental disasters, forced migrations, and economic destabilization are much more pronounced in the Global South than they are in the Global North.[3] And while there has been some tension around a westernized climate change discourse and its imperialist attitudes toward Indigenous cultures and environmental practices, climate change itself is undeniably compounded in areas that have long been exploited by the twinned mechanisms of colonialism and capitalism.[4] It is thus incumbent on the nascent field of cli-fi criticism to engage with literature from the regions most affected by climate change.

In addition to the limited geographic focus of these early assessments, most also reveal a generic limitation. The term *cli-fi*, originally coined by the self-proclaimed "cli-fi missionary" Dan Bloom, clearly invokes sci-fi, or science fiction (qtd. in Brady). As a result, many critics understand cli-fi as a genre falling under the umbrella of speculative fiction, often in conversation with dystopian forms. The texts most routinely cited in the articles mentioned above meet these criteria, from Atwood's postapocalyptic MaddAddam trilogy to Bacigalupi's young adult novel *The Wind-Up Girl*, set in the twenty-third century. In their introduction to the special issue of *Studies in the Novel*, Stef Craps and Rick Crenshaw write, "[S]eminal recent work has valorized the popular genres of science fiction and horror, and, by extension, weird and speculative fiction" (2–3), because such genres are able "to represent . . . the vast scales of time and space commensurate with the planetary processes of climate change" (3). Other scholars, however, are beginning to make the argument that any fiction addressing climate change could be considered climate fiction—in other words, that we are dealing with a topic or theme rather than a genre or particular form.[5] From this perspective, even novels that don't imagine themselves to be addressing climate change can be read with reference to climate change, just as novels that don't imagine themselves to be addressing racial dynamics can be read with reference to racial dynamics (see Morrison). Thus, I argue that critical appraisals of climate change fiction would benefit from a reevaluation of the field that addresses both the geographic and generic limitations of our current framework and from a sustained engagement with postcolonial, Global South, and Indigenous literatures.[6] This is the impetus for a course I have developed titled Global South Climate Fiction. My experience teaching this course reinforced my commitment to this project and my sense that students can be valuable contributors to it. In constructing the course, I intended to demonstrate the geographic and generic range of what might be considered cli-fi. Our primary texts, discussed in more detail in the following section, include poems, films, and works of realist and speculative fiction and are drawn from East Africa, South Asia, Latin America, and North America.

**Cli-Fi in the Classroom**

I begin the course much as I began this essay, showing students the cli-fi headlines listed above and explaining the recent emergence of the term. Climate fiction is often new to students, a fact I use to my advantage. In *The Spark of Learning*, Sarah Cavanagh presents evidence that "interest is often engaged when one realizes a gap in one's knowledge; this is appropriately called the knowledge-deprivation hypothesis" (115). For students even loosely interested in literature and the environment, realizing that this body of texts exists can be an exciting discovery, stimulating deeper engagement. Scholars who study teaching and learning also assert that "new knowledge 'sticks' better when it has prior knowledge to stick to" (Ambrose et al. 15). Thus, when introducing cli-fi, I make the connection to sci-fi and prompt students to share their impressions of that genre. From our first meeting, I let students know that what counts as cli-fi is still a matter of debate. My goal is to generate investment in the topic. Reinhard Pekrun, who studies emotional response in the classroom and its connection to motivation, proposes the control-value theory, which suggests that students' emotions can be leveraged for engagement when they are given a sense of control and value in learning (Cavanagh 145–50). By positioning students as participants in the conversation around cli-fi rather than as recipients of settled information, I aim to tap into their sense of control and value.

The course is organized around three objectives. The first of these, that students will be able to define *ecocriticism* and *postcolonial theory* and discuss how these theories advance our understanding of the relation between literature and the environment, drives our early work. After assessing students' backgrounds and interests in literature, environmental studies, and global issues, I give them a brief overview of the academic fields in which we'll be working, ecocriticism and postcolonial theory. Our semester begins with a lot of dense material. Asking students—not all of them English majors—to wrap their heads around not only two theoretical approaches but also the historical distance between these two fields requires setting aside course time and realizing that some theoretical material won't be covered in as much depth as we might like. However, providing this vocabulary and intellectual history is necessary so that we can then apply these ideas to our core texts. For a quick primer, students read Fredrik Jonsson's review of Amitav Ghosh's *The Great Derangement*, which helps students understand the concepts of the Anthropocene and the Great Acceleration and provides a succinct overview of Ghosh's argument. I pair this with a *New York Times* series, "Carbon's Casualties," that explores the effects of climate change across the globe and emphasizes its disparate effect on the Global South. We also read Anthony Carrigan's "Nature, Ecocriticism, and the Postcolonial Novel" and discuss the intersections and divergences of environmental justice and social justice.

In order to assess students' grasp of these concepts, we apply them immediately to several short texts, both in class and in a short homework assignment. In class, we conduct ecocritical readings of three very different poems: selections from William Wordsworth's *The Prelude*, Leopold Sedar Senghor's "To New York," and Juan-Carlos Galeano's "Herons." The variety of poems allows students to see how an ecocritical approach does not depend on a particular setting, period, or subject matter. At this stage of the course, my primary goal is to cultivate a mode of environmental inquiry as we approach assigned readings. As SueEllen Campbell writes, "Classrooms full of questions . . . produce students who can themselves recognize, create, and pursue good questions. . . . [I]n courses on environmental literatures, this may also mean that they produce good environmental citizens who will help create a healthy future" (222). Thus, we ask what constitutes the environment in each poem, comparing Wordsworth's awe-inspiring Alps to Senghor's personified metropolis. We ask about the relationships between animals and humans, noting their interconnectedness in Galeano's Amazon. Galeano's work, with its attendance to the ecological crisis in Colombia, Amazonian cosmologies, and the poetry of violence, is a particularly useful point of departure for our inquiries over the rest of the semester.

To round out this introductory material, students watch Kibwe Tavares's short film *Jonah* and write a response assessing the film through a postcolonial ecocritical lens. The film, which tells the story of a Zanzibari town's environmental degradation after the discovery of a tourist-attracting giant fish just offshore, is accessible to students but also rewards close readings. The images of litter-strewn beaches and offshore oil rigs, paired with the main character's descent into unsavory behavior, tell a straightforward tale of decay that students apprehend quickly. On a formal level, the narrative flash-forward, in which the town's built environment transforms quickly from seaside village to seedy hot spot by means of a series of animations, is juxtaposed against the meditative reverse-motion tracking shot of the closing credits. These effects evoke different time scales, pushing students to consider temporal registers and the pace of ecological change. Students may also recognize the more subtle extractive technologies operating alongside the exploitative tourism the movie foregrounds, offering an opportunity to connect capitalist engines in both individual and industrial modes.

The second objective of the course states that students will gain some facility with reading contemporary literature through the lens of climate change. Once we have the tools to do so, this work occupies most of our semester. We analyze three novels and two films as our primary texts. The novels we read are Amitav Ghosh's *The Hungry Tide* (2004), Yvonne Owuor's *Dust* (2014), and Alaya Dawn Johnson's *The Summer Prince* (2013); the films are Behn Zeitlin's feature *Beasts of the Southern Wild* (2012) and Wanuri Kahiu's short *Pumzi* (2009). Selecting these texts was one of the more challenging aspects of preparing the course, in large part because of the definitional issues mentioned above. It is one thing to say that any text can be read with regard to climate change but something entirely different to task students with analysis when the connections are oblique. While capitalism may serve as a "facade" for climate change, I felt it was important in an introductory course that our texts contain representations of at least some environmental phenomena related to climate change (Cohen 35). *The Rising Tide*'s floodwaters, *Dust*'s arid landscapes, *The Summer Prince*'s seasonal framework and postapocalyptic architecture, and *Beasts of the Southern Wild*'s cataclysmic hurricane offer direct engagement with climate change, while deeper readings reveal the entanglements of metaphoric and climate-adjacent phenomena such as the role of the nonhuman, cultures of silence and denial, class stratification, and supernatural mythologies.

We read slowly, affording these rich texts the careful examination they deserve. *Dust* in particular presents a challenge, but its layered narrative offers many rewards to a climate-focused reading. The novel's central themes include silence and secrecy, and the novel is elliptical and evasive in style. Likewise, its treatment of climate change is mostly implicit, although there is a derisive reference to one tangential character who serves as a "'Unique African Voice' for 'Global Climate Change conversations'" (Owuor 177). None of the major published reviews of the novel address climate change, instead focusing on its historico-political narrative and stylistic delights (Selasi; Gurnah; Charles; Dwyer). Both of these elements require some scaffolding for students, as most are neither familiar with Kenya's colonial and postindependence milieu nor accustomed to reading a nonlinear narrative with a sprawling plot, a large cast of characters, and a fragmented, lyrical style. An early activity in the class involves tracking the various characters, their relationships, and their locations, which helps students comprehend the text and points them to the broader themes we are interested in excavating. We compose a graphic that resembles a constellation, which is a recurring image in the novel as well as a useful metaphor for discussing the scale of climate change, the planet's relation to the universe, and the atmospheric ecosystems the novel's title references. Another element of the novel that can be considered with relation to climate change is the entanglement of the human and the landscape. Burial sites and the silences and secrets they contain are recurring motifs, and the ecological cycling of bodies back into the landscape by means of decay and renewal presents an opportunity to consider the relationship between humans and their environment.

Finally, our third objective is that students will be able to articulate a position on the relation between literature and current events. To that end, I have experimented with two assignments connecting course content to current events and contemporary climate change discourse. In the first, students locate two news articles covering the same climate story and present them to the class. The second version of the assignment asks students to curate a course *Twitter* feed, following organizations and journalists covering climate change and writing tweets based on readings and class discussion. This version of the assignment depends on students' facility with *Twitter*, but it could be adapted for different platforms. These assignments give students an opportunity to research climate-related topics they are interested in and to consider the rhetorical purpose and effectiveness of literature as a tool for addressing the crisis as compared with journalism and social media.

During the first semester I taught this course, the *Oxford Research Encyclopedia of Literature* published a piece by Caren Irr titled "Climate Fiction in English." Irr's essay, a robust overview of the topic, contains sections on a variety of genres, including ecocriticism, science fiction, satire, and realist hybrids. The final section of the article, titled "The Future of Cli-Fi," discusses a "turn . . . toward alternative modernities," arguing that "radically diversifying not just the stated identity and perspective of the scientist-hero but also the locations, conflicts, moods, and motives of the genre is crucial for the long-term viability of the genre." Irr cautions, however, that "recognizing and learning from the climate change activism undertaken proactively in the developing world particularly requires interested novelists to resist the metropolitan center's too frequent romanticization of an underdeveloped periphery," and she suggests that postcolonial criticism may prove useful here. The distinction between activism in the developing world and novel writing from the metropolitan center, unfortunately, makes no space for novelists from the developing world, although Irr does include novelists from a variety of postcolonial regions in her broader analysis.[7] While this elision might invite some critical discussion, it also provides an opportunity for my students in their final papers. After we read Irr's essay as our final critical work, I ask students to write a section on postcolonial climate fiction to add to Irr's piece using the texts we read in our course. Once again, this approach reinforces the idea that they are active participants in building a knowledge base for this emerging field and gives them an authentic writing situation in which to imagine themselves.

Reading Irr's piece carefully as we prepare for this assignment is useful because it contextualizes our work in relation to the broader conversation around climate fiction, helping students see the larger critical landscape and consider where our texts fit in. I also use Irr's essay as a chance to deepen our discussion of genre and medium, since we have now read and viewed a variety of texts—realist, magical realist, and speculative texts and films. We discuss whether certain genres and forms are more or less effective in addressing climate change and what these different mediums offer readers and audiences. As we turn our attention to their papers, I encourage students to see themselves as experts writing for an audience of scholars in the field. The role-playing element of this assignment appeals to them, and they enjoy mimicking Irr's tone and style while synthesizing their learning from the semester. Their final papers tend to highlight the Global North's role in contributing disproportionately to climate change and the way our texts thematize uneven power structures and global dominance. They also discuss how topics such as climate refugees and extractive economies have a deeper resonance in Global South texts because of those texts' connection to the current events we track during the course.

## Reflections and Assessment

Reflecting on my experiences teaching this course, I believe a few notes are necessary. The first concerns politics. In my first semester teaching this course, the newly assembled Trump administration began the process of removing references to climate change from federal websites and would withdraw from the Paris Agreement less than a month after the course wrapped. The second time I taught the course, a series of scandals surrounding the Environmental Protection Agency chief Scott Pruitt was in the news, and he would resign shortly after the semester concluded. For students who were often interested in, if not majoring in, environmental studies, it was a dispiriting time. It was inevitable that references to these events would find their way into the classroom. Unsettled by the political climate and the increasing polarization in some sectors over an issue that had been scientifically decided for years, I sought to calibrate my emotions in the classroom while also providing a space for students to grapple with these events. Because the course had the term *climate* in its title, students who enrolled typically accepted my statement in our first meeting that the science of climate change was not up for debate in our classroom. However, the purpose of the course was to focus on the literature and representation of this phenomenon and offer a respite, I hoped, from the increasingly contentious political maneuverings around the topic. As Anthony Vital writes, "While informing students of the scales and dimensions of environmental problems, my focus is on texts and the language we use daily and how these might affect society's relation to nature. There are no neat ways to think about any of this" (196).

Student feedback on this course has been largely positive, which is in part a reflection on the ethos of Franklin and Marshall College, where it was taught for two semesters. Additionally, however, I believe this reflects the students' awareness and acceptance of the scope of our course. We did not set out to solve the problem of climate change but to immerse ourselves in the narratives of those who are already encountering it and to ask, as Vital asks, "What role can literature and film play" in moving us "toward a more ecologically sound relation among people and planet?" (196). To that end, one of our final activities, drawing inspiration from some of the utopian threads in several of our texts, was to imagine the contours of a more environmentally just world. Moving forward, I would recommend others teaching similar courses to explore the possibilities for this kind of imaginative work earlier in the course, weaving it through as a counterbalance to some of the more dispiriting moments.

"Climate change casts a much smaller shadow within the landscape of literary fiction than it does even in the public arena," Ghosh writes in *The Great Derangement*. The word *literary* is worth unpacking here, because it allows Ghosh to develop his overarching take on the cultural representation of climate change. In other moments, he uses the term *serious* as a synonym for *literary* and states that he refers to the kind of fiction that appears in "highly regarded literary journals and book reviews" (7). I have two responses to this assertion. First, there is growing energy around critical—one might say serious—appraisals of speculative fiction.[8] Second, we are expanding the definition of climate fiction beyond the speculative, as discussed above, and reading more rigorously for references to climate and the Anthropocene in so-called realist fiction. When we reevaluate both what counts as serious and what counts as climate fiction, and when we look beyond a Euro-American framework, we see climate change casting a much larger shadow in our fictional landscapes.

Students are less burdened than critics by distinctions between literary and genre fiction. Throughout the course, their ability to move between categories is a useful reminder that what we are after in reading cli-fi is not the creation of a new set of terminological boundaries but a reckoning with our possible futures. Those of us who work in this field would do well to follow their lead.

## Notes

1. A search for "climate fiction" enclosed in quotation marks turned up two results; "climate change fiction" produced thirteen.

2. I refer to Amitav Ghosh's seminal book *The Great Derangement*.

3. It is worth noting, though, that attending to environmental justice can destabilize our notions of such categories as "Global South" and "Global North."

4. For more on imperialist tendencies in ecocriticism and intersections of ecocriticism with African literature, see William Slaymaker's "Ecoing the Other(s)" and Ogaga Okuyade's *Eco-critical Literature*.

5. I am grateful to Byron Santangelo for making this point during the panel Environmental Transformation in Literature and Criticism at the May 2019 African Literature Association Annual Conference.

6. I list these categories separately because each is distinct and useful in different ways, although teasing out their distinctions and utilities is beyond the scope of this essay.

7. The texts Irr references that might be considered from a postcolonial, Global South, or Indigenous framework include Ghosh's *The Hungry Tide*, Helon Habila's *Oil on Water*, Thomas King's *The Back of the Turtle*, Leslie Marmon Silko's *Gardens in the Dunes*, and Indra Sinha's *Animal's People*.

8. For example, a 2019 African Literature Association panel titled Realism and Its Discontents in African Literature considered Afrofuturism, pulp fiction, science fiction, and digital speculative fiction. Presenters were Carmen McCain, Ian McDonald, Mahriana Rofheart, and Matthew Omelsky.

## Works Cited

Abraham, John. "CliFi: A New Way to Talk about Climate Change." *The Guardian*, 18 Oct. 2017, www.theguardian.com/environment/climate -consensus-97-per-cent/2017/oct/18/clifi-a-new-way-to-talk-about-climate -change.

Ambrose, Susan A., et al. *How Learning Works: Seven Research-Based Principles for Smart Teaching*. Jossey-Bass, 2010.

Brady, Amy. "The Man Who Coined 'Cli-Fi' Has Some Reading Suggestions for You." *Chicago Review of Books*, 8 Feb. 2017, chireviewofbooks.com/2017/02/08/the-man-who-coined-cli-fi-has-some-reading-suggestions-for-you/.

Campbell, SueEllen. "Asking Ecocritical Questions." *Teaching North American Environmental Literature*, edited by Laird Christensen et al., Modern Language Association of America, 2008, pp. 215–22.

"Carbon's Casualties." *The New York Times*, www.nytimes.com/spotlight/climate-casualties. Accessed 9 Sept. 2020.

Carrigan, Anthony. "Nature, Ecocriticism, and the Postcolonial Novel." *The Cambridge Companion to the Postcolonial Novel*, edited by Ato Quayson, Cambridge UP, 2016, pp. 81–98.

Cavanagh, Sarah Rose. *The Spark of Learning: Energizing the College Classroom with the Science of Emotion*. West Virginia UP, 2016.

Charles, Ron. "Review: *Dust*, by Yvonne Adhiambo Owuor." *The Washington Post*, 4 Feb. 2014, www.washingtonpost.com/entertainment/books/review-dust-by-yvonne-adhiambo-owuor/2014/02/04/3347e4bc-8880-11e3-a5bd-844629433ba3_story.html.

Cohen, Tom. "Murmurations—'Climate Change' and the Defacement of Theory." *Telemorphosis: Theory in the Era of Climate Change: Vol. 1*, edited by Cohen, Open Humanities Press, 2012, pp. 13–42.

Craps, Stef, and Rick Crenshaw. Introduction. *The Rising Tide of Climate Fiction*, special issue of *Studies in the Novel*, vol. 50, no. 1, 2018, pp. 1–8. *Project Muse*, doi:10.1353/sdn.2018.0000.

Dwyer, Colin. "Through the 'Dust,' Glimmers of Brilliance." *NPR*, 1 Feb. 2014, www.npr.org/2014/02/01/264525671/through-the-dust-glimmers-of-brilliance.

Ghosh, Amitav. *The Great Derangement: Climate Change and the Unthinkable*. U of Chicago P, 2016.

Gurnah, Abdulrazak. "*Dust* by Yvonne Adhiambo Owuor Review—A Complex Vision of Kenya." *The Guardian*, 19 Mar. 2015, www.theguardian.com/books/2015/mar/19/dust-review-yvonne-adhiambo-owuor-kenya.

Irr, Caren. "Climate Fiction in English." *Oxford Research Encyclopedia of Literature*, Oxford UP, 27 Feb. 2017, doi:10.1093/acrefore/9780190201098.013.4.

Jonsson, Fredrik. "The Holocene Hangover: It Is Time for Humanity to Make Fundamental Changes." *The Guardian*, 7 Dec. 2016, theguardian.com/books/2016/dec/07/the-holocene-hangover-it-is-time-for-humanity-to-make-fundamental-changes.

Morrison, Toni. *Playing in the Dark: Whiteness and the Literary Imagination*. Harvard UP, 1992.

Okuyade, Ogaga, editor. *Eco-critical Literature: Regreening African Landscapes*. African Heritage Press, 2013.

Owuor, Yvonne Adhiambo. *Dust*. Alfred A. Knopf, 2014.

Robins, Spencer. "So Hot Right Now: Cli-Fi Comes to YA." *Los Angeles Review of Books*, 13 Mar. 2016, lareviewofbooks.org/article/so-hot-right-now-cli-fi-comes-to-ya/.

Selasi, Taiye. "The Unvanquished." *The New York Times*, 28 Feb. 2014, www.nytimes.com/2014/03/02/books/review/dust-by-yvonne-adhiambo -owuor.html.
Slaymaker, William. "Ecoing the Other(s): The Call of Global Green and Black African Responses." *African Literature: An Anthology of Criticism and Theory*, edited by Tejumola Olaniyan and Ato Quayson, Blackwell Publishing, 2007, pp. 683–97.
Tavares, Kibwe, director. *Jonah.* Factory Fifteen, 2013.
Tonn, Shara. "Cli-Fi—That's Climate Fiction—Is the New Sci-Fi." *Wired*, 17 July 2015, www.wired.com/2015/07/cli-fi-thats-climate-fiction-new-sci-fi/.
Ullrich, J. K. "Climate Fiction: Can Books Save the Planet?" *The Atlantic*, 14 Aug. 2015, www. theatlantic.com/entertainment/archive/2015/08 /climate-fiction-margaret-atwood-literature/400112/.
Vital, Anthony. "Teaching Literature as Climate Changes: Ecological Presence, a Globalized World, and Helon Habila's *Oil on Water.*" *Teaching Climate Change in the Humanities*, edited by Stephen Siperstein et al., Routledge, 2017, pp. 195–200.

**Elaine Savory**

# Toward an Interdisciplinary Symbiosis in Environmental Literary Pedagogy

*Science describes accurately from outside; poetry describes accurately from inside.*

—Ursula Le Guin, "Deep in Admiration"

My lecture course Writing the Environment models close reading of selected texts in the context of an interdisciplinary exploration of postcolonialism and environmental thinking. In its ideal form, it would best be described by the metaphor of symbiosis, drawn from the work of the ecobiologist Lynn Margulis, who argued that symbiosis was a major force in the evolution of life. Symbiotic environmental pedagogy brings into relation disciplines that usually exist in separate intellectual spaces in the university. In the course, dialogues between those disciplines transform student learning. This is a step on the way to full integration of disciplines for environmental teaching (Tsing et al.).

The course is anchored in literary studies, in conversation with chemistry, biology, design, religious studies, and history. This phase of pedagogy is only a first step toward symbiosis. Margulis thought of life as interactions between different elements. Adapting this idea, I suggest the

104

interaction of different disciplines, in this course, for the common purpose of environmental consciousness. This multidisciplinary interaction provides opportunities for new ways of thinking without discarding the diverse contributory elements, which means keeping them in kinetic balance, almost like an ecology of sorts. This symbiotic practice relates to the definition of the new field of postcolonial environmental humanities offered by Elizabeth DeLoughrey, Jill Didur, and Anthony Carrigan as multidisciplinary and deeply concerned with social justice (*Global Ecologies*). The goal is not to provide substantive instruction in disciplines outside literary studies but rather to enable students to have reliable information by which to assess the environmental content of the primary texts. This pedagogy privileges questions and exchanges of ways of knowing. It embraces the idea that to think about the environment in postcolonial space is to think globally and locally at once, beyond disciplines and across time.

Anchoring the course in literary studies affirms the idea that literature has a key role in raising environmental consciousness because it engages both imagination and empathy through skill with language. Our species is not the only one with language, but our language skills are unique in their complexity and range. Postcolonial literary studies have focused on verbal strategies for coping with and resisting formal colonialism and its heir, neocolonialism. While the role of literature in environmental studies is clearly established, the relation between the postcolonial and the environmental has only recently gained critical attention. In 2005, DeLoughrey, Renée K. Gosson, and George Handley pointed out the lack of attention to environmental matters in postcolonial criticism (*Caribbean Literature* 1–32). Five years later, Graham Huggan and Helen Tiffin, in *Postcolonial Ecocriticism*, made a similar argument: "ecocriticism has tended as a whole to prioritize the extra-human and its place in literature, whilst postcolonialism has been routinely, and at times, unthinkingly anthropocentric" (17). Rob Nixon's *Slow Violence and the Environmentalism of the Poor* demonstrated how urgent it is to recognize the simultaneous exploitation of powerless people and their environment. His succinct comment that the innate tendency of capitalism is "to abstract in order to extract" is a good way to point to economic disparities, which are major elements in despoiling the environment and at the same time harming powerless people (41). It should be inconceivable to think of any post- or neocolonial issue without environmental consciousness, or to think of exploitation of land and people separately.

Since this is a university lecture course, it is open to students from all majors and programs, and it draws students studying literature, writing, and environmental studies, as well as visual arts. All the visiting lecturers work in environmental studies within their disciplines, so the course models an integrative approach to environmental education. This pedagogical practice is forward-looking, moving away from both the silo model of disciplines and departmental organization around nations. We know that global capital flow (globalization) often damages local environmental and cultural integrity alike. We ask better questions and seek more complex, nuanced responses to environmental crisis if we think globally. Though this model validates science and social science as providing a key foundation for postcolonial environmental knowledge, it equally validates the role of imagination and empathy and of innovative, creative thinking and doing in every discipline. Since the study of literature often requires acquiring a wide range of knowledge and using it to comprehend content, this kind of pedagogy comes naturally to a postcolonial course anchored in literary studies.

## Outline of Writing the Environment

Each class consists of an hour-long lecture followed by fifteen minutes devoted to students' comments and questions. There are fifteen lectures in the semester, one per week. Weekly discussion sections, also an hour and fifteen minutes each, are run by graduate teaching assistants.

The first lecture explains the dialogic, interdisciplinary method central to the course as an iteration of the environmental humanities as well as the focus on literary analysis, postcolonial criticism, and key political, cultural, and sociohistorical contexts. Huggan and Tiffin point out that "postcolonial writers from a variety of regions have adapted environmental discourses, which have often been shaped in western (European) interests, to their own immediate ends" (15–16). The discussion of interdisciplinary method and literary analysis leads naturally to the explication of the role literary form and genre can play in environmentally engaged writing, and to the introduction of the course's primary texts—fiction, poetry, and essays. Students learn how expert and inventive use of language, scribal or oral, can reach people otherwise prepared to dismiss environmental danger, or at least to ignore it.

The first novel we read is Indra Sinha's *Animal's People*, a "visceral recreation," in the words of the ecocritic Pablo Mukherjee, of the consequences of the Union Carbide disaster in Bhopal, India, in 1984 (162). The second novel, Amitav Ghosh's environmental whodunit, *The Calcutta Chromosome*, fictionalizes the discovery of the vector for malaria in colonial India, complicating the official story of the Nobel laureate Robert Ross's work. Finally, Helon Habila's *Oil on Water* explores the huge toll, on both human and nonhuman lives, levied by the extraction of oil in Nigeria by multinational companies. Poetry is also central to the course. It is able to raise environmental awareness through its explorations beyond statement and story and, through figurative language and layered, economical poetic form, to complicate apprehension of important issues. Kamau Brathwaite's poem "9/11 Hawk," a moving and powerful elegy for those killed in the 9/11 attacks, connects the immediate, intense grief over those losses with mourning for both human-made and natural disasters that have occurred across the world throughout modern history. Brathwaite's reference to Bhopal links this elegy to *Animal's People*, and the poem, centered in New York City, brings the United States into the course. Too often, young Americans think of their nation as separate from the world, and so it is important for them to learn to imagine the local and the global in environmental and postcolonial terms. It is also important for them to realize that the United States has been both colonized and colonizer.

The last reading is the title section from the collection of essays *Braiding Sweetgrass*, by Robin Wall Kimmerer. The book's subtitle, *Indigenous Wisdom, Scientific Knowledge, and the Teaching of Plants*, will, I hope, remind students of the connections and ruptures between traditional healing and Western medicine in *The Calcutta Chromosome* and of the massive damage to health caused by chemically polluted air in Bhopal, damage resulting from an extreme violation of the balance between humans and nonhumans.

Three lectures are devoted to each dialogue: the first and third of these lectures focus on the primary text, and the middle one relates the text to another field, such as chemistry, microbiology, history, and religious studies. The second lecture on *Animal's People*, on the causes and impact of the Bhopal disaster as well as global air pollution, is given by a chemistry professor who works on atmospheric pollution with reference to climate change. For *The Calcutta Chromosome*, a biology lecture offers a detailed explanation of the life cycle of the malarial parasite and the vectors of transmission as well as the old practice of using weak malarial infection to treat tertiary syphilis. For *Oil on Water*, the middle lecture is on the history of multinational petrochemical capitalism and the connection between neocolonialism and the devastation of the environment in southern Nigeria.

Brathwaite's "9/11 Hawk" is written in what the poet calls "video style" (a dramatic use of fonts and arrangements of words and hieroglyphs on the page). It contains found material, such as transcripts of voices recorded in the aftermath of the attacks, and incorporates a strong design component. Our interdisciplinary conversation explores design strategies as an environmental tool and so enables students to consider the poem's powerful visual impact, not just as an aesthetic element but also as a directive to think about environmental issues the poem raises. The elegy is dense with historical and geographic references that reflect Brathwaite's role as a Caribbean historian and connect the poem to the significant body of Caribbean environmental scholarship interfacing culture and science (e.g., DeLoughrey et al., *Caribbean Literature*; Lakhan; Savory). Brathwaite's 9/11 elegy represents the falling of the towers as an environmental catastrophe, one in a long list of disasters that have befallen the world. Destruction is everywhere, "the tears like bees upon my fingertips like bit- / umen. the sticky black the blurr the burn(ed) the bomb(ed) the scarr(ed)" (98). The poem ends with an affirmation of love in the face of terror and loss (113).

The dialogue between literature, religious studies, and the environment is centered on Kimmerer's *Braiding Sweetgrass*. The lecture on religion and spirituality is given by a specialist in religious studies who has worked on Native American religion, culture, and the environment. Kimmerer follows the directive of her title and braids three areas of knowledge and understanding in the subtitle of her book (*Indigenous Wisdom, Scientific Knowledge, and the Teaching of Plants*), and her way of thinking and composing her text helped inspire this course's pedagogical approach.

It is necessary to pitch the techniques of literary analysis and secondary readings at the introductory level (the course is aimed at sophomores, who will not have declared their majors, though more advanced students are usually present as well). Thus, the secondary reading in each lecture is limited in scope but not in importance or value. An effective way to introduce students to relevant literary criticism and theory is through quotations posted on a screen during the lecture, with the texts of the most important secondary readings provided to the students to read in full.

The last time this course was taught, a fine arts major produced a collage as her final project, each element explained in detail by a framing essay. She said she felt the interaction between disciplines modeled in the course enabled her to think more bravely about what often seems over-whelmingly complicated and huge. The intellectual level of the course is high, and a wide range of sources are introduced through the lectures. But this kind of groundbreaking, creative thinking comes from focusing deeply on texts in an interdisciplinary way. This means limiting the amount of secondary reading within each contributing discipline.

## Approaching the Primary Texts

The course considers its central texts in three ways: as literary texts, as innovative sources of environmental awareness, and as postcolonial texts marking the degradation of environment and people by power structures that derive from colonial domination.

Animal, the narrator of *Animal's People*, walks on all fours and is extremely shrewd, vibrant, and irreverent, and it is through this consciousness that the reader encounters both the terrible effects of the chemical contamination caused by Union Carbide and the social strategies people must develop to come to terms with survival after such a disaster. Pablo Mukherjee's discussion of the novel is very helpful for teaching the text. He opens with a detailed account of the Union Carbide "gas tragedy" (134), moves into a consideration of speciesism and animal rights, and then proceeds into an analysis of the text from a literary point of view—the three approaches necessary to produce a postcolonial ecocritical reading.

Mukherjee asks us to think of the style of the novel in relation to the tradition of North Indian raga music: he offers this as an answer to those who say recent Indian fiction has "stylistic unevenness" (156), because in raga, different moods, called *rasas*, are successively aroused in the listener by certain aesthetic strategies. At one point in the novel, Animal directly invokes raga by using the term *bhayaanak rasa*, or sheer terror (157). Unlike some readers of literary texts, Mukherjee realizes that a text's formal nature is its ecology, the environment through which the story is shaped and told. Difficulty caused by student expectation of a realist narrative turns into a productive contemplation that prompts the recognition that another culture is likely to read a disaster in its own cultural and ecological terms. This further leads to an examination of the multiple languages in the novel, not only Animal's idiosyncratic speech but also that of other humans and animals. Through the intervention of a lecture by a chemistry professor, students learn that non-human elements interact with the environment. Chemicals have their own way of communicating with each other, as well as with humans, animals, and the rest of the ecosystem.

Ghosh (whose nonfiction book *The Great Derangement* justifies the need for wide-ranging environmental consciousness) centers his colonial story on a man curious about the past and living in a not-so-distant future in New York City. In *The Calcutta Chromosome*, a robot with a female voice surveils those working from home. Something similar to colonialist intrusiveness into private life is reborn in a future society where an invisible employer has access to an employee's private space. This is the doorway into the story of a disease, Western science, and Indian tradition, all entangled in colonial India. It is told as a mystery, with an urgent, page-turning pace. This popular kind of fiction writing style keeps the reader's interest.

One of the lectures on *The Calcutta Chromosome*, given by a microbiologist, permits students to imagine the vital connection between elements in the biosphere by emphasizing the role humans and other hosts play in the survival of a microscopic form of life. This encourages us to flip our perspective and see things from outside the Anthropocene in. Stephanie Browner's essay on "resocializing" literature and medicine in the postcolonial context speaks of Ghosh's narrative as "revising the traditional, linear heroic role of medieval discovery into a feverish delirium of story-telling" (82). Later, Browner says, "Ghosh challenges not only the paradigm of the scientific laboratory and scientific progress but core Western assumptions about the transmission of knowledge, practices, and even genetic material" (84–85). Browner's work provides a context for a discussion of how knowledge is shaped, claimed, and used, and by whom. The final lecture on *The Calcutta Chromosome* focuses on the issue of health and wellness in the context of formerly colonized societies, whose various traditions are often marginalized in the aftermath of colonial, racial, and cultural hierarchy; for instance, the way in which COVID-19 has affected different parts of the world exposes inequities founded in the global capitalism perpetuated by empire.

Habila's novel is written in a journalistic style that suits the story well, since his main characters are a pair of investigative journalists. *Oil on Water* provides such rich descriptions of place that when students saw a film on the Niger Delta region, they said their imagination had already seen the place through Habila's writing. But the tale needs grounding in the history of oil extraction and neocolonial alliances with multinational capitalism. This is where history helps, coming between a first encounter with the novel and the concluding lecture, which explores the whole text. History itself has to be rethought in the face of environmental crisis; as Dipesh Chakrabarty writes, "[A]nthropogenic explanations of climate change spell the collapse of the age-old humanist distinction between natural history and human history" (337). In exploring how the Delta region is devastated by reckless oil extraction, students learn to rethink historical memory when such enormous and painful changes occur in places with a long past of relative stability. Secondary readings make students aware of African ecocriticism (e.g., Iheka; Wright; Caminero-Santangelo).

Brathwaite's elegy is best understood as an oral poem as well as a poem consciously designed for the page. These are related. The poet's video style emerged after he began to use a Macintosh computer in the mid-1990s, which gave him access to a range of fonts and symbols not available on a typewriter. He uses the visual effect of different font sizes and ranges of bold to indicate sonic qualities, allowing the fonts to rise and fall, so to speak, on the page and creating a kind of musical score. Because the poem's visual and sonic range brings it close to music as well as to art, the first lecture should allow students to hear Brathwaite's voice. Though there is no available recording of "9/11 Hawk," there are many recordings of the poet reading other works on *YouTube*. In addition, the jazz saxophonist Coleman Hawkins's "Body and Soul," which is the music framing and informing the elegy, needs to be played softly as a section of the long poem is read.

Reading scribal poetry like Brathwaite's must always involve attending to its sound and its shape on the page, entering the full sensory experience of what it does with language. The grief, anger, and bafflement that 9/11 caused is reproduced by the poem's powerful language, a language riven by what it must witness and thus often changed into something close to devastatingly aware incoherence: ". . . what is the word / for this high rafter of suicide"; "ocol the cool the clear the towers falling" (101, 113). Students must come to see that the ecology of a poem is not like that of a piece of fiction. Brathwaite's poem takes the reader through the experience of grief and then offers some comfort at the end, calling for love in the moment when Hawkins's music returns as a shelter and strength, which jazz has so often been for traumatized people. But that comfort is fragile, and the chance of loss always close by. Anthony Carrigan's theorizing of "postcolonial disaster studies" cites Brathwaite's conception of catastrophe, which includes slavery, the Middle Passage, and other atrocities committed against fellow humans and the environment. Brathwaite asks what "causes nature to lunge in this cataclysmic way, and what kind of message, as I suspect it is . . . Nature [is] trying to send to us" (125). Brathwaite believes the most profound art comes often out of catastrophe.

The discussion of the ecology of the poem frames the lecture on design, which can help students read aesthetic shapes that appear abstract and consider that written language is essentially design, abstract shapes called letters that are imbued with meaning beyond their individual physical properties by their combination with other letters: an emblem of individual-collective connection that is helpful to think about as an ecological principle.

Students are asked to bring to the final lecture on "9/11 Hawk" their notes on the many proper names included in the poem, as in the cluster of Bhopal, Grenada, Guernica, Amritsar, Tajikistan, Bosnia, Sudan, Chernobyl, Aetna, and Krakatoa (101). These notes inspire a discussion of the nature and use of metonymy, and the lecture makes the case for thinking of 9/11 from a postcolonial perspective, asking how the postcolonial can be defined for an event that took place in New York City.

The next section of the course turns to a Native American writer, Robin Wall Kimmerer, also a scientist, who reflects on different modalities of thought in her experience and culture. Kimmerer's book *Braiding Sweetgrass* offers a nuanced and sophisticated understanding of Native American lifeworlds, grounded in her two worlds of science and inherited tradition.

Kimmerer retells the ancient Native American story of Nanabozho, the First Man, part man and part spirit, whose job is "to teach us how to be human" (206). Nanabozho was himself an immigrant, Kimmerer says, coming to a world already established. Kimmerer represents time for her people as a circle, not a straight line, or as "the sea itself," rather than a river "running inexorably" (206–07). So maybe the "journey of the First Man" can guide the objective of the later generations, which is "to set aside the ways of the colonist and become indigenous to place" (207). Kimmerer gives an account of taking her premed students on a walk through a local nature reserve, in an attempt to get them interested in ecology, converting their "scientific souls." At the core of her text are detailed, accurate descriptions of plants, informed not just by science and taxonomy but also by the history of human relation to them. Kimmerer creates an experience that begins to bring all kinds of knowledge together, including the knowledge shared by humans around a simple fire. The way she braids knowledges and experiences is rich and rewarding, as when she writes, "Just as old growth forests are richly complex, so too were the old growth cultures that arose at their feet" (279). Old-growth cultures were precolonial ones.

The first lecture on Kimmerer's work explores this textual braiding. The author is a scientist who is attentive to her people's traditions. She is very aware of the damage and loss caused by white incursion and settlement on Native American land. Science is a language, she says, of distance and objects (49). But something is missing in that language: she calls it "words for life," which exist in Native American languages. Pavel Cenkl's essay on "narrative currency" in an age of climate change argues that whereas environmental thinking needs to be aware of science, we should not let this become a "primary dependence" (152). So creative imagination is important. Cenkl's work helps prepare students for receiving alternative readings of the world that respect intuition, the body, and faith, not just rationality and fact. The class is also asked to consider Greg Garrard's discussion of the stereotype of the "Ecological Indian" (133), a somewhat romantic figure used to combat white eco-destruction.

The second lecture on Kimmerer's work is given by a religious studies professor. The lecture examines Native American belief systems regarding the environment, provoking questions about the nature of spirituality, oral tradition, and environmental consciousness. The third lecture focuses largely on storytelling and refers to secondary readings from other Native American writers such as Leslie Marmon Silko and Paula Gunn Allen.

The course demonstrates that focusing on a few important dialogues provides a methodology for exploring a complex and ever-growing field. Secondary readings in environmental humanities and literature introduce students to a wide variety of writers and thinkers they can further pursue (Glotfelty; Tucker and Grim; Venkatamaran; White; Winegard; Zapf). Postcolonial environmental humanities is a critically important field of study because it opens up intersectional thinking. The result can be science majors who realize the significance of close, trained analysis of literary or other creative work and literary studies or design majors who decide to take a science or social science class, and all students leave the course much more aware of the injustices and inequities embedded in a flawed world after empire. This expanded thinking is critically important to the development of responsible environmental consciousness. At this time, we are seeding this new field. Hopefully, some of those we teach now will go on to do work in the field and to challenge the very organization and evaluation of knowledge as we combat climate change and other environmental crises.

## Works Cited

Allen, Paula Gunn. "The Sacred Hoop: A Contemporary Perspective." Glotfelty and Fromm, pp. 241–63.

Brathwaite, Kamau. "9/11 Hawk." *Born to Slow Horses*, Wesleyan UP, 2005, pp. 92–118.

Browner, Stephanie P. "Resocializing Literature and Medicine: Poverty, Health and Medical Science in Postcolonial Literature." *Communicating Disease: Cultural Representations of American Medicine*, edited by Carmen Birkle and Johanna Heil, Universitätsverlag Winter, 2013, pp. 71–91.

Caminero-Santangelo, Byron. *Different Shades of Green: African Literature, Environmental Justice, and Political Ecology.* U of Virginia P, 2014.

Carrigan, Anthony. "Towards a Postcolonial Disaster Studies." DeLoughrey et al., *Global Ecologies*, pp. 117–39.

Cenkl, Pavel. "Narrative Currency in a Changing Climate: Grounding the Arctic amid Shifting Terrain." *Postcolonial Green: Environmental Politics and World Narratives*, edited by Bonnie Roos and Alex Hunt, U of Virginia P, 2010, pp. 137–56.

Chakrabarty, Dipesh. "The Climate of History: Four Theses." *Ecocriticism: The Essential Reader*, edited by Ken Hiltner, Routledge, 2015, pp. 335–52.

DeLoughrey, Elizabeth, et al., editors. *Global Ecologies and the Environmental Humanities: Postcolonial Approaches.* Routledge, 2015.

DeLoughrey, Elizabeth M., et al., editors. *Caribbean Literature and the Environment: Between Nature and Culture.* U of Virginia P, 2005.

Garrard, Greg. *Ecocriticism.* Routledge, 2004.

Ghosh, Amitav. *The Calcutta Chromosome.* HarperCollins, 1995.

———. *The Great Derangement: Climate Change and the Unthinkable.* U of Chicago P, 2017.

Glotfelty, Cheryll. "Literary Studies in an Age of Environmental Crisis." Introduction. Glotfelty and Fromm, pp. xv–xxxvi.

Glotfelty, Cheryll, and Harold Fromm, editors. *The Ecocriticism Reader.* U of Georgia P, 1996.

Habila, Helon. *Oil on Water.* W. W. Norton, 2010.

Huggan, Graham, and Helen Tiffin. *Postcolonial Ecocriticism.* Routledge, 2010.

Iheka, Cajetan. *Naturalizing Africa: Ecological Violence, Agency and Postcolonial Resistance in African Literature.* Cambridge UP, 2018.

Kimmerer, Robin Wall. *Braiding Sweetgrass: Indigenous Wisdom, Scientific Knowledge, and the Teachings of Plants.* Milkweed Editions, 2013.

Lakhan, Anu, editor. *Islands like Us: Trinidad and Tobago.* IAMovement, 2019.

Margulis, Lynn. *Symbiotic Planet: A New Look at Evolution.* Basic Books, 1999.

Mukherjee, Upamanyu Pablo. *Postcolonial Environments: Nature, Culture and the Contemporary Indian Novel in English.* Palgrave Macmillan, 2010.

Nixon, Rob. *Slow Violence and the Environmentalism of the Poor.* Harvard UP, 2011.

Savory, Elaine, editor. *Caribbean Ecocriticism.* Special issue of *Journal of West Indian Literature*, vol. 24, no. 2, Nov. 2016.

Silko, Leslie Marmon. "Landscape, History, and the Pueblo Imagination." Glotfelty and Fromm, pp. 264–75.

Sinha, Indra. *Animal's People*. Simon and Schuster, 2007.

Tsing, Anna Lowenhaupt, et al., editors. *Arts of Living on a Damaged Planet*. U of Minnesota P, 2017.

Tucker, Mary Evelyn, and John Grim. "The Movement of Religion and Ecology: Emerging Field and Dynamic Force." *The Routledge Handbook of Religion and Ecology*, edited by Willis Jenkins, Routledge, 2016, pp. 1–12.

Venkatamaran, Bhawani. "Earth's Thin Blue Line." *Air*, edited by John Knechtel, MIT Press, 2010, pp. 223–37.

White, Lynn, Jr. "The Historical Roots of Our Ecologic Crisis." Glotfelty and Fromm, pp. 3–14.

Winegard, Timothy C. *The Mosquito: A Human History of Our Deadliest Predator*. Penguin Random House, 2019.

Wright, Laura. *Wilderness into Civilized Shapes: Reading the Postcolonial Environment*. U of Georgia P, 2010.

Zapf, Hubert. *Literature as Cultural Ecology*. Bloomsbury, 2016.

# Part III

## Regional and Local Perspectives

**Christina Gerhardt**

---

# Postcolonial Cartographies, Environmental Humanities, and Sea Level Rise

Drawing on cartography (precolonial, colonial, and postcolonial), environmental studies, and the environmental humanities, as well as literary studies and creative nonfiction, this essay discusses how my teaching and the book that it dovetails with, *Atlas of Islands and Sea Level Rise*, engage the effects of climate change on low-lying islands and islanders' fight to address them. Pacific islands are responsible for producing a mere .03% of global carbon dioxide emissions, yet they are disproportionately experiencing the effects of climate-change-induced sea level rise.[1]

My research informs my teaching, and the discussions I have with students at the University of Hawai'i, Mānoa, many of whom are Pacific Islanders, inform my research. In the course Postcolonial Cartographies, Environmental Humanities, and Sea Level Rise, we open with two questions: Why environmental humanities? Why climate justice in the Pacific? That is, what work can the environmental humanities do and why is climate justice so important? Over the course of the semester, we not only read and discuss in a classroom setting but also conduct site visits with practitioners at the intersection of the environment and the arts.

In this course students write a 250- to 750-word essay of creative nonfiction about and create a map of a Pacific island. Both the essay and the map delineate the island's history, present-day situation, and predicted future shorelines. To prepare students for the mapping assignment, we compare precolonial, colonial, and postcolonial maps of the Pacific (see Jacobs). The comparison includes discussions of Polynesian voyaging and Marshall Island stick charts: of how Oceanic voyagers navigated the Pacific Ocean without the use of magnetic compasses to determine direction; without the use of sextants to measure the distance between a celestial body and the horizon; and without the use of measurements of longitude, which presupposes the Greenwich meridian (see Lewis). Instead, they steered by the stars and kept course by reading the sun, the swells, and the shifts in wind patterns. Relatedly, the Marshallese created stick charts to map ocean swells. They used the presence of birds and clouds (their color, brightness, and shape) to determine their proximity to archipelagoes and islands. They designed a sidereal compass to divide the horizon into points and map where the stars rise and set. Postcolonial mapping strategies are being revitalized, drawing on precolonial techniques—for example, by the Polynesian Voyaging Society and its journeys via the boat the *Hōkūleʻa*. Given the historical and geographic context of still-colonized Pacific islands, these considerations dovetail with ongoing struggles to decolonize (see Goodyear-Kaʻōpua et al.).

When creating a postcolonial map, we also read and discuss Pacific literature. We consider the following: How do these texts map the Pacific? Through language? Through the imaginary? What is the narrative vantage point? How do the texts engage the environment? What models do they put forward in terms of governance, resource management, and sustainability? How does this history and context give the environmental humanities a particular geographic, historical, and cultural inflection? How does it offer models for decolonizing environmental knowledge and ensuring environmental justice? Lastly, we consider how and why, following Kyle Whyte, Chris Caldwell, and Marie Schaefer, "Indigenous lessons about sustainability are not just for 'all humanity.'" These readings and discussions form the basis of the creative nonfiction writing exercise.

If the course and assignment that follow were offered at the undergraduate level, they would help open the eyes of students majoring in the sciences or other nonhumanities fields to the work of the humanities when it engages and focuses on environmental studies. To this end, the course might be well-suited for institutions that lean more toward the sciences and technologies or for institutions aiming to establish programs that bridge science, technology, engineering, arts, and mathematics (STEAM) fields. If the course were taught at the graduate level, students would also come from a range of colleges and disciplines, in particular geography, environmental studies, and English. These students would benefit from seeing the concerns of their discipline in conversation with those of another field. They would also learn to convey their discipline's concerns and methodologies to students in another field. What are the differing stakes? How are they articulated differently? How do they lead to a difference in focus, both in the research methods and in the ultimate texts, such as the papers and maps produced? Whether courses are taught at the graduate or undergraduate level, I have students work in groups, and each group includes a student from geography, from literature, and from environmental studies.

## Pacific Island Literature and Environmental Humanities

In this course, we read Pacific Island literature of various genres. We center the vantage point of Pacific Islanders' literature, whether written in the Pacific or in the diaspora, written about the Pacific or about diasporic conditions, or some combination thereof (see Hedge Coke et al.). We read and discuss selections from the volume *Indigenous Literatures from Micronesia* (Flores et al.), from Kathy Jetñil-Kijiner's *Iep Jāltok: Poems from a Marshallese Daughter*, and from Craig Santos Perez's *From Unincorporated Territory [Hacha]*.

We begin with Jetñil-Kijiner's poem "Tell Them" and Santos Perez's preface to his volume and the first two poems therein. As students begin to read the poems, I ask them to consider the following questions: What power inequities inform the text historically, currently, and with regard to the future—either in terms of inclusion and privilege, even if not explicitly named but universalized as an assumed, shared point of departure, or in terms of exclusion and marginalization? When, where, and how are whiteness and its attendant privilege presupposed? How are race and gender manifested? Who and what are centered? Students are also encouraged to consider the human and the nonhuman in terms of their differences and entanglements. In terms of the nonhuman, I ask them to consider multispecies relations and how they are structured (see Braidotti; Haraway).

We consider and discuss how Indigenous worldviews inform these multispecies ways of relating. As Whyte, Caldwell, and Schaefer write,

> [F]or many Indigenous peoples collectives are not anthropocentric. That is, they do not exclude animals, plants and ecosystems as members

with the responsibilities of active agents in the world. In many cases, plants, animals, and ecosystems are agents bound up in moral relationships of reciprocal responsibilities with humans and other nonhumans. (155)

As they argue, animals, plants, and ecosystems not only are included but also have agency, and their relationships are based on reciprocity. In fact, "Animals, plants and entities, such as water, are often considered as bearers of knowledge in their own right. Humans must exercise respect in their requesting counsel from these knowledge bearers" (156). Where do the poems we read foreground another species and its agency? How does one write this agency?

Moving from the literary analysis to the creative writing, I draw on approaches developed by Santos Perez, a Guåhan poet and a professor of creative writing at the University of Hawai'i, Mānoa. Santos Perez teaches a course on ecopoetics and has students begin by writing a poem "related to nostalgia," asking them to write "about a childhood memory in which you felt connected to nature" (Santos Perez, "Pacific Eco-poetics"). He then continues with a second assignment focused on solastalgia, a term that combines solace, desolation, and nostalgia. Solastalgia, Santos Perez writes,

> speaks to the pain and distress caused when your homeland is destroyed but you are not necessarily displaced . . . you yearn for what your home was before it was desecrated by mining, logging, fracking, military testing or oil spill; "it is the homesickness you have when you are still at home." Sadly, solastalgia is becoming more and more common, especially for peoples of color and those in developing countries.[2]

As his list highlights, due to environmental destruction home has left one, which leads to solastalgia.[3]

We then consider the ethics related to engaging Indigenous traditional ecological knowledge. Santos Perez writes that creation stories "are often encoded with eco-poetics" ("Pacific Eco-poetics"). Yet creation stories might play different roles for different peoples. "While native peoples have always looked to our creation stories for guidance and inspiration," Santos Perez writes, "many non-native peoples have turned to Indigenous stories to address the crisis of climate change" ("Creation Stories"). The observation is delicately put. But it touches on a key issue—namely, the ethics of drawing on Indigenous knowledge to address the climate crisis. Extractivism or extractive logic not only informs the conduct of oil companies but also plays out, intentionally or not, between geographies, disciplines, and peoples. What are the ethics of engaging Indigenous knowledge—in particular, Indigenous creation stories or stories that present an Indigenous cosmology? We discuss these questions in the course. At the University of Hawai'i, Mānoa, the student body's demographics in any given semester will vary, but courses will typically include students with Indigenous ancestry, particularly Hawaiians and Pacific Islanders. Addressing this ethical issue aims not only to include Indigenous knowledge, history, and culture but also to acknowledge differences in the classroom.

We read an article in which Whyte, Caldwell, and Schaefer write of how a Māori scholar uses an Indigenous creation story to gauge the environmental policies of a settler state's government. The "Māori scholar Te Kipa Kepa Brian Morgan," they write, "in Aoteoroa/New Zealand has created a model for environmental assessment based on their concept of Mauri" (165). In a presentation they cite, Morgan states that "Mauri is the binding force between the physical and the spiritual aspects. . . . Mauri is considered to be the essence of life that provides life to all living things. . . . It also establishes the interrelatedness of all living things. Linkages between all living things within the ecosystem are based on the whakapapa or genealogies of creation." "This concept," Whyte, Caldwell, and Schaefer argue, "has been used to design a metric for evaluating the environmental actions of the New Zealand settler state in terms of whether particular actions increase or decrease Mauri, instead of relying on settler notions of economic costs and health impacts" (165). Interrelatedness is vital to the concept of Mauri.

We consider this notion of interrelatedness and what role it plays in Indigenous creation stories of the Pacific, such as the Kumolipo in Hawai'i. We then reread and discuss anew Jetñil-Kijiner's poem "Tell Them" and further selections from Santos Perez's *From Unincorporated Territory [Hacha]*, considering for each one how interconnection manifests. Key to Indigenous creation stories, Santos Perez argues, is the notion of the interconnection of humans, nature, and other beings:

> Indigenous creation stories, and native eco-poetics in general, foreground how the primary themes in native texts express the idea of interconnection and interrelatedness of humans, nature and other species; the centrality of land and water in the conception of indigenous genealogy, identity and community; and the importance of knowing the indigenous histories of a place. ("Creation Stories")

Interconnectedness is key not only for Pacific Island literature but also in Indigenous literature of the United States mainland as well as in African literature.[4] This interconnectedness represents a shift in thinking about the relations among humans, nonhuman animals, land, water, and more. It also suggests a key pivot for how to think and teach the environmental humanities.

The interconnectedness put forward by Indigenous creation narratives provides an alternative model, one that recognizes, highlights, puts forward, and strengthens the relations and connections among beings. As Santos Perez puts it, "[I]ndigenous eco-poetics re-connects people to the sacredness of the earth, honors the earth as an ancestor, protests against further environmental degradation, and insists that the earth (and literary representations of the earth) are sites of healing, co-belonging, resistance, and mutual care" ("Creation Stories"). In this reconfiguration of relations, to ones of reciprocity and of "thinking with," the notion of interconnectedness is politically radical and environmentally healing. It offers the opportunity to move away from the work of settler colonialism to disconnect: from land, from knowledge, from practices, and more, and to reconnect in order to work toward a future. I ask students to consider the importance of interconnectedness not only for the texts we read but also for the essays they write.

But whose creation myth is it? And for whom is it? In asking these questions, I cycle back to Whyte, Caldwell, and Schaefer's coauthored article and grapple with how and why "Indigenous lessons about sustainability are not just for 'all humanity.'" As the coauthors argue in their article's conclusion,

> This reflection on sustainability arises from concern about how Indigenous peoples can put planning processes into practice. It is an active effort that expresses our gratitude to those before us and shows our responsibility to those who will come after us. This line of sustainability is maintained by sharing cultural values that have been passed down from generation to generation to show how we can act on the potential futurities of our peoples. (174)

The authors focus on and begin with the Menominee experience in what is now the state of Wisconsin and then branch out to other Indigenous people:

> This is different from how some non-Indigenous communities seek to understand our lessons of sustainability for the purpose of saving themselves or humankind. Instead, Indigenous planning, as a way of re-

flecting on Indigenous sustainability, is about figuring out the planning arising from the contexts that we actually live in today, when societies are greatly limited and threatened by settler colonialism and other forms of oppression. (174)

In other words, only by changing the structures that have brought about both settler colonialism and systems of oppression can Indigenous sustainability be ensured—meaning both the sustainability of Indigenous peoples and the Indigenous knowledges that ensure sustainability. With these discussions in mind, students write their short essays about an island and its history, culture, environment, and inhabitants, human and nonhuman.

## Decolonizing Mapping

Before students create the maps to accompany their essays, we discuss the relation between the map and the written text. The text might include elements that the map does not and vice versa. There should, however, be some overlap between the two. For example, if a site sacred to the Chamorro people on Guåhan will be under water due to sea level rise, the text could explain its importance and the map illustrate its location and future sea levels. Or if coral reefs and mangroves are pivotal for protecting the shoreline of a low-lying island, the text could discuss their significance and the map could illustrate their locations. The key, however, is to be mindful of the fact that each text—the essay and the map—can include other elements and that the map should not have a merely indexical relation to the essay.

We also discuss traditional Polynesian voyaging. As in the Indian Ocean, where African and Arab seafaring took place before the arrival of European colonizers, in the Pacific Ocean Polynesians voyaged, traveling distances as far as from Hawai'i to Tahiti. While maps are associated with colonization, through the surveying and mapping of land and grabbing of resources, an Indigenous tradition of mapping and countermapping challenges this history (see Jacobs). As mentioned earlier, stick charts were used by the Marshallese to identify the location of islands and the patterns of ocean swells relative to the location of islands. This intimate knowledge of the waves and winds has given rise to a different relation to them (see Ingersoll). After students consider maps, we begin to consider space. How do maps view and render space? Who and what inhabits it? Who maps it? To what end? Using which technologies? With what focus?

We visit the Hawaiian and Pacific Collections and the Map, Aerial Photographs, and GIS Collection in Hamilton Library at the University of Hawai'i, Mānoa. Many libraries have holdings of maps, such as the David Rumsey Map Center at Stanford University and the Ayer Collection at the Newberry Library. Public libraries also often have tremendous map resources, such as those at the Boston Public Library, the New York Public Library, and the San Francisco Public Library, to name only a few. Having the students view maps presented by an archivist or librarian reveals a history of cartography and is generative for the mapmaking exercise.

Next, students select an island and work in their group to map it, highlighting its features that might be affected by sea level rise. The island might be a low-lying atoll resting a mere six feet above sea level and be inundated during king tides or storm surge. It might feature a high population density located near the shore around the island's narrow perimeter. It might be highly reliant on subsistence farming and fishing. The salinization of soil resulting from storm surge might threaten crop yields. Coral or oyster reefs that once protected the island might be destroyed by ocean acidification or sedimentation, respectively, leaving the island more exposed to sea level rise and storm surge. Students consider the infrastructure that is vulnerable: Do the roads ring the island's perimeter? Is the airport near the shoreline? What about the power plants? The water treatment facility? Students are asked to go beyond an anthropocentric reading. That is, they are not to focus solely on inhabited islands and humans. After studying the island, students select three features and map them.

Over the course of their study of Pacific literature and cartography, students become attuned to differing narratives about the human and the nonhuman and the relations between them. They consider the positionality of the author and the audiences, and their own positionality: Who narrates, and for whom? They consider what is centered or emphasized, implicitly or explicitly: Who is invited in, or not, and how? They have also considered a worldview that centers interconnectedness, such as multispecies relations. They have considered different temporal frameworks; how history, politics, and economics affect them; and how they manifest in literary texts and in maps. Their ears have been more keenly attuned as they read. Responding to the readings and the class discussions of them, they consider the focus of their essays and their maps.

As they write their essays and create their maps, students are to revisit the aforementioned questions, to take note of their own positionality, the narrative point of view they adopt, and who they are addressing and how. To be aware of what they are including and why and what they are excluding and why. What are they prioritizing? For what reason? The exercises discussed are to lead not only to a closer reading of the literary texts and maps but also to different strategies of and structures informing creative writing and mapmaking. The course assignments intend to raise a broader awareness about the politics of positionality, inclusion, and exclusion, as well as the ethics of drawing on traditional ecological knowledge and temporal frameworks with an eye to interrelatedness going backward and forward for generations.

## Notes

1. Figures are similar for island nations in the Caribbean Sea, Atlantic Ocean, and Indian Ocean, with a few exceptions.

2. In this passage Santos Perez quotes Glenn Albrecht.

3. In this regard, climate change can be akin to gentrification, where it is the sense of what and who a place once was, which has now been displaced, that creates the desolation.

4. As Cajetan Iheka writes, "[T]he distancing of the Africans from their environment was carried into the practice of African literary studies and postcolonialism with an emphasis on the portrayal of rational, modern subjectivities that are often inconsistent with those indigenous practices that connect humans to their environment" (10). See also Iheka 2, 7–8.

## Works Cited

Albrecht, Glenn. "The Age of Solastalgia." *The Conversation*, 7 Aug. 2012, theconversation.com/the-age-of-solastalgia-8337.

Braidotti, Rosi. *The Posthuman*. Polity Press, 2013.

Flores, Evelyn, et al., editors. *Indigenous Literatures from Micronesia*. U of Hawai'i P, 2019.

Gerhardt, Christina. *Atlas of Islands and Sea Level Rise*. U of California P, forthcoming.

Goodyear-Ka'ōpua, Noelani, et al. *A Nation Rising: Hawaiian Movements for Life, Land, and Sovereignty*. Duke UP, 2014.

Haraway, Donna. *When Species Meet*. U of Minnesota P, 2008.

Hedge Coke, Allison Adelle, et al., editors. *Effigies III*. Salt Publishing, 2019.

Iheka, Cajetan. *Naturalizing Africa: Ecological Violence, Agency and Postcolonial Resistance in African Literature*. Cambridge UP, 2018.

Ingersoll, Karin. *Waves of Knowing: A Seascape Epistemology*. Duke UP, 2016.

Jacobs, Christian. *The Sovereign Map: Theoretical Approaches in Cartography throughout History*. Translated by Tom Conley, U of Chicago P, 2006.

Jetñil-Kijiner, Kathy. *Iep Jāltok: Poems from a Marshallese Daughter*. U of Arizona P, 2017.

Lewis, David. *We, the Navigators: The Ancient Art of Landfinding in the Pacific.* U of Hawai'i P, 1994.

Morgan, Te Kipa Kepa Brian. "A Tangata Whenua Perspective on Sustainability Using the Mauri Model: Towards Decision Making Balance with Regard to Our Social, Economic, Environmental and Cultural Well-Being." Paper presented at the International Conference on Sustainability Engineering and Science, 7–9 July 2004, Auckland, New Zealand. *The Sustainability Society,* www.thesustainabilitysociety.org.nz/conference/2004/Session5 /36%20Morgan.pdf.

Santos Perez, Craig. "Creation Stories and Indigenous Eco-poetics." *The Hawaii Independent,* 6 Oct. 2015, thehawaiiindependent.com/story /creation-stories-indigenous-eco-poetics/.

———. *From Unincorporated Territory [Hacha].* Omnidawn Publishing, 2017.

———. "Pacific Eco-poetics Week 2: Solastalgia." *The Hawaii Independent,* 7 Sept. 2015, thehawaiiindependent.com/story/pacific-eco-poetics-week-2 -solastalgia/.

Whyte, Kyle, et al. "Indigenous Lessons about Sustainability Are Not Just for 'All Humanity.'" *Sustainability Approaches to Environmental Justice and Social Power,* edited by Julie Sze, New York UP, 2018, pp. 149–79.

**Salma Monani**

# Decolonial Possibilities in an Introductory Environmental Humanities Classroom

"The growing recognition that Indigenous knowledges are emergent from the nature-culture nexus gives these knowledges a characteristic that may, in a deep sense, represent their greatest value: holistic or complex integrative thinking" (Wildcat 31). This quotation from the Yuchi, Muscogee scholar Daniel R. Wildcat's compelling *Red Alert! Saving the Planet with Indigenous Knowledge* is integral to my course Introduction to Environmental Humanities. Along with the words of numerous other Indigenous scholars and activists, it exposes my students to Indigenous peoples' environmental sensibilities and ways of being in the world. My goal in highlighting such Indigenous sensibilities in the classroom is not to "read extractively"—which, as the Unangax̂ scholar Eve Tuck describes it in her coauthored introduction to *Indigenous and Decolonizing Studies*, is the way colonial settlers often decontextualize such sensibilities from the specificities of their Indigenous situations and selectively appropriate them for settler futurity (Smith et al. 15). Instead, I want to introduce students to the problematic entanglements of Euro-American environmentalisms with Indigenous lives. By allowing Indigenous voices to tell their own specific, situated stories of environmental relations and resistance against settler colonialism's oppression, as an instructor I seek to acquaint my students with the rich epistemological possibilities decolonial pedagogies allow.

As numerous Indigenous scholars (Nakata et al.; Smith et al.; Tallbear) note, such pedagogies foreground Indigenous agency by

> engaging materials produced by contemporary Indigenous peoples that decenter Euro-American subjectivities and authority;
>
> exposing students to the settler-colonial state's historical and continuing effects on Indigenous peoples and to the active work of Indigenous peoples in resisting oppression; and
>
> inviting students to engage in open, exploratory, and creative inquiry that recognizes that knowledge production requires care and ethical responsibility toward communities involved.

In this essay, I explain how I attempt to establish these practices in Introduction to Environmental Humanities. This is a required course for my department's majors, and every spring I teach two sections of it with approximately twenty students in each. My pedagogical goal through these practices is to "provide students with more language and tools for navigating, negotiating, and thinking" about relations between knowledge and action (Nakata et al. 133). As Martin Nakata and his colleagues so eloquently write,

> By learning to focus on the conditions of the Indigenous arguments, in relation to the conditions of Western theorising, students can be led to develop awareness of the limits of various positions, the persistent pervasiveness of "all-knowing," "taken-for-granted" Western frames, an awareness of the reproduction of those frames in Indigenous analysis, and an appreciation of just how intricate and open to interpretation the dance around worldview, knowledge and practice is as a result. We suggest that in this way, students begin to understand why a rush to "understand" in order to find and "know the answers" that will overcome the colonial legacy is more likely to be evidence of not understanding sufficiently. (133)[1]

Before I elaborate on strategies for decolonial learning, I wish to highlight three challenges that contextualize my teaching and that might be familiar to others working to decolonize their introductory environmental studies or humanities courses.

First, most of my students are White Americans, and many identify politically as conservative. There are many times when I am the only identifiable person of color in my classroom.[2] Second, many of my students lack an understanding of social concepts like systemic racism that are central to environmental justice and decolonial work.

Third, while the environmental studies department at my institution is interdisciplinary, I am the only humanities faculty member (along with three social scientists and three natural scientists). The department is located in the Science Center on campus and for administrative purposes is considered part of the natural sciences division. For many of my students, Introduction to Environmental Humanities is likely the first and last humanities course they will take. Given the major's course sequence, students usually enter it after a busy fall semester in which they have taken at least two introductory natural science courses offered by the department—ecology and earth systems science.[3] They come into my class excited about environmental science and familiar with a specific pedagogy: lectures that reiterate foundational concepts from a textbook and three-hour laboratory sessions where they apply the lecture material through observation, sampling, and data collection. They are wary of the pedagogical format common to (nonlab) humanities courses: the reading of multiple primary texts and the ensuing in-class discussions that don't necessarily provide verifiable answers but instead (as more than one student has lamented) seem to suggest that everything is subjective.[4] The challenge, then, is how to inspire my students to appreciate what the humanities can offer them.

A rich body of pedagogical scholarship points to the realities of each of these challenges—the undervaluing of the humanities (Hanlon; Strauss; Massing) and the particulars of being a woman-of-color instructor in a majority-White society (Yenika-Agbaw and Hidalgo-de-Jesús; "Race/Ethnicity"). Thus, I work to craft a course that confronts these challenges even as it attempts to model decolonial practices. In the following sections, I outline my specific strategies.

## Establishing Relevance: Familiarities as Interdisciplinary and Intercultural Possibilities

Truly decolonial practices should always foreground Indigenous presence, as noted by Linda Tuhiwai Smith, Tuck, and K. Wayne Yang in their edited collection *Indigenous and Decolonizing Studies in Education: Mapping the Long View*. However, I begin the semester with an approach that appears to deprioritize such practices because I do not start with the voices of Indigenous peoples (or other non-White people). Instead, recognizing my own positionality as a perceived outsider—a minority woman of color in the majority White classroom—I begin with voices and situations familiar to my students. Beginning this way, I find, is a necessary step toward moving to more explicit decolonial pedagogies. As a number of chapters in *Teaching Climate Change in the Humanities* discuss, in the neoliberal, instrumental context of American higher education, sometimes the best way to get students to care about what seems disconnected from their lives is to reveal the inevitable, if yet invisible, connections (Siperstein et al.). Because most of my students do not identify as Indigenous, I use the first module of my class to attend to their realities, with the goal of rendering visible the connections between my course content and their lives. This strategy builds a bridge to enable students to consider lives outside their own. It is also, I believe, a step in the direction of decolonial pedagogies as I work to center "the expertise of youth and communities about the neighborhoods and institutions they inhabit, as well as the saliency of that expertise in making policy and social change" (Cammarota and Fine, qtd. in Tuck and Yang, xv).

Specifically, to confront the notion that the humanities are subjective, my goals in the first few weeks of class are to help my students recognize the value of subjectivity as an essential, and political, element in how they (and other humans) relate to our environments and to introduce them to processes of engaging critically but openly with subjectivity. To this end, I blend the close-reading and discussion format common to humanities pedagogy with the hands-on activities my students have enjoyed in their natural science courses. For example, I adapt an experiential activity from an environmental humanities course at the University of New South Wales. Each student goes on a neighborhood walk to collect six objects, which they must categorize on a spectrum ranging from "natural" to "cultural" ("Environmental Humanities"). Students bring a photograph of their categorized objects to class. I put no constraints on their choices and instead encourage them to be creative and exploratory in their collection and their processing as they connect the activity to readings that introduce them to the cultural constructions of "nature" (e.g., Corbett 1–8; Farrell 3–11; Hull).

Students enjoy this exercise because it actively engages them (their walks, their categorizations) and addresses their immediate lives (one of the readings is provocatively titled *The Nature of College*). When placed in small groups (four each) during class to compare their thoughts and photographs, they usually have plenty to say. Invariably, they observe how applying the readings to what they had initially considered a simple exercise of sorting helped complicate their assumptions of nature/culture dualities. And I am able to guide them to questions central to the environmental humanities: Why do they present a variety of responses to what is essentially the same activity in the same physical environment (our small residential college environment)? Equally important, what might be the environmental consequences of these responses? In bringing the latter question to bear, what seems a relatively frivolous and apolitical exercise—categorizing familiar everyday objects such as leaves, orange peels, feathers, and cigarette butts—takes on critical weight. Students begin to grasp the environmental value of subjectivity. We each frame our own narratives, which in turn are structured by narratives we have been taught through our exposure to specific institutional and communicative modes, historical contexts, and ethical beliefs. Individuals, but also social groups, often tell different stories about relations to their environments. I pose questions to the students like the following: What motivates a group's adherence to a particular story? Equally important, can individuals buy into more than one story? How do we make sense of these stories? Should we evaluate them? If so, how?

Thus, the introductory exercises in the first weeks of the course expose students to the value of understanding the complexities of subjective difference. I follow these exercises with the "circles of myself" activity recommended by the environmental scholars Julie Sze and Jonathan London. Students highlight multiple dimensions of their identities as interrelated circles. The activity invites students to acknowledge intersectional identities and gives them room to converse about how one defines oneself and how others label one's identity—often in harmful, stereotypical ways. Additional readings from the sociologist Andrew Hoffman's book *How Culture Shapes the Climate Change Debate* allow them to weigh the stakes of summarily dismissing difference and to ask what communicative barriers they themselves put up when faced with difference (e.g., distrust of messenger, message, process, or solution). Excerpts from the political scientist R. Bruce Hull's book *Infinite Nature*, in conjunction with a handout of discussion tips, suggest ways to negotiate difference without stymieing productive discussion. Instead of engaging the voices of Indigenous scholars or activists, this first module centers what my students are familiar with—their own perceptions of the environment, their lives as college students, what they recognize as environmental politics (e.g., debates that are intrinsically related to science, like debates about climate change), and their enjoyment of experiential learning. This tactic loosens their skepticism of the course's relevance and paves the way to grapple with topics that are less familiar to them yet more explicitly grounded in Indigenous peoples' decolonial endeavors.

## From Familiarities to Difficult Conversations: Scaffolding a Case Study

Having used the first two weeks to establish the course's relevance, I turn to topics less familiar to most of my students and more solidly grounded in Indigenous contexts. In the next two weeks, we consider a case study of the water wars in the Klamath River Basin. In this module, I engage the decolonial practices outlined in the introduction to this essay by bringing into the classroom specific, situated stories of Indigenous environmental relations and resistance against settler colonialism's oppression. To also engage the open, exploratory, and creative inquiry that constructs knowledge production as a process that must involve care and ethical responsibility, I carefully scaffold the case study by putting contextual materials into conversation with hands-on exercises.

Students begin by engaging with these contextual materials. They watch Jack Kohler's (Yurok) documentary *River of Renewal* in conjunction with excerpts from the film's coproducer Stephen Most's accompanying book *River of Renewal: Myth and History in the Klamath Basin*. The film never fails to capture my students' attention. Kohler is a soft-spoken narrator who describes himself as a "sidewalk Indian," brought up in urban California, trained as an engineer and then as an actor. The film traces his journey of self-discovery into the Klamath River Basin, the ancestral (and today greatly curtailed) homeland of the Yurok peoples, and situates itself in the water wars that pit communities of Native tribes (Yurok, Hoopa, and Karuk), settler farmers, commercial salmon fishermen, and corporate hydroelectric companies against one another. Juxtaposing Kohler's stakeholder interviews with archival footage of tense moments in the history of stakeholder relations, *River of Renewal* exposes how both nature (the river and its salmon population) and culture (of the Native tribes, the commercial fishermen, and the farmers) are threatened by resource misuse. The film ends in medias res—with a protest for the removal of hydroelectric dams.

The introduction (xxiii–xxxiv) and preface (ix–xx) in Most's book give students more background to the situation, describing how different cultures transmit specific stories about their histories to make sense of their relations to the land (whether the Yurok notion of *pikiawish* or the American settler myth of manifest destiny). The chapter "Stakeholders" provides a detailed account of procedures for resolving conflicts (244–58). Like the film, the book ends with a sense that the debate is ongoing.

The materials' high-context emphasis on community, place, and specificity piques students' interest. The materials debunk students' notions of Native peoples as "primitives of the past" by emphasizing what Nakata and his coauthors might describe as "Indigenous agency in everyday standpoints . . . premised on forms of analysis that are historically-layered, responsive to changing social conditions, often traditionally-grounded, and forward looking" (125). At the same time, because the materials cover an ongoing situation, they offer an example of problem-based learning with which I ask my students to engage through additional activities that relate the film and book to the real-world debate as it continues to unfold.

My students like problem-based learning (their science courses encourage it). However, in the experiential, role-play activity I assign, they cannot tackle the problem of resource use as if it were solely a technical one. Instead, the activity involves three discrete tasks that encourage focused yet creative exploration to foreground the processes involved in knowledge production and decision-making. First, students break into groups of four. The members imagine themselves as representatives, with names and personalities, of different stakeholder groups. In essence, each student is encouraged to populate a set of "circles of self" that traces the intersectional ways in which a member of a particular stakeholder group might relate to nature. Thus, "Sam the farmer" relates to the river not only as a source of water for crops; as a person living in this place, Sam also uses the water for drinking, perhaps for fishing, and so forth. In imagining their person's intersectionalities, students are reminded to create with care (as they did with their "circles of myself," from module one).

Second, after engaging in this individual thinking exercise, students come together in their groups to share. Here, the exercise asks them to keep in mind the first module's attention to negotiating difference and also Most's chapter on stakeholders, which clearly traces a process of respectful interaction aimed at conflict resolution (stakeholders coming together and listening openly to one another's concerns). Bringing such considerations into their own conversations, each student must be an active voice in the group's decision-making on how to resolve the debate.

For most of my students, this is their first exposure to this specific case study and to really engaging with the complex human dynamics that inform such debates. Therefore, as they deliberate, many approach the problem with a desire for equal fairness for all. To guide them to think more critically about the ethics of their decisions, the exercise's third unit asks them to collectively reflect on their decision-making process. I share the questions I pose to students at this stage below, because this step is crucial in helping students see social structures, specifically legacies of settler-colonial oppression, more clearly:

> How challenging or easy was the process of decision-making?
> How did you decide whose stories should carry the most weight in this debate?
> Did issues of power and privilege surface in your decision-making? Explain.
> Did understandings of past histories and injustices affect your decision? Explain.
> Do you take responsibility and provide support for those who might be "losers" in this decision? Should you? If so, how?
> Would adding the salmon as a stakeholder affect your decision-making?
> Finally, explain if and how these questions have altered your group's original decision.

As my students move through the three steps of the in-class exercise, I do not rush this process. Instead, I both observe their group interactions and encourage their discussions to tackle what some say are difficult questions. The activity takes an entire seventy-five-minute class period and spills over into the next class session, when we convene to compare notes. The collective conversation is inevitably productive. For most of them, their own love for nature makes the Yoruk, Hoopa, and Yaruk peoples' arguments for the rights of nature compelling, and many find consideration of the salmon as a stakeholder profoundly powerful.[5] Many enjoy the inherently philosophical yet active task of processing the ethics of decision-making. They recognize the limits of their own knowledge, especially when they see that they did not account for some of the questions in unit three. And while some find it difficult to be in spaces of uncertainty, others embrace the critical and creative possibilities that emerge from such uncertainty. Yet others appreciate hearing an environmental story they haven't heard before, especially one that portrays Indigenous peoples not only as ancestrally tied to the land but also as people of the present. Many note that history matters to the present as they see how punitive and racist policies of the past continue to structure the conditions of today.

Overall, the module is layered to emphasize attentive listening. Thus, when notions of settler-state oppression arise from their own conversations with one another and the materials, and not as something told to them by their woman-of-color instructor, students who have resisted acknowledging the structural racism of environmental injustices find it hard to ignore. As with all pedagogical tools, this module is not perfect (as I elaborate in the conclusion), but it introduces the three decolonizing methodologies that I use—critical awareness of legacies of settler-colonial oppression, Indigenous agency in resisting such oppression, and modes of creative and exploratory learning that bring care and ethical responsibility into engagements with knowledge production.

For the rest of the semester we repeatedly engage these decolonial practices through specific, historically contextualized examples of Indigenous communities' interactions with Euro-American environmentalisms. For example, we consider how Indigenous peoples continue to resist their forced removal from national parks and wilderness areas, whether in the Boundary Waters Wilderness Area (see Latiala) or in Saskatchewan (see Goulet); the resistance of Oceania's peoples to environmental injustices such as land grabs, nuclear colonialism, and climate injustices (see Goodyear-Kaʻōpua; Jetñil-Kijiner); and the way Native voices counter the devaluation of Indigenous ways of knowing by so-called objective science (see Kimmerer 39–44; Wildcat). In the spring of 2019, in the last module of the course, we brought many of these ideas together with attention to ongoing concerns at Mauna Kea, Hawaiʻi, where Kanaka peoples are fighting to protect their sacred peak from the development of a thirty-meter telescope. Greg Johnson, a religious studies professor from the University of Colorado's Center for Indigenous Studies, visited class. He shared readings and videos by his Kanaka collaborators (such as "Kapu Aloha 101") and discussed his experiences working as an ally in legal and direct action. As with the case study of the Klamath River Basin, I did not rush this discussion, and many students commented on how powerful it was to have a scholar-activist in class, as well as how the case study reiterated the need to think "in integrative, holistic" ways and see "beyond settler epistemologies" (Wildcat 31; Goodyear-Kaʻōpua 185).

## Challenges and Hope in Decolonial Pedagogies

My introductory environmental humanities course, as noted, may be the first and last humanities course my students will take during their college career. Thus, I am adamant about exposing them to the cultural complexities of environmental practice. Such complexities cannot ignore Indigenous environmentalisms. In teaching about Indigenous environmentalisms, I attempt to decolonize my classroom. However, I impose certain constraints upon my pedagogical endeavors. First, as Hoffman articulates, deep cultural ideologies invariably frame a messenger effect—and my own positionality as a woman-of-color instructor among a majority-White student population gives me pause in starting with Indigenous voices and concerns. Instead, I feel as if I have to build trust with my students through materials that are closer to their realities before we engage with Indigenous spaces.[6] I struggle with the way this pedagogical choice impinges on truly decolonial work, but I find that it enables me to do more of this work later in the semester.

Second, while I foreground numerous Indigenous voices, I do not engage my students in participatory action research that would involve them working directly with the communities whose stories they are studying. I hesitate to do so because of the introductory nature of the course and because while the course is generally well received, invariably I have students who resist its content and style. Used to learning scenarios that provide more certain "right" answers, they find unpalatable the open, exploratory, and creative inquiries that refuse certainty and raise questions about their own ideological ways of knowing. Here, I get small comfort from Tuck, who observes that she "underestimated how challenging it would be for settlers to read Indigenous work, after all these years of colonial relations" (Smith et al. 15). At the same time, I end this essay on a semihopeful note. I find that while some students don't immediately warm to the course, they surprise me when they return a year or more later and share, unsolicited, an appreciation for what the course did to shape their thinking as they advocate for "holistic, integrative thinking" and against the constraints of "settler epistemologies" in their careers.

## Notes

I would like to thank Nicole Seymour and Matt Beehr for their thoughtful feedback on drafts of the essay.

1. At this point, I would like to acknowledge that conversations and scholarship at the intersections of pedagogy and decoloniality are much richer and more vibrant than I can encapsulate in this short essay. While readers might immediately think of figures like Walter Mignolo, a stalwart in the field, here I turn to other scholars whose works I believe are as important if not always as well known.

2. I am a first-generation settler from India. I am happy to note that as the demographics of college students change, I am seeing more racial and ethnic diversity at my institution.

3. In fact, of the four courses they take per semester, many students are usually taking three natural science courses to satisfy their bachelor of science requirements.

4. Over the years I have been teaching the course, I have found students are demonstrating less enjoyment for reading. Consequently, I regularly mix reading with cinematic content. Often, I use the second to ignite interest in the first, as discussed in more detail in the next section of this essay.

5. In the interim between class periods, I provide more-recent resources to showcase the evolution of the situation (e.g., news stories from *Indian Country Today*).

6. This groundwork could include bringing in White allies to help establish credibility of the content early in the semester.

## Works Cited

Cammarota, Julio, and Michelle Fine, editors. *Revolutionizing Education: Youth Participatory Action Research in Motion*. Routledge, 2008.

Corbett, Julia B. *Communicating Nature: How We Create and Understand Environmental Messages*. Island Press, 2006.

"Environmental Humanities: Remaking Nature." *Future Learn*, www .futurelearn.com/courses/remaking-nature. Accessed 11 June 2019.

Farrell, James J. *The Nature of College: How a New Understanding of Campus Life Can Change the World*. Milkweed Editions, 2010.

Goodyear-Kaʻōpua, Noelani. "Protectors of the Future, Not Protestors of the Past: Indigenous Pacific Activism and Mauna a Wākea." *The South Atlantic Quarterly*, vol. 116, no. 1, 2017, pp.184–94.

Goulet, Danis, director. *Wapawekka*. *National Screen Institute*, 2010, www.nsi -canada.ca/2013/02/wapawekka/.

Hanlon, Aaron. "Lies about the Humanities—and the Lying Liars Who Tell Them." *The Chronicle of Higher Education*, vol. 65, no. 15, 14 Dec. 2018, p. 1.

Hoffman, Andrew. *How Culture Shapes the Climate Change Debate*. Stanford Briefs, 2015.

Hull, R. Bruce. *Infinite Nature*. U of Chicago P, 2006.

Jetñil-Kijiner, Kathy. *Iep Jāltok: Poems from a Marshallese Daughter*. U of Arizona P, 2017.

"Kapu Aloha 101: Ke Kula o Maunakea." *Vimeo*, uploaded by Ōiwi TV, 3 July 2015, vimeo.com/132507823.

Kimmerer, Robin Wall. *Braiding Sweetgrass: Indigenous Wisdom, Scientific Knowledge, and the Teaching of Plants*. Milkweed Press, 2013.

Laitala, Lynn Maria. "Jackfish Pete: Pete LaPrairie's Story." *The Wilderness Debate Rages On: Continuing the Great New Wilderness Debate*, edited by Michael P. Nelson and J. Baird Callicott, U of Georgia P, 2008, pp. 218–30.

Massing, Michael. "Are the Humanities History?" *The New York Review of Books*, 2 Apr. 2019, www.nybooks.com/daily/2019/04/02/are-the-humanities-history/.

Most, Stephen. *River of Renewal: Myth and History in the Klamath Basin*. U of Washington P, 2006.

Nakata, Martin M., et al. "Decolonial Goals and Pedagogies for Indigenous Studies." *Decolonization: Indigeneity, Education and Society*, vol. 1, no. 1, 2012, pp. 120–40.

"Race/Ethnicity of College Faculty." *National Center for Education Statistics*, nces.ed.gov/fastfacts/display.asp?id=61. Accessed 11 June 2019.

*River of Renewal*. Produced by Jack Kohler, Steve Michelson, and Stephen Most, Video Project, 2009.

Siperstein, Stephen, et al., editors. *Teaching Climate Change in the Humanities*. Routledge, 2017.

Smith, Linda Tuhiwai, et al. Introduction. *Indigenous and Decolonizing Studies in Education: Mapping the Long View*, edited by Smith et al., Routledge, 2019, pp. 1–23.

Strauss, Valerie. "Why We Still Need to Study the Humanities in a STEM World." *The Washington Post*, 18 Oct. 2018, www.washingtonpost.com/news/answer-sheet/wp/2017/10/18/why-we-still-need-to-study-the-humanities-in-a-stem-world/.

Sze, Julie, and Jonathan London. "Teaching and Learning Guide for: Environmental Justice." *Sociology Compass*, vol. 3, no. 6, 2009, pp. 1022–28.

Tallbear, Kimberly. "Standing with and Speaking as Faith: A Feminist-Indigenous Approach to Inquiry." *Journal of Research Practice*, vol. 10, no. 2, 2014, jrp.icaap.org/index.php/jrp/article/view/405.

Tuck, Eve, and K. Wayne Yang. Series editors' introduction. Smith et al., pp. x–xx.

Wildcat, Daniel R. *Red Alert! Saving the Planet with Indigenous Knowledge*. Fulcrum Press, 2009.

Yenika-Agbaw, Vivian, and Amarilis Hidalgo-de-Jesús, editors. *Race, Women of Color, and the State University System: Critical Reflections*. UP of America, 2012.

**Supriya M. Nair**

# Ecocriticism and Environmental Justice in Anglophone Caribbean Literature

Environmental pedagogies and activism are particularly vital in the Caribbean, since its entire landscapes were remade by, and still endure the consequences of, colonial invasion, genocide, displacement, slavery, indenture, and the plantation economies that reduced its verdant tropics to industrialized monocrop regimes. Fear of the dire effects of climate change, of rising oceans, coastal erosion, species extinction (which was well underway in the colonial era), and increasingly catastrophic hurricanes and earthquakes lend literary interventions an immediacy that invigorates classroom debates. The alliance of local concerns and global issues appeals to many students in the current generation, even if they are unfamiliar with Caribbean contexts at the start of the class. Although Greg Garrard claims that ecocriticism at first found a space in pedagogical instruction rather than in "elitist" research agendas (1), environmentalists were also perceived as rather preachy, privileged literati who embarked on leisurely rambles and extolled the serenity of nature, in what was identified as the first wave of the field. A postcolonial curriculum would include issues of environmental justice for populations, regions, and species that bear the brunt of global inequality and neocolonial violence, but it would also need to address the complexities of "full-stomach environmentalism" and "empty-belly environmentalism" in order to note the inequalities and differences between the Global North and the Global South that influence activism in these regions (Steinwand 155).

The so-called second wave of postcolonial interventions (if one follows the North American periodization) raised questions of privilege that would not unilaterally prioritize conservation or risk blaming victims of poverty for disastrous environmental "choices." Humans everywhere ignore scientists' warnings at our peril, but Caribbean fiction and poetry emphasize the unique precarity of the Caribbean islands, since the very existence of the vulnerable archipelagoes is at stake. Although environmental and ecocritical approaches have become increasingly purposeful in literature and literary theory in recent times, it must be noted that Caribbean writers have necessarily been preoccupied with issues of land and labor, biopolitics, social justice, and colonial destruction for centuries. Within the last century, a host of writers such as Wilson Harris and Édouard Glissant could be considered ecological theorists in virtually all their works. Despite the modern academic provenance of the environmental humanities as a field, a course designed to introduce students to anglophone Caribbean ecocriticism can select from a generative bibliography that covers a number of islands and a wide historical period. In this essay, I will discuss broad themes that could be included in a course on Caribbean ecocritical literature, with examples from some of the courses I have taught.

Like Patrick D. Murphy, one may embrace the "varieties of environmental literature" in their broadest sense and "not quibble over the distinctions between such categories as nature writing, environmental writing, ecological literature, nature-oriented literature," and other modes (25). However, since postcolonial anthropocentrism (preoccupied as it was with human rights) is symptomatic of its historical and cultural differences from the metropolis, one may want to distinguish between the "varieties" in order to challenge any settled perspective or periodization. But a catholic sensibility that would make no distinctions between taxonomies allows Caribbean literature an ecocritical turn well before the term *ecocriticism* was coined in the 1970s. As Wilfred Cartey points out, "[L]andscape actually becomes the essential foreground" for Caribbean authors, instead of being reduced to a mere framing device or inconsequential setting (9). Cartey discusses links between biology and biography; natural and social order; race, hybridity, tropical ecology, and the discourses of degeneracy; and psychic and historical testimony embedded in the land and sea. This testimony becomes a living archive, its cursed and curative memory implanted with both terror and beauty in the literature. In the first of a series of poems that begins with the phrase "Gardening in the Tropics," Olive Senior declares, "Gardening in the Tropics, you never know / what you'll turn up. Quite often bones" ("Brief Lives"). The "thriving" cemeteries and fertile composted soil of Senior's bionetworks blend culture and nature, violence and survival, death and life, in disquieting ways. Students are quick to make these connections across a range of Caribbean texts such as Edwidge Danticat's *The Farming of Bones*, a fictional account of a historical event—the 1937 massacre of Haitians in the Dominican Republic, whose victims were marked for murder by their Creole pronunciation of the Spanish word for parsley; and Jamaica Kincaid's memoir *My Brother*, a stark narrative of her sibling's death from AIDS, the physical signs of which she describes in dark, horticultural metaphors embodying a postcolonial Gothic that binds together landscape, history, and society in unsettling kinship.

Unlike the prevailing sense of harmony in nature that characterizes conventional ecocritical ideals, the topography of the Caribbean is almost always corrupted or vulnerable to despoliation. When students in my Caribbean literature courses read about early modern European incursions and about the subsequent transformation of the modern Caribbean into sugar plantations through slave labor, they understand why writers like Kincaid routinely employ Edenic and anti-Edenic tropes. The fecund vegetation incites callous greed, the genocide of the natives by the invaders, the obsessive quest for El Dorado, and what Alfred W. Crosby, Jr., rather delicately dubs "the Columbian exchange" that took place after the arrival of the European caravels. The phrase relates to a centuries-long colonial process of exploitative transplanting and trade, the dwindling of Indigenous populations, the modification of the natural landscape into plantations, and the arrival of forced labor from other continents. Even Derek Walcott, who lovingly inscribes the Caribbean's terrestrial and aqueous beauty in his poetry, is often anguished by the history of the region. When I teach his poem "Air," we discuss his startling characterization of the rain forest not as a lush paradise but as an "omnivorous" beast whose "jaws" "devour all," "grinding their disavowal / of human pain" (113). Animal extinction is ignored in this malign figuration of the land as carnivore, giving it a dubious agency that elides human accountability. The "two minor yellow races, and / half of a black" are swallowed whole, while both the "undiscriminating" forest and the "vague sea" seem indifferent to the calcified remains. "There is too much nothing here," says the final line in a damning echo of V. S. Naipaul, which should lead students to consider the potential of irony as a tactic (114). If the "poet's pen / . . . gives to airy nothing / A local habitation and a name" (Shakespeare 5.1.15–17), here the poet seems to render the region wraithlike, volatile, and ultimately self-consuming, a sinister portrayal of the "local habitation," the sense of place so crucial in the ecocritical ethos.

Walcott's bleakness may surprise students who have read his Nobel Prize speech, which, even as Walcott bemoans the commodification of the tropics, absolves history and his multiracial ancestors for the horrors they have perpetrated or endured and finds solace in the beauty of his surroundings. One key to the shift is the epigraph to "Air," which cites James Anthony Froude, the nineteenth-century English author who wrote slightingly of what he perceived as the indolent and trivial Creole lifestyles in the islands, perpetuating climatological stereotypes that negatively linked environment with epidemiology. The reference to "nothing" also sets up an acrimonious debate with Walcott's bête noire, Naipaul, whose accounts of his travels in the region rather too dutifully echoed Froude. For Naipaul and some other writers, not just brutal colonial history and the acedia-inducing climate but also the very structure of the susceptible island, reduced to a mere "dot" on the surface of the ocean, render it open to instability, misuse, and devastation.

In Caribbean texts, the piercing leaves of the sugarcane are weaponized, and the cane field, in opposition to the decorous garden and rural beauty of English lore, is a pitiless setting for even more cultural violence such as rape or murder, as in Junot Díaz's *The Brief Wondrous Life of Oscar Wao*, a text that provokes lively discussion of narrative strategies in postcolonial trauma fiction (147). While the rest of the world enjoyed Caribbean sugar in its heyday, Samuel Selvon would insist that "cane is bitter," a contention supported by Naipaul (*Middle Passage*), Harold Sonny Ladoo, and Lakshmi Persaud even after Indian indenture replaced African slavery. For Naipaul, the uncontrolled wildness of the landscape and the cultivated plantation both represented the "bush," resistant to civilization and high culture, which explains his attraction to the more pastoral and well-regulated landscapes of Wiltshire when he migrated to England. Students, however, realize the subversive potential of the wild, untamed landscape indicated in the Caribbean use of *ruinate* and familiarize themselves with Caribbean flora and fauna that clash with the bucolic symbolism of the English countryside, although there, too, Naipaul found decay and death. One could direct the class to Walcott's acerbic review of Naipaul's *The Enigma of Arrival* (categorized by some critics as a postcolonial pastoral, which can be taught in courses on Caribbean and English environmental literature), where Walcott systematically dismantles Naipaul's admissions of his unease with his disruptive Caribbean milieus and his affinity for more agreeable English landscapes. Naipaul was as much a product of the Caribbean as the sugarcane whose injurious method of harvesting he bemoans, Walcott charges: "The myth of Naipaul as a phenomenon, as a singular, contradictory genius who survived the cane fields and the bush at great cost, has long been a farce" ("Garden Path" 128).

But Walcott's indignation not only overlooks nuances in Naipaul, it also seems a bit inconsistent with his own early confessions about the deficiency of supposedly frivolous tropical Caribbean landscapes and climate and the fraught relation they have to serious writing, which partially accounts both for his exile and for the inhibitions of Caribbean writers in the diaspora, who wrote about the place at a seemingly unavoidable remove from it. However, over the years Walcott acknowledged that the perception of the Caribbean environment as an infertile canvas, a barren derivative of England inimical to writing and art, is absurd. He concludes with irony, "How dumb our nature is then. It hasn't studied Johnson and Wordsworth; it remains monosyllabic, one-dimensional, a child's, a pygmy's drawing. It defeats our artists quickly. It makes bores of our poets" ("Isla" 55). Students particularly enjoy discussing the relation between art and environment in conjunction with Kamau Brathwaite's trenchant line "The hurricane does not roar in pentameter" ("History" 265). This striking pronouncement stimulates many debates about the relation of poetry, in particular, to nature (Whitley), the concrete thisness and thereness of a place, and the appropriate rhythms, cadence, and language that best articulate a national or regional literature. Arboreal and oceanic tropes of rhizomes, mangroves, and corals that have defined Caribbean identity in recent years may then be discussed, so that antiroot discourses in favor of diasporic wandering may be balanced with the desire for local, ethnic, and national grounding (Clark; Ette; Mitsch; Torabully).

Brathwaite's anecdote about a Caribbean schoolgirl incongruously writing about "snow . . . falling on the canefields" and his critique, similar to Ngũgĩ wa Thiong'o's, of the colonial canon for making postcolonial subjects feel out of place in their own homeland galvanized his call for decolonizing "nation language," which is marked by its unique locality ("History" 264). As against the lure of the English landscape for Naipaul, kindled by the colonial canon, the Caribbean distaste for daffodils, arising from the forced recitation of William Wordsworth's famous poem by schoolchildren across British colonies, offers intertextual opportunities for not just comparing plant species but also discussing literary fidelity to local landscapes. It must be noted that Kincaid, once a stringent critic of the status of daffodils in the literary curriculum, has grown the flower in her home in Vermont and has presumably made her peace with both Wordsworth and the subject of his standardized poem. Her horticultural adventures in *Among Flowers*, which echoes colonial travelogues in its description of her plant-gathering trip to the Himalayas, contradict *A Small Place*, a critique of how tourism has further distorted the insular island plantations into gated resorts with artificial landscapes. In contrast to her earlier dismissals of imperial botany and Latin nomenclature, her subsequently uneven self-critical reflections on plant collecting in Nepal as a visitor with American citizenship stimulate provocative arguments about the postcolonial writer who metamorphoses from impoverished migrant to advantaged plant hunter from the metropolis.

In Murphy's generous construction of the field, virtually any course in Caribbean literature would inevitably involve the environment. But for those who trace the institutionalization of the field, the bibliographies of what constitute the subject would be more circumscribed. The chronology Garrard constructs for ecocriticism and "green" cultural studies in his anthology *Teaching Ecocriticism and Green Cultural Studies*, for instance, begins in 1854 with Henry David Thoreau's *Walden; or, Life in the Woods*, before the word *ecology* was coined, in 1869. The editors of another recent collection, *Global Ecologies and the Environmental Humanities*, advocate for applying "postcolonial methods to the environmental humanities—*a relatively new* but rapidly expanding interdisciplinary field" (DeLoughrey et al. 2; my emphasis). The authors of "Literature and Environment," an overview of environmental literature, acknowledge that humans have portrayed environments since "prehistory," but they echo Garrard in situating the start of the environmentalist movement proper in the late nineteenth century, flagging the 1960s and early 1990s as watershed moments for the rising global concern with the environment (Buell et al. 417).

This accessible but thorough overview would work well early in the semester, with its helpful definitions of basic terms for the novice and useful bibliography for instructors. To position the course in a postcolonial, Caribbean context, I would pair "Literature and Environment" with "Edens, Islands and Early Empires," the first chapter of Richard Grove's magisterial *Green Imperialism: Colonial Expansion, Tropical Island Edens and the Origins of Environmentalism, 1600–1860* (1995; 16–72). Although Grove mentions the 1970s as an important period, his argument that colonial invasion from its inception fundamentally influenced modern European science and Western environmental attitudes reverses the emphasis on the North as a primary incubator of the field's concerns and identifies antecedents of current discourses that were written centuries before them. He models meticulous scholarship on the earlier periods for graduate students as well, revealing how soil erosion, land management, deforestation, species extinction (including concern for human survival), and climate change in the colonies were deliberated over by colonial administrators and scientists in the governance of their overseas territories.

Another resource for the early period is the collection *The Islands and the Sea: Five Centuries of Nature Writing from the Caribbean*, which offers excerpts of writings by many authors from Christopher Columbus to Kincaid (Murray). I have often paired selections from Columbus's letters and journals with Brathwaite's poem "Colombe" and Senior's poem "Meditation on Yellow" in order to trace the source of what Graham Huggan and Helen Tiffin call "that tiresome trope," the "Caribbean 'island paradise'" (111). Students are invited to respond to the selections before or after class on *Canvas* (a course management system of online learning). They write discussion posts and read and reflect on their peers' comments, some of which inspire further discussion in class or stimulate a paper topic (see Trudeau on designing online discussion forums). In my smaller classes, I assign, sequentially, brief posts, short close-reading exercises, focused critical responses, and a final research paper, and I encourage students to develop the online posts as building blocks for the longer writing assignments. Many of my students draw attention to passages such as these in Columbus's narrative: "The breezes are very mild, the trees and fruits and vegetation are extremely beautiful and very different from ours, and there are so many rivers and harbours that are better than those in Christendom, that it is a wonder. All these islands are densely populated by the finest people under the sun, without evil or deception" (29). In their close readings, the students discuss Columbus's sweeping colonial gaze; his multiple references to plants and medicinal spices, to mastic, and to verdure; and his repeated use of the word *gold*. They pose the exultant triumph of the Columbian "discovery" of a worldly Eden against Brathwaite's native speaker in "Colombe," who predicts the coming pillage of the land and genocide of its people.

In longer papers that emerge from the posts, students discuss the relation between iconography (see, for example, "Landing"), hagiography, historiography, journeys and journals, *cartas* and travel narratives—the visual and textual productions of empire—that have all contributed not just to the celebration of Columbus but also to the persistent construction of the Caribbean as an unspoiled paradise there for the taking. When I include Senior's poem "Meditation on Yellow," we compare Columbus's obsession with gold with Senior's inversions. In contrast to the takers, Columbus and his ilk, the speaker wearily offers to give them "the gold," "the land," "the breeze," and "the beaches" (15) but eventually protests, "I want to feel / you don't own the tropics anymore" (16). We debate why the voice in the poem shifts in time, space, number, and identity, moving from the dispossessed natives to enslaved people to a subservient and then rebellious service worker in the hospitality industry, in addition to charting a disconcerting link between the arrival of the conquistador and that of the tourist. In acknowledging that tourism has wreaked further destruction on the environment, we consider the possibility of sustainable tourism and the particular problems of the Caribbean, whose spectacular beauty draws covetous visitors, as Senior's poem insists, and whose very attractions lead to the locals' displacement and damage to their ecology. The question of ownership of the land, the breeze, and the beaches, as the poem emphasizes, is still up for grabs centuries after Columbus.

Although "Colombe" begins with reveries of fame and fortune by the conquistador, the languid opening quickly dissolves when the Indigenous speaker(s) and the rest of nature protest the coming apocalypse. Birds are "harshly hawking" and "parrots scream" as the Columbus figure nears "our land." "Crabs snapped their claws / and scattered as he walked toward our shore," the poem concludes, allowing the wildlife to express its own legitimate fears in a discordant but sentient chorus. While conventional interpretations of pathetic fallacy limit the agency of the animals, such representations may be complicated by the intertextual significance of the parrot, for instance, in Caribbean literature, both as a species and as a figure that emerges in other Caribbean texts (and "screams" in alarm on more than one occasion; see Melville; Huggan). In Senior's poem "The Secret of Crusoe's Parrot" (in a section titled "A Little Bird Told Me"), "Parrot through heavy-lidded eyes, watches as the new / invader arrives," replacing the Indigenous observer in "Colombe" (18), a name that, as one of my students discussed in her post, translates as "doves"—ironically symbolizing peace—in Italian. Although zoocriticism has been belatedly appended to environmental literature, its increasing relevance merits a consideration equal to that given to human-focused texts, and we are now moving beyond anthropocentric portrayals toward depictions of multispecies lives across postcolonial contexts.

Even when the course I teach does not specifically focus on the environment, the significance of the latter is so pervasive in the literature that students often choose it as a topic. When I included Danticat's *Claire of the Sea Light*, set in Haiti, for a course called The Literature of the Americas, one wrote a final research paper on environmental crisis and another wrote on queer ecology in the novel. The first student linked the overfishing, deforestation, and destruction of terrestrial and oceanic ecosystems to the disintegration of the family unit in the novel, thus connecting the social and personal costs of environmental damage. The second analyzed the narrative of queer love in the novel through the vodou *lwa* (or spirit) of Lasiren, the mermaid accompanied by the whale, following the work of Omise'eke Natasha Tinsley. How is creaturely theology challenged, I asked this student in feedback on her draft, when the traditional habitats of magical forces, nonhuman or partially human spirits, and religious deities are at risk? I encouraged both students to research literary and nonliterary sources on religious belief and environmental catastrophe in Haiti, so they would realize that ecological disaster was not a merely fantastic scenario for the locals, whose everyday magical realist beliefs exceed the typically materialist focus of environmentalism. Lizabeth Paravisini-Gebert's essay in the collection *Caribbean Literature and the Environment* focuses on the denuding of the Haitian forests and its devastating effects on the nexus of nature and religion in vodou. The essay title "'He of the Trees'" is derived from Maya Deren's reference to Loco (or Loko), a leading vodou spirit of vegetation (Paravisini-Gebert 182). Implicitly evoking "empty-belly environmentalism," Paravisini-Gebert, like Danticat, is careful not to condemn the desperate peasants who cut trees and burn charcoal because they have no other recourse, leading to soil erosion and flooding. In graduate work, students could also focus on what the sciences, engineering, and architecture call the "built environment" for a productive interdisciplinary approach that expands the nature-focused purview of ecocriticism into areas of food, public health, transportation, and working and living spaces. (After Hurricane Katrina ravaged black neighborhoods in New Orleans, where I lived and taught, students in my undergraduate course on food and culture, which had a civic-engagement component, were drawn to community gardens and food deserts, two examples of the way nature and culture are interconnected in urban and not just rural areas.)

I would also teach Danticat's novel in a Caribbean ecocriticism course, along with Nalo Hopkinson's work, either her long or short speculative fiction, and Esther Figueroa's social realist novel *Limbo*, one of the most explicitly environmental texts in Caribbean literature. Danticat, Hopkinson, and Figueroa integrate ecofeminism and sexual politics (all three deal with queer identity) and demonstrate that different modes may be productively articulated in the struggle to save the endangered region. In the case of Figueroa, her long experience in documentary filmmaking, her interviews, and her local advocacy work in environmental justice, community empowerment, and industrial and tourist pollution in Jamaica offer multimodal material that provides context to students who, like those I teach in Michigan, may not be familiar with the debates about island ecologies. Jason de Caires Taylor's underwater museums and artificial reef sculptures off the coast of Grenada (available for viewing on *YouTube* ["Jason de Caires Taylor"]), while not without controversy, provide spectacular visual effects and mark him out as a global green activist when they are studied alongside his other aquatic projects. While conservation and ecological reparation are daunting tasks in the Caribbean in Figueroa's view, exploring her work and those of authors mentioned here would make us more aware of the region's troubled history and more mindful of our responsibilities to its imperiled environment.

## Works Cited

Brathwaite, Kamau. "Colombe." *Middle Passages*, by Brathwaite, New Directions, 1993, pp. 9–11.

———. "History of the Voice." *Roots*, by Brathwaite, U of Michigan P, 1993, pp. 259–304.

Buell, Lawrence, et al. "Literature and Environment." *Annual Review of Environmental Resources*, vol. 36, 2011, pp. 417–40. *Annual Reviews*, doi:10.1146/annurev-environ-111109-144855.

Cartey, Wilfred. *Whispers from the Caribbean: I Going Away, I Going Home.* U of California, Los Angeles, Center for Afro-American Studies, 1991.

Clarke, Richard L. W. "Root versus Rhizome: An 'Epistemological Break' in Francophone Caribbean Thought." *Journal of West Indian Literature*, vol. 9, no. 1, Apr. 2000, pp. 12–41. *JSTOR*, www.jstor.org/stable /23019767.

Columbus, Christopher. *Letter to the Monarchs (Carta a los Reyes): Columbus's First Accounts of the 1492 Voyage*. Edited and translated by B. W. Ife Cervantes, King's College, 1992.

Crosby, Alfred W., Jr. *The Columbian Exchange: Biological and Cultural Consequences of 1492*. Greenwood Press, 1972.

Danticat, Edwidge. *Claire of the Sea Light*. Vintage, 2013.

———. *The Farming of Bones*. Penguin, 1998.

DeLoughrey, Elizabeth, et al., editors. *Global Ecologies and the Environmental Humanities: Postcolonial Approaches*. Routledge, 2015.

Díaz, Junot. *The Brief Wondrous Life of Oscar Wao*. Riverhead Books, 2007.

Ette, Ottmar. "Khal Torabully: 'Coolies' and Corals; or, Living in Trans-archipelagic Worlds." *Journal of the African Literature Association*, vol. 11, no. 1, July 2017, pp. 112–19. *Taylor and Francis Online*, doi:10.1080/21674 736.2017.1335948.

Figueroa, Esther. *Limbo: A Novel about Jamaica*. Arcade Publishing, 2014.

Garrard, Greg. Introduction. *Teaching Ecocriticism and Green Cultural Studies*, edited by Garrard, Palgrave Macmillan, 2012, pp. 1–10.

Grove, Richard H. *Green Imperialism: Colonial Expansion, Tropical Island Edens and the Origins of Environmentalism, 1600–1860*. Cambridge UP, 1995.

Huggan, Graham. "A Tale of Two Parrots: Walcott, Rhys, and the Uses of Colonial Mimicry." *Contemporary Literature*, vol. 35, no. 4, U of Wisconsin P, 1994, pp. 643–60, doi:10.2307/1208702.

Huggan, Graham, and Helen Tiffin. *Postcolonial Ecocriticism: Literature, Animals, Environment*. Routledge, 2010.

"Jason de Caires Taylor Underwater Sculptures." *YouTube*, uploaded by Jason Taylor, 11 Sept. 2007, www.youtube.com/watch?v=X33698McQ7g.

Kincaid, Jamaica. *Among Flowers: A Walk in the Himalaya*. National Geographic, 2005.

———. *My Brother*. Farrar, Straus and Giroux, 1997.

Ladoo, Harold Sonny. *No Pain like This Body*. Heinemann, 1972.

"Landing of Columbus, 1492." *The Gilder Lehman Institute of American History AP US History Study Guide*, 2009–19, ap.gilderlehrman.org /resource/landing-columbus-1492.

Melville, Pauline. "The Parrot and Descartes." *The Migration of Ghosts*, by Melville, Bloomsbury, 1998, pp. 101–16.

Mitsch, Ruthmarie H. "Maryse Condé's Mangroves." *Contemporary Literary Criticism*, edited by Jeffrey W. Hunter, vol. 247, Gale, 2008. *Literature Resource Center*, gale.com/intl/c/literature-resource-center. Originally published in *Research in African Literatures*, vol. 28, no. 4, Winter 1997, pp. 54–70.

Murphy, Patrick D. "The Varieties of Environmental Literature in North America." *Teaching North American Environmental Literature*, edited by Laird Christensen et al., Modern Language Association of America, 2008, pp. 24–36.

Murray, John A., editor. *The Islands and the Sea: Five Centuries of Nature Writing in the Caribbean*. Oxford UP, 1991.

Naipaul, V. S. *The Enigma of Arrival*. Vintage, 1987.

———. *The Middle Passage: Impressions of Five Societies—British, French and Dutch—in the West Indies and South America*. Vintage, 1981.

Paravisini-Gebert, Lizabeth. "'He of the Trees': Nature, Environment, and Creole Religiosities in Caribbean Literature." *Caribbean Literature and the Environment: Between Nature and Culture*, edited by Elizabeth M. DeLoughrey et al., U of Virginia P, 2005, pp. 182–96.

Persaud, Lakshmi. *Butterfly in the Wind*. Peepal Tree, 1990.

Selvon, Samuel. "Cane Is Bitter." *Ways of Sunlight*, by Selvon, Longman, 1957, pp. 59–73.

Senior, Olive. "Brief Lives." *Gardening in the Tropics*, by Senior, McClelland and Stewart, 1994, p. 83.

———. "Meditation on Yellow." *Gardening in the Tropics*, by Senior, McClelland and Stewart, 1994, pp. 11–18.

———. "The Secret of Crusoe's Parrot." *Over the Roofs of the World*, by Senior, Insomniac Press, 2005, pp. 18–20.

Shakespeare, William. *A Midsummer Night's Dream*. Edited by Sukanta Chaudhuri, Bloomsbury Arden Shakespeare, 2017.

Steinwand, Jonathan. "Empty-Belly and Full-Stomach Environmentalism in the Introductory Literature Class: Teaching *The Hungry Tide* in the Anthropocene." *Approaches to Teaching the Works of Amitav Ghosh*, edited by Gaurav Desai and John Hawley, Modern Language Association of America, 2019, pp. 152–59.

Tinsley, Omise'eke Natasha. *Ezili's Mirrors: Imagining Black Queer Genders*. Duke UP, 2018.

Torabully, Khal. *Chair Corail, Fragments Coolies*. Ibis Rouge Éditions, 1999.

Trudeau, Robert H. "Get Them to Read, Get Them to Talk: Using Discussion Forums to Enhance Student Learning." *Journal of Political Science Education*, vol. 1, no. 3, 2005, pp. 289–322. *ResearchGate*, doi:10.1080/15512160500261178.

Walcott, Derek. "Air." *Collected Poems, 1948–1984*, by Walcott, Farrar, Straus and Giroux, 1986, pp. 113–14.

———. "The Garden Path: V. S. Naipaul." *What the Twilight Says: Essays*, by Walcott, Farrar, Straus and Giroux, 1998, pp. 121–33.

———. "Isla Incognita." *Caribbean Literature and the Environment: Between Nature and Culture*, edited by Elizabeth M. De Loughrey et al., U of Virginia P, 2005, pp. 51–57.

Whitley, David. "Poetry, Place and Environment: The Scope of Caribbean Poetry." *Teaching Caribbean Poetry*, edited by Beverley Bryan and Morag Styles, Routledge, 2014, pp. 5–16.

**Stacy Hoult-Saros**

# Humane Education and Latin American / Latinx Cultural Production

This essay offers a pedagogical framework, teaching strategies, and resources for exploring environmental issues in Latin America derived from the principles of humane education. After providing an overview of these principles, I explore intersections between this transformative, solution-focused approach to education and best practices in language teaching. Student learning objectives, cultural units, materials, assignments, activities, and teaching techniques from a model course titled Nature and Culture in Latin America demonstrate how humane educators guide language learners to engage deeply with environmental issues, experience wonder and appreciation for the natural environment, and build empathy for humans and nonhumans affected by environmental devastation in the Spanish-speaking world. These cultural products challenge students to develop a more profound understanding of the colonial legacy that continues to have an impact on relations between nature and human cultures in Latin America.

My teaching applies the mode of humane education practiced by the Institute for Humane Education (IHE) under the leadership of its president and cofounder, Zoe Weil, to the development and teaching of upper-level topics courses taught in Spanish. Weil articulates her vision of a peaceful, healthy, and just world brought about through education in a series of books, including, most recently, *The World Becomes What We Teach: Educating a Generation of Solutionaries*. The institute identifies four essential elements of humane education: humane educators prepare students to acquire knowledge by conducting effective research to "obtain accurate information about interconnected global challenges and discern fact from opinion and conjecture"; to think deeply, using critical, creative, strategic, and systems thinking; to make compassionate and responsible choices, by fostering qualities like wonder, appreciation, empathy, and a commitment to doing the most good and least harm; and to focus on solutions, by engaging in collaborative problem-solving, implementation, and assessment of ideas ("About IHE").

As an overall approach to teaching and learning, humane education overlaps naturally with best practices in language education, and IHE's areas of concern and linked activities and resources lend themselves to productive explorations of relevant topics in the Spanish language classroom. Beyond engaging with specific topics ranging from ecotourism and preservation programs to the plundering and devastation of rainforests, my approach challenges students to think about these familiar issues in new ways; as Uwe Küchler argues, "Monolingualism limits our ecological understanding by creating the illusion of a one-to-one relationship between ways of perceiving and categorizing the world around us, finding words for it . . . and, subsequently, reacting toward or against this world" (154).

Following my own first exposure to humane education through an online IHE course called Teaching for a Positive Future, I completed five semester-length courses to obtain the program's graduate certificate. As an experienced faculty member teaching Latin American literature and culture, I was inspired and challenged by IHE's focus on deep learning about complex, interconnected issues, its use of assignments and activities that empower students to research and solve problems, its emphasis on self-reflection and the development of an educator identity, and its incorporation of attitudes and behaviors into learning objectives. This experience has deeply affected my approach to teaching and course development. My course Nature and Culture in Latin America, for example, provides a curricular model for guiding students of Spanish to explore environmental themes in a range of texts that engage the ramifications of colonialism in the Spanish-speaking world. Students analyze a wide variety of canonical and contemporary cultural products to deepen their understanding of how such products both reflect and inform human attitudes toward the natural world, paying particular attention to the role of nature in history, spirituality, and race and gender relations. The first unit, "Nature, Humanity, and Culture," treats representations of nature and humanity acting upon each other, with an emphasis on narratives of conquest and colonization and of human migration; the second, "Nature, Imagination, and Ecocriticism," focuses on conflict and reconciliation through a close reading of Gioconda Belli's utopian novel *Waslala*; and the third, "Nature, Identity, and Alterity," invites critical analyses of texts depicting gendered relationships with nature and connectedness between the natural environment and the indigenous and African roots of Latin American cultures. On the value of approaching emotionally difficult themes like climate change through world literatures, Karen Thornber asserts that this type of discussion "provides [students] with a greater variety of perspectives on climate change and its likely impact on human societies" and "gives them space to envision multiple future scenarios and to think imaginatively about what changes might be made" (266).

In addition to analyzing primary texts, students complete assignments that invite them to reflect on their own relationships with nature. They produce an "archaeology of ideas" aimed at unearthing the root causes of their attitudes toward nature, in response to a series of questions focused on formative experiences, educational background, influential texts, and personal interest in environmental topics. Reflecting on these questions raises students' awareness of the impact of nature on their formation and guides them to perceive connections between their own experiences and perspectives and those encountered in the texts we explore.

Students also keep a media journal in which they record notes on images of nature encountered in their routine use of different media; these notes form the basis for conversations at the beginning of the class period. Formal in-class presentations are based on critical reviews of journal articles representing different periods and approaches to environmental literature, with the objective of raising students' awareness of the evolution of literary criticism, from more traditional interpretations of nature imagery to contemporary ecocriticism.[1] Finally, they connect with local nature through activities involving the close observation of a small area on campus and a paragraph written from the perspective of an animal or plant observed in that area.

While these assignments challenge students to describe, narrate, and reflect on topics in the target language, they also address humane education learning outcomes facilitated more easily through experiential activities than through textual analysis. The combination of analytic, reflective, and hands-on activities allows students to develop wonder and reverence not only for the majestic rain forests, volcanoes, and other iconic elements of Latin American landscapes but also for their own immediate surroundings. Moreover, as Bart H. Welling and Scottie Kapel recount of their experience teaching a course called Wild Encounters, such direct experiences of nature "challenge students to rethink animals in their daily lives as well as in literature" (107).

The literary texts I teach in Nature and Culture in Latin America illuminate aspects of the colonial past and the persistent impact of colonial attitudes, structures, and practices. They are easily and effectively paired with more experiential, humane-education-inspired teaching strategies. From the long list of assigned readings, I will choose for discussion here texts that fall into one of three rough categories: those that evoke nostalgia for an idealized precolonial past; those that depict often violent disruptions of the "natural," pre-Hispanic order of things; and those that focus on the role of nature in reconciliation and healing in an era of climate crisis. For each day's reading, students answer a set of text-specific questions in addition to five guiding questions applied to every reading. My approach to developing these orienting questions aligns with SueEllen Campbell's practice of mixing "big with small, giant generalizations with textual details," allowing her class to "zoom in and zoom out" (221). Further, in emphasizing images of individual nonhuman animals equally with forests, bodies of water, and other components of the environment, my framing of class discussions unites disparate threads in postcolonial ecocriticism; as Graham Huggan and Helen Tiffin observe, "*[E]nvironmental* literature may well appeal to broader ecological systems and processes that *animal* literature rejects in favor of more specific human-animal interactions, while *postcolonial* literature is more likely to show the conflicts that arise when different forms of advocacy are brought together . . ." (14).

If, as Timothy Brennan affirms, part of the work of postcolonial studies "is to reorient cultural values attendant upon learning to understand and appreciate aesthetically the cultural achievements of those outside the European sphere" (132), then any course on nature in Latin America should include indigenous and African-descendant voices speaking about the relationships of individual humans and societies to aspects of their natural environment. Among other types of texts, including paintings representing indigenous concepts of nature, my students read and present on selections from the Guatemalan author Flavio Herrera's *Cosmos indio*

(*Indian Cosmos*), to which they apply a series of orienting questions to reconstruct the worldview of a poet who adopted Asian forms (haikai and tanka) to transmit indigenous values. Each student is charged with summarizing one of the book's subtitled sections, analyzing Herrera's presentation of natural elements as beautiful and precious while noting how the poet invokes both Mayan history, culture, and religion and imposed Christian traditions. In the same unit, along with self-portraits by women artists with roots in Caribbean countries, students also analyze the nostalgia for a childhood spent in the company of an anthropomorphic river and, more generally, for a precolonial past, in Julia de Burgos's poem "Río Grande de Loiza." While Ana Mendieta's photographed installations and Soraida Martinez's paintings use environmental imagery to evoke both the search for origins and the objectification of the female body, Burgos's poem seeks to reestablish the poetic voice's intimate relationship with the river, characterized as a male lover and, at the same time, as a manifestation of her weeping for her enslaved people. The final stanza's social commentary, referring to both the African slave trade and Puerto Rico's continuing colonial status in the eyes of the poet and other nationalists, functions along with the artworks to contextualize intersecting preoccupations of Latin American and Latinx women of color geographically and historically. For example, students analyze how Martinez links a female figure to palm trees through color, form, and posture in *Between Two Islands* and how Mendieta explores similar linkages by photographing her own body merged with natural elements ("Silueta Works"). While Martinez locates the unclothed, vulnerable female form in the liminal space between two cultures (Puerto Rico and the continental United States), Mendieta uses natural materials to portray the female body in cycles of fertility, childbearing, and death.

Into the close examinations of these texts and artworks I incorporate activities from IHE's website that guide students in discovering and appreciating the unique treasures offered by local nature,[2] so that they can develop language proficiency while cultivating a sense of wonder at their natural surroundings. "Scavenger Hunt" invites them to find and describe various items, including animal homes, areas with distinct smells, and places of interaction between plants and animals. "The Wonder Box," credited to Lexie Greer, provides opportunities for contemplation of and written responses to found natural objects, and Christopher Greenslate's "Natural Value" prompts students to write about an image of a place of natural beauty from diverse perspectives, including that of someone who values the location mainly as a site of resource extraction. These activities can be used as prereading script activators or as opportunities to expand on and personalize themes from the readings.

My second category of texts, which present students with imaginative recreations of first contact and conquest as well as reflections on the aftermath of colonialism and the effects of neocolonialism, can help bridge the gap between Latin American studies and the broader field of postcolonialism. As Fernando Coronil affirms, arguing for the inclusion of Latin America in postcolonial studies,

> This larger frame modifies prevailing understandings of modern history. Capitalism and modernity, so often assumed both in mainstream and in postcolonial studies to be a European process marked by the Enlightenment, the dawning of industrialization, and the forging of nations in the eighteenth century, can be seen instead as a global process involving the expansion of Christendom, the formation of a global market, and the creation of transcontinental empires since the sixteenth century. (223)

When teaching Miguel Angel Asturias's conquest-era narrative, "Leyenda del tesoro del lugar florido" ("Legend of the Treasure of the Flowery Place"), I ask students to consider the importance and value of nature for the Mayan culture portrayed in the story, drawing their attention to specific elements (a volcano, clouds, a lake, cacao, feathers, and the iconic quetzal). We examine how the Guatemalan Nobel laureate's native characters ultimately depend on their connection with local nature to defeat the Spanish invaders who fail dramatically at stealing their treasure, and we give special consideration to the relation between nature images and the marvelous. Literary works that attribute magical properties to elements of nature are placed in dialogue with more recently produced materials, from the Discovery Channel's series "Latinoamérica salvaje" ("Wildest Latin America") to the animated film *The Road to El Dorado*, that perpetuate perceptions of "magical" spaces with deep roots in the original chronicles of discovery, exploration, and conquest.

Nearly all Latin American literary accounts of the conquest of Native American cultures end on a more tragic and historically correct note, with the loss of human lives and cherished traditions along with natural resources and habitats. My students read the Cuban poet Fina García Marruz's "Los indios nuestros" ("Our Indians"), in which the speaker contrasts her island nation's original human inhabitants with the denizens of the storied Aztec empire of central Mexico, simultaneously lamenting and celebrating the near-complete "escape" of the peaceful Tainos from written histories in the language of the colonizers; and they analyze Pablo Antonio Cuadra's "El aserradero de la danta" ("The Sawmill of the Tapir"), which recounts the violent death of an animal at a site of deforestation and lumber production in the poet's native Nicaragua. García Marruz's text foregrounds the diversity of indigenous cultures and the Caribbean natives' connections with the surrounding sea and undervalued, "humble" elements like ordinary stones (65), contrasted with the Aztecs' imposing temples. We explore her simile of the movements of a small, elusive fish, drawing on Father Bartolomé de Las Casas's account, in his famous three-volume *History of the Indies*, of a native musical ceremony (areito); videos of contemporary re-creations of ceremonies like this can help students visualize cultural practices based on imitations of nature. My questions on Cuadra's poem guide students to relate its images and events to original Spanish chronicles and to analyze the role of nature in the creation of these parallels; they readily identify the colonial dynamics in the careless destruction of the dark-skinned, native tapir by the white-bearded, shouting "Spanish" boss as a bewildered jaguar witnesses the fate of its intended victim. While the technologies described with devastating effect in this poem situate it in a much more recent time period, artistic and filmic portrayals of earlier contacts between white and indigenous people (like Mexican murals of conquest scenes and the films *The Road to El Dorado* and *Cabeza de Vaca*, about the eponymous sixteenth-century Spanish explorer) can lead to fruitful comparisons with contemporary exploitations of humans, nonhumans, and other natural resources.

Many texts produced by Latinx authors engage humane education's intersecting concerns through a decolonial lens. As Priscilla Ybarra observes in *Writing the Goodlife: Mexican American Literature and the Environment*, "Mexican American writing's engagement with environmental issues explicitly links environmental degradation to the larger oppressions of colonization, imperialism, modernity, and neoliberal globalization" (18). In future versions of Nature and Culture in Latin America, I will include diverse Latinx literary and artistic works produced in the United States that reflect these decolonial concerns and that have factored in my recent research, drawing on key insights from the 2019 landmark collection *Latinx Environmentalisms: Place, Justice, and the Decolonial*, which brings together interviews with influential writers and decolonial critical perspectives on texts ranging from Ester Hernández's iconic *Sun Mad* image (a parody of the well-known Sun-Maid logo) to contemporary ecopoetry and Rosaura Sánchez and Beatrice Pita's science fiction novel *Lunar Bra-ceros, 2125–2148*. As the editors of *Latinx Environmentalisms* note in their introduction, "Latinx cultures hold the potential to make visible key aspects of the exploitation of the earth (introduced and exacerbated by colonization and capital) that figure into the historical marginalization of Latinx communities" (Wald et al. 7).

The stories in *Latinx Environmentalisms* that depict the cultural and environmental impact of a series of violent confrontations can be paired successfully with IHE resources on environmental devastation and the human ability to cause and to solve serious problems. The IHE activity "Exploring Deforestation," developed by Meghan Kelly, uses the website *Global Forest Change* to engage students in the investigation of forest ecosystems, the causes and effects of deforestation, and possible solutions, while challenging them to create formats for sharing their findings. In "Council of All Beings," students role-play a conversation between animals and other elements of nature in the target language, expressing their unique identities and experiences, including those affected by human activity, and sharing their wisdom and knowledge with the other participants. In-class discussions of character development and dynamics can be enhanced by activities like "Magazine Scheme: Are We Here?," developed by Brandi Burke-Hicks, which guides students to think analytically about portrayals of women and girls. The seductive, hypersexualized Chel from *The Road to El Dorado* provides an animated example of the stereotyping of Native and Latinx women and a springboard for reflections on how magazines and films might better serve female readers.

In teaching *Waslala*, I employ a strategy adapted from a resource credited to Rachel Malchow and posted to the website *StudyLib*, designed to encourage students to actively engage with and "own" a complex reading. We form a *Waslala* book club, in which each student plays a different official role at each class meeting. While the student assigned the responsibilities of Travel Tracer, for instance, reports on Belli's descriptions of natural spaces both pristine and severely contaminated, the Illustrator creates visual representations of these scenes and the Connector underscores links between the novel and other works and themes from the class. This permits a division of labor that facilitates deep learning through Belli's narrative of a young female protagonist's search for a secluded, idyllic community in which humans live in harmony with nature. As Robert S. E. Caine observes, "Humane education encompasses sets of knowledge for transforming our society from a state of violence, chaos and fragmentation towards one of peace, tranquility and harmony, and for connecting with one another, and with non-human animals and the natural world, in more cooperative and convivial ways" (85); Belli's novel provides a literary model for this type of transformation while acknowledging the powerful forces that must be confronted in the realization of this harmonious vision.

Following the spirited protagonist Melisandra's journey, students come into contact with international journalists as well as with the capitalists, smugglers, and terrorists who represent the worst of Central America's postcolonial ills before encountering the much-sought-after hidden paradise, which shares features of its history with the artistic community of the archipelago of Solentiname in Lake Nicaragua. Founded in 1965 by the priest and poet Ernesto Cardenal, this Christian socialist society became home to artists like María Guevara Silva, Alejandro Guevara Silva, and José Arana. My students analyze Ignacio Fletes Cruz's paintings of human communities benefiting from the abundance of benevolent, exuberant nature as visual referents for Belli's vision of an egalitarian Eden in which native nature is not only preserved but improved by the touch of human hands ("Ignacio Fletes Cruz"). The novel's complex web of interconnected issues—among them environmental contamination, drug trafficking, kidnapping, torture, and war—are addressed through role-play activities that call on students to use their knowledge of characters, settings, and themes in a cooperative, "solutionary" framework ("About IHE"). In one iteration of the class, students role-played a NAFTA hearing that brought together citizens of the fictional Faguas, representatives of a multinational company based in the United States, and distinguished scholars from different countries. These in-class experiences guide students beyond either/or thinking to consider solutions that would do the most good and the least harm to all involved, in alignment with the "MOGO" principle Weil articulates in *Most Good, Least Harm: A Simple Principle for a Better World and Meaningful Life.*

Texts like Belli's can help bridge the gap between awareness and action, as the editors of *Latinx Environmentalisms* point out of texts produced in the United States: "Latinx literary and cultural environmentalisms in particular offer new ways for scholars, students, and activists to apprehend the world as it is and envision (and thus work toward) the world as it might be." Paired with works like *Waslala*, humane education activities can help students channel the negative emotions that arise in response to environmental catastrophes in positive, solution-focused ways. Heather Schooler's IHE activity "Sustainer" imagines a reality-show setting in which students must work together to overcome the challenges of surviving sustainably in a remote, self-contained biosphere. Kelly's IHE project "Forests of the Future?" provides prompts that allow students to envision future scenarios, narrate how they came about, and write hypothetically about their own experiences of these scenarios, which range from the bleakest to the most optimistic outcomes for the earth's forests.

In their introduction to *Teaching Climate Change in the Humanities*, the volume's editors comment on Jack Mezirow's concept of "disorienting dilemmas," observing that "the distressing realities of climate change constitute both obstacle and incitement to student engagement" (Siperstein et al., Introduction 5). Postcolonial Latin American cultural production immerses students in an array of complex contemporary problems that can feel overwhelming to Spanish-language learners. A humane education approach to exploring these texts demonstrates sensitivity to the emotional impact of these materials on language learners while fostering compassion, empathy, and solidarity with the human and nonhuman inhabitants of target cultures and the spaces they inhabit.

## Notes

1. Articles included Carlota Caulfield's "Canción de la verdad sencilla: Julia de Burgos y su diálogo erótico-místico con la naturaleza" ("Song of the Simple Truth: Julia de Burgos and Her Erotic-Mystic Dialogue with Nature") and Ignacio López Calvo's "La mujer en Nicolás Guillén: Símbolos botánicos y animales" ("The Woman in Nicolás Guillén: Botanical and Animal Symbols").

2. The IHE activities referred to throughout this essay can be accessed at humaneeducation.org/category/resources/types/lesson-plans-activities. Creators are attributed where named in the source.

## Works Cited

"About IHE." *Institute for Humane Education*, 2021, humaneeducation.org /about-ihe/.
Asturias, Miguel Angel. "Leyenda del tesoro del lugar florido." *Cuentos y leyendas*, edited by Mario Roberto Morales, Colección Archivos, 2000, pp. 39–43.
Belli, Gioconda. *Waslala: Memoria del futuro*. Seix Barral, 2006.
Brennan, Timothy. "From Development to Globalization: Postcolonial Studies and Globalization Theory." *The Cambridge Companion to Postcolonial Literary Studies*, edited by Neil Lazarus, Cambridge UP, 2004, pp. 120–38.
Burgos, Julia de. "Río Grande de Loiza." *El Boricua: A Monthly Bilingual Cultural Publication for Puerto Ricans*, www.elboricua.com/Poems_Burgos _RioGrandeLoiza.html.
Caine, Robert S. E. "Humane Education: A Foundation for Connecting with All of Earth's Inhabitants." *Green Teacher*, vol. 85, 2009, pp. 9–13.

Campbell, SueEllen. "Asking Ecocritical Questions." *Teaching North American Environmental Literature*, edited by Laird Christensen et al., Modern Language Association of America, 2008, pp. 215–22.

Coronil, Fernando. "Latin American Postcolonial Studies and Global Decolonization." *The Cambridge Companion to Postcolonial Literary Studies*, edited by Neil Lazarus, Cambridge UP, 2004, pp. 221–40.

Cuadra, Pablo Antonio. "El aserradero de la danta." *The Birth of the Sun*, edited and translated by Steven F. White, Unicorn, 1988, pp. 66–67.

García Marruz, Fina. "Los indios nuestros." *Antología Poética*, edited by Jorge Luis Arcos, Letras Cubanas, 1997, pp. 64–66.

Hernández, Ester. *Sun Mad*. 1982. *Smithsonian American Art Museum*, americanart.si.edu/artwork/sun-mad-34712.

Herrera, Flavio. *Cosmos indio: Hai-kais y tankas, los escribió Flavio Herrera*. Tipografía nacional, 1938.

Huggan, Graham, and Helen Tiffin. Introduction. *Postcolonial Ecocriticism: Literature, Animals, Environment*, by Huggan and Tiffin, Routledge, 2010, pp. 1–24.

"Ignacio Fletes Cruz: Nicaraguan Primitivista Painter (2007)." *Indigo Arts Gallery*, https://indigoarts.com/exhibitions/ignacio-fletes-cruz-nicaraguan -primitivista-painter-2007.

Küchler, Uwe. "Signs, Images and Narratives: Climate Change across Languages and Cultures." Siperstein et al., *Teaching*, pp. 153–60.

Malchow, Rachel. "Setting Up a Book Club Discussion for Twelfth Grade." *StudyLib*, studylib.net/doc/8063542/book-club-discussions-guide-sheet. Accessed 12 Mar. 2021.

Martinez, Soraida. *Between Two Islands*. 1996. soraida.com/islands.htm.

"Silueta Works in Mexico: Ana Mendieta 1973–77/1991." *Institute of Contemporary Art/Boston*, 2021, icaboston.org/art/ana-mendieta/silueta-works -mexico.

Siperstein, Stephen, et al. Introduction. Siperstein et al., *Teaching*, pp. 1–13.

———, editors. *Teaching Climate Change in the Humanities*. Routledge, 2017.

Thornber, Karen. "Climate Change and Changing World Literature." Siperstein et al., *Teaching*, pp. 265–71.

Wald, Sarah D., et al. Introduction. *Latinx Environmentalisms: Place, Justice, and the Decolonial*, edited by Wald et al., Temple UP, 2019, pp. 1–31.

Weil, Zoe. *Most Good, Least Harm: A Simple Principle for a Better World and Meaningful Life*. Atria, 2009.

———. *The World Becomes What We Teach: Educating a Generation of Solutionaries*. Lantern Books, 2016.

Welling, Bart H., and Scottie Kapel. "The Return of the Animal: Presenting and Representing Non-human Beings Response-ably in the (Post-)humanities Classroom." *Teaching Ecocriticism and Green Cultural Studies*, edited by Greg Garrard, Palgrave Macmillan, 2012, pp. 104–16.

Ybarra, Priscilla Solis. *Writing the Goodlife: Mexican American Literature and the Environment*. U of Arizona P, 2016.

**Simon C. Estok**

____________________

# Teaching East Asian Ecocriticisms

Teaching postcolonial East Asian ecocriticisms both outside and inside East Asia means recognizing the heterogeneity—geographic, historical, linguistic, demographic, and so on—of the region. Japan surrendered most of its colonies in 1945, but many aspects of colonialism and forms of its violence remain in many parts of East Asia. Moreover, in post-1997 (financial crisis) South Korea (much more so than in China, Japan, or Taiwan), harsh loan conditions compromised the sense of nation, reducing the country to a kind of economic and cultural colony of the West. The kinds of ecocriticisms that have developed and are evolving in the region have been determined by a wide range of factors, such as North East Asian racism against South East Asians (a racism that finds unashamed expression in the marketing of so-called lightening creams in Korea, Japan, China, and Taiwan), differing ideologies about sexuality (Taiwan is radical among East Asian countries in allowing same-sex marriage), differing religious beliefs (Confucianism, Buddhism, and Christianity, for instance, each have very different understandings of human relationships with nature), and diet. This chapter will explore the complexities and implications of teaching postcolonial East Asian ecocriticisms both outside and inside the region. The region's ecocriticisms reflect the complexities of situated histories, and teaching postcolonial East Asian ecocriticisms is an important way of resisting the one-way flow of theory from West to East.

The heterogeneity of East Asia necessitates a pedagogical approach that recognizes and encourages diversity, hybridization, dissonance, and self-determination. For example, South Korea industrialized differently than did Japan (which colonized much of the region between 1910 and 1945), China (whose huge population has historically presented unique problems), or Taiwan (a country that China still considers Chinese rather than autonomous). These histories determine the kinds of environmental concerns and critiques that develop in each nation. But while countries in East Asia share certain histories and some aspects of their respective use and development of ecocriticism, there is no one East Asian ecocriticism, any more than there is one European or African dance, or song, or food. However, one thing that modern East Asian environmental literatures share is an awareness of how industrialization is rapidly transforming the region and how industrialization has proceeded in the East much differently than it has in the West.

English translations of works from the region that address the environmental effects of industrialization are obviously of enormous use when teaching East Asian ecocriticisms.[1] For instance, a small but important fraction of the vast library of the works of Ishimure Michiko, who has been called "the Rachel Carson of Japan," is available (Allen 1). Her *Paradise in the Sea of Sorrow: Our Minamata Disease* is a collection of nonfiction stories from the victims of the mercury poisoning in Minamata Bay by the Chisso Corporation. Ishimure's *Story of the Sea of Camellias* is similarly concerned with Minamata Bay but approaches it from a much different angle. Patrick Murphy explains that "it is the same environment she depicts, but one transformed by different types of human activities founded on diametrically opposed attitudes toward humanity's place in the world and responsibility for it" (113). Ishimure's novel *Lake of Heaven* relates the stories of the people displaced by the construction of a dam. Inspired by real events, the novel offers a compelling witness to a problem with which other parts of the region are familiar—especially China, whose Three Gorges Dam displaced 1.2 million people.

Despite the magnitude of the environmental issues created by the Three Gorges Dam, there is little on the subject to be found in literary works that have been translated, and, generally, it does not seem entirely safe for writers to make explicit criticisms of important government projects in China. Nevertheless, there are useful discussions of the topic in English by Jiayan Mi, Sheldon H. Lu, Nick Kaldis, and Hongbing Zhang in the collection of essays entitled *Chinese Ecocinema in the Age of Environmental Challenge* (edited by Lu and Mi). Untranslated essays about the Three Gorges Dam have tended to be very lightly critical and heavily celebratory (Zhou; Lai; Wu Hanping; Li Hua; Wang Shiyao). A main focus of Chinese environmental literature that has been translated into English is on the losses associated with industrialization. For example, Chi Zijian's *The Last Quarter of the Moon* focuses on the disappearance of reindeer and local traditions; Guo Xuebo's collection of stories *The Desert Wolf* shows the need for protection of the vast grasslands of China and its animals; Jiang Rong's *Wolf Totem* is a monumental book both in terms of its enormous popularity and in terms of the breadth of its coverage of the dying Mongol culture and the parallel annihilation of the Mongolian wolf; and Shen Shixi's "The Last Warrior Elephant" narrativizes for an adolescent audience the dangers to elephants during the Japanese colonial period.

The effects of industrialization are an important part not only of Chinese and Japanese environmental writing but clearly of Korean and Taiwanese work too, some of which is available in English. Once heralded as a great sign of progress and growth, the industrial derogation of nature has become an object of literary environmentalism. Long gone are the days when a leader could convincingly proclaim that the "dark smoke rising from the factories is symbolic of our nation's growth and prosperity" as the former president of South Korea Park Chung Hee did in 1962 (qtd. in Lee 90). Cho Se-Hŭi's *The Dwarf* (난장이가 쏘아 올린 작은 공; literally, "a little ball that a dwarf launches") is a stinging indictment of the smoke that President Park heralded as a positive sign, culminating in the main character's suicide inside a smokestack.

The division of Korea has been a central feature of ecological discourse as well. Kim Won-Chung describes how "the imagined original unity that once defined Korea" (81) is disrupted by the division between North Korea and South Korea, an issue Kim Wonil writes about in "Dreaming of a Snipe." Wu Chan-je similarly observes the ecological issues raised by the demilitarized zone (DMZ) in his "Korea's Divided Circumstances and the Imagination of the Border." This essay analyzes three Korean novels not available in translation: Choi In-hoon's *The Square* (1960), Park Sang-yeon's *DMZ* (1997), and Kang Hui-jin's *The Ghost* (2011). Wu describes how these books reveal the ecological circumstances and the characteristics of the division of Korea in, respectively, the Cold War era, the post–Cold War era, and the digital era. Shin Dooho also addresses the topic in

"Nature under Ideological and Utopian Seizures: Recent Political and Conservationist Discourses and Literary Representations of the Korean DMZ." Food, too, has recently become a topic of considerable discussion among Korean ecocritics, perhaps in large part because Deborah Smith's translated version of Han Kang's *The Vegetarian* won the Booker Prize. Colocating issues of animal rights with women's rights and environmental matters, this book fits well into a syllabus with the Taiwanese writer Li Ang's novel *The Butcher's Wife*.

Taiwan has had to face its share of environmental issues stemming from industrialization. In their introduction to *Ecocriticism in Taiwan: Identity, Environment, and the Arts*, Chang Chia-ju and Scott Slovic explain that

> Taiwan's rapid economic growth, especially under the KMT regime, has led to . . . damage caused by industrial development in the 1970s . . . followed by a new environmental consciousness in the 1980s, especially after the lifting of martial law. Taiwan's environmental challenges, such as landslides, food safety, deforestation, water rights and contamination, air pollution, nuclear waste, and garbage disposal, to mention just a few, reflect daily, real-life concerns and struggles. (ix–x)

The problems are many, as have been the responses. Chang explains in her "Animal Writing: Taiwan's *Dongwu shuxie*" that "nature writing such as environmental reportage and other nonfictional essays began to emerge in Taiwan as a major literary genre to address the degradation of Taiwan's environmental reality" (xxi). One of the most spectacular pieces of Taiwanese climate fiction translated into English is Wu Ming-yi's *The Man with the Compound Eyes*, a startling tale about the collision of the Great Pacific Garbage Patch with Taiwan: "the trash island was spread out over an expanse of sea larger than Taiwan itself, so that when the second wave washed in it crammed trash into every discernible gap" (242). Some Taiwanese ecopoetry documenting the environmental effects of industrialization has also been translated into English (see, for instance, Liu, "Black Flight," "The Island Song," Guandu Life," "Black-Faced Spoonbill," and "Exile of the Mangrove Swamp"). Peter I-min Huang offers discussions in English and some translations of Taiwanese ecopoetry in *Linda Hogan and Contemporary Taiwanese Writers: An Ecocritical Study of Indigeneities and Environment*.

Substantial and valuable surveys of environmental writing in East Asia have appeared in diverse forms. Several useful surveys of Chinese ecocriticism are readily available in English. Wei Qingqi's essay titled "Chinese Ecocriticism in the Last Ten Years," in *The Oxford Handbook of Ecocriticism*, offers a brief history of Chinese ecocriticism, noting that "the Chinese ecocriticism we see today has two origins. Though the term itself comes from the West, it genuinely combines both native and foreign ideas" (539). Yang Jincai's influential "Environmental Dimensions in Contemporary Chinese Literature and Criticism" argues that a productive synthesis of Western ecological and ecocritical insights has inspired and encouraged a distinctly Chinese ecocritical discourse. Douglas Scott Berman's "Chinese Ecocriticism: A Survey of the Landscape" succinctly reviews the origins and influences on Chinese ecocriticism and moves quickly into a discussion about how ideologies of modernization and the controversial pushes to industrialize in China have contributed to ecological degradation. According to Berman, Chinese ecocritics have "not always [been] responsive to contemporary and social ills [but] have, in sum, successfully drawn upon the vast historical, philosophical and aesthetic resources inherent within the Chinese tradition to create a discourse that is truly cross-disciplinary" (400). The sheer breadth of cross-disciplinary Chinese ecocriticism as a growing area of study is clear not only in the numerous reviews of the field but in the increasing number both of Chinese attendees at the Association for the Study of Literature and Environment (ASLE) conferences and of special issues or clusters of essays in Western journals on the topic. The 2014 cluster in the journal *Interdisciplinary Studies in Literature and Environment*, for instance, offers another resource for teaching Chinese ecocriticism with eight essays on a variety of topics domestic and foreign, including two survey pieces: "Global in the Local: Ecocriticism in China," by Wang Ning, and "Echoes from the Opposite Shore: Chinese Ecocritical Studies as a Transpacific Dialogue Delayed," by Li Cheng.

Survey essays are useful teaching tools because they provide overviews of distinctive features. Kim Won-Chung's "Multicultural Ecocriticism and Korean Ecological Literature" and Shin Dooho's "Challenges and Promises of Asian Ecocriticism—A Case of ASLE-Korea" detail different particularities of ecocriticism in South Korea. Similarly, Yuki Masami's "Ecocriticism in Japan" is a very helpful pedagogical resource, not least for how it neatly outlines three phases of Japanese ecocriticism: translation, comparative study, and ecocritical interventions in Japanese literature. Karen Thornber also provides a convenient overview in her essay "Ishimure Michiko and Global Ecocriticism." Chang Chia-ju and Scott Slovic's

*Ecocriticism in Taiwan: Identity, Environment, and the Arts* provides a broad survey of Taiwanese ecocriticism. Broken into three main sections, this wide-ranging collection covers matters such as indigeneity and the land, deforestation, origin stories and environment, transcorporeality, animal studies, and food issues.

While the United States arguably held center stage for most of the twentieth century as a cultural, economic, and intellectual world power, many changes in the second half of the twentieth century have resulted in the strengthening of confidence and the development of cultural, economic, and intellectual independence in East Asia. In gathering the essays for the collection *East Asian Ecocriticisms: A Critical Reader*, my coeditor Kim Won-Chung and I noticed that all the submissions focused on nationhood. The centrality of nationhood to discourses about environment in East Asian literature reveals not only the various challenges to national integrity in different parts of the region but also that imagining the nation is in some ways inseparable from imagining the environment in the region. American commodification of landscapes has produced geographies that are matters of global interest, a phenomenon that has been largely absent and is only now beginning in many parts of Asia. For instance, the former president of South Korea Lee Myung-bak recognized this and sought to encourage tourism by creating a landscape in Seoul that would attract tourists from around the world: the 2005 revitalization of a stream (the Cheonggyecheon) in central Seoul that had been covered with concrete for decades. Lee removed the concrete and the expressway above the stream, investing 349 billion won (281 million US dollars in 2005) into the project. It would have been a good ecological investment, except that Lee reversed the flow of the stream. All the water in the stream is pumped in at a growing environmental and financial cost. Nevertheless, Lee (disgraced and imprisoned for bribery, embezzlement, and abuse of power) succeeded in bringing a Korean geography to global awareness. Teaching postcolonial East Asian ecocriticism—both outside and inside the region—must begin with the recognition that there is a much stronger trend toward commercializing landscapes in the West than in the East, which may have something to do with the relative importance of the individual in each region.

The dominant religions of East Asia are clear indicators that community takes precedence over the individual in the region. Thornber explains in her encyclopedic *Ecoambiguity: Environmental Crises and East Asian Literatures* that "East Asia has long been associated with belief systems advocating reverence for nature, especially Buddhism, Confucianism, Daoism, and Shinto as well as numerous indigenous philosophies and religions" (18). Daoism and Buddhism are, to be plain, more environmentally friendly than the Abrahamic religions. The long history of living on the land in Asia (certainly longer than in postcontact America) reflects entanglements of mutualism and harmony rather than heroic individualism. In the West, humanity is understood as a special creation separate from nature. Not so in Asia, where ideas about an integration of humanity and nature (articulated by Taoist philosophers twenty-five hundred years ago) remain very much a part of the culture. In contrast to the notion of individualism, the notion of the embeddedness of the individual is a key characteristic of East Asian ecological thinking. Anyone from the West traveling to East Asia will immediately notice a focus on "we" rather than "I," a focus more on the collective group of people than on the individual. In Korean, for instance, the pronoun *we* (우리; *oori*) appears before many nouns—our country (우리 나라; *oori nara*), our university (우리 대학; *oori daehak*), even a bank whose name means "our bank" (우리 은행; *oori eunheng*, branded internationally as Woori Bank).

Teachers of East Asian ecocriticisms outside the region need to recognize this significant cultural difference and the ways in which embeddedness affects not only the history of human-nonhuman (and environmental) relations but the ways in which scholarship itself is done. Yuki has argued compellingly, for instance, that the Japanese language functions much differently than written English, which requires a thesis followed by a deductive or inductive examination of the thesis. Japanese demonstrates and reveals, she explains, more than it argues and persuades ("Toward"). Yuki also pointed out to me as *East Asian Ecocriticisms* went through the pangs of production that, unlike in the West (with the exception of Hungary), people in Asia refer to each other by the last name followed by the first and second names, showing a "different value system shared by those who have their identity based on their family name more so than [on] their given name" (qtd. in Estok, "Partial Views" 13).[2]

Recognizing fundamental differences between East and West while at the same time observing and respecting the heterogeneity of East Asian regions is easier said than done. For instance, it is difficult even to apply the concept of postcoloniality to many countries in Asia, since what has occurred is perhaps more accurately thought of as a succession of colonizers in many places. A case in point is Taiwan, which has a long history of colonization. First it was colonized by the Dutch in the seventeenth century. Then the Han Chinese, the Spanish, the Japanese, and today—arguably—the Chinese again. Japan was never formally colonized by any nation, but it colonized all its neighbors. Korea bore the yoke from 1910 to 1945, and, while it has been free from formal colonization since that time, South Korea nevertheless remained under the burden of economic colonization by Western democracies for a very long time—indeed, many people in South Korea believe that the Korean War (which technically has not ended in a peace treaty and is currently in ceasefire) was a proxy war between the United States and the Soviet Union.

One of the most tangible immediate effects of the Japanese colonization of the Korean peninsula, according to the Korean Forest Service, was the slashing of the growing stock of trees "from 700 million cubic meters to 200 million cubic meters" over a thirty-five-year period (cited in Fredman 7). The Japanese stripped the land of its resources, dug mines and gutted the contents, introduced invasive species, and sought to destroy indigenous wildlife. Kim Bong-Oon's recent report in the *Korean Environment Newspaper* observes that

> 조선총독부 발행 잡지 '조선휘보'에 따르면 해수구제사업에 경찰관과 헌병은 3321명, 공무원 85명, 사냥꾼 2320명, 몰이꾼 9만1252명이 1915년부터 4220일간 동원됐다. 그 결과, 수천 마리의 야생동물이 희생당했으며 몇몇 종은 절멸로까지 내몰렸다. 일제강점기 전까지만 해도 한반도에서 종종 보이던 늑대, 표범, 호랑이 등이 일제강점기 이후 자취를 감춘 것이다. 이로 인해 한반도 생태계의 생물다양성은 큰 타격을 입었고, 아직까지도 복원되지 않고 있다.

> 3,321 police officers and soldiers, 85 civil servants, 2320 hunters, and 91,252 other operatives were mobilized for 4220 days beginning in 1915. As a result, thousands of wild animals were sacrificed, and some species were driven to extinction. Wolves, leopards, and tigers, often seen on the Korean peninsula until the Japanese occupation, disappeared during the Japanese colonial period. As a result, the biodiversity of the Korean peninsula ecosystem has suffered a major blow and has not yet been restored. (my trans.)

Information on these environmental crimes has long been difficult to find, and Japan continues to this day to distort the history it teaches its schoolchildren. Teachers of postcolonial environmental literature from Korea need to be aware of the entanglements between environmental derogation and the cultural burdens imposed by colonialism. What Japan attempted in the region is comparable to the reformatting of a hard drive, a cultural and environmental terraforming that erases everything in the service of affirming a new order. Graham Huggan and Helen Tiffin argue that "what the postcolonial/ecocritical alliance brings out, above all, is the need for a broadly materialist understanding of the changing relationship between people, animals, and the environment" (12), and this must be achieved through a carefully attentive and critical eye to the specificities of place and time. The altered postcolonial cultural and physical landscapes of Taiwan are obviously different from the geographies of eastern China or South Korea, and teaching the postcolonial environmental literatures of each of these places needs to address the specificities that define each region—and, again, this is not easy work.

There are many (and there is a growing body of) insightful discussions about the environmental and cultural colonization of the Global South, about the role and status of the privileged Global North, and about the central role of Euro-Americanism in the traumatization of cultural and geographic landscapes, but attention to the Global East both as colonizer and colonized is far from proportional in academic discourse. The exception is Thornber's wide-ranging and informative *Ecoambiguity*, by far the most thorough treatment of environmental matters in East Asian literatures.

Certainly, ecocritics have become much more attentive to postcolonial environmental writings through the efforts of a great many scholars—yet language remains an enormous obstacle preventing Western scholars from studying East Asian ecocriticisms. The unidirectionality of cultural capital no doubt has a lot to do with what Jonathan Arac has called a "global hegemony of the English language" (20). Ursula Heise has observed that "monolingualism is currently one of ecocriticism's most serious limitations. The environmentalist ambition is to think globally, but doing so in terms of a single language is inconceivable—even and especially when that language is a hegemonic one" (513). As I explained in "Discourses of Nation, National Ecopoetics, and Ecocriticism," an inability to read something means an inability to receive the information contained in that writing. 명확히 말해서, 무언가를 읽을 수 없다는 것은 그 글에 포함된 정보를 얻을 수 없 다는 것이다.[3] The previous sentence is an incomprehensible collection of lines, boxes, and circles if you can't read Korean (the Korean sentence is a repetition of the main clause of the English sentence that precedes it).

Teaching postcolonial East Asian ecocriticisms outside the region means teaching in a language and culture not of the region. Moreover, since so few Anglophones have even the most rudimentary linguistic aptitude in any of the major East Asian languages,[4] it has been the East Asian ecocritic who has translated the material for Western audiences—an awkward echo of colonialist histories in which a native guide chaperoned the colonizer through an unfamiliar and incomprehensible wilderness. Teachers of East Asian ecocriticisms outside the region need to recognize this fact and its implications. One of the most immediate implications is that a large amount of ecocritical work done on East Asian texts simply isn't translated. For instance, in South Korea, where I live and work, there are two equally balanced groups that make up ASLE-Korea: scholars of English literatures and scholars of Korean literature. Most of the scholars in Korean literature departments lack the facility or interest in translating the material for Anglophones. Certainly, there are some scholars in both camps (English literature and Korean literature) who translate the primary texts and then offer ecocritical readings in English, but much simply isn't translated.

Postcolonial East Asian ecocriticisms are a rapidly developing area. Recognizing the growth of the field may well be one of the most significant matters in teaching this material, both inside and outside the region. And there are many exciting questions. How will the topic of diet fuel theoretical developments? Taipei has many more vegan and vegetarian restaurants per capita than Seoul, Tokyo, and Beijing, evidenced by the hundreds of restaurants that show up on the website *Happy Cow* ("Find Vegan Options in Taipei"). How will social liberties (or oppressions) influence progressive thinking about environmental matters? Taiwan's legalization of same-sex marriage stands in shockingly sharp contrast to Beijing's stand against LGBTQ rights. What will be the role of justice movements for indigenous people in the region? Korea has no indigenous population at all. The International Work Group for Indigenous Affairs categorizes approximately 112 million people in China, or 8.4 percent of the country's population, as "indigenous people," while China terms them "ethnic minorities" ("China"). Japan has approximately 1.4 million indigenous people (the Ryūkyūans on Okinawa and the Ainu of Hokkaido ["Japan"]). Taiwan has some 569,000, or 2.4 percent of the population ("Taiwan"). The Taiwanese ecocritic Huang (who is indigenous) has done some of the only work about East Asian environmentalisms with a focus on indigenous justice issues, and he has connected that work with scholarship on American indigenous environmental writers such as Linda Hogan. So it is not only heterogeneous development patterns, histories, religions, relations of people with each other and the land, and language, but also diet, sexuality, and indigeneity that need to be on the radar in the classroom.

## Notes

1. A partial list current to 2007 can be found at the website *ASLE-Japan*: www.asle-japan.org/english/resources/.

2. Parts of this paragraph appear in a slightly different form in my "Discourses of Nation" (93).

3. I am indebted to Lee Young-Hyun of Sungkyunkwan University for proofing my grammar here.

4. In an essay about representations of climate change across languages and cultures, Uwe Küchler argues that "giving more attention to the role of foreign languages and cultures within the conceptualization of knowledge promises insights into the effect of language diversity on the choice of research questions, theoretical pervasiveness, as well as methodological diversity" (154). While Küchler is not suggesting that everyone go out and learn every language, clearly he has pinpointed a problem relevant to the discussion of postcolonial East Asian ecocriticisms in this essay—namely, that the lack of facility with these languages among scholars in the West is a severe limitation.

## Works Cited

Allen, Bruce. "Introduction to 'Ishimure Michiko and Global Ecocriticism.'" *The Asia Pacific Journal*, vol. 14, issue 13, no. 6, 1 July 2016, pp. 1–2.

Arac, Jonathan. "Global and Babel: Language and Planet in American Literature." *Shades of the Planet: American Literature as World Literature*, edited by Wai Chee Dimock and Lawrence Buell, Princeton UP, 2017, pp. 17–38.

Berman, Douglas Scott. "Chinese Ecocriticism: A Survey of the Landscape." *Literature Compass*, vol. 12, no. 8, 2015, pp. 396–403.

Chang, Chia-ju. "Animal Writing: Taiwan's *Dongwu shuxie*." *Taiwan Literature: Special Issue on Animal Writing in Taiwan Literature*, edited by Kuo-ch'ing Tu and Terence Russell, National Taiwan UP, 2018, pp. xix–xxxviii.

Chang, Chia-ju, and Scott Slovic. Introduction. *Ecocriticism in Taiwan: Identity, Environment, and the Arts*, edited by Chang and Slovic, Lexington Books, 2016, pp. ix–xxii.

"China." *IWGIA*, www.iwgia.org/en/china. Accessed 2 Oct. 2020.

Chi Zijian. *The Last Quarter of the Moon*. Translated by Bruce Humes, Vintage Books, 2014.

Cho Se-hŭi. *The Dwarf*. Translated by Ju-Chan Fulton and Bruce Fulton, U of Hawai'i P, 2006.

Estok, Simon C. "Discourses of Nation, National Ecopoetics, and Ecocriticism: Canada and Korea versus the US as Case Studies." *Comparative American Studies*, vol. 7, no. 2, June 2009, pp. 85–97, doi: 10.1179/147757008X280803.

———. "Partial Views: An Introduction to East Asian Ecocriticisms." Estok and Kim, pp. 1–13.

Estok, Simon C., and Won-Chung Kim, editors. *East Asian Ecocriticisms: A Critical Reader*. Palgrave Macmillan, 2013.

"Find Vegan Options in Taipei." *Happy Cow*, 2020, www.happycow.net/asia /taiwan/taipei/. Accessed 2 Oct. 2020.

Fredman, David. *Seeds of Control: Japan's Empire of Forestry in Colonial Korea.* U of Washington P, 2020.

Guo Xuebo. *The Desert Wolf.* Translated by Ma Ruofen, Chinese Literature Press, 1996.

Heise, Ursula K. "The Hitchhiker's Guide to Ecocriticism." *PMLA*, vol. 121, no. 2, Mar. 2006, pp. 503–16.

Huang, Peter I-min. *Linda Hogan and Contemporary Taiwanese Writers: An Ecocritical Study of Indigeneities and Environment.* Lexington Books, 2015.

Huggan, Graham, and Helen Tiffin. *Postcolonial Ecocriticism: Literature, Animals, Environment.* 2nd ed., Routledge, 2015.

Ishimure Michiko. *Lake of Heaven.* Translated by Bruce Allen, Lexington Books, 2008.

———. *Paradise in the Sea of Sorrow: Our Minamata Disease.* Translated by Livia Monnet, U of Michigan Center for Japanese Studies, 2003.

———. *Story of the Sea of Camellias.* Translated by Livia Monnet, Yamaguchi Publishing House, 1983.

"Japan." *IWGIA*, www.iwgia.org/en/japan. Accessed 2 Oct. 2020.

Kaldis, Nick. "Submerged Ecology and Depth Psychology in *Wushan yunyu*: Aesthetic Insight into National Development." Lu and Mi, pp. 57–72.

Kang, Han. *The Vegetarian.* Translated by Deborah Smith, Portobello, 2015.

Kim Bong-Oon. 일제강점기 때 사라진 소중한 우리 동물 ["Il jay gang jeom gee dae sa ra jin so joong han oori dong mool"]. 환경일보 [*Hwan kyung il bo*], 30 July 2019, www.hkbs.co.kr/news/articleView.html?idxno=524501.

Kim, Won-Chung. "Multicultural Ecocriticism and Korean Ecological Litera-ture." Estok and Kim, pp. 77–90.

Kim Wonil. "Dreaming of a Snipe." Translated by Brendon MacHale. *Anthology of Korean Literature*, vol. 2, edited by Seunggil Paik, Dong-Suh-Munhak-Sa, 1988, pp. 141–227.

Küchler, Uwe. "Signs, Images, and Narratives: Climate Change across Lan-guages and Cultures." *Teaching Climate Change in the Humanities*, edited by Stephen Siperstein et al., Routledge, 2017, pp. 153–60.

Lai Yongbing. 浅析杨吉甫三峡乡土叙事的生命情怀 ["Qianxi yangjifu sanxia xiangtu xushide shengmingqinghuai"]. 大众文艺 [*Dà zhòng wén yì*], no. 6, 2019, pp. 28–29.

Lee, Su-Hoon. "Environmental Movements in South Korea." *Asia's Environ-mental Movements: Comparative Perspectives*, edited by Yok-shui Lee and Alvin Y. Yo, M. E. Sharpe, 1999, pp. 90–119.

Li Ang. *The Butcher's Wife.* Translated by Howard Goldblatt, Peter Owen, 2002.

Li, Cheng. "Echoes from the Opposite Shore: Chinese Ecocritical Studies as a Transpacific Dialogue Delayed." *ISLE: Interdisciplinary Studies in Literature and Environment*, vol. 11, no. 4, Autumn 2014, pp. 821–43.

Li Hua. 三峡移民美术创作题材乡愁意象的审美价值探究 ["Sanxiayiming meishuchuangzuoticai xiangchouyixiangde shenmeijiazhiyanjiu"]. 2012. Xi'nan U, master's dissertation.

Liu Kexiang. "Black-Faced Spoonbill." *ISLE: Interdisciplinary Studies in Literature and Environment*, vol. 11, no. 2, Summer 2004, pp. 268–69.

———. "Black Flight." *ISLE: Interdisciplinary Studies in Literature and Environment*, vol. 11, no. 2, Summer 2004, p. 267.

———. "Exile of the Mangrove Swamp." *ISLE: Interdisciplinary Studies in Literature and Environment*, vol. 11, no. 2, Summer 2004, p. 269.

———. "Guandu Life." *ISLE: Interdisciplinary Studies in Literature and Environment*, vol. 11, no. 2, Summer 2004, p. 268.

———. "The Island Song." *ISLE: Interdisciplinary Studies in Literature and Environment*, vol. 11, no. 2, Summer 2004, p. 267.

Lu, Sheldon H. "Gorgeous Three Gorges at Last Sight: Cinematic Remembrance and the Dialectic of Modernization." Lu and Mi, pp. 39–56.

Lu, Sheldon H., and Jiayan Mi, editors. *Chinese Ecocinema in the Age of Environmental Challenge*. Hong Kong UP, 2009.

Mi, Jiayan. "Framing Ambient *Unheimlich*: Ecoggedon, Ecological Unconscious, and Water Pathology in New Chinese Cinema." Lu and Mi, pp. 17–38.

Murphy, Patrick. "Atonement and At-one-ment from *The Story of the Sea of Camellias* to *Lake of Heaven*." *Ishimure Michiko's Writing in Ecocritical Perspective*, edited by Bruce Allen and Masami Yuki, Lexington Books, pp. 105–22.

Rong, Jiang. *Wolf Totem*. Translated by Howard Goldblatt, Penguin Books, 2008.

Shen Shixi. "The Last Warrior Elephant." *"The Last Warrior Elephant" and Other Stories*, e-book ed., Blue Peacock Press, 2014.

Shin, Dooho. "Challenges and Promises of Asian Ecocriticism—A Case of ASLE-Korea." 2008. *ASLE-Japan*, www.asle-japan.org/app/download /7140080915/ASLEJjointspeech2008Wuhen.pdf?t=1376016698.

———. "Nature under Ideological and Utopian Seizures: Recent Political and Conservationist Discourses and Literary Representations of the Korean DMZ." *Mushroom Clouds: Ecocritical Approaches to Militarization and the Environment in East Asia*, edited by Simon C. Estok et al., Routledge, 2021, pp. 9–24.

"Taiwan." *IWGIA*, www.iwgia.org/en/taiwan. Accessed 2 Oct. 2020.

Thornber, Karen. *Ecoambiguity: Environmental Crises and East Asian Literatures*. U of Michigan P, 2012.

———. "Ishimure Michiko and Global Ecocriticism." *The Asia Pacific Journal*, vol. 14, issue 13, no. 6, 1 July 2016, pp. 3–23.

Wang, Ning. "Global in the Local: Ecocriticism in China." *ISLE: Interdisciplinary Studies in Literature and Environment*, vol. 11, no. 4, Autumn 2014, pp. 739–48.

Wang Shiyao [王诗瑶]. 三峡移民文艺作品中的"家园"主题 ["Sanxiayiming wenyizuopingzhongde jiayuan zhuti"]. *Journal of Zhejiang Shuren University*, no. 1, 2015, pp. 84–87.

Wei, Qinqi. "Chinese Ecocriticism in the Last Ten Years." *The Oxford Handbook of Ecocriticism*, edited by Greg Garrard, Oxford UP, 2014, pp. 537–46.

Wu, Chan-Je. "Korea's Divided Circumstances and the Imagination of the Border." Estok and Kim, pp. 111–22.

Wu Hanping. 三峡工程题材文学作品述评 ["Sanxiagongchengticai wenxue
    zuoping shuping"]. 长江文史论丛 [*Changjiang Wenshi Luncong*], no. 5, 2019,
    pp. 230–36.
Wu Ming-yi. *The Man with the Compound Eyes.* Translated by Darryl Sterk,
    Harvill Secker, 2013.
Yang Jincai. "Environmental Dimensions in Contemporary Chinese Literature
    and Criticism." Estok and Kim, pp. 187–204.
Yuki Masami. "Ecocriticism in Japan." *The Oxford Handbook of Ecocriticism*,
    edited by Greg Garrard, Oxford UP, 2014, pp. 519–26.
———. "Toward a Language of Life: Ecological Identity in the Work of Kazue
    Morisaki." Estok and Kim, pp. 17–33.
Zhang, Hongbing. "Ruins and Grassroots: Jia Zhangke's Cinematic Discontents
    in the Age of Globalization." Lu and Mi, pp. 129–53.
Zhou Jiawei [周佳唯]. 城市居住空间布局和消费对三峡移民身份建构的意义
    ["Chengshijuzhukingjian bujuhexiaofei dui sanxiayiming shenfen jiangoude
    yiyi"]. 美与时代 [*Měi yǔ shí dài*], no. 4, 2015, pp. 113–14.

# Part IV

## The Lives of Animals

**Jonathan Steinwand**

# Teaching Multispecies Entanglement

*Entanglement with others makes life possible, but when one relationship goes awry, the repercussions ripple.*

—Anna Lowenhaupt Tsing, Heather Anne Swanson,
Elaine Gan, and Nils Bubandt,
*Arts of Living on a Damaged Planet*

I teach at a small residential college historically dedicated to liberal education grounded in the humanities at a time when student and public interest in literature and other humanities fields is on the wane. In this context, I am foraging for strategies to test and demonstrate the relevance of the subjects I teach. At the confluence of my interest in postcolonial ecocriticism and my students' concerns about their own futures, I find that questions involving multispecies entanglement draw students into the environmental humanities. In what follows, I sketch some ideas for how indigenous, postcolonial, and ecocritical perspectives can be infused throughout the curriculum rather than reserved for upper-level seminars in postcolonial literatures or ecocriticism. Three such lower-level undergraduate courses—Global Literature and Environmental Justice; Animal

Stories: Kinship, Rivalry, and Alterity; and Plant Stories: Forests, Prairies, and Gardens in Literature—offer spaces in which I can work with students coming at these questions from various disciplines, vocations, and cultures. I developed the animal-stories course to deepen experiences students were having in Global Literature and Environmental Justice while emphasizing a new college-wide integrative-learning goal to get students out into the community to work alongside people grappling with real-world problems—in this case people who work with animals and human-animal relationships. I am only just beginning to develop the plant-stories class as an online summer course bookended by community site visits, workshops, place-based hikes, and campouts.

Postcolonial, indigenous, and ecocritical studies have robust traditions of human engagement with the more-than-human world. To dig deep into such entanglement in my upper-level postcolonial literatures course, I teach such works as Linda Hogan's *Solar Storms*, Alexis Wright's *The Swan Book*, Zakes Mda's *The Heart of Redness*, Mahasweta Devi's stories (*Imaginary Maps*, "Strange Children"), and Patricia Grace's *Potiki*. In the lower-level classes, the broader questions about how each of us in the room relates to the natural world around us provide the point of entry. Such questions are then enriched and complicated as we dig deeper into cultural contexts, colonial history, and postcolonial resistance. In Global Literature and Environmental Justice, for example, I introduce students to the concept of charismatic megafauna (dolphins, tigers, lions, hyenas, rhinos, and gorillas) and how it is used in environmental activism and the stories we are reading. As we get further into these readings, we explore questions and examples of environmental racism in the treatment of war, development, and conservation refugees—using Nadine Gordimer's "The Ultimate Safari," Nicholas Ellenbogen's *Horn of Sorrow*, Orlando von Einsiedel's *Virunga*, and Amitav Ghosh's *The Hungry Tide* as the key texts (as I describe in my essay "Empty-Belly and Full-Stomach Environmentalism in the Introductory Literature Class"). In the animal- and plant-stories classes, I include indigenous stories of how humans are descended from culturally significant plants and animals—such as Victoria Kneubuhl's *Ka Wai Ola* (which traces Hawaiian genealogy to the kalo plant); Linda Hogan's *People of the Whale* (in which a fictional Pacific Northwest tribe traces its ancestry to whales); or Robin Wall Kimmerer's version of the Mayan creation story (in which humans are created from corn after failed attempts with mud, wood, reed, and sunlight [*Braiding* 341–43]). Such stories emphasize what Cajetan Iheka calls an "aesthetics of proximity," where multispecies entanglement and interspecies relationships become central to indigenous and animist ecocosmologies. I use the word *ecocosmology* here to emphasize how indigenous and animist cosmologies overlap with traditional indigenous ecological knowledge and ethics.[1] When we teach traditions that attend to multispecies proximity and entanglement, Iheka suggests, we challenge "discourses that legitimate environmental violence in the name of human exceptionalism" (5). The learning activities that follow are inspired by place-based and community-based pedagogies.[2] These activities are attempts to show students how to expand environmental justice into what Iheka, following Ursula Heise, calls "multispecies justice" (15), which challenges both environmental racism and human exceptionalism (see Heise 198).

Settler-colonial and neoliberal capitalist cultures tend to relegate encounters with other species to the periphery as symbolic, anthropomorphic, primitive, triumphant, or inconsequential. Nevertheless, consumer culture depends on multiple species that serve as entertainment, sustenance, research subjects, symbols, companions, and guides. As the climate changes and extinctions proliferate, however, human alienation from other species becomes a more urgent concern. Where else in American higher education, outside our specialized courses in postcolonial and indigenous studies, do students have opportunities to encounter traditions of multispecies entanglement, kinship, and empathy? Can thematic environmental humanities courses reach a broader segment of the population? When asked by her physicist son whether she believes that poetry classes are going to shut down the slaughterhouses, J. M. Coetzee's Elizabeth Costello gives an emphatic "No" (58). But, if anything is going to get us to confront the violence of the slaughterhouse, I say why not poetry? Why not literary fiction? Why not animal stories that get us to rethink our interspecies relationships and challenge our human exceptionalism and consumption patterns? Basing her observations in her experience living among baboons, gorillas, and dogs, Barbara Smuts responds to Coetzee and Costello by proposing that we treat individuals of other species as persons:

> Relating to other beings as persons has nothing to do with whether or not we attribute human characteristics to them. It has to do, instead, with recognizing that they are social subjects, like us, whose idiosyncratic, subjective experience of us plays the same role in their relations with us that our subjective experience of them plays in our relations with them. If they relate to us as individuals, and we relate to them as individuals, it is possible for us to have a personal relationship.

> If either party fails to take into account the other's social subjectivity, such a relationship is precluded. (Smuts 118)

Timothy Morton takes a similar approach to interspecies entanglement by calling for "human-kindness" that fosters "solidarity with nonhuman people" (144–45). Morton and Kimmerer object to the way many human languages deny personhood and sometimes animacy and agency to more-than-human living organisms. In search of what Morton calls "the ecological pronoun" (3–4), Kimmerer finds "a grammar of animacy" in Potawatomi, the native language she is working to reclaim from settler-colonial endangerment (*Braiding* 48–59). With her students, she explores how different our relationships with other species might be if we used pronouns like *ki* and *kin* rather than *it* ("Speaking" 23–27). Kimmerer, Donna Haraway (*Staying*, *When Species Meet*), and Anna Tsing (*Mushroom*, *Arts*) prefer to talk about kinship, while Hogan emphasizes sovereignty and Morton focuses on solidarity.[3] Each in their own way emphasizes multispecies entanglement and interspecies relationships. The trouble begins whenever humans take too much comfort and pleasure in domination over other species. For Kimmerer, such arrogance turns humans into monsters like those in the Windigo stories told by the Anishinaabe people (*Braiding* 303–09, 374–79).[4] For the editors of *Arts of Living on a Damaged Planet*, an environmental humanities approach focusing on "ghosts and monsters" can "unsettle *anthropos*, the Greek term for 'human,' from its presumed center stage in the Anthropocene by highlighting the webs of histories and bodies from which all life, including human life, emerges" (Tsing et al. M3). If, as Kimmerer maintains, we humans are the younger siblings of creation, we also "have the least experience with how to live and thus the most to learn—we must look to our teachers among the other species for guidance" (*Braiding* 9). To equip our students to be participatory citizens in a world facing an extinction crisis, I urge us to infuse postcolonial environmental literature and media of multispecies entanglement into our courses and programs wherever possible.

Through literature, the narrative and poetic imagination has always transgressed our presumed individual boundaries in order to get to know, to understand, to live the experience of our intimate companions, our neighbors, our fellow earthlings, our distant relations, our friends, and our enemies. As readers, writers, and critics, we navigate between the hazards of projecting too much of ourselves, on the one hand, and of othering to the point of rejection, banishment, or delegitimization, on the other. We know our transgressions render us doomed to fall short of perfect understanding. We need humility to avoid misrepresenting or caricaturing the other by recklessly projecting our own assumptions, proclivities, fantasies, and fears.

Maybe you too have noticed that young people seem increasingly invested in companion species and in charismatic megafauna they encounter, especially in social media. A survey conducted in 2018 estimates that an astonishing seventy-two percent of millennials own pets and that most treat them as family (TD Ameritrade). Hotels, retailers, airlines, workplaces, and colleges are adjusting to accommodate emotional-support animals and companion species. When I ask students about a favorite pet or the latest kitten or puppy video they have seen, the energy in the room changes dramatically. Why are these relationships and encounters so appealing? To what extent is such appeal shared or not shared across cultures and communities? This interspecies attraction comes, paradoxically, at a time when one million species of plants and animals are on the verge of extinction (Fears). Humans and domesticated mammals are now estimated to make up ninety-six percent of mammal biomass on earth, which means only four percent remains wild (Bar-On et al.). Is it possible that the more alienated we become from nature in our daily lives, the more we tend to latch on to charismatic creatures for their heroic, powerful, poignant, dramatic, or just darn cute antics and dispositions? Now is a good moment for literature programs, faculty members, and courses to foreground representations of more-than-human persons, interspecies relationships, and multispecies entanglement.[5] Poetry and fiction can help us unpack these feelings and encounters as we connect them to larger issues facing postcolonial, indigenous, and animal studies in a world of ecological endangerment. What does it mean to be human, what does it mean to be animal, and how can the humanities help us practice the "arts of living on a damaged planet" (Tsing et al.)?

My teaching and research have generated a range of activities for exploring these questions, for delving deeper into how the narrative and poetic imagination help us embrace multispecies entanglement, and for prompting students to take action in response to the conclusions they draw.[6]

## Interspecies Encounter Log

Ask each participant to keep a log tracking all their encounters with animals in a week, divided into categories by type of animal: living, dead, cooked, symbolic, metaphoric (think, for example, of when we call someone or something sluggish, beefy, or chicken-livered), and so on. After students share their logs, assign a reading about the science of the human microbiota and the many more-than-human organisms that live in each of our supposedly exceptional and singular human bodies (e.g., Stein; Sender et al.). Then, ask how reflecting on this activity helps them think about what it means to be human. How does this knowledge affect the way they relate to other species and experience multispecies entanglement?

## Meme of the Day Activity

Ask one student each day to share a meme they found or created related to the topic. This activity can be enriched with discussion about the role of humor, irony, and irreverence in environmental discourse (Seymour).

## News Forum Post

Ask students to sign up to share a news article connected to the course theme a couple of times in the semester on an online discussion forum. Pull these into class discussion whenever appropriate.

## Community Site Visits

Arrange visits to local organizations and sites that will demonstrate community approaches to challenges discussed in the course. For an animal-stories class, sites might include a pet-rescue shelter, zoo, experimental animal-research lab, sustainable farm, factory farm, farm-animal-rescue sanctuary, service-animal training center, pet cemetery, or hippotherapy center. Additional resource people might include a veterinarian, an animal-rights advocate, a vegan organizer, and a pet psychic. For a plant-stories class, visit a community-garden project, botanical society, wilderness-restoration project, sugar-beet-processing factory, medical-marijuana dispensary, herbal-medicine center, plant-pathology lab, or farmers market. Additionally, this class could undertake a wild-food-foraging hike, forest-bathing experience, prairie-biodiversity hike, or gleaning activity. Each visit can be paired with readings and reflection to make vivid for students the living complexity of these issues and the beauty of interspecies engagement in the task of standing for multispecies justice.

## Community-Based Service or Research Project

Carrie Rohman explains how caring for animals at local shelters is an integral part of her students' experience in her course on animals in twentieth-century literature and culture (54–55). Following up on the community site visits in the animal-stories class, I ask students to work with their preferred community partner on a research project that furthers the human-animal encounter at work in the organization.

## Social Media Dive

Invoking the controversy over Walter Palmer's shooting of Cecil the lion, Morton writes that "the year 2015 was when a very large number of humans figured out that they had more in common with a lion than with a dentist" (33). Assign groups to investigate more-than-human social media superstars: Cecil the lion; Harambe; Sudan, the last male rhino of his subspecies; Kokito, the dog who died in the overhead bin of a United Airlines flight; Tahlequah, the grieving orca; Spitfire, the Yellowstone wolf; Lewis the koala; and the gay penguin foster dads in Berlin. The reports on *Instagram* of photographers "loving nature to death" during the California super bloom add some flora to the fauna in this list (Gammon). I like to keep these groups small, two or three students per group, so that everyone can engage with the topic. Introduce the main list of social media stars and then invite students to add to it to share ownership and to catch some of the latest popular figures. Although figures like Grumpy Cat might take discussion away from ecological devastation, climate change, and the extinction crisis, indulging in some discussion of social-media-distraction manufacturing and obsessive-pet-persona generation can nevertheless be worthwhile. To historicize how narratives of the last of its species on earth play out, you can explore the case of Martha, the last carrier pigeon; read Joe Balaz's "Da Last Squid"; or investigate how social-structure breakdown affects young male elephants and their human counterparts (Bradshaw; Siebert; Willett). To emphasize the value of the narrative imagination in such discussion and the slow extinguishing violence of climate change, you might also add reports lacking an individual protagonist, like the recently reported extinction of the Bramble Cay melomys (Guarino and Bever). Each group should be given a set of questions that help them delve deeper into the historical and environmental implications of each species extinction. For example, How does the story of this one individual being or species represent the larger historical narrative of the ecosystem to which it belongs? How does the story connect animals and humans around experiences and emotions related to life and death, surviving and thriving, consumption and overconsumption, and so on? How do the local community and culture respond to the story of this creature? How complicit are the curators of the information and the retweeters in the causes that build toward the story and the effects that result from sharing it?

## Roadkill Photography, Art, and Poetry

I like to follow our section on social-media-celebrity animals with an acknowledgment of the anonymous animal deaths we experience through roadkill. After asking students to share reflections on their own encounters with roadkill, introduce poetry ranging from William Stafford's "Traveling through the Dark" to Gary Snyder's "The Dead by the Side of the Road," Athena Kildegaard's "Raccoon," and Margaret Atwood's "The Animals in That Country." And to examine how we cope—or refuse to cope—with animal deaths in our midst, consider the photography of Stephen Paternite, Joy Hunsberger, Viivi Häkkinen, Emma Kisiel, Lilla Dent, Kimberly Witham, or Marcel Huijser. For more extended treatment, consider Barry Lopez's *Apologia*, with woodcuts by Robin Eschner; Chris Jordan's photographic elegy on the Pacific garbage patch, *Midway: Message from the Gyre*; and Thom van Dooren's thoughts about "learning to grieve with" (Haraway, *Staying* 38–39). The rhetoric and activism of the global environmental civil-disobedience movement known as Extinction Rebellion presses the multispecies-entanglement conversation to call for multispecies justice in the extinction crisis.

## Poetry Explication

In each of the classes mentioned, I include a student-led poem-of-the-day discussion that can lead to a more developed poetry explication essay (see my essay "Teaching Environmental Justice Poetry"). It helps to select several dozen poems in advance for students to choose from or to assign a relevant collection, such as *Birds, Beasts, and Seas: Nature Poems from New Directions*, edited by Jeffrey Yang, or *Ghost Fishing: An Eco-Justice Anthology*, edited by Melissa Tuckey. Onno Oerlemans's *Poetry and Animals:*

*Blurring the Boundaries with the Human* is a good resource for selecting poems and for guiding students' approaches to animal poems, though postcolonial poems should be added to supplement that collection.

## Book Clubs

Focusing these classes on fiction, poetry, and drama risks overlooking creative and critical environmental justice nonfiction. To sample some of this work for the global literature and environmental justice class, I prepare a list of a dozen or more books related to the topic, ask students to rank them by preference, and pair up students based on their rankings.[7] Student pairs then read the book and explain to the class what the author did to make them understand and care about the environmental justice case presented in the book. In the animal-stories class, we read and discuss Philip Armstrong's cultural history of sheep together before pairs of students dive into the cultural history of another species chosen from other works like Armstrong's in the Reaktion Animal Series. For advanced classes, book clubs could explore theoretical, academic, or disciplinary perspectives on the topic.[8]

## Revisit Favorite Childhood Stories

In the animal-stories class, students revisit a favorite children's or young adult story that features an animal as a central character. Then they share with the class what they love about the story and what they find problematic about its animal depictions, such as its anthropomorphism. We follow the reports with a discussion of the concept of and concerns about anthropomorphism in its various forms (de Waal; Garrard 154–70; Hediger; Małecki et al.; Urquiza-Haas and Kotrschal). If representations of other animals will mostly fail by overemphasizing our similarities to or differences from them, should we not then try to understand them in every way that we can? As Ryan Hediger puts the question, "How can texts representing nonhuman animals be useful to us and to them?" (35).

## "Dreaded Comparisons"

An animal-stories class might challenge students to design an experiment to test what Marjorie Spiegel calls the "dreaded comparison" of racism and speciesism: Under what conditions and at what costs does a nonhuman animal achieve agency that surpasses a dehumanized human being in value? Jonathan Swift's Houyhnhnms and Yahoos in book 4 of *Gulliver's Travels* provide a stunning satirical exploration of this question (187–250). To what extent can solidarity between human people and animal people disarm strategies to disempower?[9] To what extent can human-animal studies find constructive connections between the work of decolonization and healing the interspecies and intraspecies social trauma that spread as a result of violent and destructive forces of colonialism, imperialism, resource extraction, unsustainable development, and environmental racism? To what extent do racist colonial mindsets intersect with human exceptionalism, speciesism, sexism, predator extermination, factory farming, pest control, and habitat destruction?

## Epistolary Activism

Toward the end of the global literature and environmental justice class, we read Margaret Atwood's *The Year of the Flood*. Instead of writing a literary analysis, students write a letter calling on an influencer, leader, or gatekeeper to take specific action in relation to one issue explored in the novel. The range of topics and audiences students imagine for this assignment exceeds what I imagined when I developed the activity. When they share their letters in class, students are often surprised by how well-equipped and inspired their classmates are to be participatory citizens.

## Design a New Ceremony

For a plant-stories class, after reading about indigenous ceremonies that celebrate reciprocity with the land, one could ask students to design—without cultural appropriation—a new ceremony that celebrates the kind of reciprocity suggested by Kimmerer in *Braiding Sweetgrass* (250–51).

Although, like many of my environmentalist friends, I might like to teach the world to sing in perfect harmony, my primary goal for these assignments and teaching strategies is not to convert students to my preferred response to the ecological crisis. Rather, the goal is to come up with worthwhile assignments that challenge students as participatory citizens to confront the questions and issues at stake in the environmental crisis and to take ownership and responsibility for the future. Too often, traditions of human exceptionalism, individualism, and overconsumption distract us from our entanglements on this earth. We forget that our relations are human people and more-than-human people. If a few students can be inspired by these strategies to continue to read and think about multispecies entanglement in the years ahead, they may take more care in representing and nourishing interspecies and intraspecies relationships of many kinds.

## Notes

1. It is important to respect each story in its own local context and complexity. As Donna Haraway warns, "Animism cannot be donned like a magic cape by visitors." And many descendants of animist cultures are "wary of animism in their own heritage" (*Staying* 89). Advanced classes could attend to postcolonial and indigenous forays into magic realism with such animist and indigenous ecocosmologies in mind (see Bowers; Iheka 16–47; Quayson; Strass; Strass and Steinwand).

2. For scholarship and examples of placed-based pedagogy, see Ball and Lai; Crimmel; and Gruenewald. For scholarship and examples of community-based pedagogy, see Cooke and Thorme; Halseth et al.; and Rohman.

3. Hogan writes, "In the traditional and historic past, we recognized the sovereignty of other species, animal and plant. We held treaties with the animals, treaties shaped by mutual respect and knowledge of the complex workings of the world, and these were laws the legal system will never come close to" ("Reckoning with the Spirit of the Whale" 153).

4. Kimmerer describes the Windigo as the insatiably greedy, cannibalistic monster of Anishinaabe legends whose footprints are evident in ecological destruction all over the world (*Braiding* 304–06). She goes on to say that "an economy that grants personhood to corporations but denies it to the more-than-human beings: this is a Windigo economy. . . . Gratitude for all the earth has given us lends us courage to turn and face the Windigo that stalks us, to refuse to participate in an economy that destroys the beloved earth to line the pockets of the greedy, to demand an economy that is aligned with life, not stacked against it" (376–77).

5. On the program level, for example, my English department has redesigned a historical gateway-to-the-major course as a course on how literature cultivates imagination and empathy across difference. Readings and class activities emphasize how such empathy can be interpersonal, intercultural, and interspecies.

6. For further discussion of multispecies entanglement and additional teaching ideas, see Alaimo; Armbruster; James; Rohman; and Welling and Kapel.

7. Such a reading list might include Anna Clark's *The Poisoned City: Flint's Water and the American Urban Tragedy*; Nick Estes's *Our History Is the Future: Standing Rock versus the Dakota Access Pipeline, and the Long Tradition of*

*Indigenous Resistance*; Dan Fagin's *Toms River: A Story of Science and Salvation*; David Gessner's *The Tarball Chronicles: A Journey beyond the Oiled Pelican and into the Heart of the Gulf Oil Spill*; Kristen Iverson's *Full Body Burden: Growing Up in the Nuclear Shadow of Rocky Flats*; Kimmerer's *Braiding Sweetgrass: Indigenous Wisdom, Scientific Knowledge, and the Teachings of Plants*; William Kamkwamba and Bryan Mealer's *The Boy Who Harnessed the Wind: Creating Currents of Electricity and Hope*; Wangari Maathai's *Unbowed: A Memoir*; Bill McKibben's *Oil and Honey: The Education of an Unlikely Activist*; Arundhati Roy's *The Cost of Living*; Lauret Savoy's *Trace: Memory, History, Race, and the American Landscape*; and Terry Tempest Williams's *Refuge: An Unnatural History of Family and Place*.

8. Such groups could select from works on interspecies relations like Marc Bekoff's *The Animal Manifesto: Six Reasons for Expanding Our Compassion Footprint*; Jonathan Safran Foer's *Eating Animals*; Erica Fudge's *Animal*; Haraway's *Staying with the Trouble: Making Kin in the Chthulucene*; Hal Herzog's *Some We Love, Some We Hate, Some We Eat: Why It's So Hard to Think about Animals*; T. J. Kasperbauer's *Subhuman: The Moral Psychology of Human Attitudes to Animals*; Susan McHugh's *Animal Stories: Narrating across the Species Line*; Erin McKenna's *Livestock: Food, Fiber, and Friends*; Wojciech Małecki, Piotr Sorokowski, Bogusław Pawłowski, and Marcin Cieński's *Human Minds and Animal Stories: How Narratives Make Us Care about Other Species*; Jon Mooallem's *Wild Ones: A Sometimes Dismaying, Weirdly Reassuring Story about Looking at People Looking at Animals in America*; Morton's *Humankind: Solidarity with Nonhuman People*; Oerlemans's *Poetry and Animals: Blurring the Boundaries with the Human*; Tsing's *The Mushroom at the End of the World: On the Possibility of Life in Capitalist Ruins*; Tsing, Swanson, Gan, and Bubandt's *Arts of Living on a Damaged Planet*; Cynthia Willett's *Interspecies Ethics*; and Peter Wohlleben's *Inner Lives of Animals: Love, Grief, and Compassion—Surprising Observations of a Hidden World*.

9. Students conducting an experiment on the "dreaded comparison" could be guided by Neel Ahuja's "Postcolonial Critique in a Multispecies World"; Coetzee's *The Lives of Animals*; Iheka's *Naturalizing Africa: Ecological Violence, Agency, and Postcolonial Resistance in African Literature*; Witi Ihimaera's *The Whale Rider*; Morton's *Humankind: Solidarity with Nonhuman People*; Spiegel's *The Dreaded Comparison: Human and Animal Slavery*; Swift's *Gulliver's Travels*; Wendy Woodward's "Pedagogies of Discomfort: Teaching Coetzee's *The Lives of Animals*"; and Alexis Wright's *The Swan Book*. Another approach could involve a more extended comparative study of elephant and human social structures with the help of G. A. Bradshaw's *Elephants on the Edge: What Animals Teach Us about Humanity*; Barbara Gowdy's *The White Bone*; Charles Siebert's "An Elephant Crack-up?"; and Willett's *Interspecies Ethics*.

## Works Cited

Ahuja, Neel. "Postcolonial Critique in a Multispecies World." *PMLA*, vol. 124, no. 2, Mar. 2009, pp. 556–63.

Alaimo, Stacy. "When the Newt Shut Off the Lights: Scale, Practice, Politics."
*Teaching Climate Change in the Humanities*, edited by Stephen Siperstein
et al., Routledge, 2017, pp. 31–36.

Armbruster, Karla. "Thinking with Animals: Teaching Animal Studies–Based
Literature Classes." *Teaching North American Environmental Literature*,
edited by Laird Christensen et al., Modern Language Association of
America, 2008, pp. 72–90.

Armstrong, Philip. *Sheep*. Reaktion, 2016.

Atwood, Margaret. "The Animals in That Country." *Selected Poems, 1965–1975*,
Houghton Mifflin, 1976, pp. 48–49.

———. *The Year of the Flood*. Anchor Books, 2010.

Balaz, Joe. "Da Last Squid." *Whetu Moana: Contemporary Polynesian Poems in
English*, edited by Albert Wendt et al., U of Hawai'i P, 2003, pp. 8–10.

Ball, Eric, and Alice Lai. "Place-Based Pedagogy for the Arts and Humanities."
*Pedagogy: Critical Approaches to Teaching Literature, Language, Composition,
and Culture*, vol. 6, no. 2, Spring 2006, pp. 261–87. *Academic Search
Premier*, doi:10.1215/15314200-2005-004.

Bar-On, Yinon M., et al. "The Biomass Distribution on Earth." *Proceedings of
the National Academy of Sciences*, vol. 115, no. 25, June 2018, pp. 6506–11.
*Academic Search Premier*, doi:10.1073/pnas.1711842115.

Bekoff, Marc. *The Animal Manifesto: Six Reasons for Expanding our Compassion
Footprint*. New World Library, 2010.

Bowers, Maggie A. *Magic(al) Realism*. Routledge, 2004.

Bradshaw, G. A. *Elephants on the Edge: What Animals Teach Us about Humanity*. Yale UP, 2009.

Clark, Anna. *The Poisoned City: Flint's Water and the American Urban Tragedy*.
Henry Holt, 2018.

Coetzee, J. M. *The Lives of Animals*. Edited by Amy Gutmann, Princeton UP,
1999.

Cooke, Deanna, and Trisha Thorme. *A Practical Handbook for Supporting
Community-Based Research with Undergraduate Students*. Council on
Undergraduate Research, 2011.

Crimmel, Hal, editor. *Teaching in the Field: Working with Students in the
Outdoor Classroom*. U of Utah P, 2003.

Dent, Lilla. *Expired*. 2017. bibelotecamollusca.com/art/expired.

Devi, Mahasweta. *Imaginary Maps*. Translated by Gayatri Spivak, Routledge,
1995.

———. "Strange Children." *Of Women, Outcastes, Peasants, and Rebels: A
Selection of Bengali Short Stories*, edited by Kalpana Bardhan, U of California
P, 1990, pp. 229–41.

de Waal, Frans. "Are We in Anthropodenial?" *Discover*, 18 Jan. 1997, www
.discovermagazine.com/planet-earth/are-we-in-anthropodenial.

Ellenbogen, Nicholas. *Horn of Sorrow. Drama for a New South Africa: Seven
Plays*, edited by David Graver, Indiana UP, 2000, pp. 79–91.

Estes, Nick. *Our History Is the Future: Standing Rock versus the Dakota Access
Pipeline, and the Long Tradition of Indigenous Resistance*. Verso, 2019.

Fagin, Dan. *Toms River: A Story of Science and Salvation*. Island Press, 2015.

Fears, Daryl. "One Million Species Face Extinction, U.N. Report Says: And Humans Will Suffer as a Result." *The Washington Post*, 6 May 2019, www.washingtonpost.com/climate-environment/2019/05/06/one-million-species-face-extinction-un-panel-says-humans-will-suffer-result/?utm_term=.3dabe160b38b.

Foer, Jonathan Safran. *Eating Animals*. Little, Brown, 2010.

Fudge, Erica. *Animal*. Reaktion, 2002.

Gammon, Katharine. "Superbloom: Can This Tiny California Town Avoid Another 'Flowermageddon'?" *The Guardian*, 15 Mar. 2019, www.theguardian.com/environment/2019/mar/15/california-superbloom-flowergeddon-anza-borrego.

Garrard, Greg. *Ecocriticism*. 2nd ed., Routledge, 2012.

Gessner, David. *The Tarball Chronicles: A Journey beyond the Oiled Pelican and into the Heart of the Gulf Oil Spill*. Milkweed Editions, 2011.

Ghosh, Amitav. *The Hungry Tide*. Houghton Mifflin Harcourt, 2005.

Gordimer, Nadine. "The Ultimate Safari." *"Jump" and Other Stories*, by Gordimer, Penguin, 1991, pp. 31–46.

Gowdy, Barbara. *The White Bone*. Picador, 2000.

Grace, Patricia. *Potiki*. U of Hawai'i P, 1995.

Gruenewald, David A. "The Best of Both Worlds: A Critical Pedagogy of Place." *Environmental Education Research*, vol. 14, no. 3, June 2008, pp. 308–324. *Academic Search Premier*, doi:10.1080/13504620802193572.

Guarino, Ben, and Lindsey Bever. "Climate Change Officially Claims Its First Mammal: The Bramble Cay Melomys Is Declared Extinct." *The Washington Post*, 20 Feb. 2019, www.washingtonpost.com/science/2019/02/20/climate-change-officially-claims-its-first-mammal-bramble-cay-melomys-is-declared-extinct/?utm_term=.51968cfc5e22.

Häkkinen, Viivi. *Forget Me Not*. 2016. *Instagram*, instagram.com/forgetme_not_photography/.

Halseth, Greg, et al. *Doing Community-Based Research: Perspectives from the Field*. McGill-Queen's UP, 2016.

Haraway, Donna. *Staying with the Trouble: Making Kin in the Chthulucene*. Duke UP, 2016.

———. *When Species Meet*. U of Minnesota P, 2008.

Hediger, Ryan. "Our Animals, Ourselves: Representing Animal Minds in *Timothy* and *The White Bone*." *Speaking for Animals: Animal Autobiographical Writing*, edited by Margo DeMello, Routledge, 2013, pp. 35–47.

Heise, Ursula. *Imagining Extinction: The Cultural Meanings of Endangered Species*. U of Chicago P, 2016.

Herzog, Hal. *Some We Love, Some We Hate, Some We Eat: Why It's So Hard to Think about Animals*. HarperCollins, 2010.

Hogan, Linda. *People of the Whale*. W. W. Norton, 2009.

———. "Reckoning with the Spirit of the Whale." *Sightings: The Gray Whales' Mysterious Journey*, by Brenda Peterson and Hogan, National Geographic, 2002, pp. 153–54.

———. *Solar Storms.* Scribner, 1997.

Huijser, Marcel. "Road-Killed Animals." *Marcel Huijser,* www
.marcelhuijserphotography.com/roadkilledanimals. Photographs.

Hunsberger, Joy. "Just Because It's in Slow Motion Doesn't Mean You Can
Stop It." *Joy Hunsberger,* joyh.com/PHOTO/ROADKILL/body_roadkill
.html.

Iheka, Cajetan. *Naturalizing Africa: Ecological Violence, Agency, and Postcolonial Resistance in African Literature.* Cambridge UP, 2018.

Ihimaera, Witi. *The Whale Rider.* Harcourt, 2003.

Iversen, Kristen. *Full Body Burden: Growing Up in the Nuclear Shadow of Rocky Flats.* Crown Publishers, 2012.

James, Erin. "Teaching the Ecocritical/Postcolonial Dialogue." *Teaching Ecocriticism and Green Cultural Studies,* edited by Greg Garrard, Palgrave Macmillan, 2012, pp. 60–71.

Jordan, Chris. *Midway: Message from the Gyre. Chris Jordan: Photographic Arts,* 2009–present, www.chrisjordan.com/gallery/midway/#about.

Kamkwamba, William, and Bryan Mealer. *The Boy Who Harnessed the Wind: Creating Currents of Electricity and Hope.* HarperCollins, 2010.

Kasperbauer, T. J. *Subhuman: The Moral Psychology of Human Attitudes to Animals.* Oxford UP, 2018.

Kildegaard, Athena. "Raccoon." *Bodies of Light,* Red Dragonfly Press, 2011, p. 56.

Kimmerer, Robin Wall. *Braiding Sweetgrass: Indigenous Wisdom, Scientific Knowledge, and the Teachings of Plants.* Milkweed Editions, 2013.

———. "Speaking of Nature: Finding a Language That Affirms Our Kinship with the Natural World." *Orion,* Mar.-Apr. 2017, pp. 14–27.

Kisiel, Emma. *At Rest.* 2011. www.emmakisiel.com/work#/at-rest/.

Kneubuhl, Victoria. *Ka Wai Ola: The Living Water. He Leo Hou / A New Voice: Hawaiian Playwrights,* edited by John H. Y. Wat and Meredith M. Desha, Bamboo Ridge Press, 2003, pp. 209–87.

Lopez, Barry, and Robin Eschner. *Apologia.* U of Georgia P, 1998.

Maathai, Wangari. *Unbowed: A Memoir.* Knopf Doubleday, 2007.

Małecki, Wojciech, et al. *Human Minds and Animal Stories: How Narratives Make Us Care about Other Species.* Routledge, 2019.

McHugh, Susan. *Animal Stories: Narrating across the Species Line.* U of Minnesota P, 2011.

McKenna, Erin. *Livestock: Food, Fiber, and Friends.* U of Georgia P, 2018.

McKibben, Bill. *Oil and Honey: The Education of an Unlikely Activist.* St. Martin's Press, 2014.

Mda, Zakes. *The Heart of Redness.* Farrar, Straus and Giroux, 2000.

Mooallem, Jon. *Wild Ones: A Sometimes Dismaying, Weirdly Reassuring Story about Looking at People Looking at Animals in America.* Penguin, 2014.

Morton, Timothy. *Humankind: Solidarity with Nonhuman People.* Verso, 2019.

Oerlemans, Onno. *Poetry and Animals: Blurring the Boundaries with the Human.* Columbia UP, 2018.

Paternite, Stephen. "Roadkill." *The Fine Art of Stephen Paternite,* www
.spaternite.com/frame/frames/fr/fr_0700.html.

Quayson, Ato. "Magical Realism and the African Novel." *The Cambridge Companion to the African Novel*, edited by F. Abiola Irele, Cambridge UP, 2009, pp. 159–76.

Rohman, Carrie. "Animal Writes: Literature and the Discourse of Species." *Teaching the Animal: Human-Animal Studies across the Disciplines*, edited by Margo DeMello, Lantern Books, 2010, pp. 48–59.

Roy, Arundhati. *The Cost of Living*. Random House, 1999.

Savoy, Lauret. *Trace: Memory, History, Race, and the American Landscape*. Counterpoint Press, 2015.

Sender, Ron, et al. "Revised Estimates for the Number of Human and Bacteria Cells in the Body." *PLOS Biology*, vol. 14, no. 8, Aug. 2016, pp. 1–14. *Academic Search Premier*, doi.org/10.1371/journal.pbio.1002533.

Seymour, Nicole. *Bad Environmentalism: Irony and Irreverence in the Ecological Age*. U of Minnesota P, 2018.

Siebert, Charles. "An Elephant Crack-up?" *The New York Times*, 8 Oct. 2006, www.nytimes.com/2006/10/08/magazine/08elephant.html.

Smuts, Barbara. "Barbara Smuts." Coetzee, pp. 107–20.

Snyder, Gary. "The Dead by the Side of the Road." *Turtle Island*, New Directions, pp. 7–8.

Spiegel, Marjorie. *The Dreaded Comparison: Human and Animal Slavery*. Mirror Books, 1996.

Stafford, William. "Traveling through the Dark." *Contemporary American Poetry*, edited by A. Poulin, Jr., 4th ed., Houghton Mifflin, 1985, pp. 509–10.

Stein, Rob. "Finally, a Map of All of the Microbes on Your Body." *NPR*, 13 June 2012, www.npr.org/sections/health-shots/2012/06/13/154913334/finally-a-map-of-all-the-microbes-on-your-body.

Steinwand, Jonathan. "Empty-Belly and Full-Stomach Environmentalism in the Introductory Literature Class: Teaching *The Hungry Tide* in the Anthropocene." *Approaches to Teaching the Works of Amitav Ghosh*, edited by Gaurav Desai and John Hawley, Modern Language Association of America, 2019, pp. 152–59.

———. "Teaching Environmental Justice Poetry in the Anthropocene." *The Journal of Commonwealth and Postcolonial Studies*, vol. 2, no. 2, Fall 2014, pp. 47–60.

Strass, Hanna. "'A Living Death, Life Inside-Out': The Postcolonial Toxic Gothic in Robert Barclay's *Meḻaḻ: A Novel of the Pacific*." *Globalizing Literary Genres: Literature, History, Modernity*, edited by Jernej Habjan and Fabienne Imlinger, Routledge, 2016, pp. 228–40.

Strass, Hanna, and Jonathan Steinwand. "Das Motiv der verzauberten Giftigkeit und die Darstellung schleichender Gewalt im postkolonialen Roman." *Komparatistik: Jahrbuch der deutschen Gesellschaft für allgemeine und vergleichende Literaturwissenschaft 2013*, Synchron, 2014, pp. 53–65.

Swift, Jonathan. *Gulliver's Travels: A Norton Critical Edition*. W. W. Norton, 2002.

TD Ameritrade. "Millennials and Their Fur Babies." *TD Ameritrade*, 2018, s1.q4cdn.com/959385532/files/doc_downloads/research/2018/Millennials-and-Their-Fur-Babies.pdf.

Tsing, Anna Lowenhaupt. *The Mushroom at the End of the World: On the Possibility of Life in Capitalist Ruins.* Princeton UP, 2017.

Tsing, Anna Lowenhaupt, et al., editors. *Arts of Living on a Damaged Planet.* U of Minnesota P, 2017.

Tuckey, Melissa, editor. *Ghost Fishing: An Eco-Justice Anthology.* U of Georgia P, 2018.

Urquiza-Haas, Esmeralda G., and Kurt Kotrschal. "The Mind behind Anthropomorphic Thinking: Attribution of Mental States to Other Species." *Animal Behavior,* vol. 109, Nov. 2015, pp. 167–76. *ScienceDirect,* dx.doi.org/10.1016/j.anbehav.2015.08.011.

von Einsiedel, Orlando, director. *Virunga.* Ro*co Films Educational, 2017.

Welling, Bart H., and Scottie Kapel. "The Return of the Animal: Presenting and Representing Non-human Beings Response-ably in the (Post-)humanities Classroom." *Teaching Ecocriticism and Green Cultural Studies,* edited by Greg Garrard, Palgrave Macmillan, 2012, pp. 104–16.

Willett, Cynthia. *Interspecies Ethics.* Columbia UP, 2014.

Williams, Terry Tempest. *Refuge: An Unnatural History of Family and Place.* Knopf Doubleday, 1992.

Witham, Kimberly. *Domestic Arrangements. Lensculture,* www.lensculture.com/projects/5733-domestic-arrangements.

Wohlleben, Peter. *Inner Lives of Animals: Love, Grief, and Compassion— Surprising Observations of a Hidden World.* Greystone Books, 2016.

Woodward, Wendy. "Pedagogies of Discomfort: Teaching Coetzee's *The Lives of Animals.*" *Approaches to Teaching Coetzee's* Disgrace *and Other Works,* edited by Laura Wright et al., Modern Language Association of America, 2014, pp. 139–45.

Wright, Alexis. *The Swan Book.* Washington Square Press, 2013.

Yang, Jeffrey, editor. *Birds, Beasts, and Seas: Nature Poems from New Directions.* New Directions Publishing, 2011.

**Amit R. Baishya**

# The Lives of Animals in Postcolonial Cultural Production

In *Animal Intimacies*, Radhika Govindarajan writes, "[T]he promise of posthumanism must engage the lessons of postcolonialism and vice versa" (179). However, scholars who fuse postcolonial theory with approaches like animal studies and environmental studies have discussed reasons for which postcolonial criticism has been wary of posthumanisms (Huggan and Tiffin; Nixon, "Environmentalism"). Since this essay is about animals and animality, I reiterate the four factors that, according to the postcolonial zoocritics Graham Huggan and Helen Tiffin, explain the reluctance to treat animals in postcolonial theory:[1] anxieties about questioning the species boundary; the either/or situations that arise when "humans are pitted against animals in a competition over decreasing resources"; the differential value of particular animals in various cultures; and the "first-things-first" approach, which prioritizes certain forms of life over others (135–38).

Lately, a steady trickle of publications has appeared at the intersection of postcolonial theory and animal theory (Ahuja; Boisseron; Deckha; Kim; Mwangi; Sinha and Baishya). I have recently contributed to this conversation, and the impetus to create the collection of essays *Postcolonial Animalities* with Suvadip Sinha stemmed from a panel I had co-organized at

198

the MLA convention in 2016 and, more important, from a graduate course I taught titled Humans and Animals in Postcolonial Literature and Theory at the University of Oklahoma in spring 2018.

## Planning the Course

A few guiding principles have been useful when I frame classes on postcolonial studies at all levels of instruction. The first is to construct courses as simultaneously linear and multiperspectival narratives. A course on postcolonial literature should tell a story chronologically encompassing the colonial encounter, anticolonialism, neocolonialism, and postcolonialism. Each move forward in the narrative trajectory also makes us look back antidiachronically at what we discussed earlier. Second, instead of focusing on a particular locale, I juxtapose texts from various colonial and postcolonial locations, incorporating both Europhone and non-Europhone texts. While this approach can be criticized as insufficiently grounded in local specificities, such cross-cultural juxtapositions give us the ability to map the history of a theoretical field by focusing on key concepts and a comparative perspective.

Humans and Animals in Postcolonial Literature and Theory posed a few unique challenges. How could I make students take animal representations seriously while still grounding them in key concepts in postcolonial studies? This course partly arose from my dissatisfaction with the tendency in postcolonial criticism to transform discussions of animals into the vector of the animalization of the human. While we should emphasize the continuing importance of the grammar of animality in the colony and postcolony, resorting exclusively to this approach erases the material presence of animals, reducing them to metaphors and allegories. I also didn't want the class to be only about advocacy and the "better treatment of nonhuman animals" (Lundblad 4)—a tendency common in critical animal studies. While better treatment of animals is a desirable goal, I concur with Michael Lundblad that "any environmentalist narrative that fails to take into account the human-rights issues involved" can have malignant effects (qtd. in Iheka 38). Treatment of animals within a postcolonial framework must consider the mutual constitutiveness of the human and the animal instead of treating these categories as autonomous. Moreover, inspired by multispecies ethnography, Sinha and I argue in the introduction to *Postcolonial Animalities* that "[h]uman-animal relationships can only be studied in [their] complexities . . . if we consider the vertiginous range of affective states instead of focusing exclusively on narratives of care and relatedness . . ." (3). These theses also serve as touchstones for my teaching.

I found Claire Jean Kim's notion of "multi-optic vision" useful for any pedagogic endeavor that tries to connect the competing claims of postcolonial theory and animal studies. For Kim, "multi-optic vision is a way of seeing that takes disparate justice claims seriously without privileging any one presumptively" (19). Such lenses reorient us toward an "ethics of mutual avowal, or open and active acknowledgement of connection with other struggles" (20). Categories like race and species impose taxonomic hierarchies, but multi-optic vision reveals a "dense web of relationships" that undercut Manichean human-animal binaries.

Achieving such intersectionality meant jettisoning the usual chronological narrative structure I followed, while keeping the comparative focus intact. Moreover, examining animals and animality through a postcolonial lens also necessitated, following Upamanyu Mukherjee and colleagues, "pedagogy . . . as feral communication . . . , modes of knowledge capable of scavenging from, and transporting knowledge between, the institutions that ultimately fail them" (64). I like this allusion to "scavenging," a figure Jack Halberstam uses to describe queer methodologies: "a scavenger methodology," he writes, "uses different methods to collect and produce information on subjects who have been deliberately or accidentally excluded from traditional studies of human behavior." A scavenger methodology "combines methods often cast as being at odds with each other" while refusing the "compulsion towards disciplinary coherence" (13). Accordingly, I fused established forms of postcolonial inquiry with a welter of different approaches emerging from critical animal studies, disability studies, biosemiotics, media theory, multispecies ethnography, ethology, and queer theory. Indeed, the passages I quote above about "feral communication" and "scavenging" share affinities with Carrie Rohman's arguments in her pedagogic essay on literature and the discourse of species—"The question of our relationship to animals is so pressing in terms of contemporary ethics, biomedicine, conservation, and ecological values, that some context in these areas seems necessary to show students what an astonishing range of issues are at stake in the literary and cultural representations of animals" (49). I provided such context, for example, by assigning the chapter "Of Cetaceans and Ships" from the communication theorist John Peters's book *The Marvelous Clouds* when we discussed Zakes Mda's *The Whale Caller*. Peters's chapter is informed by recent research on the sonic aspects of cetacean communication, and it reconsiders water as an elemental form of media. This chapter added a different dimension to our discussion of the representation of soundscapes in the text, which complemented literary criticism's focus on the relations between the topoi of sea and shore in Mda's novel. The best student paper compared the sonic elements in *The Whale Caller* and Henrietta Rose-Innes's "insect" text *Nineveh* using studies on sound and its importance for animal communication.

## Organization and Execution

While I jettisoned chronological organization and adopted a scavenger methodology, the texts I chose for the course's five units created a narrative trajectory. The readings in unit 1, "Humanimals," were Joseph Conrad's *Heart of Darkness*, Frantz Fanon's *The Wretched of the Earth*, Sembène Ousmane's *Xala*, and Indra Sinha's *Animal's People*; in unit 2, "The Humanized Animal?: Dogs," they were J. M. Coetzee's *Disgrace*, Saadat Hasan Manto's "The Dog of Tetwal," and the films *Chienne d'histoire* (*Barking Island*) and *Taskafa, Stories of the Street* (both about stray dogs in Istanbul); in unit 3, "Charismatic Animals," texts discussed were *The Whale Caller*, Amitav Ghosh's *The Hungry Tide* (about tigers), and Ibrahim al-Koni's *Gold Dust* (about camels); in unit 4, "Anthropomorphism and Mythical Animals," they were Eka Kurniawan's *Man Tiger* and Mahasweta Devi's "Pterodactyl, Puran Sahay and Pirtha"; and in unit 5, "Small Animals," we discussed *Nineveh* (about beetles) and Jehirul Hussain's "Minor Preludes, Major Preludes" (about snails).

The narrative was designed to make students move from discussions of the blurred interzone between the biopolitical and the zoopolitical (the first two units) to a consideration of nonhuman agency and the entanglement of human and nonhuman worlds (the last three units). The focus on blurred interzones and entanglement echoes Cajetan Iheka's formulation of "aesthetics of proximity," understood here both as "a spatial sense of nearness" and as "a form of proximity brought about by similarities and shared characteristics" (22). Possibilities for studying interspecies entanglements emerge through such proximities in interzones. For example, in our discussion of Manto's Urdu short story "The Dog of Tetwal," we focused on how the wagging of a stray dog's tail establishes a mode of relationality between humans and the canine. Deploying Jacques Derrida's ideas on hospitality, we concluded that the move toward the thingification of the dog, its treatment as mere inert matter by hypernationalist masculine figures, occurs precisely when this proximity between human and animal—signified in the story by the wagging tail—is disregarded and negated. The fragile possibility of hospitality toward the animal stranger is shattered by the violence perpetrated by the Indian and Pakistani soldiers.

We also jumped scale, moving from large animals to miniscule ones in an attempt to challenge animal studies' limiting focus on charismatic animals. Sinha and I present a critique of that focus in our introduction to *Postcolonial Animalities* (14), as does Evan Mwangi, who writes, "The vitality of the insect emphasizes that humans do not have complete control of the universe . . ." (102). Our class arrived at a conclusion similar to Mwangi's when we discussed *Nineveh* alongside passages on "swarm intelligence" from Michael Hardt and Antonio Negri's *Multitude* (91–93) and from the media theorist Jussi Parikka's *Insect Media* (27–56). *Nineveh*'s differentiation between the "sterile" housing complex of Nineveh in Cape Town and the vitality of the surrounding swamp, where "everything is insistently alive and pushing to enter," emphasizes Mwangi's point about humans' not having complete control of the universe (53). Indeed, this is underscored at the end of *Nineveh* when gogga beetles overrun the housing complex, leading to its eventual abandonment.

Rose-Innes depicts the vitality of insects wonderfully in *Nineveh*, one of the last texts discussed. But mention of insects takes me back to the beginning of my course and the section on humanimals. Recall what Fanon says about the colonist's racio-speciesist language in *The Wretched of the Earth*: "when the colonist speaks of the colonized he uses zoological terms. Allusion is made to the slithery movements of the yellow race, the odors from the 'native' quarters, to the hordes, the stink, the swarming, the seething, and the gesticulations" (7). This is a classic instance of the animalization of the human. *Heart of Darkness* was a wonderful text with which to initiate this discussion on animalization. Conrad's novel participates in the racist denigration of Africans, who are relegated to the level of the animal. However, *Heart of Darkness* also reverses some Eurocentric metaphysical shibboleths that distinguish human from animal being. In *Civilization and Its Discontents*, Sigmund Freud writes that "the fateful process of civilization would thus have set in with man's adoption of an erect posture" (78). The shift from quadruped to biped emerges as the threshold that separates the human from states of animality. Notice how the reversion from biped to quadruped marks a descent into animality in *Heart of Darkness*: "While I stood horror-struck one of these creatures rose to his hands and knees and went off on all-fours towards the river to drink" (17). Moving on all fours here represents absolute dehumanization—a person is described as a "creature." However, Conrad interestingly reverses this perspective in the Inner Station when Marlow narrates, "He [Kurtz] can't walk—he is crawling on all-fours . . ." (64). Both the *homines sacri* (people who can be killed but not sacrificed) on the outer circle of the colonial Inferno and the sovereign (Kurtz) at its center become manifestations of the animalized human—an apt illustration of Aimé Césaire's famous thesis about the *choc en retour* ("boomerang effect"; 37) of colonialism. The *choc en retour* reveals that the colonial order of things dehumanizes both colonizer and colonized.

But what if walking on all fours is read as a sign not of animality but of a different sort of humanness? This is where a contrast between the two texts that bookended the section on humanimals—*Heart of Darkness* and *Animal's People*—worked well. Animal, the disabled protagonist of Sinha's novel on the Bhopal gas disaster of 1984, walks on all fours. Influential readings, such as Rob Nixon's first chapter on the novel in *Slow Violence* (45–67), gloss over the material dimensions of Animal's disability. Juxtaposing Nixon's chapter with a chapter on the intersections between disability and animality in Sunaura Taylor's *Beasts of Burden* helped us to reconsider Animal's repeated refusal to be considered human, to see it not as a mournful form of disavowal but as an affirmative statement that reclaimed animality within the calculus of the human. Taylor was born with arthrogryposis and uses a wheelchair. In a chapter titled "Claiming Animal," she narrates, "I feel animal in my embodiment, and this feeling is one of connection, not shame. Recognizing my animality has been . . . a way of claiming the dignity in the way my body and other nonnormative and vulnerable bodies move, look and experience the world around them. It is . . . an assertion that my animality is integral to my humanity" (115). Taylor emphasizes that the analogy between animality and humanity shouldn't be read metaphorically; instead, these experiences gesture toward alternative ways of being in the world. When Taylor rummages through her purse for her phone with her face, she is reminded of "pigs who root with their noses, birds who build nests with their beaks, and Bailey, my dog . . . who likes to make his bed" (116). Since Bailey doesn't have hands—hands being another metaphysical shibboleth ostensibly distinguishing humans from animals—he uses his mouth to create his sleeping pile. Taylor recognizes that despite their "sensorial species differences," she and these animals share a kinship. Our discussions emphasized this kinship in Animal's characterization, enabling us to move away from reductive grammars of animality and contend with affirmative representations of alternative states of being. Another student paper in the course emerged from the willingness to take seriously Animal's claim that "I am an Animal fierce and free / in all the world is none like me" (366).

The hybrid methodology we adopted also made us reconsider representations of animals. Take, for instance, *Disgrace*. While we read Gayatri Chakravorty Spivak's essay on the novel, what excited the class were two takes on the novel from the perspectives of posthumanism and disability studies. Calina Ciobanu's essay on *Disgrace*'s "posthumanist ethics" reads Coetzee's novel alongside a key intertext—Kafka's *The Trial*. In Kafka's novel, the protagonist, Josef K, is eventually executed "[l]ike a dog" (196). This is echoed in *Disgrace* in a conversation between the protagonist, David Lurie, and his daughter Lucy when they are discussing the aftermath of the brutal assault on Lucy's farm:

> "Yes, I agree, it is humiliating. But perhaps that is a good point to start from again. Perhaps that is what I must learn to accept. To start at ground level. With nothing. Not with nothing but. With nothing. No cards, no weapons, no property, no rights, no dignity."
> "Like a dog."
> "Yes, like a dog." (200)

One of Ciobanu's comments on this passage led to a lively discussion about seemingly pejorative depictions of animality ("like a dog") necessarily being a "fall" from humanness. Ciobanu suggestively claims that a different reading of animality is possible if we consider "the novel's interspecies ethical imaginary," which "derives from the possibility of taking a phrase like 'like a dog' and making it mean something new—something that levels hierarchies and stresses the elements of sameness in the simile ('like a dog') over its points of exclusion and difference ('like a dog [as opposed to a human]')" (687).

Such affiliations with alternative forms of being—also an important discourse in disability studies—were emphasized further when we discussed the disabled status of Driepoot, the dog Lurie gives up. Taylor's discussion of "animal crips" was useful here. While Taylor agrees that identifying nonhuman animals as disabled figures may be an anthropocentric projection, she argues that naming "animals as crips is a way of challenging us to question our ideas about how bodies move, think, and feel and what makes a body valuable, exploitable, useful or disposable" (43). Consider one of the last sentences in *Disgrace*: "One by one he brings in the cats, then the dogs: the old, the blind, the halt, the crippled, the maimed, but also the young, the sound—all those whose term has come" (213). The sentence, crucially, begins with a list of disabilities before the "but also" posits the able-bodied animals as possible exceptions. We pondered whether this "but also" naturalizes the euthanasia of disabled animals. Is this prior naturalization of disabled animality as a form of disposable life essential to the pathos of the concluding scene, where Lurie gives up Driepoot as a "lamb" for sacrifice?

> He opens the cage door. "Come," he says, bends, opens his arms. The dog wags its crippled rear, sniffs his face, licks his cheeks, his lips, his ears. He does nothing to stop it. "Come."
> Bearing him in his arms like a lamb, he re-enters the surgery. (214)

While there is hardly any discussion of Driepoot's disabled figuration in the copious critical literature on *Disgrace*, it seemed to us that Coetzee's sacrificial ethics in the novel deployed disability to accentuate pathos. This possibility is rarely discussed, but could it be that this critical silence comes from equations of "disability only with suffering and a fear of contagion" (Taylor 24)?

While we began with discussions of dehumanization through animalization, and of points of intersection among race, species, and disability, I steered discussions toward an appraisal of the concrete materiality of animal presences, interspecies entanglements, and animal modes of communication. This isn't another instance of making the animal subaltern speak; instead, it is a contention about how we live with alterity in all its messy and uninnocent dimensions. I am influenced by Lauren Corman and Tereza Vandrovcová's intersectional approach: the "question of the animal," they write, "is not only intersectional but complicated by the multiplicity of . . . life experiences that cannot be reduced to victimhood or voicelessness. Instead of thinking of animals as voiceless, we must pay closer attention to their complex subjectivities in our work, including our pedagogy" (138–39). I glean two lessons from Corman and Vandrovcová's quote for my pedagogical goals. First, regarding the question of the "multiplicity of . . . life experiences" that can't be reduced to voicelessness—my attempts at localizing human-animal interfaces, such as the human-tiger entanglements in *The Hungry Tide*, contend with the multiplicity of life experiences. We pondered what it would mean to take the story of the folk goddess of the Sundarbans folk, Bon Bibi, and the tiger, Dakkhin Rai—the crux of Ghosh's novel—seriously as an instance of human-tiger entanglement in a multispecies ecosystem, instead of dismissing it as mere superstition. This would also entail taking the villagers' killing of the tiger that trespasses their territory—an act that horrifies the American-born marine biologist Piya (242–44)—seriously, without reducing it to yet another act of human barbarity against voiceless animals. In her fine ethnographic account of human-tiger relationships in the Sundarbans—sections of which we read alongside the novel—Annu Jalais summarizes a conversation about tiger-conservation efforts with an impoverished old woman: "due to the legitimizing of killings in their name, they (the tigers) had turned egotistical and did not hesitate to attack people. Now tigers were no longer the neighbors with whom the forest had to be shared, but 'state-property', and backed by the ruling elite, they had begun to treat the islanders as 'tiger-food'" (172). Far more interesting than the implicit anthropomorphism in this passage is the woman's mournful apprehension of shifting interspecies relationships, of "neighbors" transforming into predators. This led us to some complex discussions of interspecies relationships that abjured simplistic dichotomies of human wickedness and animal innocence and voicelessness.

Second, regarding the complex subjectivity of animals, work in biosemiotics and biosemiotically inflected ethnography offers us pathways toward a consideration of animal communication (Kohn). Eduardo Kohn draws on Piercian biosemiotics to outline an "anthropology beyond the human," and he calls for "provincializ[ing] language"—for delinking semiotic processes from the symbolic limits of human language. Indeed, in our discussions of the wagging tail in "Dog of Tetwal," of the point-of-view shots attempting to show how a dog sees the world in *Taskafa*, and of cetacean communication in *The Whale Caller* and *The Hungry Tide*, we asked what the wagging of a dog's tail or the song of a whale or dolphin could signify as a form of communication and way of establishing relationality.

## Back to the Future

I believe that the two iterations of the class—in 2018 and 2020—were largely successful. Class sessions were characterized by an "affective slide" (Szeman 49). Students would begin the class with intellectual energy and frequently leave feeling depressed by the vicissitudes of political violence and its impact on human and nonhuman lives, climate change, and species extinction. However, they were also energized by unexpected encounters with alternative forms of agency—for instance, the stray dogs' capacity for survival in *Taskafa*.

I made a few changes to Humans and Animals in Postcolonial Literature and Theory when I taught it for the second time, in spring 2020, the semester when I completed this essay. A lot more had been published in the interim on conjunctions between postcolonial and animal theory. Moreover, the focus of my work had shifted to species extinction and the inhuman dimensions of time reaching beyond the animal (to the virus, for instance) in the era of the Anthropocene. We touched on these aspects pertaining to Anthropocene discourse briefly in spring 2018 in our discussions of the figuration of the pterodactyl in "Pterodactyl" and the representation of lithic time inhering in the ancient petroglyphs in the Tadrart Acacus caves in Libya in *Gold Dust*. However, I am pushing discussions of such nonhuman and inhuman dimensions further through a consideration of texts like Mayra Montero's *In the Palm of Darkness* (on frogs) and Keri Hulme's *Stonefish* (featuring shellfish).

Adding such works also helped me address one major lacuna in the first articulation of the course. I didn't pay enough attention to small animals, thereby inadvertently replicating postcolonial theory's bias for charismatic animals. Focusing on small animals such as frogs, insects, and shellfish like the crabs in *The Hungry Tide* brings us face-to-face with Spivak's notion of planetarity, what Gautam Basu Thakur calls the "irrevocable subject-destabilizing unhomeliness (*unheimlich*) of the planet" (31). Small animals alert us to destabilizing unhomeliness as we have the unsettling realization that our time exists conterminously with many other temporalities. Further, they show that while "the multispecies and ontological turn is new to Anthropocene discourse, it has a long history in feminist and Indigenous studies" (DeLoughrey 30). Unsettling our anthropocentric tendencies and exploring the genealogy of multispecies imaginaries in other global traditions—these signposts will continue to guide my pedagogical endeavors in postcolonial animal studies.

## Note

1. Despite this reluctance, postcolonial theory frequently deploys the metaphoric "grammar of animality" to discuss conditions of dehumanization (Mbembe 236).

## Works Cited

Ahuja, Neel. *Bioinsecurities: Disease, Interventions, Empire, and the Government of Species*. Duke UP, 2016.

Basu Thakur, Gautam. "'A Strangeness beyond Reckoning': The Animal as Surplus in Postcolonial Literature." Sinha and Baishya, *Postcolonial Animalities*, pp. 29–47.

Boisseron, Bénédicte. *Afro-Dog: Blackness and the Animal Question.* Columbia UP, 2018.

Césaire, Aimé. *Discourse on Colonialism.* Translated by Joan Pinkham, Monthly Review Press, 2001.

*Chienne d'histoire.* Directed by Serge Avekidian, Sacrebleu Productions, 2010. *YouTube*, uploaded by Karin Arustamyan, 22 Dec. 2016, youtube.com /watch?app=desktop&v=GgDspl_nFgc.

Ciobanu, Calina. "Coetzee's Posthumanist Ethics." *MFS: Modern Fiction Studies,* vol. 58, no. 4, Winter 2012, pp. 668–98.

Coetzee, J. M. *Disgrace.* Penguin, 2000.

Conrad, Joseph. *Heart of Darkness.* Edited by Paul Armstrong, W. W. Norton, 2005.

Corman, Lauren, and Tereza Vandrovcová. "Radical Humility: Towards a More Holistic Animal Studies Pedagogy." *Counterpoints,* vol. 448, 2014, pp. 135–57.

Deckha, Maneesha. "Postcolonial." *Critical Terms for Animal Studies,* edited by Lori Gruen, U of Chicago P, 2018, pp. 280–93.

DeLoughrey, Elizabeth M. *Allegories of the Anthropocene.* Duke UP, 2019.

Derrida, Jacques. *Of Hospitality.* Translated by Rachel Bowlby, Stanford UP, 2000.

Devi, Mahasweta. "Pterodactyl, Puran Sahay and Pirtha." *Imaginary Maps,* translated by Gayatri C. Spivak, Routledge, 1994, pp. 95–196.

Fanon, Frantz. *The Wretched of the Earth.* Translated by Richard Philcox, Grove Press, 2004.

Freud, Sigmund. *Civilization and Its Discontents.* Translated by James Strachey, W. W. Norton, 2010.

Ghosh, Amitav. *The Hungry Tide: A Novel.* Mariner Books, 2006.

Govindarajan, Radhika. *Animal Intimacies: Interspecies Relatedness in India's Central Himalayas.* U of Chicago P, 2018.

Halberstam, Jack. *Female Masculinity.* Duke UP, 1998.

Hardt, Michael, and Antonio Negri. *Multitude: War and Democracy in the Age of Empire.* Penguin Press, 2005.

Huggan, Graham, and Helen Tiffin. *Postcolonial Ecocriticism: Literature, Animals, Environment.* Routledge, 2010.

Hulme, Keri. *Stonefish.* HUA Publishers, 2007.

Hussain, Jehirul. "Minor Preludes, Major Preludes." Translated by Amit R. Baishya, *museindia.com,* no. 63, Sept.–Oct. 2015, museindia.com/Home /ViewContentData?arttype=focus&issid=63&menuid=6016.

Iheka, Cajetan. *Naturalizing Africa: Ecological Violence, Agency, and Postcolonial Resistance in African Literature.* Cambridge UP, 2018.

Jalais, Annu. *Forest of Tigers: People, Politics and Environment in the Sundarbans.* Routledge, 2011.

Kafka, Franz. *The Trial.* Translated by Breon Mitchell, Schocken Books, 1998.

Kim, Claire Jean. *Dangerous Crossings: Race, Species, and Nature in a Multicultural World.* Cambridge UP, 2015.

Kohn, Eduardo. *How Forests Think: Towards an Anthropology beyond the Human.* U of California P, 2013.

Koni, Ibrahim al-. *Gold Dust.* Translated by Elliott Colla, American U in Cairo P, 2008.

Kurniawan, Eka. *Man Tiger: A Novel.* Translated by Labodalih Sembiring, Verso, 2015.

Lundblad, Michael. "The End of the Animal—Literary and Cultural Animalities." Introduction. *Animalities: Literary and Cultural Studies beyond the Human,* edited by Lundblad, Edinburgh UP, 2018, pp. 1–21.

Manto, Saadat Hasan. "The Dog of Tetwal." Translated by Ravikant and Tarun K. Saint, *Manoa,* vol. 19, no. 1, 2007, pp. 80–87.

Mbembe, Achille. *On the Postcolony.* U of California P, 2001.

Mda, Zakes. *The Whale Caller: A Novel.* Picador, 2006.

Montero, Mayra. *In the Palm of Darkness: A Novel.* Harper Perennial, 1998.

Mukherjee, Upamanyu P., et al. "Teaching Climate Crisis in the Neoliberal University: On the Poverty of Environmental Humanities." *Teaching Climate Change in the Humanities,* edited by Stephen Siperstein et al., Routledge, 2017, pp. 59–66.

Mwangi, Evan. *The Postcolonial Animal: African Literature and Posthuman Ethics.* U of Michigan P, 2019.

Nixon, Rob. "Environmentalism and Postcolonialism." *Postcolonial Studies and Beyond,* edited by Ania Loomba et al., Duke UP, 2005, pp. 233–51.

———. *Slow Violence and the Environmentalism of the Poor.* Harvard UP, 2013.

Ousmane, Sembène. *Xala.* Translated by Clive Wake, Chicago Review Press, 1997.

Parikka, Jussi. *Insect Media: An Archeology of Animals and Media.* U of Minnesota P, 2011.

Peters, John Durham. *The Marvelous Clouds: Towards a Philosophy of Elemental Media.* U of Chicago P, 2016.

Rohman, Carrie. "Animal Writes: Literature and the Discourse of Species." *Teaching the Animal: Human-Animal Studies across the Disciplines,* edited by Margo DeMello, Lantern Books, 2010, pp. 48–59.

Rose-Innes, Henrietta. *Nineveh.* Unnamed Press, 2016.

Sinha, Indra. *Animal's People: A Novel.* Simon and Schuster, 2007.

Sinha, Suvadip, and Amit R. Baishya. Introduction. Sinha and Baishya, *Postcolonial Animalities,* pp. 1–25.

———, editors. *Postcolonial Animalities.* Routledge, 2020.

Spivak, Gayatri Chakravorty. "Ethics and Politics in Tagore, Coetzee, and Certain Scenes of Teaching." *Diacritics,* vol. 32, no. 3–4, Autumn–Winter, 2002, pp. 17–31.

Szeman, Imre. "Energy, Climate and the Classroom: A Letter." *Teaching Climate Change in the Humanities,* edited by Stephen Siperstein et al., Routledge, 2017, pp. 46–52.

*Taskafa, Stories of the Street.* Directed by Andrea Luka Zimmerman, Grasshopper Film, 2013.

Taylor, Sunaura. *Beasts of Burden: Animal and Disability Liberation.* New Press, 2017.

**Jason Price**

---

# Postcolonial Animal Studies: Animal and Animist Codes

In teaching courses such as Animals in Postcolonial Literature, or in teaching animal-centric narratives in postcolonial literature courses, a pedagogical problem arises when giving students the critical tools to read postcolonial animals. The problem stems, in part, from the prevalence of European and North American scholarship in animal studies. While such a course or unit should perhaps properly include key works of theory in animal studies, how relevant are such works to students' readings of animals in African literatures? Providing students with North American and European approaches to reading animals can help them recognize their limits when it comes to African literary texts, an experience that also helps students reflect on their own worldviews and cultural assumptions about animals. In this essay, I assess the relevance of Euro-American animal studies scholarship for reading animals in postcolonial literatures, gesture to exciting new work in postcolonial ecocriticism, and finally offer suggestions for teaching the debate about animals and meaning in response to the challenges posed by animals in animist-realist African literature.

This essay comes from my observations of students' tendency to read spiritualized animals in works of magical realism almost exclusively as fantastic or as psychologically fabricated (as hallucinations and so on)—modes of reading that risk a neocolonial denial of indigenous spiritualities. To address this proclivity, I recommend Harry Garuba's concept of "animist materialism," which, while not focused on animals, offers ways of reading spiritualized animals in African literature. Ultimately, this approach challenges students to decide which insights from animal studies and postcolonial theory are useful for doing postcolonial ecocriticism, which concepts need adapting, and which new concepts need to be created.

I often begin the semester in postcolonial animal studies courses by screening clips from *The Ghost and the Darkness*, a film about lions interrupting the British Empire's construction of a railroad bridge in the Tsavo region of Kenya during the late Victorian period. The film is based in part on real events: two lions notoriously attacked and killed laborers building the bridge in 1898. Centered on a British engineer's attempt to complete the bridge, the film dramatizes the lions' disruptive attacks and hunters' efforts to kill the "man-eaters." The movie is less than stellar, but, despite its flaws, such as its celebration of the colonial hunters' killing lions and overcoming disgruntled colonized laborers to complete the bridge, it nonetheless opens up a discussion about the role of animals in colonial logic. The film helps students appreciate how colonialism visited violence not only on humans in colonized places but also on nonhuman animals. I also point out that the Tsavo lions have been made into taxidermy and are on display in the Field Museum in Chicago, which helps students see the strange ways that animal bodies get caught up in human meaning and connects African animals and colonial history to the American classroom.

More important, *The Ghost and the Darkness* invites questions about animals and meaning. An Indian laborer, Abdullah, says of the lions, "The devil has come to Tsavo." A Kenyan character, Samuel, later suggests that "they are not lions. They are the ghost and the darkness." He also offers various spiritual understandings of the animals as evil, as the spirits of medicine men, and so on. Such competing readings of the lions begin to help students appreciate the complexity of animal representations. I pose questions such as, What are the implications of reading animals in terms of religion or as the spirits of ancestors? Does the spiritualization risk backgrounding the animals? Do such understandings contribute to or detract from developing more ethical ways of relating to postcolonial animals?

## Decolonizing Relationships with Animals

Given the negative views of animals and the violence visited on them historically, as a film like *The Ghost and the Darkness* well shows, I begin the class with a theoretical question: How do writers decolonize relationships with animals or otherwise critique colonialist instrumentalization and violence? The question serves as a challenge for students to develop ways of reading and thinking about animals and is inspired by Val Plumwood's essay "Decolonizing Relationships with Nature." Plumwood challenges some of the assumptions that inform Western philosophy and colonial understandings of nature. She uses terms like "hyper-separation" and "backgrounding" to critique anthropocentrism and assumptions of mastery (54, 56). In opposition to the arbitrary practice of renaming lands and natural features in Western colonialism, Plumwood advocates listening and respecting indigenous narratives and naming practices that import meaning to the environment to check colonial instrumentalizations. Philip Armstrong's brief essay "The Postcolonial Animal" is another early attempt to bring together animal studies and postcolonial studies, arguing that the two fields might be best connected through a shared critique of the humanist, Cartesian self. Bénédicte Boisseron's *Afro-Dog* offers a more robust overview of the relation between the fields of postcolonial studies and animal studies in the chapter "Is the Animal the New Black?" In their introduction to *Postcolonial Animalities*, Suvadip Sinha and Amit R. Baishya critique some strands of postcolonial animal studies and posthumanism, noting the need for more engagement with non-Western understandings of the human and cultural renderings of animals; they also recommend the more intersectional animal studies work of Neel Ahuja and Mel Chen.


## Teaching Postcolonial Animal Studies

Karla Armbruster's "Thinking with Animals" reviews works by several European and American scholars such as Cary Wolfe, Jacques Derrida, Gilles Deleuze and Félix Guattari, Donna Haraway, Steve Baker, Akira Mizuta Lippit, and Nigel Rothfels. Similarly, Bart H. Welling and Scottie Kapel discuss their course Wild Encounters in "The Return of the Animal," where they attempt to "denaturalize animal imagery" (110). While such classes nicely call attention to how a general animal studies course might be taught, my essay emphasizes how such a class must be tailored for a postcolonial animal studies literature class.

Some of the animal studies scholars recommended by Armbruster lend themselves nicely to a postcolonial literature course. For example, Wolfe's *Before the Law* can be fruitfully taught alongside Achille Mbembe's "Necropolitics," which explains the colonial logic that equated "savage life" with "animal life" (24). However, as Erin James puts it, "Postcolonial ecocriticism courses . . . pose the significant pedagogical challenge of asking students to engage with potentially unfamiliar terrains, languages, and customs" (64–65). Providing students with histories of animals and environmentalism in postcolonial contexts is helpful here: selections from Rob Nixon's *Slow Violence*, Byron Caminero-Santangelo and Garth Andrew Myers's *Environment at the Margins*, Caminero-Santangelo's *Different Shades of Green*, Lance van Sittert and Sandra Swart's *Canis Africanis*, and so on. Instructors might also find it useful to offer articles or books on specific animist cultures, such as Harry West's work on Muedan sorcery (*Ethnographic Sorcery*). Other sources of recent postcolonial animal studies include Evan Mwangi's *The Postcolonial Animal*, Wendy Woodward's *The Animal Gaze*, and Woodward and Susan McHugh's collection *Indigenous Creatures, Native Knowledges, and the Arts*.

## Animals and the Animist Code: Debating Animals and Meaning

I've found that American college students tend to have some familiarity with the use of animals as symbols and with racist, dehumanizing uses of animal metaphors; however, many are less familiar with African spirituality. For example, in K. Sello Duiker's *Thirteen Cents* a character's experiences of animal transformation or supernatural phenomena can be read as the effects of hallucinogenic drugs or trauma. While such readings are plausible, students tend to opt for them alone, excluding and ignoring the spiritual elements of the text (Duiker's protagonist Azure experiences supernatural encounters with the San god Mantis, thinks he's transforming into a lizard, and so on as he rejects a Western-capitalist *Bildung* for a more traditional formation of self). This is not true of all students, however, and those with knowledge of Native American cultures and literatures or other traditional knowledges express greater ease with reading animist-realist works of African literature. Yet, as Anthony Lioi notes, "the inclusion of an ostensibly archaic spirituality in a contemporary context . . . [is] difficult for . . . students to face" (139). Providing students with Garuba's work on "animist materialism" and the scholarly dialogue about animals and meaning offers students a footing to help them understand the animist-coded animals in African texts.

Many animal studies theorists would balk at Samuel's claim from *The Ghost and the Darkness* that the lions "are not lions" but something else. After all, a major strand of thought in animal studies scholarship criticizes the use of animals as stand-ins for human meaning and instead emphasizes animal materiality in attempting to think about animals outside human meaning systems. Baker's *Picturing the Beast*, for example, warns against the "denial of the animal" and criticizes the tendency of humans to use animals for signification, as in his metonymic example of the bald eagle standing in for the United States. Baker observes how in work on fairy tales and "Disney comics there was a common tendency to deny the animal, by proposing that the stories must be properly understood not to be about animals but about something else entirely" (211). Similarly, in their introduction to zoocriticism in the second half of *Postcolonial Ecocriticism*, a useful primer on key issues for thinking about postcolonial animals, Graham Huggan and Helen Tiffin criticize the fact that many cultures' only or primary relation to animals is to use them for human meaning, citing the history of racist animal metaphors.

Kari Weil's chapter "A Report on the Animal Turn" from *Thinking Animals* offers a succinct overview of the question of animals, language, and meaning (3–24). Weil describes the "counterlinguistic turn" in animal studies, citing Deleuze and Guattari, who seek a way of relating to animals more materially and affectively, outside language and human meaning. Deleuze and Guattari's antisignification stance comes from their reading of Kafka's animals, where they criticize the dominant culture's use of signification and prefer Kafka's strategy of relating to animals outside language or in a language that makes no sense to humans (*Kafka*). Deleuze and Guattari praise both Kafka's use of metamorphosis and his refusal to employ metaphors. Looking to animals for a way to escape our all-too-human ways of thinking and being, which are often oppressive, Deleuze and Guattari value literatures that deterritorialize language through the intensities of asignifying animal sounds.

Similarly, the Deleuzean philosopher Rosi Braidotti calls for a more literal treatment of animals and argues against using animals as metaphors. Braidotti criticizes Freudian psychoanalysis for the way it oedipalizes animals as stand-ins for family members. She wants to recognize an animal code or how animals have "code systems of their own" to approach an understanding of animals in all their differences from humans (528). The attempt to strip animals of cultural meaning to ensure we respond ethically to them offers one strategy of preventing animal instrumentalization. Yet we might expand this debate by gesturing to the strategies of the animist code: a practice in African material culture of adding social and spiritual meaning and metaphor to objects.

For instructors offering a course on animist-realist African literature featuring animals, I suggest teaching this antimeaning stance in animal studies scholarship alongside Garuba's "animist materialism," which adopts a more positive stance on metaphor and meaning. While not specifically about animals, Garuba's "Explorations in Animist Materialism" theorizes the animist code in African material culture. For Garuba, animist materialism involves a "re-traditionalization" of objects in contemporary life (264), coding them to have "a social and spiritual meaning" that enables a "re-enchantment" of the world (267). Garuba explains that a key feature of the animist code is "the 'locking' of spirit within matter or the merger of the material and the metaphorical" (267). In teaching Garuba's essay, I emphasize how an animist worldview differs from a secular one and explain the history of Western philosophers dismissing animism in racist fashion, something Marisol de la Cadena notes in her "Indigenous Cosmopolitics in the Andes." De la Cadena offers another introduction to animism and a helpful example in her discussion of a spiritualized understanding of a mountain in Peru that is thought to be capable of feeling and acting on rage. Because such examples can be new for students and they may be skeptical about such beliefs and their relevance to the readings, I emphasize Garuba's footnote about the influence of animism on daily life in animist cultures: "this does not necessarily mean that the individual has to believe in magic or animism. In predominantly animist societies, the animist unconscious conditions being and structures subjectivity" (271n21). His note demonstrates the significant role that animism continues to play in coding social relations and culture and challenges students who may dismiss such codings as mere archaic beliefs or who want to read spiritual elements only as hallucinations. After students understand how animist cultures code the material world with spiritual and social meaning, I ask them to think about animism's potential, and, ultimately, we arrive at Garuba's point that "an animistic understanding of the world applied to the practice of everyday life has often provided avenues of agency for the dispossessed in colonial and postcolonial Africa" (285). Examining postcolonial animals in animist-realist fiction, we can assess the role that animals play. We ask ourselves, Are animals included in the category of the dispossessed? Are they recognized as part of the community and its distributed animist agency—spiritual, material, social—in texts of postcolonial resistance?

Garuba provides several examples of the merger of meaning and material in the animist code, such as in his reading of Toni Morrison's *Beloved* and Niyi Osundare's poem "The Rocks Rose to Meet Me." Students familiar with Morrison's work find Garuba's discussion of it helpful, and Osundare's poem offers accessible evidence of the potential of animist-materialist readings. Garuba explains how Osundare's speaker finds meaning in rocks upon his return home, a meaning that he suggests strengthens the speaker's environmentalism. Students also find Garuba's examples of present-day appeals to Yoruba gods revelatory. For example, they appreciate his explanation of how Sango, the god of lightning, is invoked by an electric company to retraditionalize a modern technology.

De la Cadena warns scholars against the flawed approaches of either dismissing indigenous politics as being too dangerous or valorizing them as all good (360), and instructors might also prompt students to think about the risks posed by animism or traditional spirituality for animal ethics. For instance, Garuba mentions literary and cultural examples of dogs being sacrificed to Ogun, the god of iron, sometimes as a kind of "traditional 'insurance policy'" to protect cars (269). Might certain codings or spiritualizations of animals make ethical relationships with postcolonial animals more difficult? As his essay makes clear, people make use of the animist code vastly differently, and not all retraditionalizations work to challenge oppression or to give agency to the dispossessed, such as when calculating politicians strategically perform traditionalism to garner voter support.

With Garuba's concept in mind, students are better able to see the limitations of Euro-American animal studies scholarship when it comes to reading African fiction in which animals are often treated simultaneously as material, spiritual, and metaphoric. In reading animals portrayed according to the animist code in works by authors such as Zakes Mda and Mia Couto, it becomes clear that paying attention to the many meanings given to animals in these texts enhances our understanding of postcolonial animals.

Instructors might also gesture to animal studies scholarship that embraces metaphor and otherwise has affinities with the animist code. For example, John Berger's canonical essay "Why Look at Animals?" finds no fault with animal metaphors. For Berger, "if the first metaphor was animal, it was because the essential relation between man and animal was metaphoric" (7). While Berger mourns the loss of interaction with real animals in North America and Europe beginning in the nineteenth century, he finds the metaphoric relations to animals in the past unproblematic. Further, where others criticize anthropomorphism, Berger questions why anthropomorphism (at least in the past) should be viewed negatively: "Until the 19th century, . . . anthropomorphism was integral to the relation between man and animal and was an expression of their *proximity*. Anthropomorphism was the residue of the continuous use of *animal metaphor*. In the last two centuries, animals have gradually disappeared. Today we live without them" (11; my emphasis). Berger's nostalgia for traditional ways of living closely with animals resonates with Garuba's description of animist materialism as retraditionalizing contemporary life.

Like Berger, Cajetan Iheka in his recent book *Naturalizing Africa* advocates for a "strategic anthropomorphism" that occurs "when the lines between humans and nonhumans are blurred to undercut notions of superiority" (14). In elaborating on the "aesthetics of proximity" he observes in African literature (22), Iheka develops a concept in line with Berger's desire that animals be "with man at the center of his world" (Berger 3) rather than mere background. Iheka asks, "if colonial modernity elevated the human as the avatar, the center of the universe, often to the detriment of the nonhuman worlds, both seen and unseen, how has African literature reinstated the nonhuman in relation to the human?" (22). For Iheka, proximity has to do not only with the close relations of humans and animals but also with the nearness of both to the spiritual: "humans share their environment with plants, animals, and other material forms. Moreover, although the supernatural world is generally understood as the 'great beyond,' outside the reach of humans, many [literary works] . . . problematize this distance by bringing both material and immaterial worlds together" (22). The aesthetics of proximity offer another approach to the problem of instrumentalizing animals that doesn't necessarily require doing away with metaphor or meaning altogether.

Jean Langford's "Wilder Powers" also looks at the role of magical or spiritualized animals by way of his analysis of a Cambodian poem about a forced laborer's encounter with a magical snake. Langford reviews several Southeast Asian animist codings of animals and wonders about the potential of spiritualized animals: "What might such animals offer to those who are threatened with a social violence unrestrained by law and 'humanitarian' ethics?" (203). Langford argues that such magical animals provide the dispossessed opportunities for alliances with "moral beasts" (213) that have powers that, as Garuba suggests, might provide them with agency to deal with their otherwise seemingly impotent positions of oppression.

## Animals in Animist-Realist Fiction

In closing, I'll gesture briefly to a few southern African literary texts that engage the question of literary animals and meaning. In the interest of brevity, I'll discuss only two novels, one by Zakes Mda and one by Mia Couto, in some depth. Of course, many African literary works offer animist codings of animals and the environment, and I can name only a few here. For other relevant literary texts, instructors might wish to consult literature cited by Woodward, Iheka, and Mwangi or choose from the following list: Mda's *The Whale Caller* and *The Heart of Redness* for their emphasis on the importance of spiritualized snakes and animist traditions, Couto's *The Last Flight of the Flamingo* for its mythological and spiritualized flamingos, J. M. Coetzee's *Disgrace* for its discussion of dogs and meaning, Es'kia Mphahlele's indictment of racism and white characters' oedipalization of animals in "Mrs. Plum," Duiker's *Thirteen Cents* for its critique of dehumanizing animal metaphors and its portrayal of San spirituality, and Alex La Guma's *The Time of the Butcherbird* for its contrasting portrayals of Christian understandings of animals and animist codings of animals.

Much of Mda's work portrays postcolonial animals, and Mda writes about his interest in animals in "The Pink Mountain," an essay that responds to critiques of animal conservation as a colonial import. As Louise Bethlehem argues, Mda's fiction resists the pronouncement by some South African critics that antiapartheid literature should adopt realist, mimetic aesthetics to be political. As Bethlehem observes, instead of writing about South African life in this more literal fashion, Mda (along with Coetzee, Achmat Dangor, and others) opts for more magical-realist aesthetics.

In Mda's *Sculptors of Mapungubwe*, an artist named Chata creates fantastic sculptures of animals that don't exist on earth—fictional and hybrid animals he sees during trance dances. Unlike his half brother Rendani, who makes mimetic sculptures of animals and attempts to tame leopards, Chata through his sculptures and dances taps into an animist unconscious, using San trances to contact the spirit world of the animals and ancestors. Making Chata the more ecocentric of the brothers in his respect for animals, Mda dramatizes the debate about realist and nonmimetic animal art. Students find the novel accessible as they follow the sibling rivalry between the status-driven and power-hungry Rendani and the outsider Chata, the unacknowledged child of Rendani's father and a !Kung woman (a people Mapungubweans dehumanize as animal-like and use as slaves). Students also criticize Rendani for making beautiful sculptures of animals like the famous artwork the Mapungubwean Golden Rhinoceros while also hunting sacred rhinos to sell their horns for profit. Chata, the nonmimetic artist, by contrast demonstrates great respect for animals, recognizing their spiritual sacredness and recalling traditional knowledge that animals "were once people" (34).

I prompt students to think about how Garuba's notion of the animist code operates in the novel with questions like the following: What is the importance of traditional practices like Chata's !Kung trance dance? Why might Mda emphasize Chata's !Kung traditions as secret and rather different from other Mapungubweans' spirituality? How do characters' treatments of animals relate to the other concerns of the novel (art, power, politics, drought, etc.)? Taking note of Garuba's emphasis on the agency that animism offers the dispossessed, students observe how the increasingly tyrannical Rendani attempts to control the outsider Chata and his art; yet Chata's trance dances, his traditional knowledge, and his spirituality grant him a degree of freedom because his knowledge remains unknown and therefore less easily managed. The novel portrays the animist coding of the environment in a moment of crisis: a drought is thought to have been caused by the failure of the kingdom's elites to perform rituals to please the gods. Chata and Marubini, a rain dancer, employ their animist traditions as a kind of agency against the controlling and corrupt ruling elite, protecting the community while their leaders endanger it. Students also find Harry Sewlall's essay on *Sculptors*, "Love in the Time of Mirrors," insightful for explaining the connection of Mda's precolonial novel to aspects of contemporary South African life, such as the illegal rhino-horn trade.

Another author whose work proves fruitful for exploring the debate about postcolonial animals and meaning is Couto, who is Mozambican. His *Confessions of the Lioness* offers a striking example of animist realism in its invocations of Muedan spirituality and sorcery in Mozambique. The text invokes animism's blurring of the spiritual, metaphoric, and the material as characters at times get lost trying to decipher which register is being used in referring to lions. For example, there are bush lions, invented lions, "and then there are the lion-people," and "they're all real" (86). As the village women suffer under a violent patriarchy and rape culture, the novel engages in wordplay with the lion attacks. Are the lions metaphors for men? Or are they real lions created by sorcerers? Or are the lion attacks simply literal or plain-old lion attacks? Animist materialism's embrace of myth, magic, and metaphor can shed light on how characters are thinking about the lion attacks, since, as Garuba explains, "animist cultures generate meanings that cast an otherworldly veil over natural phenomena as much as over human activities" (283). Characters' animist codings of the lion attacks and of patriarchal violence ask readers to interpret the lions' spiritual and cultural meanings.

The protagonist of *Confessions*, Mariamar, uses the animist code to understand the violent power relations at work in her village, asserting a kind of resistance through her sorcery. West's "Sorcery of Construction and Socialist Modernization" can offer context for interpreting *Confessions*. West provides a history of the Mozambican Civil War and describes how the Marxist guerilla fighters of the Mozambique Liberation Front dismissed animism as false consciousness. By contrast, West argues that sorcery is a "cultural schema" through which Muedans interpret the ambiguous nature of power and is often used to capture or resist new forms of power (122). He writes about the Muedan practice of creating lions through sorcery and further distinguishes between healing and violent uses of sorcery. Mariamar appears to transform into an animal at times in the novel, and animist materialism adds to the possible interpretations available for thinking about supernatural phenomena. Instructors might pose the following questions: Are her experiences a result of her being a victim of dehumanizing language and her psychological reactions to trauma? Are the metamorphoses she describes what Deleuze and Guattari call "becoming animal," which therefore don't involve really turning into an animal, as the philosophers define their concept (*Thousand Plateaus* 273)? Or, from an animist-materialist perspective, might her transformations be read as real in the context of the material-spiritual animist worldview? We might argue that combinations of these various interpretive approaches in these questions are at work simultaneously in this constantly shifting narrative. As Langford suggests, "we should be wary of presuming any firm distinction between actual and fabulous animalities" (211). Characters sort through the material evidence left after a lion attack and attempt to discern its cause as spiritual, material, or otherwise, rather like the treatment of lion attacks in *The Ghost and the Darkness*. The way the women in the novel identify with lionesses can lead to discussions about the merits of the novel for thinking about animal ethics, since the lions can also be seen as threatening man-eaters. Because Mariamar's phenomenological understanding of the lionesses' strength and rage informs her identification with the animals, the novel emphasizes Garuba's point about the agency that animism offers the dispossessed—an agency made available in the novel through spirituality as well as animality.

As a review of Mda's and Couto's novels shows, not all metaphoric or nonmetaphoric treatments of animals are the same, and there are many shades of animal, meaning in between. Reading lions as "not lions" risks denying the animal, yet other metaphoric-material approaches might successfully blend treatments of animals as literal and nonliteral without denying or backgrounding the animal. Tracing the debates about animals and meaning can help students recognize that context and genre matter and that a metaphoric animal in an animist-realist text might be valuable for thinking about animal ethics and decolonizing relationships, whereas that same metaphoric practice in a text not operating in an aesthetics of proximity might be less useful or even detrimental to decolonizing relationships with animals. Further, not all animist codings challenge the oppression of humans and animals or give them a source of agency, but some animist treatments of animals do have the potential to do so. Using this dialogue about animals and meaning, students are better prepared to think through the difficulties that reading postcolonial literary animals presents.

## Works Cited

Armbruster, Karla. "Thinking with Animals: Teaching Animal Studies–Based Literature Courses." *Teaching North American Environmental Literature*, edited by Laird Christensen et al., Modern Language Association of America, 2008, pp. 72–90.

Armstrong, Philip. "The Postcolonial Animal." *Society and Animals*, vol. 10, no. 4, 2002, pp. 413–19.

Baker, Steve. *Picturing the Beast: Animals, Identity, and Representation.* Manchester UP, 1993.

Berger, John. "Why Look at Animals?" *About Looking*, reprint ed., Vintage Books, 1992, pp. 3–28.

Bethlehem, Louise. "The Pleasures of the Political: Apartheid and Postapartheid South African Fiction." *Teaching the African Novel*, edited by Guarav Desai, Modern Language Association of America, 2009, pp. 222–45.

Boisseron, Bénédicte. *Afro-Dog: Blackness and the Animal Question.* Columbia UP, 2018.

Braidotti, Rosi. "Animals, Anomalies, and Inorganic Others." *PMLA*, vol. 124, no. 2, Mar. 2009, pp. 526–32.

Caminero-Santangelo, Byron. *Different Shades of Green: African Literature, Environmental Justice, and Political Ecology*. U of Virginia P, 2014.

Caminero-Santangelo, Byron, and Garth Andrew Myers, editors. *Environment at the Margins: Literary and Environmental Studies in Africa*. Ohio UP, 2011.

Coetzee, J. M. *Disgrace*. Penguin Books, 1999.

Couto, Mia. *Confession of the Lioness*. Translated by David Brookshaw, Picador, 2016.

———. *The Last Flight of the Flamingo*. Translated by David Brookshaw, Serpent's Tail, 2004.

de la Cadena, Marisol. "Indigenous Cosmopolitics in the Andes: Conceptual Reflections beyond 'Politics.'" *Cultural Anthropology*, vol. 25, no. 2, 2010, pp. 334–70.

Deleuze, Gilles, and Félix Guattari. *Kafka: Toward a Minor Literature*. Translated by Dana Polan, U of Minnesota P, 1986.

———. *A Thousand Plateaus*. Translated by Brian Massumi, U of Minnesota P, 1987.

Duiker, K. Sello. *Thirteen Cents*. Ohio UP, 2013.

Garrard, Greg, editor. *Teaching Ecocriticism and Green Cultural Studies*. Palgrave Macmillan, 2012.

Garuba, Harry. "Explorations in Animist Materialism: Notes on Reading/Writing African Literature, Culture, and Society." *Public Culture*, vol. 15, no. 2, 2003, pp. 261–85.

*The Ghost and the Darkness*. Directed by Stephen Hopkins, Paramount, 1998.

Huggan, Graham, and Helen Tiffin. *Postcolonial Ecocriticism: Literature, Animals, Environment*. Routledge, 2010.

Iheka, Cajetan. *Naturalizing Africa: Ecological Violence, Agency, and Postcolonial Resistance in African Literature*. Cambridge UP, 2017.

James, Erin. "Teaching the Postcolonial/Ecocritical Dialogue." Garrard, pp. 60–71.

La Guma, Alex. *Time of the Butcherbird*. Pearson Education, 1987.

Langford, Jean M. "Wilder Powers: Magical Animality in Tales of War and Terror." *Postcolonial Animalities*, edited by Suvadip Sinha and Amit R. Baishya, Routledge, 2020, pp. 201–20.

Lioi, Anthony. "Teaching Green Cultural Studies and New Media." Garrard, pp. 133–43.

Mbembe, Achille. "Necropolitics." *Public Culture*, vol. 15, no. 1, Jan. 2003, pp. 11–40.

Mda, Zakes. *The Heart of Redness*. Picador, 2000.

———. "The Pink Mountain: Landscapes and the Conception of a Literature of Public Action." *Journal of the African Literature Association*, vol. 3, no. 2, 2009, pp. 97–109.

———. *The Sculptors of Mapungubwe*. Kwela Books, 2013.

———. *The Whale Caller*. Picador, 2005.

Mphahlele, Es'kia. "Mrs. Plum." *Renewal Time*, Readers International, 1988, pp. 161–208.

Mwangi, Evan. *The Postcolonial Animal.* U of Michigan P, 2019.

Nixon, Rob. *Slow Violence and the Environmentalism of the Poor.* Harvard UP, 2011.

Osundare, Niyi. "The Rocks Rose to Meet Me." *The Eye of the Earth*, HEBN, 1987, pp. 13–17.

Plumwood, Val. "Decolonizing Relationships with Nature." *Decolonizing Nature: Strategies for Conservation in a Post-colonial Era*, edited by William Mark Adams and Martin Mulligan, Earthscan, 2003, pp. 51–78.

Sewlall, Harry. "Love in the Time of Mirrors: The Real and the Imaginary in Zakes Mda's *The Sculptors of Mapungubwe.*" *English Academy Review*, vol. 33, no. 1, 2016, pp. 24–37.

Sinha, Suvadip, and Amit R. Baishya. Introduction. *Postcolonial Animalities*, edited by Sinha and Baishya, Routledge, 2020, pp. 1–25.

Sittert, Lance van, and Sandra Swart, editors. *Canis Africanis: A Dog History of Southern Africa.* Brill, 2007.

Weil, Kari. *Thinking Animals: Why Animal Studies Now?* Columbia UP, 2012.

Welling, Bart H., and Scottie Kapel. "The Return of the Animal: Presenting and Representing Non-human Beings Response-ably in the (Post-)humanities Classroom." Garrard, pp. 104–16.

West, Harry. *Ethnographic Sorcery.* U of Chicago P, 2007.

———. "Sorcery of Construction and Socialist Modernization: Ways of Understanding Power in Postcolonial Mozambique." *American Ethnologist*, vol. 28, no. 1, 2001, pp. 119–50.

Wolfe, Cary. *Before the Law: Humans and Other Animals in a Biopolitical Frame.* U of Chicago P, 2013.

Woodward, Wendy. *The Animal Gaze: Animal Subjectivities in Southern African Narratives.* Wits UP, 2008.

Woodward, Wendy, and Susan McHugh, editors. *Indigenous Creatures, Native Knowledges, and the Arts: Animal Studies in Modern Worlds.* Springer, 2017.

# Part V

Extractive Ecologies,
Environmental Justice,
and Postcolonial Ecomedia

**Rhonda Knight and Mary Laffidy**

# Examining Speculative Petrofiction through Journaling and Blogging

Genre Studies: Postcolonial Speculative Fiction is an upper-level literature course developed to fulfill several curricular needs, including genre and diversity requirements, and a college-wide elective for students pursuing a specialization in African American studies at Coker University.[1] The course texts are divided into themed units—petrofiction, monsters, other worlds, and steampunk—offering varied postcolonial and diasporic perspectives, which indicate how stories and cultures are transmitted, how dominant cultures create otherness, and how economic imperialism continues to control formerly colonized countries (see Knight). The speculative works of the Nigerian American author Nnedi Okorafor explore this latter perspective, showing how Big Oil shapes the lives of Nigerians. Her novel *Lagoon* and the short stories in her collection *Kabu Kabu* form the core of the petrofiction unit, which examines humanity's varied relationships to oil—as fuel, mode of manufacturing, pollutant, and scarce resource. The speculative spaces Okorafor creates bear the weight of Nigeria's historical resistance to imperialism and Big Oil by normalizing the violence and discomfort this resistance brings with it.

Speculative fiction, by nature, creates or recreates a world. Even though many students grow up reading fantasy or dystopic fiction, they need help understanding how world building functions in speculative fiction. Because the new worlds in this course are based on African and Caribbean cultures and locations, students needed even more guidance. Cora Agatucci suggests that for Western students "[e]ffective study of African novels" requires apparatuses, such as "guides and glossaries, historical and cultural contextual materials" (311). Instead of creating such apparatuses, we developed a multimodal assignment that compelled students to build their own knowledge bases by looking up words and concepts unfamiliar to them and situate that knowledge within the course's multiple frameworks of petrofiction and postcolonial and speculative fiction. The first step of the multimodal assignment required them to write in journals to build their knowledge. In the second step, they revised selections from their journals into blogs, written for a broad audience, and uploaded them to our course site, *Postcolonial Speculative Fiction* (scalar.usc.edu/works /postcolonial/index?path=index). The two modes in this conjoined assignment produced different learning outcomes: journaling fostered students' skill at reading unfamiliar content, and blogging cultivated their ability to write for outside audiences and enhanced their awareness of themselves as global digital citizens.

## Petrofiction and Global Digital Citizenship

Amitav Ghosh coined the term *petrofiction* in his 1992 review of two novels from Abdelrahman Munif's *Cities of Salt* series. Ghosh famously claims that Americans do not, nor will they ever, write about "the Oil Encounter" (29) because it is too messy, too multicultural, too violent, and "verging on the unspeakable, the *pornographic*" (30). He also implies that the West is too busy consuming oil and its associated products to care about their origins or manufacturing processes. This ignorance engenders the anthropologist Fernando Coronil's concept of "petro-magic"—the illusion that petroleum provides "wealth without work" (Wenzel 451). Jennifer Wenzel adapts Coronil's concept in her term *petro-magical-realism*. The genre of petro-magical-realism depicts fantastic events and landscapes but grounds them in worlds where current and historical modes of production and exploitation are neither forgotten nor erased (Wenzel 457–58). Similarly grounded in revealing exploitative practices, Okorafor's stories in *Kabu Kabu* mirror the "real-life tactics" of postcolonial resistance, such as bunkering, that Nigerians must deploy to survive in their oil-rich and fuel-scarce land, poisoned by the extraction of oil (Kapstein 2). Okorafor exposes the false narratives that the West and Big Oil construct about themselves in the Niger Delta: as peaceful, well-meaning, and responsible institutions undermined by the work of pirates and thieves (Caminero-Santangelo 226, 230–31). She does not deny the violence of Ghosh's "The Oil Encounter" that Michael Watts calls "palpable and existential" but shows how the West and Big Oil force the neocolonial citizens into roles—pirates and thieves—shaped by narratives that highlight the need of surveillance in an area of lawlessness (Watts 258). Her works do not attempt to make these complex encounters look simple.

The same can be said for the other texts in the petrofiction unit—short stories that offer varied geographic perspectives, focus on different methods of oil extraction, and demonstrate overt and covert types of pollution, corruption, and violence, thus introducing the readers to the multitude of ways petroculture is situated within culture. British author China Miéville's "Covehithe," set in the North Sea, showcases historical oil-refinery tragedies by portraying capsized rigs as sentient beings that rise from the sea. The American author Deji Bryce Olukotun's "Four Lions" depicts the violent business of taxi gangs in Cape Town through the eyes of a reporter looking for a big story. In "Wishful Thinking," the Ugandan author Acan Innocent Immaculate writes about the effect that loud and chaotic traffic, especially *boda-bodas* (motorcycle taxis), have on one man as he walks through Kampala. The South African writer Henrietta Rose-Innes portrays race and privilege in her short story "Poison," in which a cross-section of Cape Town's population becomes stranded at a gas station as they try to escape a poisonous cloud caused by the explosion of a chemical plant. "An Athabasca Story," by Warren Cariou, a Métis author, calls attention to surface mining in the Athabasca Tar Sands through the allegory of a First Nations man, Elder Brother, who becomes ensnared in the mining equipment.[2]

These texts challenge their readers to situate themselves in a petro-global context and thus to cultivate their own global competencies. According to Madelyn Flammia, individuals who are globally competent are able to connect "the global and the local," to communicate with "intercultural awareness and sensitivity," and to "manage knowledge to create shared understandings." Flammia emphasizes that globally competent individuals must have information fluency so that they can "use technology for research and for collaboration across cultures." Globally competent, information-fluent individuals possess the skill of presenting ideas "in an appropriate and effective manner" (701; see also Agatucci 316). In its publication *Global Digital Citizen: Teacher's Companion,* the commercial learning platform Wabisabi outlines competencies and fluencies similar to Flammia's and offers five tenets of global digital citizenship. The students identified specific goals related to three of these five tenets—global citizenship, digital citizenship, and environmental stewardship—that they wanted to address in their blogs. All members of the class collaborated to compose a content rubric, using selected terminology from *Global Digital Citizen*, requiring that the blogs demonstrate two of the following forms of global competency and information fluency:

> an awareness of their own ability to reach diverse readers through a medium in which "the barriers of time and distance no longer exist" and, therefore, show respect for the "various traditions, values, faiths, beliefs, opinions and practices" of these potentially diverse readers;
>
> an ability to display the author's critical thinking about the short- and long-term effects of the ideas, information, and images posted and, therefore, to correctly credit "creators of intellectual properties," to seek permission from creators when appropriate, and to utilize "fair use" sites when possible;
>
> the means to address values of fairness and equality in the texts under consideration, in order to inform readers about relevant issues included in the texts; and
>
> an ability to discuss or provide information about the unequal distribution of wealth in natural-resource industries and cultural industries, such as tourism, the marketing of handicrafts, and other areas we might explore, and about the cultures and languages that the authors address, with a goal of educating the readers about specific expressions and traditions of cultures.

These goals encouraged the students to explore the new cultures they encountered, their own place in the global economy, and their responsibilities when writing about their discoveries through journaling. This process provided them with the space to explore their thoughts before their ideas became blog posts.

## Writing Pedagogy: Journaling to Learn and Blogging to Inform

As a pedagogical tool, journaling can support many different learning outcomes because it is reflective, asking students to engage personally with the course material. Charles Bazerman explains that journals often ask students to "[t]hink about the ideas and information of the course," "find what is relevant to [them]," relate the course to their own experiences, engage with "divergent viewpoints," and discuss aspects of the material they consider challenging or interesting. This course altered these usual expectations for journaling. Instead of only reflecting on their engagement with the texts, students recorded their acquisition of knowledge and wrote to teach themselves about the cultures (real and imagined) that they were encountering. This journal assignment was not prescriptive. Instead, it offered the students various suggestions of ways to engage with the texts and encouraged them to use visual-learning techniques, such as lists, drawings, and colored text. Notebooks were provided to each student, but one student quickly abandoned the notebook for a word processor. Another alternately used word processing and handwriting. An explicit goal of this assignment was to force the students to slow down their reading process as they paused to record their acquisition of knowledge, such as new and unfamiliar words, including the names of locations, tribes, and mythological figures. Students were encouraged to write down questions for class and to record connections between texts. Each student was assigned a theme to trace throughout the works, so the journals also became a place they documented their discoveries about it.

The journaling assignment encouraged students to use a method of active reading and recording that combines methods used in writing-to-learn (WTL) and writing-to-engage (WTE) activities. The pedagogical strategy of WTL emerged through the practice known as writing across the curriculum. In 1982, Toby Fulwiler and Art Young emphasized WTL as a way for readers to prepare themselves to write. For them, the writer's language provides "a unique way of knowing and becomes a tool for discovering, for shaping meaning, and for reaching understanding." As such, WTL produces "first-draft writing, necessary before more formal, finished writing can be done" (x). Yet WTL should not always be a step toward what the authors of *The Development of Writing Abilities (11–18)* call *transactional writing*, which informs, advises, persuades, or instructs others (Britton et al. 88). WTL "is learning to think, on paper, about what students already know and how that fits with new information" (Forsman 162), and as a result "better written products" are "a side benefit" of WTL (Gere 5).

Closely related to WTL, WTE fosters students' abilities to process newly learned information. If WTL enables students to remember, understand, and apply information, then WTE adds the skills of analyzing and evaluating ("What"). Grounded in active reading practices, WTE requires more time and effort than students are used to expending on assignments (Bean 161–66). Judith C. Roberts and Keith A. Roberts explain that throughout students' educational careers they have developed reading strategies that merely mine "factual information to regurgitate" (125). Contrasting these strategies is deep reading, which encourages students to perform higher order cognitive practices, such as "predict[ing] what will happen next, ask[ing] questions, and think[ing] about the use of language" (126). In the case of Genre Studies, deep reading helped the students not only trace themes across texts but also learn new vocabularies and syntaxes particular to speculative world building and postcolonial writing (Bean 163–66).

College students often know how to practice deep reading, but they may choose not to. David Perkins explains that classrooms operate within a cognitive economy of "gains and costs" (156). Students' largest "costs" are time and cognitive effort—the requirements of deep reading (157). John Tagg, building on Perkins's model, elucidates a clear cost-benefit strategy many students employ. As "rational agents," students weigh "their time and effort" against the benefit of a grade, trying to accomplish the highest possible grade while retaining most of their "available resources"; thus, "the highest value class is one that produces the highest grade for the least effort" (102).

Despite curricular efforts to indicate the value of deep reading, students in Genre Studies demonstrated Tagg's cost-benefit analysis. This course contained students who were heavily involved in extracurricular activities requiring them to dedicate their time to many areas of collegiate life. One student's first journal entry initially contained evidence of deep-reading practices (questions, predictions, lists, and doodles), but the student only sustained this level of engagement for a few classes. After that early journaling period, many entries were missing. The student explained that stopping to look things up took too long, so they opted to finish the reading rather than do the journaling. Other students demonstrated the same behavior at the end of the semester, dedicating their time to completing the readings instead of writing in their journals. Sometimes, just before journal checks, students would complete several entries by recycling class discussions instead of providing their own content. One student simply did not turn in the last set of journal entries, saying they were too busy to complete the assignment.

Although some students flagged in their journaling efforts during the semester, having several due dates generally helped them stay on track. Instructors should plan to check students' journaling progress frequently and offer timely feedback. Students will often be concerned that they may not be "doing it correctly," so timely check-ins combat their worries. Also, encouraging students to speak in class about what they have written proves to be a good conversation starter and demonstrates to the other students a variety of ways to engage with the texts. While missing and regurgitated journal entries should be heavily penalized, all sincere engagement with the material should be rewarded. Instructors should respect the personal and creative aspects of the handwritten journals. They may want to use sticky notes to add comments and suggestions. Instructors might want to set up a coded system in which small colored flags point out exemplary content related to course themes. All of these methods of feedback will encourage better student engagement.

The students' graded journals provided them with solid platforms from which they could compose transactional writing. The authors of *The Development of Writing Abilities (11–18)* explain that the transactional writing process is itself a "means to an end" with an ingrained purpose characterizing the writing's form and organization (Britton et al. 93). Transactional writers consider their audience's "relevant knowledge, experience, [and] interests" and provide appropriate context (94). When the audience is unknown, the writer demonstrates "a desire to conform to some cultural norm or trend" (128). The students in Genre Studies demonstrated these traits of transactional writing as they transformed their WTL and WTE journal entries into public blog posts for an indeterminate audience.

## Examples of Journaling to Learn and Blogging to Inform

Student 1's journal demonstrates the thought processes of a student who is writing to learn *and* engage. Their journal's guiding factor is the theme that they were assigned during the course—West African spider gods and Anansi folklore. They used sticky tabs in their journal notebook to divide their writing into separate themes. Their writing about one book or short story might appear under different tabs. For example, on a page near the beginning of the journal with the tab "Spider Tracker," they list websites about the spider gods and Anansi folklore. An envelope attached to the page is filled with printouts of articles and pictures that they found helpful or interesting. Their journal entries contain quotations they gathered from the class texts or independent research, their own drawings that represent concepts important to them, and their reflections and opinions. By amassing this multimodal collection, student 1 cultivated knowledge about this topic that enabled them to make spider and Anansi connections among almost all the texts the class read. They were constantly looking for commonalities between the knowledge they had sought on their own and the references to spiders and Anansi folklore in the texts. When it was time to start blogging, student 1 had such a deep connection to and understanding of the theme that they were more than prepared to engage with an audience through their writing.

The students' blogs are thoughtful and visually interesting and often exceeded our expectations in their explorations of petrocultures, otherness, and identity. Their most powerful blog posts call attention to Rob Nixon's "slow violence" by depicting the damage Big Oil does to individuals and cultures. They show how slow violence works through attrition and "occurs gradually and out of sight," as actions that most hegemonies would not define "as violence at all" (Nixon 2).

In their journal entry on "Spider the Artist" from *Kabu Kabu*, student 1 compiled their favorite quotations from the story and unwittingly created a found poem that we discussed later in class. This was the source for their blog post "Spider the Artist," which exemplified their process of WTL by demonstrating their understanding of the ways Big Oil affected the narrator, such as causing her infertility. Student 1 quotes the narrator, Eme, who says, "My life is shit" (108) and "Nigeria supplies 25% of U.S. oil and we get nothing in return" (105). These two quotations led student 1 to research the current state of the oil industry in Nigeria. By including photos and referring to news articles in their post, they illustrate the devastation that the oil industry has brought to the region.

In the blog post "Udide and Friends in Nnedi Okorafor's *Lagoon*," student 1 connects quotations that refer to cultural symbols and deities with photos that depict these symbols and deities in some way. The visual representations were meant to help readers understand aspects of Nigerian culture they might not have encountered. For example, student 1 was able to find photos of an Ijele Masquerade in Nigeria, which is an event that the narrator witnesses in *Lagoon*. Both of student 1's blog posts demonstrate how WTL and WTE led them to provide meaningful contexts for their readers. They used all the resources they collected during their journaling and condensed them into readable and visually appealing blog posts focusing on the petrospeculative genre. They found a way to intertwine the texts' depiction of Big Oil with their own understanding and present it in a way that encourages their readers' interpretation and engages their imagination. Student 1's work exemplifies what WTL and WTE should look like and how commonplace journaling provides a greater learning experience than the "reading to regurgitate" that Bean describes.

In their interaction with the blogs, students demonstrated their positions as global digital citizens and "address[ed] values of fairness and equality in the texts." Journal writing is both an opportunity for students to deepen their understanding of texts by comparing them to their own experiences and a vehicle for them to convey their realizations to others (Rose and Theilheimer 26–27). Student 2's post "The Real Poison in Henrietta Rose-Innes's 'Poison'" demonstrates this. The protagonist of "Poison" is a young woman who remains at an empty gas station after others have found means to escape. While she fantasizes that she is leading an outlaw lifestyle, she also believes that emergency personnel will soon arrive to rescue her. Student 2 compares the story's toxic chemical poison to what they believe is even more toxic to humans—social poison. For student 2 the protagonist shows "willful ignorance" of climate change and is an example of people's reluctance to accept responsibility or acknowledge important issues. In sharing their own knowledge about the politics of climate change, student 2 opened the conversation for other classmates to do the same in their responses. An English major tied the character's willful ignorance to white privilege. A biology major continued student 2's theme of climate change and discussed myths relating to the phenomenon. By exchanging ideas, students contributed new perspectives and reinforced the author's original position.

Student 3's blog post "Evolving over Time: Nature versus Industry" focuses on Big Oil's exploitation of nature, comparing survival of the fittest in the natural world with survival of the fittest in an industrialized world. In chapter 2 of *Lagoon*, a tarantula finds himself facing the daunting task of trying to cross a busy road. As he tries to safely navigate it, he tells a story of how he lost a leg in a fight with a wasp. Okorafor shows that the spider, despite having survived a run-in with one of his greatest predators, is no match for monstrous vehicles, which flatten him before he can reach the other side. Student 3 sets the tarantula's two challenges up as "nature vs. nature" and "nature vs. industry," interpreting the story as an allegory about how nature becomes less capable of survival as humans continue to exploit natural resources in ways that destroy the environment.

In a world untouched by human beings, the spider still faces challenges like wasps and other predators but is able to survive. However, in a petroculture, small insects and other creatures have no chance of survival against machines. Student 3 makes the point that however quickly nature tries to evolve to live in an industrialized environment, it will never be able to keep up. Student 3 depicts the spider's life as just one small outcome of the destructive chain of events set in motion by the Nigerian oil industry.

Okorafor's "Icon" forced the students to reevaluate what it means to be a spectator of another culture, particularly when that spectator is from a colonizing and exploitative culture. Two American journalists travel to the Niger Delta to observe a group that protests the oil industry through terrorist acts. The Americans quickly learn that they are trespassers in a culture that they know nothing about. Student 4, in class discussions and in their journal, used the term *hyphen porn* to refer to a glamorized portrayal of identities or actions created to validate the audience's perception of its place in the social hierarchy. In *hyphen porn*, the term before the hyphen signals the identity or action that evokes the interest and voyeurism in the spectator. Examples are *poverty-porn*, such as commercials that exploit images of people of low socioeconomic classes in order to evoke emotional responses in privileged viewers, and *war-porn*, which similarly portrays images of death, violence, and torture to elicit viewers' reactions. Student 4 chose to expand on this idea in their blog entry "'Icon': What Happens When You Stare into the Abyss?" by discussing American journalists who risk their lives to create war-porn by exploiting international conflicts. The post states, "Strangely, [journalists] often have the idea that their Western culture exceptionalism will protect them from harm. Sure, they know intellectually that it's dangerous, but they don't internalize it." Student 4's blog demonstrates a connection between economic imperialism and American ignorance by reflecting real conflicts that occur in the Nigerian oil industry.

One of the goals in this course was to get students to think about the motives of outsiders entering the African continent and the negative effects they can have on the physical environment and many cultures that exist there. WTL and WTE processes enabled these students to explore petrocultures from their initial positions of unfamiliarity. Therefore, their blogs demonstrate the outcomes of their knowledge acquisition and communicate to an audience the repercussions of oil companies, tourists, or even journalists who exploit natural resources and indigenous cultures for profit or status.

## Two Perspectives

### Teacher's Perspective

I invited Mary, an English major, to help me plan this class because she was considering graduate work in sustainability studies; thus, the focus on petrofiction fits her interests. As a former education major, she knew about journaling pedagogy and had herself completed a variety of journal and commonplace-book assignments in classes. She suggested affective journaling as a means to combine personal reflections with connections to the wider world. Drawing on Mary's experience, we built a journal assignment that required almost daily commitment but offered the students more agency by giving them the freedom to choose their subject matter and approach. My experience with Mary and the assignment helped me understand how students read and deal with unfamiliar information. In future classes, I want to foreground deep reading more deliberately and incorporate focused, low-stakes assignments promoting that skill.

### Student's Perspective

Collaborating with someone whom I view as a mentor was something that I approached eagerly but cautiously. My biggest concern was preparing to participate as a student and an observer, to learn while simultaneously documenting the class pedagogy. However, as we discussed the class, I realized that my perspective as a participant allowed me to help tailor the course to students' desires, and my professor allowed me to take control in areas where I had insight and experience. During this process, I realized that my voice and experience were not only powerful but valued. A professor's new idea for an assignment may not always be what works best for students, and throughout this collaborative project I was able to understand how multifaceted and valuable students' perspectives can be in developing interactive and effective assignments.

## Notes

1. As professor (Knight) and student (Laffidy), we collaborated in planning the assignment outlined here before the semester began. Our thanks to the course participants, Jennifer Heusel (auditor), Dawn Hicks, Matthew Hicks, Kiisha Hilliard, and Chelsea Larymore.

2. In retrospect, I wish I had also assigned Imre Szeman's "Energy, Climate and the Classroom: A Letter" as a secondary text that clearly outlines petrofiction's

background and the factors of climate change pedagogy (something I did through lecture).

## Works Cited

Agatucci, Cora. "Introducing African Novels in a Web-Enhanced Community College Survey Course." *Teaching the African Novel*, edited by Gaurav Desai, Modern Language Association of America, 2009, pp. 311–20.

Bazerman, Charles. *Involved: Writing for College, Writing for Your Self.* WAC Clearinghouse, 2015, wac.colostate.edu/books/practice/involved/.

Bean, John C. *Engaging Ideas: The Professor's Guide to Integrating Writing, Critical Thinking, and Active Learning in the Classroom.* 2nd ed., Jossey-Bass, 2011.

Britton, James, et al. *The Development of Writing Abilities (11–18).* Macmillan Education, 1975.

Caminero-Santangelo, Byron. "Witnessing the Nature of Violence: Resource Extraction and Political Ecologies in the Contemporary African Novel." *Global Ecologies and the Environmental Humanities: Postcolonial Approaches*, edited by Elizabeth DeLoughrey et al., Routledge, 2015, pp. 226–41.

Flammia, Madelyn. "WAC or WAG: Should Writing across the Curriculum (WAC) Be Expanded to Writing across the Globe (WAG)?" *College Composition and Communication*, vol. 66, no. 4, 2015, pp. 700–05.

Forsman, Syrene. "Writing to Learn Means Learning to Think." *Roots in the Sawdust: Writing to Learn across the Disciplines*, edited by Anne Ruggles Gere, National Council of Teachers of English, 1985, pp. 162–74.

Fulwiler, Toby, and Art Young. Introduction. *Language Connections: Writing and Reading across the Curriculum*, edited by Fulwiler and Young, National Council of Teachers of English, 1982, pp. ix–xiii.

Gere, Anne Ruggles. Introduction. *Roots in the Sawdust: Writing to Learn across the Disciplines*, edited by Gere, National Council of Teachers of English, 1985, pp. 1–8.

Ghosh, Amitav. "Petrofiction: The Oil Encounter and the Novel." *The New Republic*, 2 Mar. 1992, pp. 29–34.

*Global Digital Citizen: Teacher's Companion.* Wabisabi Learning, 2018.

Kapstein, Helen. "Crude Fictions: How New Nigerian Short Stories Sabotage Big Oil's Master Narrative." *Postcolonial Text*, vol. 11, no. 1, 2016, pp. 1–18.

Knight, Rhonda. "Course Texts." *Postcolonial Speculative Fiction*, 9 May 2019, scalar.usc.edu/works/postcolonial/course-texts?path=index.

Nixon, Rob. *Slow Violence and the Environmentalism of the Poor.* Harvard UP, 2011.

Okorafor, Nnedi. *Kabu Kabu.* Prime Books, 2013.

Perkins, David. *Smart Schools: Better Thinking and Learning for Every Child.* Free Press, 1995.

Roberts, Judith C., and Keith A. Roberts. "Deep Reading, Cost/Benefit, and the Construction of Meaning: Enhancing Reading Comprehension and Deep Learning in Sociology Courses." *Teaching Sociology*, vol. 36, 2008, pp. 125–40.

Rose, Lisa, and Rachel Theilheimer. "You Write What You Know: Writing, Learning, and Student Construction of Knowledge." *WAC Journal*, vol. 13, 2002, pp. 17–29.

Szeman, Imre. "Energy, Climate, and the Classroom: A Letter." *Teaching Climate Change in the Humanities*, edited by Stephen Siperstein et al., Routledge, 2017, pp. 46–52.

Tagg, John. *The Learning Paradigm College*. Anker Publishing, 2003.

Watts, Michael. "Petro-violence." *Fueling Culture: One Hundred and One Words for Energy and Environment*, edited by Imre Szeman et al., Fordham UP, 2017, pp. 255–58.

Wenzel, Jennifer. "Petro-Magic-Realism: Toward a Political Ecology of Nigerian Literature." *Postcolonial Studies*, vol. 9, no. 4, 2006, pp. 449–64.

"What Is Writing to Engage?" *WAC Clearinghouse*, wac.colostate.edu /resources/wac/intro/wte/.

**Sofia Ahlberg**

# The Colonial Relation between Digitization and Migration in Mohsin Hamid's *Exit West*

At the end of the spring 2019 semester, working in my office in the English department at Uppsala University, in Sweden, I could look through my window past freshly watered indoor plants to see students tending the gardens across the way. These seasonal activities brought a sense of calm, and the world's problems seemed remote. I was in the planning stages for my course in English literary studies in a program that hosts Swedish teacher-training students for part of their degree. Their required exposure to English literature in the education program for upper-secondary teachers in training offers them the chance to reach educational goals beyond language proficiency and reading and writing skills. But what might those teacherly goals be, I asked myself after a restless spring in which schoolchildren, in a movement started by the Swedish fifteen-year-old Greta Thunberg, had gone on strike every Friday to draw attention to what they saw as a worldwide generalized lack of action on the part of politicians in response to climate change. The strikes, although universities did not formally join them, jolted me into thinking more about how well we prepare our students for social upheaval associated with climate change. What tools do we give our vocational teachers to help them create or imagine a more equitable and sustainable future, tools that they can then impart to their pupils? In this essay, I examine the way literary narrative can make the connections between global processes easier to understand. My example is Mohsin Hamid's novel *Exit West*, which invites readers to comprehend the fraught and fluctuating relations between energy supplies, digital communication, population movements, and climate change. The novel's subject matter helps justify my inclusion of postcolonial ecofiction in an otherwise pretty canonical course for Swedish secondary school teachers that ranges from William Shakespeare's plays to Toni Morrison's *Song of Solomon*. I also reflect in this essay on the learning potential of the various activities I incorporate into the classes.

There are many texts that would support energy pedagogies similar to or consistent with what I propose here.[1] I chose to teach *Exit West* in the fall 2019 semester because of the book's relevance. Extreme weather conditions seemed ubiquitous in June 2019. Severe heat affected northern India and Pakistan, and deadly dust storms smothered New Delhi and Lahore, resulting in death and injury, poor air quality, and prolonged power outages. Europe also suffered a sweltering heat wave, and an unprecedented number of fires broke out there. Strong evidence suggests that these weather anomalies are caused by anthropogenic climate change (Rahmstorf and Coumou). Moreover, the Global South is likely to suffer disproportionately from climate change because this region is among the most heavily affected and does not have sufficient infrastructure for mitigating the damaging effects of extreme weather. The ecological effect of the continued use and extraction of fossil fuel anywhere is now obvious to many, though the burden of responsibility for the problem should be on populations in the Global North that most benefit from the kind of industries that cause the problem. A transition to renewable energy by means of fuel substitution and a significant reduction in energy usage is key to ameliorating global warming. Our computing practices are often overlooked as causes of high energy dependence and a consequent carbon footprint (Nardi et al.). According to Sean Cubitt, the "myth of immaterial media," which assumes that digital communication is largely independent of its material basis and therefore has little ecological effect, is due for revision (13). If the climate crisis is to be understood in the light of human institutions and practices, our relationship to information communication technology would seem particularly relevant.

## Mohsin Hamid's *Exit West*

*Exit West* is an excellent teaching text because it brings together a complex set of issues. The novel portrays the equitable distribution of energy resources as an issue of social justice, imagines the future viability of life on a shared planet, provokes reflections on border control and migration in a postcolonial context, and underlines technology's role in mediating our understanding of our world. *Exit West* invites students to consider the ecological footprint of their own uses of portable digital technology through the lens of neocolonialism. Typically, vocational teaching students are already comfortable working across contexts. It is second nature to them not only to focus on mastering the content of a given topic but also to consider practically how they would impart this content to their future students. These students see the future staging or performance of the knowledge they are acquiring as part of "a process that is inherently entangled with the material, the social, the political and the discursive" (Bayley 40). As natural "boundary crossers," these future teachers are familiar with "taking information from one place to the other, and raising questions in one context and discuss[ing] answers in the other" (Bakker and Akkerman 362).

Hamid's novel tells of two migrants, Saeed and Nadia, who depart from an unnamed Middle Eastern country and make their way first to the Greek island Mykonos, then to London, and lastly to Sausalito, California—with little to no travail. Intriguingly, and unlike actual migrants, they travel directly, inexplicably, and almost instantly, as though distance were nothing. Despite this magical element, the novel invites serious reflection on population displacement, especially in the light of the sharp rise in the rates of migration to Europe since 2015. *Exit West* argues that a significant cause of population displacement is unjust energy distribution and the exploitation of the Global South to sustain digital connectivity in the Global North. The novel encodes the movement of people as a trajectory for social change that aims to remedy such injustices. A teacher's task is to give students keys for decoding the social truths behind the fiction. In the novel, access to the web becomes a metonym for access to the West, and it is possible to teach *Exit West* as an allegory of Western anxieties about the breaching of immigration borders as though they were back doors in software.

How these back doors work is never explained—all we know is that refugees magically pass through doors in poor countries directly into places in the West with considerably higher energy consumption. By making my students conscious of resource production, distribution, and consumption, I aim to challenge the prevalent belief that digital products and services exist wirelessly, free of material conditions. At the same time, I want to make visible how the earth is being despoiled in a colonial pattern of exploitation. I wish to reveal that the vulnerability of human communities is to a large extent historically determined and that there is an ongoing exploitation of the Global South that benefits the North. My overall intent is to foreground consumer patterns that contribute to this exploitation of the Global South. In this essay I demonstrate ways of enhancing teaching and learning along the lines of a social construction approach to education in which "the notion of a learner gradually moving from peripheral to full participation implies a stronger emphasis on what kind of person a learner aims to be—not merely an emphasis on the knowledge they need to pick up" (Machanick 10). I am mindful of the twenty-first-century teaching and learning skills defined by Marilyn Binkley and her coauthors, which focus on living in the world and emphasize citizenship (local and global), life and career, personal and social responsibility, and cultural awareness and competence (18–19).

My Swedish teacher-training students are typically involved in their local communities and connected to global events through social media and sophisticated communication technologies. But they rarely reflect on the connection between what Hilary Janks calls Politics with a big *P*, which includes climate change, global markets, and so forth, and politics with a small *p*, meaning personal, local power relations (188). Hamid's novel teaches us that access to the Internet stands for all the affordances of the industrialized world as well as the largely automated security measures that ensure that those affordances are available only to a few. In the course, students learn that alternative fuel power presents opportunities not just for technological innovation but also for social reform that pursues energy transition and resists ongoing colonialism. Ultimately, I hope the course makes students more aware of the uneven distribution of energy and its affordances and encourages them to take more responsibility for their digital consumerism and its environmental effects.

## Learning Goals

Seeing a world on the brink of catastrophic climate change, students are now challenging their teachers to make literature relevant to their lives and futures. In addressing this concern, I emphasize the acute sensitivity of Hamid's novel to pressing global issues. In class, the aim is for discussions to be not merely critical but creative, forward-looking, and responsive to the entanglements and complexities of our world. Close readings focus on the discovery of a more complex set of images that model alternative forms of resource distribution. To enhance transformative learning practices, these classes in postcolonial ecofiction for vocational students focus on narrative as a means of imagining alternative futures. I emphasize narrative as a construction through which important meanings are generated and negotiated, policies are thought through and envisioned, and politics analyzed and possibly even practiced. Narrative becomes a means for giving students a coherent alternative to the world as it appears, what Cubitt calls "an exterior" to the often inward-looking and fragmented computational assemblages of our lives (62). The intended learning outcomes include the ability to identify narrative relations between the private and the public and between micro- and macropolitics; to discover new models for economic well-being and social justice based on acknowledging limits to economic growth; and to mobilize a range of pedagogical methods that demonstrate an appreciation of the purposes of teaching literature.

The study of literature I promote offers a social constructivist approach to learning in which readers are invited to see their interpretations of texts as part of the world and not external to it. Moreover, these worldviews can take on a fuller existence when shared with others. To reach the intended learning outcomes listed above, the teaching of literature must ask students to produce new knowledge rather than to consume knowledge as in a transmission model of learning. The learning activities I have in mind for this unit test *Gestaltungskompetenz*, or "design abilities." These activities teach "the skills, competencies and knowledge to change economic, ecological and social behaviour" with the view of making "an open future possible that can be actively shaped and in which various options exist" (Haan 320).

## Guiding Questions

The thirteen-week literature course in the teaching-training program is taught in classes of fifteen to twenty students. There are no formal lectures, only seminars in which we spend about forty percent of the time practicing close reading and the rest of the time meeting the objectives of the program specifically relevant to future teachers, such as literary didactics and pedagogy.[2] I teach *Exit West* during two of the thirteen weeks and introduce the students to the topic of energy humanities (Szeman and Boyer), without necessarily referring to it as such, by means of the following guiding questions:

> How do fictional characters register fears about energy, such as fears about pollution, securitization (the protection of privileges through defense measures and border control), and contamination?
>
> Is there a difference between how male and female characters view energy expenditure?
>
> How does the novel depict the way energy issues affect intimate relationships?
>
> How does the cost of energy affect the decisions that characters make?
>
> How are energy sources described in terms of their effects on families, communities, and minority groups?
>
> How does the novel represent the different means of accessing affordances in the Global North and the Global South?
>
> Does the writing aestheticize aspects of energy production? If so, how?
>
> What ethical choices about energy do the characters make?

These questions are intended to stimulate broader discussion on issues of social justice and energy in the novel. In *Exit West*, access to energy divides the rich from the poor, the Global North from the Global South. Although energy confers many benefits—including wealth, freedom, and progress—it often prevents access to these benefits for the population of the Global South. By creating magical portals into the West, Hamid troubles an assumed secure divide separating the Global South from the North. The learning potential is tremendous, since the novel combines topics that are often treated separately but actually need to be treated together. The novel clearly shows that the physicality of our experience is mediated by digital technology. It then considers, in a magical-realist way, what would happen if the energy used to protect many familiar benefits became scarce. This is one way to read the significance of the inexplicably open portals into the West—they register a sharp decrease in the resources available to securely close access to energy affordances to all but a privileged few. Thus, in Hamid's vision, there are surprising benefits to energy scarcity, since it reveals the weakness of systems that restrict access to energy. In the novel, divisions between the North and the South, and between the rich and the poor, collapse. The conclusion of the novel, which we read closely in class, bears out the novel's overall premise. It strongly suggests that if energy scarcity diminishes the strength of national borders, then a resulting energy transition will counter postcolonial injustice as well as bring ecological benefits.

## Learning Activities

I give students a couple of preliminary texts in order to invite them to reflect on the link between climate change and migration. The prereading texts I have selected come from a range of genres and give students a broad discursive model. The texts have been selected in a scaffolding sense to prompt students to rediscover and activate in their mental archives a set of images that they already possess. They include an opinion piece by Myles Allen, a professor of geosystem science and the leader of the Environmental Change Institute Climate Research Programme at the University of Oxford, who writes about why "geopolitical breakdown" as a consequence of "injustices of climate change" is of greater concern to him than rising temperatures as such. I ask students to read the poet Athena Farrokhzad's polemical open letter to Europe, in which Farrokhzad reflects on the recent treatment of refugees. When students begin reading *Exit West*, I invite them to raise their eyes from the plight of the refugees to consider their own online activities.

I also ask students to track their online activity while they are taking the course. First, they work out how much data they consume when scrolling on their phone and through downloads. Second, they try to work out the cost in carbon dioxide emissions of their activity. There are several websites out there that calculate how much your lifestyle contributes to carbon dioxide emissions, including *Kilo What?* and *Global Footprint Network*. Finally, students imagine which part of the world their finger actually affects as they click and drag on their devices. This question is key to bringing resource-extraction politics into view, as argued by Pramod K. Nayar, who notes, "We need to locate technological 'devices' and processes within ideologies, economic policies and politics" (205). During our seminars, we closely read selected passages from the novel as a group. I discuss key passages and themes below.

We start by examining social media and the uneven distribution of energy's affordances. At the beginning of chapter 3, the injustices of the distribution of the world's resources can no longer be kept hidden from those who do not benefit from energy affordances (Hamid 35–39). The digital world has made it impossible to keep secret the unfair distribution of wealth. This difference between East and West becomes all the more apparent as basic services cease to exist in Nadia and Saeed's country of origin. We also discuss the theme of dark versus light in London during the electricity blackout at the beginning of chapter 8 (141–43). London's population is segregated based on access to energy.

We move on to discuss the description of the makeshift refugee settlement in Marin County, California (191–92). Hamid lets us imagine a surprisingly comfortable postcarbon future as an alternative to the future imagined by growth-obsessed Silicon Valley. This passage offers an alternative set of relations between humans and objects with an attention to vulnerability and scarcity. In a postcarbon economy, it seems likely that infrastructure, as well as private and public institutions, would be repurposed with greater thought given to how systems block or enable intimacy (Wilson 248). More broadly, my reading of *Exit West* sees the novel reprising the critique of imperialism and militant nationalism. It achieves this by linking energy scarcity to an opening up of borders that in part keep colonized populations and people of the Global South at a distance. In Hamid's vision of the fledgling encampment, alternative energy sources are pooled by necessity. One might share with students AbdouMaliq Simone and Edgar Pieterse's notion that those with little access to resources and opportunities "prefigure, in their making something out of difficult conditions, what many urban futures may need to look like" (110). For example, do-it-yourself technology and the repurposing of technologies and resources might make it possible to adapt to new conditions of living.

Chapter 11 of *Exit West* contains a powerful description of a radically altered future (Hamid 215–16). In the conclusion of the novel, Hamid presents readers with a postenergy future that is religiously, ethnically, and sexually diverse. Yes, the apocalypse has arrived, yet it is not apocalyptic. Worth discussing with students is the power of narrative in determining the future. The future in the novel is narrated as cautiously triumphal, and the novel shifts its narrative perspective from what is lost to what is gained. Instead of signifying an end to all things, this apocalypse brings with it opportunities to unearth alternative forms of living and loving. *Exit West* ends with an affirmation that celebrates the collapse of gender, class, and cultural barriers. In its conclusion, we are all portrayed as migrants who embrace our humanity by yielding to the socioeconomic and environmental realities of our moment.

The reading of *Exit West* presents a set of provocations. One anticipated outcome of the discussion of *Exit West* is the realization that it is not possible to view the arrival of migrants in Europe in 2015 and 2016 as an unexpected and unwelcome arrival of strangers from elsewhere, since they in an important sense were already here. For all practical purposes, although Westerners have refused entry to offshore workers' bodies, the reliance on what Jason Moore calls "Cheap Natures," which includes labor power, to maintain affluent lifestyles means that the workers' labor as a form of natural resource is pervasively present in the West (10).

As an alternative to the current apocalyptic tenor of the climate change discourse, which proposes solving the problem of weather-induced migration by erecting bulwarks against it, the conclusion of Hamid's novel shows us that our survival must be based on solidarity and smart growth (Bullard). Collaboration between the Global North and the Global South is envisaged through real-life initiatives such as participatory cultures (Cammaerts), digital inclusion, and free software (Schoonmaker). Along the lines of Joanna Zylinska's feminist counterapocalypse, Hamid's conclusion emphasizes new intimate clusters and communities in lieu of competitive social configurations.

Narrative's role in making the world meaningful has never been more important. As Donna Haraway insists, "[W]e need to write stories and live lives for flourishing and for abundance, especially in the teeth of rampaging destruction" (136). Haraway sees stories as helping to generate what is "not yet but might be." The sophisticated reading practices that literary studies teaches provide a way to counter the claim made by some secondary and tertiary students that the insights offered by the humanities have no bearing on their reality and do not address the urgency of climate change.

To summarize, literary pedagogies aim to impart reading skills on which the communities and social relations of the future might be based. Careful and caring communication will always require negotiation between the distant and the near, whether that communication happens in person or on digital media. Students of *Exit West* will discover that loving relations as well as neighborly ones are inseparable from the energy economy. Hamid's novel introduces readers and students to some of the hidden costs of inequity and the unexpected benefits of fair and just global relations.

## Notes

1. For other postcolonial texts that in a classroom situation could facilitate discussions on energy pedagogies in relation to gender, the energy economics of community, and global trade politics, see El-Saadawi; Habila; Mujila; Okri; Pirzad; and Yamashita.

2. I distinguish the two firstly by seeing didactics as a field of research as well as a set of teaching principles or skills that exist to an extent independently of specific classroom situations. It is generally held that the teacher or researcher is at the center of didactics. The term *pedagogy* emphasizes the strategic deployment of didactic principles and skills in specific classroom situations so as to impart knowledge. Pedagogy has to take students and their contexts into account in order to effectively practice didactics.

## Works Cited

Allen, Myles. "Why Protesters Should be Wary of 'Twelve Years to Climate Breakdown' Rhetoric." *The Conversation*, 18 Apr. 2019, theconversation .com/why-protesters-should-be-wary-of-12-years-to-climate-breakdown -rhetoric-115489.

Bakker, Arthur, and Sanne Akkerman. "The Learning Potential of Boundary Crossing in the Vocational Curriculum." *Handbook on Vocational Education*, edited by Lorna Unwin and David Guile, Wiley, 2017, pp. 351–72.

Bayley, Annouchka. *Posthuman Pedagogies in Practice: Arts Based Approaches for Developing Participatory Futures*. Palgrave MacMillan, 2018.

Binkley, Marilyn, et al. "Defining Twenty-First-Century Skills." *Assessment and Teaching of Twenty-First-Century Skills*, edited by Patrick Griffin et al., Springer, 2012, pp. 17–66.

Bullard, Robert D. "Smart Growth Meets Environmental Justice." *Growing Smarter: Achievable Livable Communities, Environmental Justice, and Regional Equality*, edited by Bullard, MIT Press, 2007, pp. 23–50.

Cammaerts, Bart. "Disruptive Sharing in a Digital Age: Rejecting Neoliberalism?" *Continuum: Journal of Media and Cultural Studies*, vol. 25, no. 1, Feb. 2011, pp. 47–62.

Cubitt, Sean. *Finite Media: Environmental Implications of Digital Technologies*. Duke UP, 2017.

El-Saadawi, Nawal. *Love in the Kingdom of Oil*. Saaqi Books, 1992.

Farrokhzad, Athena. "Europe, Where Have You Misplaced Love? An Open Letter from a Poet." *Literary Hub*, 23 Aug. 2018, lithub.com/athena -farrokhzad-europe-where-have-you-misplaced-love/.

*Global Footprint Network: Advancing the Science of Sustainability*. www .footprintnetwork.org.

Haan, Gerhard de. "The Development of ESD-Related Competencies in Supportive Institutional Frameworks." *International Review of Education*, vol. 56, no. 2, 2010, pp. 315–28.

Habila, Helon. *Oil on Water*. Penguin Books, 2010.

Hamid, Mohsin. *Exit West*. Penguin Books, 2017.

Haraway, Donna J. *Staying with the Trouble: Making Kin in the Chthulucene.* Duke UP, 2016.

Janks, Hilary. *Literacy and Power.* Routledge, 2009.

*Kilo What?* KTH Royal Institute of Technology / Linnaeus U, kilowh.at.

Machanick, Philip. "A Social Construction Approach to Computer Science Education." *Computer Science Education*, vol. 17, no. 1, Mar. 2007, pp. 1–20.

Moore, Jason W. "Nature in the Limits to Capital (and Vice Versa)." *Radical Philosophy*, vol. 193, 2015, pp. 9–19.

Mujila, Fiston Mwanza. *Tram 83.* Translated by Roland Glasser, Deep Vellum, 2015.

Nardie, Bonnie, et al. "Computing within Limits." *Communications of the ACM*, vol. 61, no. 10, Oct. 2018, pp. 86–93.

Nayar, Pramod K. *Postcolonialism: A Guide for the Perplexed.* Continuum, 2010.

Okri, Ben. "What the Tapster Saw." *Stars of the New Curfew*, Random House, 1999, pp. 181–94.

Pirzad, Zoya. *Things We Left Unsaid.* OneWorld Publications, 2012.

Rahmstorf, Stefan, and Dim Coumou. "Increase of Extreme Events in a Warming World." *PNAS*, vol. 108, no. 44, 1 Nov. 2011, doi:10.1073/pnas.1101766108.

Schoonmaker, Sara. "Globalization from Below: Free Software and Alternatives to Neoliberalism." *Development and Change*, vol. 38, no. 6, Nov. 2007, pp. 999–1020.

Simone, AbdouMaliq, and Edgar Pieterse. *New Urban Worlds: Inhabiting Dissonant Times.* Polity Press, 2017.

Szeman, Imre, and Dominic Boyer, editors. *Energy Humanities.* Johns Hopkins UP, 2017.

Wilson, Ara. "The Infrastructure of Intimacy." *Signs: Journal of Women in Culture and Society*, vol. 41, no. 2, 2016, pp. 247–80.

Yamashita, Karen Tei. *Through the Arc of the Rainforest.* Coffee House Press, 1990.

Zylinska, Joanna. *The End of Man: A Feminist Counterapocalypse.* U of Minnesota P, 2018.

**Charly Verstraet**

# For a dEcolonization of the Caribbean: Edouard Duval-Carrié's *Imagined Landscapes*

The Caribbean embodies an image. While historically and culturally diverse, the region is often described using the "sea, sun, and sand" trope. Corporations such as cruise lines, hotel chains, and travel agencies depict the region as a paradise on social media and in their television commercials and cruise brochures. The visual representations of the Caribbean raise questions of environmental ethics, cultural agency, and global capitalism. In her acclaimed book *Consuming the Caribbean*, the sociologist Mimi Sheller investigates European and North American consumption of the Caribbean through products, landscapes, and bodies from the fifteenth to the early twenty-first century. Sheller considers how "Europeans moved through the Caribbean, introduced exotic species, removed seeds, fruits, and timber, and represented Caribbean plants and landscapes verbally and visually." The Caribbean landscape has been reshaped throughout its history to become a visual construction for "Northern Atlantic inhabitants' pleasure and use" (36). In their introduction to *Caribbean Literature and the Environment*, the literary critics Elizabeth M. DeLoughrey, Renée K. Gosson, and George B. Handley claim that "there is probably no other region in the world that has been more radically altered in terms of human and botanic migration, transplantation, and settlement than the

251

Caribbean" (1). The history of the Caribbean is thus a history of how humans have remodeled the region's landscape. In *An Eye for the Tropics*, the art historian Krista A. Thompson describes how British colonial administrators framed the Bahamas and Jamaica as tropical paradises through photographs in order to encourage tourism. Using her notion of "tropicalization," Thompson exposes how the "very particular concept of what a tropical Caribbean island should look like developed in the visual economies of tourism" (6). The global capitalist system creates a visual system that reinforces the capitalist narrative about the Caribbean.

The visual representations of the Caribbean embody the connection between imperialism and ecocriticism. Key questions about representations of the Caribbean include the following: What are the visual legacies of colonization in the contemporary Caribbean landscape? How has the model of colonization shifted in the global capitalist system? In what ways do contemporary writers and artists reclaim the space they were alienated from? How do they break with cultural imperialism and reinsert the landscape into the history of the Caribbean? Many artists, such as the Trinidadian artist Christopher Cozier, the English photographer David Bailey, the Trinidadian artist Irénée Shaw, and the Dominican artist Tony Capellán, have dismantled the tropical-paradise images of the Caribbean in their works. In this essay, I will explain how I teach the Haitian artist and sculptor Edouard Duval-Carrié's exhibit *Imagined Landscapes*. Duval-Carrié makes an interesting choice in depriving his paintings of vivid colors to renounce the exoticization of the Caribbean landscape. This artistic choice presents the landscape as a site of cultural formation and expression. As the Martinican poet Edouard Glissant writes, "Our landscape is its own monument: its meaning can only be traced on the underside. It is all history" (11). History is felt through the landscape in the Caribbean.

This essay reflects on the pedagogical methods, outcomes, and challenges of teaching works that contain representations of the Caribbean environment. It also discusses a weeklong unit in my French studies undergraduate survey course, Hi/stories of Camouflage, taught at Emory University, which focused on the politics of environmental representation in the French-speaking world. The class attracted students who were majoring or minoring in French studies and who were aiming to develop their fluency in French. It was centered on a specific theme—ecocamouflage—in French-speaking literature, film, and art. The intent of the course was to survey multiple French-speaking countries across centuries and artistic or literary forms, paying particular attention to the cultural and political messages embedded in images of the environment. The course proposed modules on film, art, and literature in French from the seventeenth to the twenty-first century. A few examples of texts studied were the French fabulist Jean de La Fontaine's fables, the French poet Arthur Rimbaud's "Le dormeur du val" (1870; "The Sleeper in the Valley"), and excerpts from Alain Mabanckou's *Mémoires de porc-épic* (2006; *Memoirs of a Porcupine*). The study of Duval-Carrié's exhibit was in a unit on the Caribbean that included extracts of Glissant's *Poetics of Relation* (1990) and Suzanne Césaire's "Le grand camouflage" (1945; "The Great Camouflage"). These works struggle against global representations of the Caribbean and resist producing generic portraits of the region.

Duval-Carrié's exhibit *Imagined Landscapes* aimed at revealing the social construction of the Caribbean environment from the colonial period to the present day. The exhibit featured eleven mural-sized paintings and two chandelier sculptures that revisit the imperialist and expansionist motifs of nineteenth-century paintings by American artists of the Hudson River School (HRS). The objective of my course was for students to identify the politicized representations of the Caribbean through its landscape and the resistance offered by a Caribbean immigrant artist (Duval-Carrié lives in Miami). The learning outcomes emphasize how neocolonialism controls spaces through narratives, whether those be linguistic or visual, and uncover what I call dEcolonization, or the act of dismantling a politicized and hegemonic representation of the landscape to relocate Caribbean spaces in the historical and cultural imaginary of the Caribbean itself. The term *dEcolonization* combines the prefix *eco-* and the term *decolonization* to indicate the resistance to an ecological colonization of a space—that is to say, an aesthetic consumption of the landscape by Western nations, corporations, and consumers. Through dEcolonization, artists and writers bypass external hegemonic narratives of the landscape to form new accounts of Caribbean history and culture.

## Visual Politics of the Caribbean

First displayed in 2014 at Pérez Art Museum Miami (PAMM), Duval-Carrié's *Imagined Landscapes* alludes to nineteenth-century paintings from the United States that defined the Caribbean space with lush tropical scenery. The representation of the Caribbean as an untouched land was closely tied to the political, economic, and ecological colonization of the region by the United States at the end of the nineteenth century. Art participated in the ecological colonization of the Caribbean by portraying an image of its landscape that helped establish control over the region and its people. This ecological colonization continues to exist; these very same depictions still affect the Caribbean today. The consumption of the landscape through stereotypical images is an essential part of the tourist resort system. Through his paintings, Duval-Carrié points out the politics of continuing to portray the Caribbean through its landscape. In addition to critiquing the neocolonial discourse embedded in the tropical paradise trope, the artist applies a modern aesthetic to the nineteenth-century paintings. *Imagined Landscapes* shifts the historical role of the landscape to present the history and culture of the Caribbean in a different light. The purpose of Duval-Carrié's exhibit is therefore twofold: it points out the violent dissimulation of imperialist motives through art and proposes to reveal the histories, and stories, that were silenced in the process of altering the Caribbean environment for economic and political purposes. *Imagined Landscapes* offers a compelling invitation for students to examine the relation between land and imperialism, culture and expansion, art and politics.

*Imagined Landscapes* was a response to paintings by HRS artists, who participated in a nineteenth-century artistic movement that produced romantic images of landscapes. Painters such as Martin Johnson Heade, Frederic Edwin Church, and Albert Bierstadt traveled to the Caribbean and other areas of Latin America to create large-scale paintings of landscapes praising the power of nature. To intensify the vastness of the land, HRS artists often omitted humans in their paintings. The artists also chose lighter colors to accentuate the reflection of the sky in the water. The idea was to create "an emotional and sensual engagement with the world" (Ostrander 104). However, the artists' romantic portrayal of the environment had a more pecuniary motive as well. In the nineteenth century, Heade, Church, and Bierstadt were commissioned by the United States government to create an image of an exotic and picturesque Caribbean. The purpose was to attract investors to the region to buy land and industrialize the area. Ostrander explains that the HRS painters' "engagement with the region was economically motivated and directly tied to the United States' economic interests" (104). The paintings were required to display an attractive landscape to entice investors to its profit potential, to define and sell the Caribbean. Art can be a tool of imperialism. An ecological colonization is about consuming the landscape artistically and enticing investors to do the same financially.

Although my students and I examined the HRS movement in depth, I will focus on the work we did on two paintings in particular. We closely examined Bierstadt's *The Landing of Columbus* and Duval-Carrié's *After Bierstadt—The Landing of Columbus*. Students were asked to outline the romantic characteristics of Bierstadt's rendition of Christopher Columbus's arrival on the island of Hispaniola and indicate how the painting enticed investors to come to the Caribbean. Students were asked to collaboratively consider the colors, the positioning of the landscape, and the behaviors of the invaders and natives. The analysis centered on a couple of key points. First, the colors are light and warm, complementing the friendly encounter displayed in the painting. The landscape plays its role in welcoming the invaders: the white beach, blue sea, rich environment, and palm trees with coconuts arching around the newcomers. Second, Columbus and his crew seem to celebrate their new acquisition with joyous screams, fists and flags up in the air. The "Indians" bow to the invaders, occupying a subordinate position vis-à-vis the foreigners. Students determined that the romantic vision of the painting was made possible by the subjection of the local population and the illustration of the beauty and virginity of the land.

Students then turned to Duval-Carrié's transformation of Bierstadt's work and paid particular attention to the gunboat and the rowboat, on which eight famous figures appear. Among them are Columbus, easily recognizable at the front of the boat, followed by Daffy Duck, Mickey Mouse, Marie Antoinette, Bugs Bunny, Mr. Potato Head, Batman, and Minnie Mouse. Looming behind is a menacing gunboat, reminiscent of "the USS Machias," which "dropped anchor in the harbor of Port-au-Prince" in December 1914, marking the beginning of a twenty-year-long occupation of Haiti by the United States (Dubois 204).[1] The juxtaposition articulates a sense of continuity of invasion from the past to the present, from a military colonization to cultural globalization. Duval-Carrié draws similarities between political and commercialized expansions, notably their power to impose global culture on domestic culture.

## Artistic Technique

This section of the class, which students later indicated was their favorite, focuses on two of Duval-Carrié's artistic choices in *Imagined Landscapes*: colors and glitter. These two complementary features reveal how the artist intended to show a Caribbean that tends to be silenced. Through the use of colors usually absent in the representation of the Caribbean and the glitter technique, Duval-Carrié reinscribes a history and culture proper to the region in the landscape. I argue that Duval-Carrié's paintings dEcolonize the Caribbean environment by pointing out the hegemonic, systematic, and politicized structural violence performed through the landscape and by forming ecological accounts linked to Caribbean history and culture. Aesthetically, the dEcolonization in Duval-Carrié's art materializes through the shift from a sunny day to a rainy night, from vivid to dark colors. Students were tasked with performing comparative analyses of the colors used in HRS paintings and those used in Duval-Carrié's paintings, responding to queries such as, What colors dominate in each painting? Are there colors that are more often associated with the Caribbean? Are there any colors missing?

In his foreword to the book *Prismatic Ecology*, the literary critic Lawrence Buell indicates how our imagination associates colors with concepts. He points out "the speciousness of reducing 'ecology' or 'ecocriticism' to 'green'" (ix). The essays in that book imagine other colors that form the ecological world. In the same vein, the Caribbean has always been associated with vivid colors. In the touristic imaginary, a rainbow of colors emerges: the turquoise blue water; the white, sandy beach; the brown trunks of coconut trees; their yellowish-green leaves; the blue sky; the white clouds; and the vegetation, green as far as the eye can see. This multicolored portrait depicts a warm, welcoming, and paradisiacal place attractive to foreigners.

In *Imagined Landscapes*, Duval-Carrié reacts to the colors that defined the Caribbean in HRS paintings. The Haitian artist privileges black, gray, and purple. Through this choice, Duval-Carrié shows how darker colors, more than just representing the Caribbean, *indeed are the Caribbean*. Students examined short excerpts of Duval-Carrié's interview with Tobias Ostrander, the chief curator at PAMM ("'Imagined Landscapes'"). The interview gave insight on Duval-Carrié's provocative use of colors as a way to reclaim the representation of the Caribbean space. Duval-Carrié provides details about his thorough understanding of Haitian and Caribbean history, which can be seen in his paintings. The artist also questions the geographic notion of the Caribbean and its limits and borders, linking Miami to the Caribbean space. If my class had been limited by language, I would, however, have suggested that anglophone readers consult Ostrander's essay "Tropical Values," which situates Duval-Carrié's artistic reaction vis-à-vis the romantic depictions of the Caribbean by the HRS painters, as well as the other essays in the book *From Revolution in the Tropics to Imagined Landscapes: The Art of Edouard Duval-Carrié*.

Students were asked to compare and contrast the colors in the paintings of the HRS artists and those of Duval-Carrié. They were also asked to focus on the stereotypical images (sea, sun, sand) that were transformed in the Haitian artist's works. From these guided instructions, students drew three conclusions about the colors Duval-Carrié uses in his paintings. The first was about the color black, which students described as symbolizing the bodies and narratives that are repeatedly erased in recounting the history of the Caribbean. The second emphasized the color purple, which Duval-Carrié discussed in his interview with Ostrander at PAMM. The artist states that his choice of purple was drawn from the vodou religion, in which purple represents spirits and death ("'Imagined Landscapes'" 00:35:07). The appearance of purple gives a sort of spectral effect to the paintings, which, though they do not clearly portray a human shape, display an abstract presence nonetheless. Duval-Carrié, through the color purple, transmits a mysterious aspect to his paintings, where the dead appear among the trees and are commemorated by the living, and where spirits are inscribed into the environment.

The third conclusion, and perhaps the most interesting, centered on the color gray, a result of the material the artist used and his glitter technique. Duval-Carrié uses aluminum sheets, which he spray-paints black and royal blue. He then draws over the sheets with silver glitter glue and seals them with clear resin. The glitter stands out in his work because it is in direct contrast to the black background of his paintings.[2] In the painting, glitter provides a bright, shimmering, reflective light. The students concluded that glitter has two effects in Duval-Carrié's exhibit. First, the glistening image portrays rain. Duval-Carrié proposes a rupture with the usual depiction of Caribbean weather. When the sun is replaced with rain, the transformed landscape acts as a refusal of the exoticization of the Caribbean and reaffirms a less idealized picture of the region. Second, glitter produces a reflection of the spectators looking at the canvas. The painter introduces a white and Western audience to its own gaze, the detrimental eye of the tourist that frames the Caribbean with the beach trope. Glitter therefore positions Western viewers in front of their damaging discourse. Through his choice of colors and techniques, Duval-Carrié gives voice and visibility to subjects that are dismissed in neocolonial artistic representations, tropes, and narratives, confronting a Western audience with its own actions.

After examining colors and glitter in Duval-Carrié's paintings, many students expressed a sense of guilt and responsibility. They remarked on their unconscious contribution to promoting the stereotypical images of the Caribbean and their lack of critical thinking to challenge these assumptions. In offering different images of the Caribbean through colors and glitter, Duval-Carrié does not deny the tourist representation of the Caribbean but resists its systematization in global discourses. Adrienne Cassel states "there is room for critical thinking . . . without the shaming that is often associated with asking students to engage in an ecological assessment of any aspect of their lives" (29). Teachers of postcolonial ecocriticism must tackle the importance of empowering students to change their values. The dEcolonization of the Caribbean revolves around questioning our very own visual assumptions of the region's landscape, a step I incorporate into my pedagogical approach to Duval-Carrié's painting and describe in the next section of this essay.

## Pedagogical Approaches to the Caribbean Landscape

Earlier in this essay, I mentioned that the glitter technique reflects the audience in Duval-Carrié's paintings. The artist creates a deeper level of interaction between the viewer and the painting, which I also tried to bring into the classroom. My motive was to see how Duval-Carrié's paintings reflected the students. The activity I proposed had two objectives: to acknowledge the visual systemization of the Caribbean in a North American setting and to measure how course materials allowed students to move beyond the standard imaginary of the Caribbean. The exercise consisted of preclass and postclass drawings. The instructions were fairly simple: "Draw me the Caribbean." The preclass drawing offered the results expected. In every drawing, the sand, sun, and sea were prominent. Most students added a palm tree with a few coconuts at its top. Every drawing but one was empty of people. The only student who drew a beach with people had them lying on towels, wearing sunglasses. One student depicted a visit to a luxurious resort hotel in Punta Cana, in the Dominican Republic. This activity can be expanded at different levels, for example by asking students to add colors to their drawings or to include words that define the Caribbean. I encouraged my students to do a *Google* search of the Caribbean on their laptops in the evening and send me screenshots of their findings. These exercises offer a point of entry into the global capitalist representation of the Caribbean environment.

The postclass drawing followed the same instructions as the preclass drawing but ended with very different results. One student drew an island with the French flag on it to symbolize the neocolonization of our images of the region. Another student, inspired by Duval-Carrié, colored his piece of paper all black, underlining the invisibility of the Caribbean. One student portrayed a volcano that turned the sand of the beach black. One other student illustrated a hurricane hitting the shore. The different representations of the Caribbean exposed not only Duval-Carrié's influence on the students' drawings but also, and more important, the need to detach from a standardized portrait of the region. Neocolonialism in the tourism industry in the Caribbean is about the literal control of spaces through narratives and tropes, whether those are linguistic or visual. Duval-Carrié, among other writers and artists, reinvents the Caribbean space in an attempt to create alternative narratives and tropes. Assessing my students' postclass drawings was an exciting part of my teaching, because it showed the positive effects of sharing my current research in a classroom setting. The students' illustrations were evidence that students had gained knowledge and critical-thinking skills from the study of the artist's work. My course evaluations also provided encouraging feedback about teaching Duval-Carrié's exhibit.

Another pedagogical approach involves the study of cruise ads, *Instagram* images, *Google* searches, and works by other artists. Online visual content is a great resource to teach the representations of the Caribbean landscape for two reasons. First, the proliferation of social media in recent decades has transcended geographic borders and experiences. Most of my students had never been to the Caribbean, except for Miami, but felt they had experienced the region through social networking (friends, family, or other people they follow online). Second, digital public images can become the basis of an engaging discussion on the importance of global representations on the Internet. Students were able to tackle the notion of responsibility and power by examining images associated with the Caribbean landscape. Other visual works for discussing global images of the Caribbean landscape include the Mexican multimedia artist Alejandro Duran's *Washed Up* series. One could also teach works by the Barbadian multimedia artist Annalee Davis, the Haitian American photographer Carl Juste, Haitian artists such as Wilson Bigaud and André Pierre, the Dominican painter Hulda Guzmán, the Cuban artist Wilfredo Lam, and the Cuban sculptor Jenny Feal. Projects by the Martinican sculptor and painter Laurent Valère, Victor Anicet, Patricia Donatien-Yssa, and the Guyanese British artist Jason deCaires Taylor, among others, would also work.

If the course focuses on literature, the pre- and postclass assessments about the Caribbean landscape discussed above might be transformed linguistically. Students can be asked to write down three words describing the Caribbean. If repetition of words or a certain pattern arises among students, instructors might ask students to compare those words to the literary works examined in class. Examples of literary works dealing with the environment in the francophone Caribbean that one might draw on are Aimé Césaire's *Cahier d'un retour au pays natal* (1939; *Journal of a Homecoming*), Suzanne Césaire's *The Great Camouflage* (1945), Patrick Chamoiseau's *Texaco* (1992) or *Les neufs consciences du malfini* (2009; *The Nine Consciences of the Frigatebird*), Maryse Condé's *Traversée de la mangrove* (1989; *Crossing the Mangrove*), Gisèle Pineau's *L'exil selon Julia* (1997; *Exile: According to Julia*), Jacques Roumain's *Gouverneurs de la rosée* (1944; *Masters of the Dew*), Edwidge Danticat's short story collection *Krik? Krak!* (1996) or her novel *Claire of the Sea Light* (2013), Yannick Lahens's *Failles* (2010; *Cracks*) or *Bain de lune* (2014; *Moonbath*), and anything from Glissant's oeuvre. These texts introduce themes of environmental justice, deforestation, urbanization, ecofeminism, ecological vulnerability, ecoculture, and ecohistory, and they depict ecosystems and phenomena such as Creole gardens, trees, seascapes, shorelines, hurricanes, and earthquakes.

To complement primary texts on the francophone Caribbean environment, instructors may find it useful to assign secondary materials such as DeLoughrey, Gosson, and Handley's *Caribbean Literature and the Environment*, particularly the essays by Jana Evans Braziel ("'Caribbean Genesis': Language, Gardens, Worlds") and Eric Prieto ("The Use of Landscape: Ecocriticism and Martinican Cultural Theory"). Other possibilities include DeLoughrey and Handley's *Postcolonial Ecologies: Literatures of the Environment*, which includes contributions on Haiti. The literary critics Valérie Loichot and Carrie Noland each address the limitations of language for alluding to the Caribbean environment and draw upon Glissant, who finds a way to overcome the insufficiency of the word *environment* in the Creole language. Loichot and Noland highlight Glissant's use of the Creole word *antou* (literally, "surroundings"), adapted into French as *entour*, to discuss the Caribbean landscape. Glissant rejects words such as *environment*, *nature*, and *ecology* and uses *entour* instead for two reasons. First, adapting a Creole word allows for a geographic reimagining of the landscape in the Caribbean, in opposition to images evoked by a term like *beach*, which alienates Caribbean residents from their own islands. For Glissant, landscape and history exist on a continuum. Noland states that Glissant "is mobilizing an unremarkable, symbolically neutral word (as opposed to 'paysage,' 'nature,' or 'environment') and charging it with a new meaning and function within the economy of his own text" (163). The word *antou* abolishes the division between the human and nonhuman worlds. The history of the Caribbean has been marked by the separation between the land and its people, first with the crossing of the Middle Passage, then with the brutal plantation system, but Glissant connects the imaginary of humans to the land in the Caribbean through the word *entour*. The dEcolonization of the Caribbean landscape must involve changing the visual representations of the region, but it starts with language.

## Notes

This essay is indebted in many ways to Valérie Loichot, Cajetan Iheka, and Nathan Dize for their support throughout the writing process.

1. In his interview with Tobias Ostrander at PAMM, Duval-Carrié relates stories of fear that circulate around gunboats, which symbolize foreign invasion and the disappearance of self-governance, on his native island of Haiti: "if there is a rumor of political instability in Haiti, [people say that] a gunboat would be standing right outside the port" ("'Imagined Landscapes'" 00:24:08).

2. Duval-Carrié has said that he would have used sugar instead of glitter if it had been possible: "I just wanted to sugarcoat the whole thing! Had I been able to do it with sugar, I would have made it with sugar" (qtd. in Turner).

## Works Cited

Bierstadt, Albert. *The Landing of Columbus*. 1893. *Albert Bierstadt: The Complete Works*, albertbierstadt.org/The-Landing-Of-Columbus.html.

Braziel, Jana Evans. "'Caribbean Genesis': Language, Gardens, Worlds." DeLoughrey et al., *Caribbean Literature*, pp. 110–26.

Buell, Lawrence. Foreword. *Prismatic Ecology: Ecotheory beyond Green*, edited by Jeffrey Jerome Cohen, U of Minnesota P, 2013, pp. ix–xii.

Cassel, Adrienne. "Walking in the Weathered World." *Teaching Ecocriticism and Green Cultural Studies*, edited by Greg Garrard, Palgrave Macmillan, 2012, pp. 27–36.

DeLoughrey, Elizabeth M., and George B. Handley, editors. *Postcolonial Ecologies: Literatures of the Environment*. Oxford UP, 2011.

DeLoughrey, Elizabeth M., et al. *Caribbean Literature and the Environment: Between Nature and Culture*, U of Virginia P, 2005.

———. Introduction. DeLoughrey et al., *Caribbean Literature*, pp. 1–30.

Dubois, Laurent. *Haiti: The Aftershocks of History*. Picador, 2012.

Duval-Carrié, Edouard. *After Bierstadt—The Landing of Columbus*. 2013. Pérez Art Museum Miami, 2014, pamm.org/exhibitions/edouard-duval-carrié-imagined-landscapes.

———. *Imagined Landscapes*. 13 Mar.–31 Aug. 2014, Pérez Art Museum Miami.

Glissant, Edouard. *Caribbean Discourse: Selected Essays*. Translated by J. Michael Dash, U of Virginia P, 1989.

"'Imagined Landscapes' with Edouard Duval-Carrié and Tobias Ostrander." *YouTube*, uploaded by Pérez Art Museum Miami, 30 Apr. 2014, www.youtube.com/watch?v=2kZQ-kDZEfw.

Loichot, Valérie, editor. *Entours d'Edouard Glissant. Revue des sciences humaines*, vol. 309, no. 1, Jan.–Mar. 2013.

Noland, Carrie. "Edouard Glissant: A Poetics of the Entour." *Poetry after Cultural Studies*, edited by Heidi R. Bean and Mike Chasar, U of Iowa P, 2011, pp. 143–72

Ostrander, Tobias. "Tropical Values: The Imagined Landscapes of Edouard Duval-Carrié." *From Revolution in the Tropics to Imagined Landscapes: The Art of Edouard Duval-Carrié*, edited by Anthony Bogues, Pérez Art Museum Miami, 2014, pp. 100–07.

Prieto, Eric. "The Use of Landscape: Ecocriticism and Martinican Cultural Theory." DeLoughrey et al., *Caribbean Literature*, pp. 236–46.

Sheller, Mimi. *Consuming the Caribbean: From Arawaks to Zombies*. Routledge, 2003.

Thompson, Krista A. *An Eye for the Tropics: Tourism, Photography, and Framing the Caribbean Picturesque*. Duke UP, 2007.

Turner, Elisa. "Art Review: Glitter Flirts in 'Edouard Duval-Carrié: Imagined Landscapes.'" *Hamptons Art Hub*, 15 July 2014, hamptonsarthub.com/2014/07/15/art-review-glitter-flirts-in-edouard-duval-carrie-imagined-landscapes/.

**Juan Meneses**

# The Visuality of Environmental Disasters

One of the main challenges in conveying to students the impact and scope of an environmental disaster lies in finding ways for them to visualize it fully. Visualization literally means registering specific events through one's eyes. Looking at images (from film to photography, from realistic renditions to creative interpretations) allows students to familiarize themselves with a disaster's attributes as well as its spatial and temporal contexts. The sheer number and ready availability of images make it easy to incorporate this process into one's teaching practice, at least when it comes to modern disasters. Yet visualization also involves comprehending such disasters using the mind's eye. Given that it depends on students' ability to work at a more abstract level, forming a mental image of a disaster can be more difficult. Analysis at this level, most often a language-based form of interpretation, allows students to fill gaps that may appear regarding matters such as agency, historicity, socioeconomic relations, and racism that some images do not reveal at first glance, especially when they are not properly contextualized. This essay posits that teaching these two ways of seeing disasters can help students develop a set of ecological "multiliteracies"— an ability to decipher the meaning of an array of environmental issues across various media and representational modes (New London Group 63–67).

While they are sensorially and intellectually distinct, the components of this "dual" approach that incorporates linguistic and visual images (Sadoski and Paivio) have a positive impact on the cultivation of students' interpretive skills. In particular, this approach engages their imaginations by facilitating a more comprehensive understanding of environmental disasters. This is especially useful when one is dealing with postcolonial materials in the West, as I do in my teaching, because it reveals the position from which students learn about such disasters. Indeed, I have found it extremely productive to start by urging students, following Peggy McIntosh, to "understand that their ideas and experiences, material circumstances and life quandaries are illuminated by understanding the privilege systems that have been working in and around them" (xiv). Only then will the complexities of a privilege that is neither obvious nor absolute begin to become apparent to them. This first step is crucial to establishing, as Greg Garrard has put it, "methodologies suited to new developments in ecocritical theory, questioning learners' perceptions, meaning systems and discursive locations" (242). Thus, while it may be hard for certain students to connect with texts from postcolonial and Global South contexts, they tend to respond positively once they begin by reflecting on their own position in the world.

I teach at a large urban campus and I have students from a variety of backgrounds. One thing many of them have in common, however, is that, apart from enrolling in full course loads and fulfilling extracurricular educational roles, they assume a number of added responsibilities. Because they often do not come from wealthy, or even "comfortable," backgrounds, a large number of my students, like many across the United States, must balance their education with those other life commitments, such as financially supporting their families or taking care of dependents. Students experiencing such economic and personal challenges, and standing at a historical and geographic distance that separates them from the kinds of experiences that the literature I teach illuminates, may not readily see their position as privileged. Therefore, the method I describe here has been helpful in bridging that distance in graduate courses such as Postcolonial Literature, Contemporary Literature and the Environment: Fictions of the Anthropocene, and Contemporary Global Fiction, which I teach at the master's level but are open to a small number of undergraduate seniors. In these courses, I include texts by Ngũgĩ wa Thiong'o, Jean Rhys, Amitav Ghosh, and J. M.

Coetzee, among others, as well as films ranging from postcolonial classics by Ousmane Sembène to documentaries such as *Chasing Ice*. Yet I do not simply assign literature and visual material separately. Instead, I try to cultivate this dual literacy when my students and I tackle the representation of environmental disasters, drawing on the critical language traditionally associated with one medium to analyze the other. Perhaps predictably, it has been in my experience easier to teach narrative and textual issues occurring in visual media; what students find more intriguing and unexpectedly rewarding is an exploration of visual matters in literary texts.

Indra Sinha's *Animal's People* is a novel that can easily be taught in this dual manner.[1] Whereas I also point to its countless literary merits, in the classroom I primarily explore the ways in which *Animal's People* combats the idea that literary and visual images are radically different. On the surface, of course, they engage us in their own distinct ways. Yet, as W. J. T. Mitchell has argued, there is a continuity between them that stems from the ways we decipher their meaning:

> Ordinary, not philosophical, language leads us to think of images as a family of immaterial symbolic forms, ranging from well-defined geometrical shapes to shapeless masses or spaces, to recognizable figures and likenesses, to repeatable characters such as pictograms and alphabetic letters. Images are also, in common parlance, mental things, residing in the psychological media of dreams, memory, and fantasy; or they are linguistic expressions ("verbal images") that name concrete objects that may or may not be metaphoric or allegorical. They are, finally (and most abstractly), "likenesses" or "analogies" that invite more or less systematic correlations of resemblance in a variety of media and sensory channels. (84–85)

As a fictionalized account of the 1984 gas leak that took place in the city of Bhopal, India, *Animal's People* reveals this continuity by allowing its readers to visualize more than the environmental disaster at its center. While it is written as a direct address aimed at a Western audience by a victim of the gas leak, the novel works on a larger scale too. It facilitates the visualization of the Anthropocene in a way that, instead of reducing it to its most visible manifestation, climate change,[2] opens it up "to discussion, so as to enable closer reflection on the particularities of our representations of the world" (Bonneuil and Fressoz 48).

In teaching *Animal's People*, then, I pursue a double instructional goal regarding both content and theory. On the one hand, I can show students the realities of a well-documented disaster and its ongoing impact as well as its place within the larger narrative of the Anthropocene. On the other, I can teach them to practice an alternative form of literary analysis, one that incorporates visual theory and enables them to think of the visibility of this and other disasters in the Global South. In the age of ultimate exposure, as Jonathan Crary would put it, this allows me to urge students to reflect on the way that many disasters are not absolutely, neutrally, or easily visible, especially as they are perceived in the Global North. Instead, as the Bhopal disaster itself has proven, the visibility of such ecological events in the West is subordinated to the interest they can garner among audiences; they are visible only in the selected ways in which they appear to us halfway around the world; they run the risk of becoming normalized; and they are, in turn, threatened by competing shocking visual images as well as the unavoidable effects of the passage of time.

In preparing to teach *Animal's People*, I do not provide students with any specific directions on how to read the novel because my intention is to build a bridge between reading texts in the traditional sense (which they are already good at) and the kind of visual analysis that is crucial for students to learn. As Anahit Falihi and Linda Wason-Ellam suggest, "The power of text and image in today's communications media is undeniable, and a lack of critical evaluation has made it possible for capital corporations to promote a consumer culture by manipulating the content of transmissions. This gives visual literacy an ever-increasing importance" (412). To get students ready for class discussion, I assign a set of secondary texts that depends on the number of class periods devoted to the novel. A good companion piece is, of course, Rob Nixon's introduction to *Slow Violence*, which explores the invisibility of certain forms of environmental suffering in the Global South.[3] Another text that helps prepare students to discuss these visual dimensions is the introduction to T. J. Demos's *Decolonizing Nature*. Finally, Roland Barthes's "The Great Family of Man," which places visual-literacy skills at its center through a discussion of an art exhibition, offers a useful starting point for an analysis of the impossibility of considering all human life as universal or monolithic.

I teach *Animal's People* in four stages. First, I briefly introduce the notions pertaining to visual theory that we will use in our later discussion. This can be rather daunting, because many students are not very well versed in the discipline of visual studies. Instead of providing a general overview, however, I try to zero in on the kinds of reflections on visuality that the novel offers textually: what things and people are seen, what medium or channel they are seen through, who sees them, and what relationship is formed as those three elements are connected to one another. Introducing the notion of what Ariella Azoulay calls "the civil contract of photography" has been very helpful, because it convincingly explains the political tensions underlying a photograph. Azoulay defines this civil contract as a relationship among a number of participants—active and passive—by means of a specific technology of capture, which can then be easily extrapolated to other visual relations. In this short lecture, I also incorporate a few short excerpts from Susan Sontag's *Regarding the Pain of Others* and a few passages from Nicholas Mirzoeff's *The Right to Look* to complement this problematization of the ways in which images are produced, disseminated, and consumed.

In the second stage I provide key data to contextualize quickly the human impact of the Bhopal gas leak in a way that students can easily assimilate it. I do this with the help of a handout that includes information about the number of casualties (between 15,000 and 30,000 people killed, 1,700 to 10,000 of them instantly) and the number of people (over 500,000) affected by long-term and hereditary illnesses and disabilities, such as cancer and birth defects ("Basic Facts"). Introducing the incident presents the first major difficulty for students. As a general rule, students tend to know nothing about Bhopal, and they need substantial background information about the dimensions of the disaster. To help them put this information in perspective, I provide comparable data they are more familiar with, such as the number of students attending our university and the population of our and other major cities, so they can more fully imagine the disaster and its impact. Following this contextualization, I show images of Bhopal and the disaster, and I explore the political ramifications of looking at them. In order to encourage students to see the city in a three-dimensional and complex way, I begin by showing pictures of contemporary Bhopal that purposely exclude imagery related to the catastrophe. Despite their obvious representational limitations, the state of Madhya Pradesh's Department of Tourism's official website (www.mptourism .com) as well as the websites of international travel companies help students consider the city as more than the site of the gas leak, as does its *Wikipedia* page ("Bhopal"). After students have become familiar with Bhopal's geography, architecture, climate, and general environmental characteristics, I show them images of the disaster itself and invite them to discuss why they find some of these images shocking. Getty Images' site—which allows users to search specific terms and contains images captured both immediately after the explosion and many years later under the category "Bhopal"—and the photographer Raghu Rai's Magnum collection are good sources (Rai). In presenting the images in this sequence, I encourage students to examine Bhopal's visual representation in a way that directly confronts the environmental violence caused by the gas leak without reducing the city to a spectacularized disaster site or casting its inhabitants as faceless victims in a distant, underdeveloped land.[4]

I devote the third part to a close reading of several passages from the novel. My goal in this portion is to get students to participate actively in the narrative moment that Sinha creates. To do so, I ask them to articulate how the novel involves them in the relationship that emerges between Animal (the narrator) and the imaginary audience to whom he addresses his account, Eyes. This encourages them to contemplate the power of literature to have an impact on the "real world," and I reinforce their sense of this power by reminding them of the main events that are fictionalized in the novel. Reflecting on how the novel asks them to identify themselves as part of the narrative also helps students explore the visuality of the disaster in Bhopal, represented in the novel by the city of Khaufpur. Students often ponder the parallels between the images I have shown them and Animal's reflections on the ways the gas leak has been depicted across the world. To explore this, I select for close reading a number of excerpts that feature the many modes of visuality deployed in the novel, from the spectacularization of ecological disasters—against which the novel works—to the visual dimensions of what Animal calls "jamisponding" (a term derived from the fictional secret agent James Bond's name that he uses to describe his work spying for an activist group) to the manner in which Elli, an American doctor who sets up a free clinic, first struggles to be recognized as an ally by Khaufpur's inhabitants and later disguises herself to play a key role in interrupting the secret meeting between the lawyers for the company responsible for the disaster and representatives of the local government. During this portion, I also encourage discussion of other major themes and topics that are crucial to the novel, such as Animal's ontological self-examination—which can be placed in relation to ideas of animality, posthumanism, and human dignity—and the novel's reflections on certain representations of poverty in the Global South.

Finally, I devote the fourth stage to assessing the novel in terms of what David Orr calls "ecological design"—that is, "the careful meshing of human purposes with the larger patterns and flows of the natural world, and the careful study of those patterns and flows to inform human purposes" (19). Thus, I invite students to take some time during class to think on their own about a few or all of the following questions: In what ways does Animal challenge our notions of what is to be a human being and what is to be an animal? How is the continuum between those two onto-logical categories visualized in the novel? How does the novel critique the kinds of images of the poorer parts of the Global South that we consume in the Global North? This is followed by a short period in which the whole group reconvenes, and students address these and other questions that may have arisen from my initial prompt.

This four-step structure allows me to discuss the novel's main stakes while exploring how it interrogates the visibility and visuality of the Bho-pal gas leak and, by extension, ecological disasters at large. Focusing on the continuities between image and text provides a helpful platform to study the novel and its textual intricacies. I have, however, encountered some difficulties in implementing this approach. As I have mentioned, one of the main challenges is to introduce clearly and effectively certain aspects related to visual theory, and to put them in practice in service of a literary analysis of the novel. Students tend to separate the strictly visual material we handle in preparation for class discussion from the textual critique of visuality that the novel proposes. They also struggle initially to translate ideas from one representational modality to another. I employ two differ-ent but related strategies to deal with these challenges. One is working with key terms and keeping them present on the classroom's blackboard so that they are readily available; the other entails presenting a step-by-step ar-ticulation of the ways in which the language of visuality is useful not only as a metaphoric tool (e.g., when we talk about literary images) but also as an analytical tool in its own right, that is, as an instrument to examine the visual dynamics at play in a text. Another challenge I have encoun-tered is finding ways to encourage students, who are often visually very adept, to question their own assumptions about how they see the world and the visual relations in which they participate every day. A breakdown of the processes and mechanisms of representation and their manifesta-tion on the visual plane has proven to be extremely helpful. Ultimately, these and other challenges can be met by carefully laying out the theo-retical and analytic connections between visual theory and literary analysis.

There are many ways to teach *Animal's People* successfully. The visual framework I have described here provides a solid structure that, while it focuses on one major thematic strand, can easily incorporate other themes related to the environmental violence at the center of the narrative. Yet the many times I have followed this approach in teaching the novel, I have seen that *Animal's People* offers students sufficient primary material to disentangle and a clear vocabulary to use in describing and analyzing the visual and narrative relations with which it is concerned. In addition, I have seen that teaching the novel in this way has further pedagogical benefits. While tackling the continuities between image and text provides a way to analyze the novel as well as environmental disasters in general, students have adopted such an approach in discussions of other novels without being prompted to do so. Finally, because the production, dissemination, and consumption of images and narratives consistently follow a specific arrangement of participants and operations, this approach has been extremely powerful in encouraging students to reflect on the dynamics of narrative as a primarily relational enterprise.

This pedagogical strategy, to conclude, can be usefully applied to many other texts. Visual material showing the destructive presence of extractive industries in Congo and along the banks of the Congo River, for instance, could be analyzed alongside Joseph Conrad's *Heart of Darkness* and may be of great use in exploring, in particular, Conrad's employment of perspective and point of view to critique the colonial gaze that the novella deploys. It can also be used for the study of more recent texts. Images of the Sundarbans, in the Bay of Bengal, for example, could be successfully incorporated into a study of Amitav Ghosh's *The Hungry Tide*. Climate change and the tensions between human and nonhuman life in the mangrove forests described in the novel could be productively illuminated by images of the swamps, which would provide a basis for exploring notions central to the narrative, such as the ecological threats posed by human activity. Finally, Helon Habila's novel *Oil on Water* would also fit well into this pedagogical framework. Images that reflect the violence of the oil-extraction industry (spills, gas flares, dead matter, etc.) could be effectively used in both direct and oblique (or allusive) ways in teaching this narrative, which is often invested in complicating rather than clarifying the visuality of the ecological destruction caused by this industry in the Niger Delta.[5]

This is just a sample of the ways in which the approach I have described in this essay could be productively used in the classroom. In fact, given its political and theoretical emphasis on issues of representation, the study of the intersection of images and texts may be adopted as the main lens for a course in postcolonial or Global South environmental literature. Whether employed as one of many analytic techniques or as the main critical apparatus, this approach offers ways not only to facilitate a differential analysis of literary texts and visual images concerned with ecological disasters but also to investigate the semiotic and interpretive processes common to both kinds of cultural production.

## Notes

1. I draw here on the argument I present in the last chapter of my book *Resisting Dialogue: Modern Fiction and the Future of Dissent* (171–218). The larger goal of the book is to show how certain novels published in the last hundred years or so offer ways to counter the depoliticization of dialogue, or the employment of what I call "illusory dialogue" (15). The last chapter demonstrates this idea in relation to the representation of ecological disasters in the Anthropocene.

2. For an excellent discussion of the challenge of teaching the visualization of climate change, see Houser.

3. To avoid influencing students' evaluation of the representational characteristics of *Animal's People*, I do not assign Nixon's chapter on the novel.

4. Pramod K. Nayar's *Bhopal's Ecological Gothic*, in particular its final chapter (107–138), helps readers consider problems arising from the transformation of visual representations of Bhopal's catastrophe into reductive icons and the dynamics at play as these images mediate the event and allow us to imagine similar future catastrophes.

5. I investigate this issue too in the last chapter of *Resisting Dialogue*.

## Works Cited

Azoulay, Ariella. *The Civil Contract of Photography*. Zone Books, 2008.

Barthes, Roland. "The Great Family of Man." *Mythologies*, Hill and Wang, 2012, pp. 196–99.

"Basic Facts and Figures, Numbers of Dead and Injured, Bhopal Disaster." *The Bhopal Medical Appeal*, www.bhopal.org/basic-facts-figures-numbers-of -dead-and-injured-bhopal-disaster. Accessed 15 Jan. 2021.

"Bhopal." *Wikipedia: The Free Encyclopedia*. www.en.wikipedia.org/wiki /Bhopal. Accessed 15 Jan. 2021.

Bonneuil, Christophe, and Jean-Baptiste Fressoz. *The Shock of the Anthropocene: The Earth, History and Us*. Verso, 2015.

*Chasing Ice*. Directed by Jeff Orlowski, Submarine Deluxe, 2012.

Conrad, Joseph. *Heart of Darkness*. Heart of Darkness *and Other Tales*, Oxford UP, 2008, pp. 101–87.

Crary, Jonathan. *24/7: Late Capitalism and the Ends of Sleep*. Verso, 2013.

Demos, T. J. Introduction. *Decolonizing Nature: Contemporary Art and the Politics of Ecology*. Sternberg Press, 2016, pp. 7–30.

Falihi, Anahit, and Linda Wason-Ellam. "Critical Visuality: On the Development of Critical Visual Literacy for Learners' Empowerment." *The International Journal of Learning*, vol. 16, no. 3, 2009, pp. 409–17.

Garrard, Gregory. "Problems and Prospects in Ecocritical Pedagogy." *Environmental Education Research*, vol. 16, no. 2, 2010, pp. 233–45.

Ghosh, Amitav. *The Hungry Tide*. HarperCollins, 2004.

Habila, Helon. *Oil on Water*. W. W. Norton, 2010.

Houser, Heather. "Climate Visualizations as Cultural Objects." *Teaching Climate Change in the Humanities*, edited by Stephen Siperstein et al., Routledge, 2017, pp. 136–45.

McIntosh, Peggy. "Teaching about Privilege: Transforming Learned Ignorance into Usable Knowledge." Foreword. *Deconstructing Privilege: Teaching and Learning as Allies in the Classroom*, edited by Kim A. Case, Routledge, 2013, pp. xi–xvi.

Meneses, Juan. *Resisting Dialogue: Modern Fiction and the Future of Dissent.* U of Minnesota P, 2019.

Mirzoeff, Nicholas. *The Right to Look: A Counterhistory of Visuality*. Duke UP, 2011.

Mitchell, W. J. T. *What Do Pictures Want? The Lives and Loves of Images*. U of Chicago P, 2005.

Nayar, Pramod K. *Bhopal's Ecological Gothic: Disaster, Precarity, and the Biopolitical Uncanny*. Lexington Books, 2017.

New London Group. "A Pedagogy of Multiliteracies: Designing Social Futures." *Harvard Educational Review*, vol. 66, no. 1, 1996, pp. 60–92.

Nixon, Rob. Introduction. *Slow Violence and the Environmentalism of the Poor.* Harvard UP, 2011, pp. 1–44.

Orr, David. "Reinventing Higher Education." *Greening the College Curriculum: A Guide to Environmental Teaching in the Liberal Arts*, edited by Jonathan Collett and Stephen Karakashian, Island Press, 1995, pp. 8–23.

Rai, Raghu. "Exposure: Portrait of a Corporate Crime." *Magnum Photos*, www.magnumphotos.com/newsroom/exposure-portrait-corporate-crime-raghu-rai. Accessed 15 Jan. 2021.

Sadoski, Mark, and Allan Paivio. *Image and Text: A Dual Coding Theory of Reading and Writing*. Routledge, 2013.

Sinha, Indra. *Animal's People*. Simon and Schuster, 2007.

Sontag, Susan. *Regarding the Pain of Others*. Picador, 2003.

**Rachel Rochester**

# *Colonize Mars*: Precolonial Pedagogies for Anticolonial Praxis

There are myriad digital tools designed to educate students about the on-going legacy of colonialism and about the implications of climate chaos, but few interrogate the link between the two.[1] I created the digital project *Colonize Mars* to help students engage with postcolonial environmental literatures in innovative ways. *Colonize Mars* is part choose-your-own-adventure novel, part nonfiction account of Mars exploration past and future, and part video game. Users explore an immersive, three-dimensional digital map of Mars. As they investigate, they come upon a growing body of visual, literary, auditory, fictional, and nonfictional narratives that grapple with the ethical implications of a hypothetical colonization of Mars and its drivers, and they are also invited to contribute their own content. In this essay I detail my rationale for pursuing the project, outline its theoretical basis, address its pedagogical implications, and summarize its development.

Catalyzing students to become active champions of effective environmental policies that also consider the power inequalities and histories of colonialism is one of the most important and challenging tasks facing educators today. Ninety-seven percent of actively publishing climate scientists agree that "[c]limate-warming trends over the past century are extremely likely due to human activities" ("Scientific Consensus"). The scientific community has been outspoken about this causation for quite some time, imploring governments around the globe to enact strict, specific targets for reducing greenhouse gas emissions since the 1980s (Weart 149). Recent technology that allows for more sophisticated modeling and a larger body of research affirms scientific conviction that the climate is warming as a result of human activity. Despite decades of scientific warnings, however, public opinion and scientific opinion about climate disruption and environmental conditions differ dramatically; in 2018, just sixty-two percent of Americans believed climate change was human-caused, and only seventy-three percent believed it was happening at all (Gustafson et al.). Much excellent research attempting to account for mainstream environmental apathy and misconception suggests that the traditional model of environmental education, which assumes that information motivates investment in environmental welfare, is flawed. Instead, researchers find that information alone is inadequate to prompt the public to take meaningful environmental action in the face of anthropogenically motivated climate change (Norgaard 72–73). We need new strategies and tools to combat the aggressive disinformation campaign that misleads the populace about climate collapse, its causes, and its link to existing global inequalities and power dynamics. Moreover, to fully understand how to limit and rectify grave environmental devastation, we must study colonial (and neocolonial) stories that showcase the structures that buttress human and environmental exploitation. To paraphrase Graham Huggan and Helen Tiffin, humans can only become fully liberated by taking a two-pronged approach to restructuring our societies: we must acknowledge our long history of positioning ourselves as superior to other human and nonhuman societies, and we must disrupt that history by prioritizing societal reconfigurations that are ecologically connected (22). Effective environmental pedagogy must expose the ideological miasma that normalizes colonial violence and its trail of environmental and social catastrophe while invigorating learners to identify alternative means of inhabiting the world.

The postcolonial novel is an effective starting point, because it can help students explore the relation between colonialism and environmental destruction. The novel has long been credited with triggering seismic changes in public belief, self-perception, and behavior.[2] In colonial India, for example, the novel encouraged colonial subjects to face their condition and to reconceive the culture of the colonizer, and the novel became a space in which discourses of colonial resistance and colonial obeisance waged war (Mukherjee 16–17). Climate fiction novels, or "cli-fi," are well equipped to harness the rhetorical techniques of their literary forebears to help readers face another existential threat: climate change and environmental degradation. Cli-fi focuses on humanity's impact on the environment, and a growing cadre of postcolonial novelists are using cli-fi to spotlight the ineluctable interdependency of environmental issues and colonialism and neocolonialism. Cli-fi allows readers to cocreate desirable futures that are worth working toward. The more I brought postcolonial cli-fi into the classroom, the more convinced I became that students would benefit even further from becoming informed, active participants in the creation of their own cli-fi narratives and from taking part in collaborative future building and reworlding. I wondered how, in the postcolonial environmental classroom, I could best emphasize the structural and systemic relation between colonization and environmental exploitation and show students how to push back against ongoing neocolonial projects repeating the same violent histories.

I created *Colonize Mars* to inspire students and the public to cocreate anticolonial cli-fi by interrogating proposed and ongoing schemes for colonizing Mars. Most interplanetary colonization plans evidence little historical awareness, and inviting students to explore those plans in an unfamiliar context distances them from their preconceptions about particular regions. Mars is currently incapable of supporting carbon-based life, and therefore all plans for its settlement demand that the planet be terraformed by releasing large quantities of greenhouse gases into the atmosphere. There is a strange poetry in the idea that the process making Earth uninhabitable might do the opposite to Mars, but this irony also reveals an alarming legacy of lessons left unlearned. Humans know little about Martian ecosystems, and one of the major arguments for sending people there is to gain a better understanding of how other planetary systems function. Terraforming proposes to disrupt those systems as soon as people arrive to study them. While recent research suggests that there is not enough carbon dioxide on Mars to make terraforming possible, the fact that it features in the plans of aspirational Martian colonizers like SpaceX and the United Arab Emirates reveals ignorance of the devastating heritage of terrestrial terraforming projects (Jakosky and Edwards).

The desire to overwrite the landscape of a new colonial outpost is one of the oldest and best-established ways of wrenching control from the indigenous population. The practice of changing the landscape and its ecosystemic relations is multiplex in its aims—it diminishes the value of local knowledge, it disorients the indigenous populations even within their familiar territories, it ensures that colonizers can proceed with less humility and desire to learn about a new locale—but it also has unintended ramifications. Legacies of kudzu, Asian carp, and hundreds of other invasive species that outcompete native plants and animals for resources should warn aspirational Martians against interfering with local ecosystemic relations before understanding them. In the light of the recent controversy over tardigrades that crash-landed on the moon, humans are clearly overdue to revisit the ethics of interplanetary interference (Weisberger). Equally important, the echoes of terrestrial imperialism that reverberate from the plan to terraform first and ask questions later indicate that interplanetary colonization plans are constructed on the same ideological underpinnings that made imperialism on Earth such a destructive and exploitative practice.

Although the novel is a powerful tool of environmental education, the genre has some limitations that may restrict its ability to get readers to fully consider the cascading effects of colonization. In *The Great Derangement*, Amitav Ghosh argues that the limited scope of novels inhibits their ability to adequately address climate change. The world of novels, he maintains, is created by boundaries of time and space—they don't take place over eons and epochs and rarely cover more than a few generations. Their settings generally represent larger milieus, while remaining specific. Ghosh writes, "It is through the imposition of these boundaries, in time and space, that the world of a novel is created: like the margins of a page, these borders render places into texts, so that they can be read" (59). Ghosh goes on to describe how other kinds of narratives have historically been better at depicting spans of time and space that exceed human experience, noting that only within the confines of the modern novel is such an expansive perspective impossible (61–62). When I conceptualized *Colonize Mars* it was with these shortcomings in mind: I wanted to create a digital tool that could challenge contemporary narrative forms to encompass both deep time and expansive geography.

In recent discussions of genres and mediums that are well qualified to drive imaginative conceptualizations of sustainable futures, video games have come to the fore. Ghosh's critique of the novel concludes that the "act of reading itself" will adapt to better engage with climate change and other environmental issues (84). For Ghosh, this is a response to how the Anthropocene thinks through humans through images, and therefore we must depart from "our accustomed logocentricism" (83). The potential collaboration between textual narratives, which allow readers to creatively envision certain aspects of climate change and characters, and the immersive experience of video game play seems like a rich site for climate change communication. While there is an abundance of evidence that the misuse of technology—such as uncritically typing lecture notes verbatim—can hinder the learning process in the college classroom (Mueller and Oppenheimer 8), credible studies overwhelmingly suggest that multimedia learning that catalyzes student participation dramatically increases student retention of material.[3]

Video games are often perceived as capable of succeeding where traditional modes of delivering climate change information falter. Recent studies have criticized conventional media as a means of climate change communication for encouraging the passive reception of information as opposed to collaboration, for an inability to adequately contextualize the issues of climate change, and for being apocalyptic or nihilistic, leading the audience to feel as if it is already too late to mitigate the adverse effects of climate change (see Aparici and Silva; Moser). In contrast, virtual game environments create interactive sites of communication that can lead to elevated comprehension of environmental issues and climate change. Virtual environments can communicate difficult concepts because they curate interactive simulations. The combination of audio, visual, storytelling, and active participation can prompt learning that is both rational and emotional—and credible scholarship in the field suggests that cocreating alternative futures in response to the threats of environmental harms is most effective when it is a simultaneously affective and logical process (Dulic et al. 58). Video games can catalyze emotional reactions, a sense of agency, and ontological reflexivity.

Video games also have the potential to foster positive collaborations among players. In his consideration of procedural literacy, Ian Bogost posits that video game play, not just development, can nurture technological literacy, intellectual experimentation, and social cooperation. Bogost notes that by playing games like *Animal Crossing*, which are tethered to real time and incorporate extratextual seasonal cues, players can interact in meaningful ways even when living physically separate lives: "This binding of the real world to the game world creates opportunities for families or friends to collaborate in a way that might be impossible in a simultaneous multiplayer game. . . . [T]he game's persistent state facilitates natural collaboration between family members with different schedules" (36). Considering that climate chaos is a problem that cannot be solved by individual action alone, the potential of video games to model and promote social problem-solving may make them more effective tools of environmental education.

Although art, imagery, and participation contribute to the ways in which video games engage players in environmental issues, experts agree that strong storytelling is essential. Recent studies indicate that the efficacy of climate change games must be assessed through the lens of both narratology, or reading games as a form of narrative expression, and ludology, or analyzing games for their rules, worlds, and play (Ouariachi et al. 14). Tania Ouariachi, María Dolores Olvera-Lobo, and José Gutiérrez-Pérez's recent research on the subject notes that while gameplay, visual, and interactive aspects of video games cultivate more active user engagement, storytelling is nevertheless one of the most effective means of communicating climate change because it "makes climate impacts and solutions more real, it influences people's beliefs because they shift the frames of reference for emotional and cognitive processes, and it increases people's capacity for empathy because it can connect with values and social identities" (31). The team crafted a questionnaire designed to help assess the success of various climate change games, in which they ask many of the same questions one might about postcolonial cli-fi novels: What is their geographic and temporal scope? Does the narrative imbricate real and speculative climate change scenarios, and to what ends? But it also contends with an issue that is particularly difficult for novels alone to grapple with: Does the story lead to a single end point or to multiple possible conclusions? Or is it gnoseological, with no clearly defined conclusion? (21).

If one goal of climate change education is to inspire participants to creatively envision alternative futures, and to imagine their part in cocreating those futures, then the way climate change narratives end is critical. If the ending of a narrative is too clearly delineated, it can restrict the freedom of readers and game players to consider possible alternatives. Donna Haraway theorizes that the vast majority of serious fiction, and the reading norms surrounding it, prohibits the type of creative rewriting that encourages readers to productively imagine conclusions other than those offered by the text. In her consideration of the environmental potentials of SF, which encompasses science fiction, science fantasy, speculative futures, and speculative fiction, Haraway contends that the anti-elitist culture built around SF allows readers to more freely reconceive of possible endings (108). While Haraway feels authorized to test the worlds of SF, however, she's aware that the reader's ability to project their own fantasies onto another's narrative dissolves when it has a conclusive ending (110).

While the novel can largely refuse to give readers the type of closure that would foreclose imaginative reworlding, that goal presents unique challenges within the confines of video game technology. The climate change video games that are most often cited as superb examples of their genre, like *CityOne*, *Clim'Way*, *Climate Challenge*, *EnerCities*, *Future Delta*, and *Habitat*, allow limited user choice within the game because they are all confined by available animation. More pervasive games like *Greenify* and *PowerAgent*, which include a hybrid of online and offline activity by sending users on real-world environmental missions, offer more player choice but less narrative depth. Although some restriction of choice can be a boon in climate change education—infinite possibilities have the potential to overload users and confound action—video games may offer too few, despite being lauded for offering users agency in developing plot.

In contrast, a digital novel-game hybrid might be able to engage the full potential of user imagination, even while incorporating digital, immersive experiences, and I built *Colonize Mars* around these principles of design. After much research, I decided to build the project onto *Google Maps* because it contained a preexisting and extremely detailed three-dimensional Martian landscape that was also widely accessible, broadly supported, and free and allowed users to take an existing KMZ or KML file and change it, thus creating a unique artifact. Before piloting the project in An Introduction to Cli-Fi, a course I was teaching to non-English-major undergraduates at the University of Oregon in 2018, I composed a few fictional accounts of various Martian colonists and created the shell of a narrative that could be explored alongside a regularly updating wealth of information about the surface of the planet and missions that have already begun there, provided by NASA. As one possible capstone project, I invited students to contribute to the project by writing a character study of a new Martian colonist that accounted for their environmental motivations for becoming interplanetary and their involvement in colonial processes.[4] Students could also create multimedia supplements to their stories, including illustrations, audio recordings, and digital movies (see, for example, "Climate Change"). This technique engaged their imaginations, encouraging them to consider how and if human behavior might adapt to the even more extremely limited resources available on the red planet to which humans have pinned their hopes of planetary redundancy. The project is now available to the public at rachelrochester.com/colonize-mars, and users can drop their own pins and add to ongoing narratives or create new ones, contributing to an ever-expanding polyvocal digital novel. The effect is a collaborative, three-dimensional world-building experience that is not limited by any single creative team's imaginative vision.

The project has turned out to be a rich site for environmental education for the students who have chosen to participate, and it will only become richer as other users add to its discourse. Students proved enthusiastic about contributing to a digital creative project, and many participants sought permission to write final papers that exceeded the assigned length, revised multiple drafts, conducted outside research both on colonization efforts and on environmental projections for earth, and developed a wildly diverse population of colonists who might be the first to (fictionally) set foot on Mars. As students revised their initial drafts based on peer and instructor feedback, it became clear that their comprehension of the nuances of climate change and its relation to sociopolitical philosophies, and their conceptualization of what sustainable human civilization might look like on Earth and Mars, had grown exponentially. In student evaluations, comments about the project were unanimously positive, and many students indicated that the project had an impact on their previously held worldviews.[5]

By mapping out the precolonial situation unfolding on Mars, students can employ digital tools to explore previously impossible or largely inaccessible lines of humanist inquiry; they can use postcolonial conventions to make precolonial interventions. This type of digital narrative can build on the work of forms like graphic novels and choose-your-own-adventure books, and the immersive agency cultivated by video games, to create an innovative experience that drives critical thinking about the links among colonialism, climate change, and other forms of environmental degradation. The project aims to offer Mars as a site where humans might end the cycle of social and environmental exploitation that makes astronautical pioneers so convinced that Earth will eventually be uninhabitable, but it also encourages students to apply their solutions designed for the red planet to local contexts. By expanding the novel in innovative ways to present colonial histories, speculative futures, and the means of resistance to neoliberal systems of exploitation, students may learn to recognize and interrupt destructive cycles for a more sustainable means of inhabiting earth.

Implementing digital humanities (DH) projects like *Colonize Mars* in the classroom can be immensely rewarding, and surprisingly manageable, but success depends on a few fundamental guidelines. Carefully consider how digital tools drive pedagogical objectives and set aside the allure of novelty for its own sake. Part of the appeal of DH, particularly for the already interdisciplinary field of postcolonial environmental humanities, is that it is designed to be interdisciplinary and collaborative. Enlist assistance from and partner with people who are already doing DH work, attend workshops both digitally and physically, and solicit the input of your students with an open mind. Our students are often digital natives who may savor the opportunity to share their expertise. Most important, be willing to take risks and to fail. Reconfiguring human societies to be socially and ecologically equitable will be full of false starts and experimentation, just like scholarly research. Good pedagogy requires educators to model problem-solving and critical-thinking skills, particularly when projects don't work out as planned.

## Notes

1. Roopika Risam's *New Digital Worlds* showcases a wealth of excellent #DHPoco projects (as does that hashtag on *Twitter*). Examples of digital tools for the classroom grappling with climate chaos can be found later in this essay.

2. The efficacy of narrative persuasion is well documented, particularly regarding antiextremism and attitudes toward stigmatized groups (Igartua and Frutos), business (O'Connor), health care (Hinyard and Kreuter), environmental concerns (Hillier; Hoeken et al.), and animal welfare (Małecki et al.). As archetypal examples like *Uncle Tom's Cabin* demonstrate, novels can trigger a groundswell of public action.

3. See Sawyer et al. for an excellent review of recent findings on this topic.

4. Students could choose to keep their narratives offline, but most elected to contribute to the project.

5. While the use of student evaluations of teaching (SETs) to gauge teaching effectiveness is increasingly contentious, since many universities still use SETs in consideration of employment decisions, they feel relevant in this context. See Uttl et al. for an effective summary of the controversies surrounding SET.

## Works Cited

Aparici, Roberto, and Marco Silva. "Pedagogy of Interactivity." *Comunicar*, vol. 19, no. 38, 2012, pp. 51–58.

Bogost, Ian. "Procedural Literacy: Problem Solving with Programming, Systems, and Play." *Telemedium: The Journal of Media Literacy*, vol. 52, nos. 1–2, 2005, pp. 32–36.

*CityOne*. IBM, 2011.

*Climate Challenge*. Red Redemption, 2006.

"Climate Change Audio Log." *YouTube*, uploaded by Xtrocity Films, 19 Mar. 2018, youtube.com/watch?v=a1pPP6aYI8A.

*Clim'Way*. Cap-Sciences, 2010.

Dulic, Aleksandra, et al. "Designing Futures: Inquiry in Climate Change Communication." *Futures*, vol. 81, Aug. 2016, pp. 54–67.

*EnerCities.* Intelligent Energy Europe, 2011.

*Future Delta.* Collaborative for Advanced Landscape Planning, U of British Columbia, 2011.

Ghosh, Amitav. *The Great Derangement: Climate Change and the Unthinkable.* U of Chicago P, 2016.

*Greenify.* PoLAR Projects, 2013.

Gustafson, Abel, et al. "A Growing Majority of Americans Think Global Warming Is Happening and Are Worried." *Climate Note: Yale Program on Climate Change Communication,* Yale U / George Mason U, 21 Feb. 2019, climatecommunication.yale.edu/publications/a-growing-majority-of-americans-think-global-warming-is-happening-and-are-worried/.

*Habitat.* Elevator Entertainment, 2013.

Haraway, Donna Jeanne. "The Promises of Monsters: A Regenerative Politics for Inappropriate/d Others." *The Haraway Reader,* edited by Haraway, Routledge, 2004, pp. 63–124.

Hillier, Ann, et al. "Narrative Style Influences Citation Frequency in Climate Change Science." *PLOS One,* vol. 11, no. 12, 2016, p. e0167983.

Hinyard, Leslie J., and Matthew W. Kreuter. "Using Narrative Communication as a Tool for Health Behavior Change: A Conceptual, Theoretical, and Empirical Overview." *Health Education and Behavior,* vol. 34, no. 5, Oct. 2007, pp. 777–92, doi:10.1177/1090198106291963.

Hoeken, Hans, et al. "Story Perspective and Character Similarity as Drivers of Identification and Narrative Persuasion." *Human Communication Research,* vol. 42, no. 2, 2016, pp. 292–311.

Huggan, Graham, and Helen Tiffin. *Postcolonial Ecocriticism: Literature, Animals, Environment.* Routledge, 2010.

Igartua, Juan-Jose, and Francisco J. Frutos. "Enhancing Attitudes toward Stigmatized Groups with Movies: Mediating and Moderating Processes of Narrative Persuasion." *International Journal of Communication,* vol. 11, 2017, pp. 158–77.

Jakosky, Bruce M., and Christopher S. Edwards. "Inventory of $CO_2$ Available for Terraforming Mars." *Nature Astronomy,* vol. 2, no. 8, 2018, pp. 634–39.

Małecki, Wojciech, et al. *Human Minds and Animal Stories.* Routledge, 2019.

Moser, Susanne C. "Communicating Climate Change: History, Challenges, Process and Future Directions." *WIREs,* vol. 1, no. 1, 2009, pp. 31–53.

Mueller, Pam A., and Daniel M. Oppenheimer. "The Pen Is Mightier than the Keyboard: Advantages of Longhand over Laptop Note Taking." *Psychological Science,* 22 May 2014, pp. 1–10. *Sage Journals,* doi:10.1177/0956797614524581.

Mukherjee, Meenakshi. *The Perishable Empire: Essays on Indian Writing in English.* Oxford UP, 2000.

Norgaard, K. M. *Living in Denial: Climate Change, Emotions, and Everyday Life.* MIT Press, 2011.

O'Connor, Ellen. "Storied Business: Typology, Intertextuality, and Traffic in Entrepreneurial Narrative." *The Journal of Business Communication,* vol. 39, no. 1, Jan. 2002, pp. 36–54, doi:10.1177/002194360203900103.

Ouariachi, Tania, et al. "Analyzing Climate Change Communication through Online Games: Development and Application of Validated Criteria." *Science Communication*, vol. 39, no. 1, Feb. 2017, pp. 10–44. *Sage Journals*, doi-org .libproxy.uoregon.edu/10.1177/1075547016687998.

*PowerAgent*. Interactive Institute, 2008.

Risam, Roopika. *New Digital Worlds*. Northwestern UP, 2018.

Sawyer, Jeremy E., et al. "Which Forms of Active Learning Are Most Effective: Cooperative Learning, Writing-to-Learn, Multimedia Instruction, or Some Combination?" *Scholarship of Teaching and Learning in Psychology*, vol. 3, no. 4, 2017, pp. 257–71. *APA Psycnet*, dx.doi.org/10.1037/stl0000095.

"Scientific Consensus: Earth's Climate Is Warming." *NASA: Global Climate Change, Vital Signs of the Planet*, 15 Mar. 2018, climate.nasa.gov/scientific -consensus/.

Weart, Spencer R. *The Discovery of Global Warming*. Harvard UP, 2008.

Weisberger, Mindy. "There Are Thousands of Tardigrades on the Moon: Now What?" *LiveScience*, 15 Aug. 2019, www.livescience.com/moon-tardigrades -future.html.

Uttl, Bob, et al. "Meta-Analysis of Faculty's Teaching Effectiveness: Student Evaluation of Teaching Ratings and Student Learning Are Not Related." *Studies in Educational Evaluation*, vol. 54, Sept. 2017, pp. 22–24.

Hanna Musiol

# Postcolonial Environmental Fiction, Media, and Pedagogy in the North of the Global North

"How would you speak," asks Ánde Somby, "if the birth gift you were given implied that your language is drying away, . . . your rights were evaporating, . . . [and] all your means of expression, your clothing, your language, your singing . . . were all covered under a thick blanket of shame?" (00:00:40–00:01:37). In his 2015 Venice Biennale performance, Somby speaks, ironically, about Norway, which routinely tops global indexes of prosperity, happiness, and quality of civic life but where Sámi "means of expression" and even the very language, one of the country's official languages, is nearly impossible to study at public universities[1] and where the conversations about decolonization and racism in academia are only now, slowly, gaining public traction (Bangstad; "Decolonial Critique"). "Would you speak legalese and focus on rights?" muses Somby, or "academese and focus on discourse?" or "artese to communicate . . . through art?" as he reflects on animal culling in an ongoing conflict between Sámis and environmentalists and the Norwegian state (00:01:43, 00:02:10; see Ravna). He ultimately plays with all three modalities as a scholar of environmental law, theorist, and self-proclaimed "*shame*man" (00:07:25) artist in his critique of Nordic colonialism, concluding his talk with a yoik (or joik), an "ancient way of singing" (00:02:28) and transspecies storytelling,[2] a "precious" (00:02:26), dangerous political art, banned in the churches of the North and attacked by "the state system . . . because it made *spaces* for other ways to think" (00:02:59–00:03:10; emphasis mine). Somby's performance narrates the familiar "aberrations of the postcolonial state" in an unfamiliar setting in the North of the Global North, rarely framed by narratives of colonial dispossession and domestic environmental injustice (Iheka 159). Yet he also points to local forms of transmodal, narrative, and embodied resistance to them (e.g., Arke, *Stories*; Reinert). His lecture-yoik is, then, also instructive. It models how postcolonial environmental humanities (EH) fiction, theory, and media art could be taught in transdisciplinary, transmodal, and postcolonial ways. Geopolitical location and transmodality are therefore key preoccupations in this essay, as is the counterprospecting impulse.[3] They were my main considerations when reimagining what environmental literature and media courses and pedagogy could look like in the Nordic Global North.

## Theory and Praxis—In Space

Space matters crucially to EH and postcolonial theory scholars,[4] not just as a theme or subject but as a stage, a foreground for research and learning, a cultural territory to be reclaimed. Place-based transdisciplinary pedagogical approaches work well, therefore, not only as techniques of classroom organization but also as approaches to the archival recovery of local postcolonial theory and praxis. Yet site-specific pedagogy grounded in postcolonial theory poses different challenges in Norway (see Arke, *Stories*; Eriksen; McEachrane; Ravna; Somby). Since local postcolonial epistemologies are rarely taught across discipline, and media courses are limited to "modern" and "new" technologies of storytelling and communication, which exclude nondigital forms of transmodal storytelling and theorizing, reproducing colonialist knowledge categories is common. Of course, free public education means fewer economic barriers to access, especially for citizens of Nordic countries and the European Union. Yet public universities are also impervious to community-engaged pedagogical praxis. Grassroots-initiated changes to institutional curricula are rare, and the humanities, especially philosophy departments, are as resistant to intersectional postcolonial theory as they are to its producers.[5] Anglophone literature (mainly British and American) and media courses are more common than postcolonial theory or Nordic postcolonial literature and culture courses at Norwegian universities. Accordingly, they are important vehicles for the popularization of postcolonial environmental literature and media and postcolonial theory, in general. However, Elizabeth DeLoughrey and George Handley rightly worry that such a welcome "expansion" of "American ecocriticism" and its "increasing relevance in the context of our global environmental crisis" has the blinding, perhaps unintentional effect of "producing a more narrow and nationalist genealogy" and archive (Introduction 7). American literature classes can, and often do, overshadow rich and local postcolonial theoretical practice, relevant environmental contexts, and histories of ongoing resistance to, for instance, state-mandated culling of wolves and reindeer in Norway, land seizures, and other reiterations of local "green violence" and colonialism (Peluso and Watts 23; see also Bergh; Reinert).

Mindful of that, together with collaborators, I designed two elective courses—the BA-level Literature, Environmental Humanities, and *Arts of Living on a Damaged Planet* and the MA-level Ghosts, Memories, Landscapes, on literature, spectrality, and space[6]—to teach American and other anglophone literature explicitly as postcolonial literature and to address the absence of postcolonial theory and EH instruction at my home institution.[7] Another ambition was to rethink the disciplinary place of media in a postcolonial environmental literature classroom in order to reclaim transmodality as a postcolonial method. We also tried to consciously situate our courses at the moment of "late" or, one could say, "high Nordic" colonialism and extractivism in Trondheim, in Norway, the oil and aquaculture welfare state, at the Norwegian University of Science and Technology (NTNU), the largest university in the country (Lars Kiel Bertelsen qtd. in Arke, *Ethno-Aesthetics* 9). We were working in an English literature program in a language and literature department, which required no postcolonial literature or theory training of its majors in English and other literatures, even around the time of the Tråante (Trondheim) Sámi Assembly centennial (the 1917 meeting is a pivotal event in the Sámi rights struggle in the region).

We set out to read anglophone texts in different genres—well-known works by Helon Habila, Paolo Bacigalupi, Jesmyn Ward, Celeste Ng, Ursula Le Guin, Leslie Marmon Silko, Jamaica Kincaid, and Joy Harjo—to fulfill the institutional English-language requirements and, clandestinely, added some works in English translation (by Svetlana Alexievich and Ahmed Saadawi). Since institutional criteria left ample room for pedagogical experiments, we also incorporated different theoretical paradigms, media, and in- and out-of-class collaborative activities with external partners. This broadened the focus of the courses from a national literary corpus to a critical, contextual, comparatist, transdisciplinary, and "undisciplined"[8] exploration of transmodal and postcolonial art, media, and "literatures of the environment" (DeLoughrey and Handley, *Postcolonial Ecologies*). Paradoxically, NTNU, with its shrinking of humanities offerings, institutionalized gospel of technological innovation, and strong focus on new media and environmental studies—predominantly tied to extractive industries—became a platform for building more rhizomatic knowledge communities and for experimenting with postcolonial theory, environmental literature, transmedia storytelling, and the city as "tools," archives, and "spaces for other ways to think" (Somby 00:03:10).

The first, BA-level course, inspired by Anna Tsing and her coeditors' groundbreaking book *Arts of Living on a Damaged Planet*, paved the way for experiments in transdisciplinary creativity, storytelling, and research initiatives, which are needed, together with the sciences, "for Earthly survival" (*Donna Haraway*). We began by reflecting on the different modalities of storytelling, using Sissel Bergh's forensic cartographies of disavowed historical Sámi presence in the region, Miwa Matreyek's multimedia environmental performances, and Kincaid's experiments with the tourist guidebook form, in order to develop complex understandings of environmental concepts (environment, nature, extraction, extinction, toxicity, human exceptionalism, colonial and "green violence," etc.) through the prisms of literary studies, environmental history, anthropology, geography, disability studies, biology, art, and postcolonial theory. For instance, we read Arturo Escobar, Tobin Siebers, and *Arts of Living on a Damaged Planet* alongside novels by Le Guin, Habila, and Kincaid. Michael Watts, Nancy Peluso, and Hannes Bergthaller framed our discussions of Habila's novel, Edward Burtynsky's visual oilscapes, and our local petroculture fictions. Each week, we also blogged about our new readings, reflecting on and experimenting with "storytelling beyond [human] individuals" (Swanson et al. M9), and often held classes and workshops at Kunsthall Trondheim, interacting with the bio art exhibit devoted to transspecies and multimedia storytelling and postcolonial knowledge. Speculative works by Harjo and Le Guin and theory by Donna Haraway, Kyle Powys Whyte, and Rob Nixon guided our experiments, especially in digital EH workshops devoted to prototyping new worlds. These prototyping sessions, led by Henry Mainsah, a digital media scholar, and devoted to imagining different futures, focused on play-making and multimodal creativity in embodied spaces. They allowed us to experience—often with our skin, fingers, and ears—and to reflect on the modalities of knowing that we often disavow in the humanities classroom (Eriksen; Reinert). Other consequences of our pedagogical experiments included leveling of the hierarchies of participation: NTNU administrators, senior scholars, students, temporary residents of the city, humanists, and technologists alike played and collaborated and often experienced vulnerability in equal measure when writing poems, reciting them, and prototyping speculative, futuristic objects together. The workshops and postcourse reflections emphasized the impact of these immersive activities on participants, who developed new relationships to the environment, local archives, companion species, and one another, in addition to honing their skills as literary scholars.

The second, MA-level course borrowed from the first course's toolbox but focused explicitly on necropolitics, landscapes, and memory. Thus, it took a spectral, performative, cartographic approach to literary geographies of disappearing or disappeared archives, bodies, and landscapes and to the legacies of colonial and environmental devastation and "survivance" (Vizenor 7; also see Blanco and Peeren; Keir; Langford; Stoler; Thacker; Tsing et al.). As we followed the trope of haunting in literatures of place, we reflected on the gothic as a postcolonial and environmental optic (in Morrison; Mbembe; Saadawi; Hayes; and Wideman, for example) and tried to use it in our own cartographies of local cultural histories. One of the course's creative tasks involved interpreting a local space and its cultural charge and narrating and mapping it in any genre or medium (a sonnet, a speculative story, a visual or sonic map, etc.). The final workshop, Spectral Landscapes: Archives, Senses, Cocreation, synthesized our approaches. Led by the artist-archivists Lena Gudd and Antonin Pons Braley, whose project *An Archive of Norths* examines extraction-company towns in the Arctic, in collaboration with the performance artists Alex Murray-Leslie, Ada Hoel, and Amanda Fayant, and framed by the project *A Generative Archive*, by Raphaël Grisey and Bouba Touré, on the histories of postcolonial resistance in France and Mali, Spectral Landscapes allowed participants to reflect on the presence of postcolonial memory in local environmental and cultural archives (parks, streets, libraries, syllabi, and landscapes) in comparatist, transnational, performative, and embodied ways.


**Preproduction and Knowledge Communities**

The preparations for both courses took several months and drew heavily on previous experiences and academic and nonacademic networks in the city, in Norway, and abroad (Musiol). The creators of the course ultimately became a large collective, including me, the instructor of record of the course at NTNU; senior EH mentors from abroad who volunteered advice and time (Stephanie LeMenager and Armiero); local and international institutional partners, the Trondheim municipality, the Trondheim Kommune (its immigrant integration division, in particular), and the Falstad Human Rights Center; the NTNU Academic Guest Network and NTNU for Refugees;[9] NTNU ARTEC, the university-wide arts and technology initiative, led by Andrew Perkis; local grassroots literature and arts collectives (Literature for Inclusion and Trondheim Poetry Nights); and invited guests and collaborators (Bergh, Krista Caballero, Armiero, Henry Mainsah, Gudd and Pons Braley, and the director-curator duo Helena Holmberg and Carl Faurby at Kunsthall Trondheim).[10] NTNU students and Trondheim-based refugee academic guests, several having intimate knowledge of the visceral effects of the global resource-extraction networks and heritages of colonial rule on their home environments, were equally important participants and cocreators. We also offered a granular model of access to the courses and all activities—more formal for registered students, and more flexible and still free for others, with no selection criteria other than a self-reported interest in the subject and a sufficient knowledge of English to follow our course material[11]—and opened all class sessions and related events to the public. This meant that a typical class of twenty students could attract twenty additional participants, or sixty more during public off-campus workshops and screenings. Kunsthall Trondheim, the city's art institution cum postcolonial and decolonial theory hub, led then by Holmberg, was central to our undertaking. It hosted several large events—the exhibit *A New We*, on bio art and transspecies storytelling, cocurated with Dea Antonsen and Ida Bencke of the Laboratory for Aesthetics and Ecology; the Indigenous Knowledge Seminar, with local and international scholars, artists, activists, and policy makers; a screening of *Donna Haraway: Story Telling for Earthly Survival*; the exhibit *Rivers of Emotions, Bodies of Ore*, curated by Lisa Rosendahl, on the arts of Nordic extractivism; and several public debates. As we collaborated closely on programming and syllabus development, Kunsthall also connected us to the environmental artists whose works were included in our course materials—Caballero's, on art "as praxis for ecological futures"; Bergh's, on language, cartography, and the arts as tools for forensic recovery of local indigenous history; and Gudd and Pons Braley's, on archiving the Arctic through artistic research. Ultimately, both courses were collaborative enterprises, and their diverse participants and cocreators contributed differently to the art programming and reading lists, shaped the format of activities and the content and outcomes of workshops, and affected future iterations of these courses through weekly blog comments and pre-, mid-, and end-of-course assessments.

However, logistical decisions and the radically open-access course format were first and foremost indebted to the work of, and debates with, postcolonial and EH scholars, artists, and theorists about desegregating theoretical, material, and place-based teaching practices (see Arke, *Stories*; Arsenijević; Armiero; Brennan; Christensen et al.; Musiol; Somby). It is noteworthy that critics of Nordic colonialism often pay tribute to literary studies (see Arke, *Ethno-Aesthetics* 7) and to American studies and critical race theory, specifically—for instance, Gloria Wekker's acknowledgment of Toni Morrison's influence on her pioneering work on "white innocence" and Danish racial politics (Wekker 3)—yet these theoretical transactions are rarely reciprocal or multilateral. Our ambition was to promote reciprocal postcolonial theory flows, aiming to rebalance the "hereness and thereness" of postcolonial theory (Ngũgĩ 60) and to make the entanglement of environmental fiction and colonialism "personal" and situational in the North, too (Arke, *Stories* 13; Søstrene Suse). In other words, we understood Ngũgĩ wa Thiong'o's call to read texts "globalectically" to require a reflection on how our own position and Nordic postcolonial epistemic heritage might affect what we read, and how. To this end, global postcolonial theory (for instance Kincaid, in addition to Ngũgĩ) became an important interpretive instrument for tackling local orature, such as Somby's or Søstrene Suse's work. We also explored how local theoretical practice (e.g., Arke, *Stories*; Bergh; Somby) can help us read more traditional textual fiction with greater sensitivity to postcolonial space, an ear for oral storytelling and transmodality, and greater scrutiny of how our own position in the Nordic country frames our understanding of, say, Gerald Vizenor's work.

## The Classroom beyond the Lecture Hall

Since there is little space for local postcolonial theory in traditional institutional spaces, finding local critical praxis where it happens meant moving across disciplinary and institutional boundaries that segregate bodies of humans and bodies of theory, literature, and media (Eriksen). Scholarship on EH and postcolonial ecocriticism pedagogy is a treasure trove of diverse teaching approaches (see Alaimo; Armiero; Christensen et al.; Glotfelty; Huggan and Tiffin; Keir; Sandlin et al.; Thacker; Tsing et al.), and transdisciplinary public pedagogy and "place-based" practices were key influences in our courses at the university in Norway, where instruction in large lecture halls is the pedagogical default and civic engagement and critical post- and decolonial thought (see "Decolonial Critique"; Bangstad) are not. We soon became aware that Trondheim—located at the core of the world's new environmental extraction frontier and a hub for migrants and economic, climate, and tech entrepreneurs alike—made its own claims on us, too, and that we should explore "learning beyond schooling" in epistemic and practical senses (Sandlin et al.). Yet when we joked that we had "engineered" an escape from the lecture hall, it was not a metaphor. Paradoxically, the NTNU art and engineering networks NTNU ARTEC helped us fund and organize transmodal environmental digital humanities workshops, introduced us to design-studio cocreation and prototyping methods, and connected us to local heritage and art institutions (Trondheim Fine Art Academy, Kunsthall Trondheim, the Falstad Center, and the NTNU Gunnerus Library Archive) and other places where the city's diverse residents, including migrant and refugee academics, could participate without fees or other access barriers.

## Transmodality as a Postcolonial Method

In our aspiring silicon fjord city, and at a technology and science university, *multimodality* and *interdisciplinarity* have been popular buzzwords, yet they are used mainly in the context of tech entrepreneurship and ocean-resource extraction and prospecting. A course on literature, theory, and media, then, can be used to complicate this singular genealogy that ties multimodality and interdisciplinarity mainly to twentieth- and twenty-first-century technological progress by revealing other local or indigenous genealogies. For example, the Nordic artist-thinkers Somby, Arke, and Bergh model embodied, transdisciplinary, transmodal, and spatial "geographies of learning" (Somby) and draw on a presettler (and postcolonial) yet very transmodal and interdisciplinary archive of storytelling and theory making. They forced us to recognize the North as a colonial site (Keskinen; Søstrene Suse) and to reconsider our own "prospecting" impulses toward the North or the Arctic as exotic landscapes, models for a "clean" and humane extraction (Uhre), or merely as a background for epistemologies of elsewhere. In our classes, we claimed *transmodality* and *transdisciplinarity*, using them as keywords, bridges for communication, during transmedia and immersive design events with digital media scholars, architects, computer scientists, and music technology artists, who actively participated in all public-facing postcolonial EH workshops. Yet we also reclaimed them as postcolonial praxes. The welcome if unexpected consequence of working with thinkers who theorize in multimodal ways[12] was making postcolonial theory legible to students and scholars of diverse disciplines (literature, architecture, art, and immersive design). Of course, we used traditional literature-classroom methods, lectures, reading and academic writing assignments, communal blogging, creative, speculative (and, less common, transspecies and transmodal) writing sessions, critical reflections on material read and produced (compiled in an end-of-term portfolio), and more. But our unique access to local cultural and tech networks allowed us to hold classes and workshops at the university and in the city, where we could play with critical design and art and use interpretive and creative writing skills gained in the literature classrooms to prototype fictive "theory devices" and environmental futures in inclusive ways. In a convoluted way, then, our encounters and playing with contemporary new media art led participants to recognize the different genealogies of transmodal storytelling and theorizing in postcolonial settings, beyond new technology—yoik being just one example, Bergh's visual and linguistic cartographies of Trondheim another.

Postcolonial and environmental literature is unruly and escapes the classroom; it draws links that extend beyond the university, that travel across disciplinary, linguistic, and national borders, but it is also tied to the materiality of the soil, water, air, and human and nonhuman bodies, touching on specific, local settler histories, the geopolitics of extraction and migration, the embodied ways of being, grieving, and reimagining trauma, resistance, and futurity, always in a particular place and in a particular way (Arke, *Stories*; Søstrene Suse; Somby; Uhre). It demands that we challenge aesthetic values and approved modes and functions of storytelling and reclaim "shameful" aesthetics as tools for inquiry, documentation, critique, protest, legal advocacy, and as expressions of creativity and political and environmental imagination.

Trondheim and NTNU have a uniquely robust cultural, tech, and art infrastructure but are also entangled in colonial knowledge reproduction in unique ways, so our literature or media courses might not be easily replicable elsewhere. Perhaps should not be. What we learned from working within narrow institutional parameters is that unpredictable logistical and collaborative opportunities are always possible. In our case, we simply could not teach such rich and textured courses in a literature department alone, especially if we wanted to link literature and media from diverse postcolonial sites, including our own. Anglophone literature educators interested in adopting a place-based pedagogy and Arke's or Somby's transmodal approach in the Arctic, Norway, and in Europe more broadly must also be prepared to deal with the well-resourced but also monodisciplinary, instrumentalist, and, often, surprisingly colonial institutional environments (Bangstad; Eriksen) in which English literature courses unfortunately play a starring role. Moreover, experimenting with collective knowledge making and storytelling in an academic setting that does not reward or facilitate such experimentation is extremely labor- and resource-intensive and should be recommended for junior or untenured scholars with caution, although it certainly became easier for us with the second course. Public outreach may also be less desirable or feasible in other settings. However, recognizing the weight of the sociocultural and institutional place of teaching is a step toward moving postcolonial EH pedagogy away from teaching postcolonial environmental literature simply as a subject and into a postcolonial environmental "counter-prospecting" praxis (Uhre). In our case, in addition to official and measurable academic success and high attendance and retention rates in both classes, the public-outreach element of both courses had institutional and local effects that persisted after teaching concluded, including pushing EH into NTNU's institutional orbit in 2019. The number of MA theses on postcolonial literature and the environment increased, feeding the newly established NTNU Environmental Humanities Research Group, which, in turn, contributed to establishing the EH doctoral teaching and research consortium called NorRS-EH shared among five universities in Norway.[13] More important, reading anglophone fiction texts, conducting on-site explorations, and performing local postcolonial spectral cartographies helped us think of postcolonial literacy as a profoundly spatial and embodied practice and as a mode of transnational solidarity, attentive to the over- and undernarrated spectral landscapes of environmental devastation, colonialism, extractivism, and resistance—Habila's oil violence in Nigeria, the Sámi North, Arsenijević's sites of mass graves and toxic dumping in Bosnia and Herzegovina, Ward's Hurricane Katrina, Vizenor's White Earth reservation, and Saadawi's Baghdad. It also made us reflect on our positionality as reader-actors onstage in Trondheim and in the Global North-South.

## Notes

I thank my mentors and the course participants, artists, and collaborators for their commitment to expanding communities of knowledge beyond academia. I also thank Cajetan Iheka for making room for Arke, Somby, Bergh, and the postcolonial North in this volume and for his feedback on earlier versions of this essay.

1. The University of Tromsø and the Sámi University of Applied Sciences are exceptions.

2. Yoik singing is both humanistic and animalistic and, often, lyricless; Somby frames the yoik as the nearly lost language of human-nonhuman communication of "Sámi dreamtime" (00:03:51).

3. "Counter prospecting is an experimental and interpretative praxis-based method that operates on two intersecting planes: It resists dominant and already given prospects, while on a plane of anticipation, it reaches beyond these prospective exchanges toward possible alternative futures" (Uhre).

4. For works that address the fraught encounter between ecocriticism and postcolonial studies, see DeLoughrey and Handley, *Postcolonial Ecologies*; Iheka; Nixon; Tsing et al.; or Whyte.

5. The most egregious recent case at the institution where I teach, the Norwegian University of Science and Technology, was an all-male cluster hire of ten in philosophy in 2019. Expertise in feminist, queer, postcolonial, or Sámi epistemologies was not required for the jobs and might have been, in fact, a liability (Schei).

6. Their abbreviated syllabi are available at www.ntnu.no/documents/10234 /1275341294/ENG_H2017.pdf/9e8d5b44-50ca-4566-8df1-f497e2ef6a7f and www.ntnu.no/documents/10234/1282489869/ENG_V19.pdf/0e59261e -4d69-43ea-807e-039ad32f655e.

7. Also, postcolonial and EH theory modules were added to MA-level literary theory courses in 2017.

8. "Undisciplining the Humanities since 2011, Naturally" is an institutional slogan at the KTH Royal Institute of Technology's Environmental Humanities Laboratory, directed by Marco Armiero.

9. NTNU offers some flexibility for informal participation of permanent or more-transient city residents, and we invited Trondheim-based refugee academic guests not enrolled as NTNU students into the course. They could receive NTNU's noncredit certificates of attendance if they followed classes and submitted required work, or they could attend any session or event without credit.

10. We usually collaborated with guests who had prior plans to visit the city, so tying their talks to the class and inviting them to lead discussions with our students demanded minimal financial resources.

11. Sessions were often attended by junior and senior academics from other disciplines, undergraduate and doctoral students, city residents, and NTNU administrators, all motivated by different needs and interests.

12. For more-textual approaches, see Wekker; and Huggan and Tiffin.

13. The initiative allows doctoral students to take any PhD courses in environmental history, anthropology, literature, cultural studies, and the arts across the partner institutions, and, for the first time in Norway, it provides a space for advanced postcolonial EH training.

## Works Cited

Alaimo Stacy. "The Trouble with Texts; or, Green Cultural Studies in Texas." Christensen et al., pp. 369–76.

Arke, Pia. *Ethno-Aesthetics / Etnoæstetik.* Ark, 2010.

———. *Stories from Scorebysund: Photographs, Colonisation and Mapping.* Kuratorisk Aktion, 2010.

Armiero, Marco. "An Environmental Historian among the Activists: The Political, the Personal, and a Project of Guerilla Narrative." *Italy and the Environmental Humanities: Landscapes, Natures, Ecologies,* edited by Serenella Iovino et al., U of Virginia P, 2018, pp. 163–72.

Arsenijević, Damir. "Gendering the Bone: The Politics of Memory in Bosnia and Herzegovina." *Journal for Cultural Research,* vol. 15, no. 2, 2011, pp. 193–205.

Bangstad, Sindre. "Decolonizing the Academy." *Africa Is a Country,* 9 Apr. 2018, africasacountry.com/2018/09/decolonizing-the-academy.

Bergh, Sissel. sisselmbergh.net/. Accessed 14 June 2019.

Blanco, Maria del Pilar, and Esther Peeren, editors. *The Spectralities Reader: Ghosts and Haunting in Contemporary Cultural Theory.* Bloomsbury, 2013.

Brennan, Sheila A. "Public, First." *Debates in the Digital Humanities 2016,* edited by Lauren F. Klein and Matthew K. Gold, U of Minnesota P, 2016, pp. 384–89.

Caballero, Krista. "Transdisciplinary Imagination: Praxis for Ecological Futures." 12 Sept. 2017, Norwegian University of Science and Technology, Trondheim. NTNU ARTEC Seminar Series.

Christensen, Laird, et al., editors. *Teaching North American Environmental Literature.* Modern Language Association of America, 2008.

"Decolonial Critique, Knowledge Production, and Social Change in the Nordic Countries (DENOR) Research Project." *Göteborgs Universitet,* 2021, gu.se/forskning/decolonial-critique-knowledge-production-and-social-change-in-the-nordic-countries-denor.

DeLoughrey, Elizabeth, and George B. Handley. Introduction. DeLoughrey and Handley, *Postcolonial Ecologies,* pp. 3–39.

———, editors. *Postcolonial Ecologies: Literatures of the Environment.* Oxford UP, 2011.

*Donna Haraway: Story Telling for Earthly Survival.* Directed by Fabrizio Terranova, Icarus Films, 2017.

Eriksen, Kristin Gregers. "Education for Sustainable Development and Narratives of Nordic Exceptionalism: The Contributions of Decolonialism." *Nordidactica,* vol. 4, 2018, pp. 21–42.

Glotfelty, Cheryll. "Finding Home in Nevada? Teaching the Literature of Place, on Location." Christensen et al., pp. 345–53.

Habila, Helon. *Oil on Water.* W. W. Norton, 2010.

Hayes, Terrance. *American Sonnets for My Past and Future Assassin.* Penguin Poets, 2018.

Huggan, Graham, and Helen Tiffin. *Postcolonial Ecocriticism: Literature, Animals, Environment.* Routledge, 2010.

Iheka, Cajetan. *Naturalizing Africa: Ecological Violence, Agency, and Postcolonial Resistance in African Literature.* Cambridge UP, 2018.

Keir, Jerry. "'Come to Paradise—While It Lasts': Teaching Literary Ecology on Mexico's Costa Alegre." Christensen et al., pp. 403–13.

Keskinen, Suvi, et al., editors. *Complying with Colonialism: Gender, Race and Ethnicity in the Nordic Region.* Routledge, 2009.

Kincaid, Jamaica. *A Small Place.* Farrar, Straus and Giroux, 1988.

Langford, Jean. *Consoling Ghosts: Stories of Medicine and Mourning from Southeast Asians in Exile.* U of Minnesota P, 2013.

Mbembe. Achille. *Necropolitics.* Duke UP, 2019.

McEachrane, Michael, editor. *Afro-Nordic Landscapes: Equality and Race in Northern Europe.* Routledge, 2014.

Morrison, Toni. *Playing in the Dark: Whiteness and the Literary Imagination.* Vintage, 1993.

Musiol, Hanna. "On Migration Research, Humanities Education, and Storytelling." *Border Criminologies,* Oxford U Faculty of Law, 24 June 2017, www.law.ox.ac.uk/research-subject-groups/centre-criminology/centreborder-criminologies/blog/2017/06/migration.

*A New We / Ett Nytt Vi.* Cocurated with Laboratory for Aesthetics and Ecology, 14 Sept.–21 Dec. 2017, Kunsthall Trondheim, Norway, kunsthalltrondheim.no/en/utstillinger/et-nytt-vi.

Ngũgĩ wa Thiong'o. *Globalectics: Theory and the Politics of Knowing.* Columbia UP, 2012.

Nixon, Rob. *Slow Violence and the Environmentalism of the Poor.* Harvard UP, 2011.

Peluso, Nancy Lee, and Michael Watts. *Violent Environments.* Cornell UP, 2001.

Ravna, Øyvind. "Menneskerettigheter og moral ofres for statlig prestisje." *Ságat—Samisk Avis,* 24 Aug. 2019, www.sagat.no/mening/menneskerettigheter-og-moral-ofres-for-statlig-prestisje/19.18189.

Reinert, Hugo. "The Skulls and the Dancing Pig: Notes on Apocalyptic Violence." *Terrain: Anthropologies and Sciences Humaine,* vol. 71, Apr. 2019, journals.openedition.org/terrain/18051?lang=en#authors.

Saadawi, Ahmed. *Frankenstein in Baghdad: A Novel.* Penguin Books, 2018.

Sandlin, Jennifer, et al., editors. *Handbook of Public Pedagogy: Education and Learning beyond Schooling.* Routledge, 2010.

Schei, Amanda. "NTNU lyste ut 10 stillinger i filosofi og ansatte 10 menn." *Khrono,* 13 May 2019, khrono.no/anne-marie-lund-ansettelse-filosofi/ntnu-lyste-ut-10-stillinger-i-filosofi-og-ansatte-10-menn/279134.

Somby, Ánde. "Creative Time Summit 2015: The Geography of Learning: Ánde Somby." *YouTube,* uploaded by Creative Time, 2 Sept. 2015, www.youtube.com/watch?v=nmK6ZGyf1w0.

Søstrene Suse. *I Elsa Laulas Fotspor Gjennom Sápmi.* elsalaulasfotspor.com. Accessed 15 Jan. 2021.

Spectral Landscapes: Senses, Archives, Cocreation. 19 Feb. 2019, Kunsthall Trondheim, Norway, kunsthalltrondheim.no/no/arrangementer/spectral-landscapes. NTNU ARTEC Seminar Series.

Stoler, Ann. *Haunted by Empire: Geographies of Intimacy in North American History.* Duke UP, 2006.

Swanson, Heather, et al. "Introduction: Bodies Tumbled into Bodies." Tsing et al., pp. M1–M12.

Thacker, Andrew. "The Idea of a Critical Literary Geography." *New Formations,* no. 57, 2005, pp. 56–73.

Tsing, Anna Lowenhaupt, et al., editors. *Arts of Living on a Damaged Planet: Ghosts and Monsters of the Anthropocene.* U of Minnesota P, 2017.

Uhre, Kjerstin. "Oceanic Openings: Counter Prospecting." The New Arctic and the Digital Ocean (NADO) Workshop, 20 June 2019, Norwegian University of Science and Technology, Trondheim, Norway. Conference presentation.

Vizenor, Gerald. *Shrouds of White Earth.* State U of New York P, 2011.

Ward, Jesmyn. *Salvage the Bones.* Bloomsbury, 2012.

Wekker, Gloria. *White Innocence: Paradoxes of Colonialism and Race.* Duke UP, 2016.

Whyte, Kyle Powys. "Our Ancestors' Dystopia Now: Indigenous Conservation and the Anthropocene." *The Routledge Companion to the Environmental Humanities,* edited by Ursula Heise et al., Routledge, 2017, pp. 206–15.

Wideman, John Edgar. "Art of Story." *The New Yorker,* 19 July 2018, www.newyorker.com/books/flash-fiction/art-of-story.

**Kirk B. Sides and Tjawangwa Dema**

---

# Anthropocene Storytelling: Ecological Writing and Pedagogies of Planetary Change

*To listen to and to tell a rush of stories is a method.*

—Anna Lowenhaupt Tsing, *The Mushroom at the End of the World: On the Possibility of Life in Capitalist Ruins*

This essay traces the evolution of a series of workshops on academic and creative writing and pedagogy based in modes of ecowriting specifically and teaching in the environmental humanities more broadly. A collaboration between an academic writer and university lecturer (Kirk B. Sides) and a poet and teaching artist (Tjawangwa Dema), these workshops asked participants to explore various ways of thinking and writing about environmental change and planetary precarity. The workshops focused on how we as academics and researchers, as well as writers, artists, and cultural producers, think about, represent, and tell stories of and in the Anthropocene. Whether you locate its origins in the seventeenth-century advent of modern colonial enslavement or after a twentieth-century, postnuclear consciousness, the Anthropocene is defined by an increasing planetary precarity. In these workshops, we asked how planetary and climate change affect our modes of knowledge production, storytelling, and aesthetic practice from both an academic and a creative perspective. The participants in the workshops were graduate students, postdoctoral fellows, and professors from across the humanities—fields such as art education, African studies, comparative literature, and geography—as well as from the sciences, including entomology, plant biology, and ecosystems sciences. These participants worked through a series of engagements with what we call Anthropocene storytelling, a pedagogical methodology that can be integrated into both the university teaching classroom and the creative writing workshop.

Drawing on what we learned from these workshops, we reflect in this essay on what it means to do academic and cultural work in an age of environmental crisis and possible planet death, when otherwise established ideas of authorship, subjectivity, and even individual sovereignty are up for debate. We explore issues of planetary and climate change at an analytic and creative level, as well as from a pedagogical point of view, in order to consider how best to write about and teach from various ecocritical perspectives. The essay also looks at how the workshops themselves employed creative writing and the methodology of speculative and science fiction (SF) as a mode of Anthropocene storytelling that might offer an ecoethics based in narrative practice for writing and thinking about environmental and planetary change. Anthropocene storytelling aspires to bridge the sciences and the humanities, to be a methodology for creative as well as critical practice, both listening to and telling stories about the earth and our relationships to it. But perhaps more important, this storytelling is an epistemological shift toward foregrounding narrative as a mode of thinking with the ecological precarities of the planet. One of the animating ideas of the workshop is that climate change alters the architecture of knowledge and that its alterations in turn ask us to rethink how we might construct literary pedagogy (see Baucom and Omlesky).

We begin with a brief summary of what each of us tried to accomplish in the workshops, with one set of interventions focusing on SF as a method for apprehending some of the uncanny horror of environmental breakdown, and the other exploring the confluences between poetry and a planetary ecological consciousness. For the sake of space we will describe two workshops, which took place at Pennsylvania State University, on 19 April 2019. During this set of engagements, Kirk facilitated a workshop that asked participants to think about how SF narrative modes captured some of the generic junctures of realism, fantasy, and animism. This interrogation of genre also allowed for what might be seen as a crucial coming to the fore of creation mythologies in ecologically oriented works of fiction and films, especially those dealing in postapocalyptic imaginative terrains.

The premise of this workshop, Science Fiction as Method, was based on Donna J. Haraway's claims that SF is "crucial to the practice of thinking" precisely because the genre allows for "thinking-with" and that SF offers a "sympoietic," or "making-with-others," mode of storytelling that pushes against the bounded, autonomous individualism characteristic of our neoliberal moment (39). This workshop asked participants to think with the notion that SF is particularly suited—as critical and pedagogical method—to approaching the environmental catastrophes characterizing the Anthropocene. It began with examples of SF based in differing modes of empathy and continued with the idea that empathy is a crucial method for practicing what Anna Tsing and her collaborators call the "arts of living on a damaged planet" (Tsing et al.). Employing some of these arts as writing and pedagogical practices, the workshop explored how SF can offer us, as critics and educators, a mode of thinking that is open to various aesthetic and disciplinary approaches to histories of world thinking, as well as to imagined planetary futures. Participants experimented with SF writing in order to better understand how academic practice—writing and teaching—might continue to take account of our rapidly changing planet while also foregrounding the fact that these environmental calamities are not new but rather linked to longer histories of colonial exploitation (Whyte).

The workshop began with a screening of the Kenyan filmmaker Wanuri Kahiu's 2009 short film *Pumzi*. The film is set in a postapocalyptic desertscape thirty-five years after what we are told is World War III, the "Water War." Set inside a compound sealed from the surrounding desert, the film shows us the inner workings of this microcosm of precarity and survival. The compound is named after the fictional Maitu seed, or mother seed, a relic of the time before nature died. After witnessing the harsh realities of life in a compound governed by extreme water rationing, we watch as the film's protagonist, Asha, steals the Maitu seed and escapes to find the source of a mysterious soil sample sent to her at the film's beginning and to eventually plant the seed.

The film allowed the workshop to highlight a few key tenets of writing and thinking about climate change and environmental precarity. First, we discussed how environmental damage and ecological apocalypse foster thinking about political economy and the relation between modes of production and accompanying ideologies and their environmental impact. We focused on a key moment in the film, when Asha breaks the autonomous energy-feedback loops of fluid recycling in the compound in order to share water with another inhabitant and thereby short-circuits the economies and ideologies of the bounded (biological) self that subtend the compound. This moment of sharing points toward what Haraway terms sympoietic, or "making-together," modes of production for sustainable living on a damaged planet (58).

In the workshop, we practiced the kind of poiesis (making) that Haraway suggests is reflective of all ecological assemblages, sympoiesis, or "making-together," through a writing exercise that asked participants to cocreate stories. The exercise was structured to encourage students to take account of the SF imagination mentioned above as well as to reflect on environmental precarity and even apocalypse. In groups, workshop participants were asked to create a world that was either missing an element or had too much of it—that either had no water or was flooded with it, that had no oxygen or an excess of it, that had no sunlight or was ablaze, and so on. They were asked to populate this world, not necessarily with humans but with a resident species, and to imagine ways in which the residents reacted to and organized responses to their changed environments. Again, most important, these stories were cowritten and, because of the wide range of transdisciplinary, creative input, produced a diverse set of possibilities for imagining life and lives on a damaged planet. We hoped to achieve a sense of what the editors of *Arts of Living on a Damaged Planet* call being "purposefully promiscuous" (Swanson et al. M7). In the formulation of cocreational writing practices, we tried to take note of the editors' point that "[t]he rigid segregation of the humanities and natural sciences was an ideology for modern Man's conquest, but it is a poor tool for collaborative survival. Co-species survival requires arts of imagination as much as scientific specifications" (M7–M8). Our goal was to push beyond interdisciplinary conversation and aim instead for transdisciplinary creation, for creativity at the intersection of different disciplinary backgrounds and narrative-making practices.

After discussing the possibilities of sympoiesis in the film and taking time to coproduce stories, groups shared the narratives they had written, which in turn led to conversations that focused on speculative and alternative mythologies as well as future-oriented, global shifts toward sustainable modes of production. Kirk closed by reflecting on these surprising and productive moments in the conversation, emphasizing how the workshop exercises could be used in the undergraduate classroom, where complicated subjects (ecological connectivity, materialist critique, etc.) could be addressed through a kind of SF writing exercise that tried to take account of an ecologically damaged world, such as our own. These workshops are ideally suited to many undergraduate classrooms, especially to those that are made up of a cross section of nonmajors, who bring differing interests and disciplinary knowledges to class.

In a workshop entitled Poetry and the Planet, Tjawangwa began from the premise that planetary and environmental shifts—characteristic of climate change in the Anthropocene—present an opportunity to think about how and why we tell stories, and how practice-based poetry workshops present ways to explore and complicate how poets think about, represent, and tell stories of and in the Anthropocene. Participants were invited to ask themselves why "it matters what stories tell stories," as Haraway suggests (35). Working from the premise of George Monbiot's idea of the "pollution paradox," which details the relation between environmentally harmful economic practice and corresponding investment in influence and political power, the workshop explored the role of creative mediums, such as poetry, and what they might offer us at a time that necessitates increasing scrutiny of the objectivity and truth telling of the news media.

Similar to Kirk's intervention, this workshop encouraged participants to think with the notion that creative writing, in this case poetry, is particularly suited to articulating issues connected to environmental and planetary precarities. Students discovered that poetry allows for a language of multiplicity, one that can capture varied perspectives, unlike more singular narratives of environmental experience. More specifically, poetry in this instance allowed for a mediating between the nuances of stories that are, as Tsing writes, "simultaneously true and fabulous" (viii). As a way to marry local ecological experience with the vastness of global environmental precarity, workshop writing prompts required participants to imagine being one of the few people chosen for transplant to "Planet B" as earth collapses and to consider carefully what single object, animal, or human being they might choose to take with them. Participants answered a series of questions to build up an inventory describing their chosen object, animal, or human being, from which they began to write their poems. This exercise proved productive, and the discussion following it was rich with emotion and curiosity as well as surprise at the choice of subject and imagery that participants made. The goal of this workshop was to explore how poetry lends itself comfortably to what Stephen Jay Gould terms "intellectual promiscuity." Tjawangwa's workshop foregrounded inquiry alongside close readings as a way to invite multiple perspectives. Participants also explored intersectionality in times of planetary precarity, asking in what ways race, gender, or class might complicate ecopoetry and help us to think about how we tell stories of both the global and the individual in a changing world.

Tjawangwa also foregrounded questions of spatiality and logistics in structuring her workshop. Inspired by what the artist and educator Toni Blackman calls a "cipher/cypher" ("Cipher"), Tjawangwa arranged the participants' chairs in a loose oval, and she envisioned herself more as a guide than as a lecturer or teacher. Hip-hop ciphers encourage improvisation and responsiveness in the moment, which requires facilitators to ready themselves to accommodate this; spectator and practitioner are interchangeable, which in turn supports active listening and cocreation. At any one point every participant can see the speaker's face regardless of where the speaker is placed in the room, or cipher, which is an attempt to hold space for all those in the room by encouraging listening and respect while decentering the flows of knowledge. Similar to the Harkness teaching methodology, which "inculcates a culture of enquiry, driven by students in dialogue around a table" (Williams 58), this model can complement performance- and outcome-based teaching. If it truly matters what stories we use to tell other stories, is it not possible that some of those stories will come from peer thinking and engaging with one another?

Participants in Tjawangwa's workshop viewed the Marshallese poet and climate change activist Kathy Jetñil-Kijiner's video poem "Anointed." The video begins with the sound of water and an epigraph firmly locating the Marshall Islands as a postcolonial space with a violent history of environmental degradation: "After World War II the United States tested 67 nuclear weapons in the Marshall Islands." This beginning and the poem itself not only offered participants a way to imagine a kind of "apocalypse" as having already occurred in various places, they also created "survivance" scenarios. This shift in focus away from (Western) conceptions of the apocalypse as end also opens up space for comparison with writers such as the Mvskoke Nation poet Joy Harjo, especially her poem "When the World as We Knew It Ended," which imagines the ongoingness of life after the apocalypse of colonial encounter. Jetñil-Kijiner's scenario also allowed the workshop to ask whether the "sudden" panic over environmental precarity surrounding Anthropocene discourses is just another example of a canon-shaping selective amnesia. In *A Billion Black Anthropocenes or None*,

Kathryn Yusoff writes, "The Anthropocene might seem to offer a dystopic future that laments the end of the world, but imperialism and on-going settler colonialisms have been ending worlds for as long as they have been in existence" (xiii).

Jetñil-Kijiner's poem allowed participants to engage not only with ecological precarity and cocreation, or sympoiesis (opening with "I'm coming to meet you . . . what stories will I find"), but also with the idea of a story within a story. Within the poem, Jetñil-Kijiner tells us the tale of a turtle goddess and her son Letao as a way to enter into a conversation about stories, power, and consequence. Through a refrain of questions Jetñil-Kijiner asks, "Who gave them this power? Who anointed them with the power to burn?" The poem thinks through the shifting trope of fire (figured as both a gift from the turtle goddess to her son and the nuclear blasts of the mid–twentieth century) in order to reposition the symbolic landscapes of the Marshall Islands in a postnuclear world. In doing so it also captures mythology's ability to create a safe pedagogical space, or distance, for the listener/viewer. Jetñil-Kijiner performs a kind of intellectual promiscuity through this exploration of the island as ecological archive, which holds the statistical histories of nuclear aggression and colonization as well as the more expansive symbolic landscapes of creation tales. Near the poem's end, a kind of epilogue sets up a structural juxtaposition between the soundscape created by the musical score and the statistics of nuclear testing on the islands. Participants also read Jetñil-Kijiner's poem closely through the ecopoet Helen Moore's lenses of reconnection, witnessing, resistance, and visioning, in order to think about the ways ecopoetry benefits from human and nonhuman entanglements.

Tjawangwa's workshop also interrogated what it means to think and write about the natural world as a minority, formerly oppressed person, or person of color. Are the historical relations between Blackness and nature ever characterized by bucolic leisure, or are they always complicated by the politics of race and what Camille T. Dungy calls "negative or at least compromised experiences" ("Camille Dungy")?


## Ecopedagogies, Cocreation, and Multiplicity in the Classroom

The workshops, we hope, also open up works that are often taught in the contexts of other courses, while offering possibilities for including lesser-taught, noncanonical works; because to think ecocritically requires multiple and expanded modes of observation. For Kirk this means finding articulations of ecocritical (and anticolonial) politics in the African literary archive much earlier than the decolonial, or independence, expressions of the mid–twentieth century. Kirk argues for teaching writers such as Thomas Mofolo and Sol Plaatje, from the early twentieth century, for the ways in which they articulate ecological imaginings of the southern African landscape as a version of an African modernity and as an ecological, anticolonial politics. This way of reading for the long duration of ecological (and anticolonial) imagination in literary archives—at least in various African contexts—might also be an impetus to consider writers such as Amos Tutuola for his particular ecohistorical investments in the landscapes of Nigeria as an ecoscape populated with historical trauma and fantastical and folkloric characters.

This approach to expanding the ecocritical field is also based in notions of intellectual promiscuity, which as a pedagogical approach arises from a perspectival shift regarding what, or rather who, is the focus of analysis from an ecocritical standpoint. In trying to move away from anthropocentric orientations to the various textual lifeworlds we deal with, we encounter the beings and spaces against which (human) protagonists define themselves. In his groundbreaking work *Myth, Literature and the African World*, Wole Soyinka speaks of the "chthonic realm," which he describes as a

> storehouse for creative and destructive essences, [which] required a challenger, a human representative. . . . The stage, the ritual arena of confrontation, came to represent the symbolic chthonic space and the presence of the challenger within it is the earliest physical expression of man's fearful awareness of the cosmic context of his existence. (2–3)

Soyinka goes on to describe "the gradual erosion of Earth in the European metaphysic scope" and attributes this to the "growth and influence of the Platonic-Christian tradition" (3). This "disappearance" of, or dissociation from, the earth in the Western tradition was accompanied by a transference of cosmological significance to "the sky deities" and away from the grounded, earthly—and earthy—terrestrial investments.

It is imperative to teach cultural and literary imaginings of the environment and ecologies through discussions of ontological shifts *within* cultural systems of thought, as well as through comparisons *across* these systems, to see the ways in which ecological imaginaries have remained "enchanted" or animated. An ecopedagogical approach such as this provides a space in the undergraduate classroom not only to think *from* the lifeworlds, Soyinka's "chthonic space," of texts, but to do so in order to critique ideological narratives such as Western modernity's relation to secularization and disenchantment of the (natural) world. This also suggests that approaching climate change and ecological breakdown, as well as the environmental apocalypses of indigenous communities globally, brings form and genre sharply into focus. Such epistemological boundaries (the novel, realism, etc.) might be read as entangled imaginaries when read ecocritically. We want to suggest that form and genre are best taught through the kind of promiscuity that would transgress these boundaries. Think of all the arguments about genre that follow the fields of world literatures, postcolonial literatures, and so on, as well as the controversial ascriptions of "magical realism" to African literatures. Might we find better pedagogical tools in the works themselves, in these literary lifeworlds that are based in deep ecological imaginaries? In this way Anthropocene storytelling might offer an ecopedagogical approach situated at the intersections of texts and their lifeworlds.

Soyinka's "accommodationism" at the level of teaching content and pedagogical approach is reflected in what Harry Garuba writes about animist materialism (Soyinka 54). Garuba claims that an "animist logic subverts this binarism and destabilizes the hierarchy of science over magic and the secularist narrative of modernity by reabsorbing historical time into the matrices of myth and magic" (270). In approaching various ecological imaginaries from the perspective of intellectual promiscuity and cocreation, we begin the work needed in destabilizing Western epistemological renderings of the relation between human culture and nature. An ecopedagogical approach must attend to the ways in which not only Western literary texts but also Western criticism and education can be shown in large part to be caught up in disenchanting the world. This could be said to be true in the Western canon long before Enlightenment rationality.[1] Promiscuity and accommodationism, on the other hand, help us to see how the undergraduate literature classroom can be a space of "multiple practices of knowing, from vernacular to standardized science, and [can] draw inspiration from both the arts and sciences to work across genres of observation and storytelling" (Swanson et al. M3); we see how questions of genre and form here can extend to the disciplinary, epistemological, and even ontological level.

We conclude with one final thought—that much of the cultural and epistemological impact of colonialism around the world has been the systemic erasure of multiplicity. As Achille Mbembe has said of Africa:

> [W]hen we look at the cultural history of the continent, it seems to me it is characterized by at least three attributes that can be conceptually deemed creative. The first one is the idea of multiplicity. . . . One of the tragedies of colonialism has been to erase that element of multiplicity which was a resource for social development in pre-colonial Africa and which was replaced by the paradigm of "the one," the kind of monotheistic paradigm. So how do we recapture the idea of multiplicity as precisely a resource for the making of the continent, its remaking, but also for the making of the world?

Much of the work of ecocriticism and ecocreativity involves foregrounding these cultural archives of multiplicity. Thinking across boundaries and thinking with many narrative practices allows the ecological imaginary we are proposing in the notion of Anthropocene storytelling to offer spaces of sympoietic, collaborative thinking and creative production.

## Note

1. Think of texts such as *Sir Gawain and the Green Knight*, in which Gawain's struggles, on both a symbolic and quite literal level, are figured as a battle against natural forces that are brought to life through magic. Gawain's battle against the Green Knight in many ways encapsulates a larger epistemological transition away from an enchanted nature and marks a shift toward the Platonism of the European early modern period.

## Works Cited

Baucom, Ian, and Matthew Omlesky. "Knowledge in the Age of Climate Change." *Climate Change and the Production of Knowledge*, edited by Baucom and Omelsky, special issue of *South Atlantic Quarterly*, vol. 116, no. 1, 2017, pp. 1–18.

"Camille Dungy—On Black Nature." *YouTube*, uploaded by ACCArtsand DigitalMedia, 20 Oct. 2011, youtube.com/watch?v=nNo4x1LuL5I. Interview.

"The Cipher, the Circle and Its Wisdom: Toni Blackman at TEDxUMassAmherst." *YouTube*, uploaded by TedX Talks, 14 May 2013, youtube.com/watch?v=WYdb5snA1Jc.

Garuba, Harry. "Explorations in Animist Materialism: Notes on Reading/Writing African Literature, Culture and Society." *Public Culture*, vol. 15, no. 2, 2003, pp. 261–85.

Gould, Stephen Jay. "The Paradox of Intellectual Promiscuity." *I Have Landed: The End of a Beginning in Natural History*, Harvard UP, 2011, pp. 29–53.

Haraway, Donna J. *Staying with the Trouble: Making Kin in the Chthulucene.* Duke UP, 2016.

Harjo, Joy. "When the World as We Knew It Ended." *Poetry Foundation*, www.poetryfoundation.org/poems/49619/when-the-world-as-we-knew-it-ended.

Jetñil-Kijiner, Kathy. "Anointed." Directed by Dan Lin, Pacific Storytellers Cooperative. *Kathy Jetñil-Kijiner*, www.kathyjetnilkijiner.com/videos -featuring-kathy/.

Mbembe, Achille. "Africa and the Future." Interview by Thomas Blaser, *Africa Is a Country*, 20 Nov. 2013, africasacountry.com/2013/11/africa-and-the -future-an-interview-with-achille-mbembe/.

Monbiot, George. "The Pollution Paradox." *George Monbiot*, 20 Jan. 2017, www.monbiot.com/2017/01/20/the-pollution-paradox/.

Moore, Helen. "What Is Ecopoetry?" *International Times*, 12 Apr. 2012, internationaltimes.it/what-is-ecopoetry.

*Pumzi*. Directed by Wanuri Kahiu. Awali Entertainment, 2009.

Soyinka, Wole. *Myth, Literature and the African World*. Cambridge UP, 1976.

Swanson, Heather, et al. "Bodies Tumbled into Bodies." Tsing et al., pp. M1–M12.

Tsing, Anna Lowenhaupt. *The Mushroom at the End of the World: On the Possibility of Life in Capitalist Ruins*. Princeton UP, 2015.

Tsing, Anna Lowenhaupt, et al., editors. *Arts of Living on a Damaged Planet*. U of Minnesota P, 2017.

Whyte, Kyle. "Indigenous Climate Change Studies: Indigenizing Futures, Decolonizing the Anthropocene." *English Language Notes*, vol. 55, nos. 1–2, 2017, pp. 153–62.

Williams, Guy J. "Harkness Learning: Principles of a Radical American Pedagogy." *Journal of Pedagogic Development*, vol. 4, no. 3, 2014.

Yusoff, Kathryn. *A Billion Black Anthropocenes or None*. U of Minnesota P, 2018.

# Part VI

# Place-Based Approaches

**Sule Emmanuel Egya**

# Ecocriticism in Nigeria:
# Toward a Transformative Pedagogy

Ecocriticism is a relatively new field of study in Nigeria, as it is in other parts of Africa. Not many English departments here offer courses in ecocriticism, although there is a growing awareness of its relevance in African literary studies. Mostly regarded as a literary theory, it usually comes at the bottom of the list of theories, being considered new, and is usually not explored in the way the theory teacher explores, say, Marxism or feminism in relation to African literature. As a literary scholar with an interest in ecocriticism, I have over the years been teaching it, nudging students to undertake their undergraduate and postgraduate research in the field. In this essay, I explain my approach to teaching ecocriticism, which moves from the classroom to the field, or from the text to reality—an approach not favored by many teachers of literature, who mostly consider it suitable only to the natural and social sciences. My main objective in teaching ecocriticism is to close the gap between text or imagination and reality, even if it means problematizing the notion of referentiality, and to get my students to see that the worlds in the texts are not absolute fictions. This is not usually difficult for them because their training in African literature has, mostly through social realism, exposed them to the connections between texts and sociopolitical realities around them.

However symbolic its gestures, African literature always historicizes (to echo Fredric Jameson) the human condition. Given this premise, it is not hard to convince students that literature also historicizes the ecological condition, if we choose to look beyond the human condition, or if we choose to see the ecological in the human. My other objective is to raise the students' consciousness of proenvironment activities, to translate knowledge into advocacy, so that they not only see how writers have used their writings as an instrument for advocacy but also take a position that enables them to read ecowritings in an empathic manner that initiates a healthy relation between them and their environments. In other words, their analytic thinking on ecowritings should engender a sense of advocacy. The pedagogy I propose uses the argument generated by a text to transform students from mere consumers of the text to active advocates. Or, as Hayden Gabriel and Greg Garrard put it, my teaching "aims both to enlighten and empower" the students (122). I will explain what I think is the most viable approach for achieving this transformation. Although broadly speaking most of the situations I describe here are common to Africa as a continent, I cite examples and details specific to Nigeria, where I live and work. Perhaps except for South Africa, the general levels of education, political stability, and economic prosperity, as well as general attitudes toward ecological issues, are similar across the continent. My approach embodies what I would like to see as African ecocriticism—an ecocriticism informed by the continent's economic, political, and social dynamics.

Definition, vague and parochial as it can be, is important to the design of this approach. By definition, I mean a set of statements that describes and maps out the philosophical ground for the study of literature and the environment. This is usually arrived at after sampling and discussing definitional statements on ecocriticism made by ecocritics such as Cheryll Glotfelty, Lawrence Buell, Simon C. Estok, William Slaymaker, Byron Caminero-Santangelo, Graham Huggan, and Helen Tiffin. My approach foregrounds two crucial notions that underpin my formulation of a Nigeria-centred ecocriticism: that of difference, developed by Caminero-Santangelo in "Different Shades of Green: Ecocriticism and African Literature," and that of advocacy, discussed by Huggan and Tiffin in *Postcolonial Ecocriticism: Literature, Animal, Environment*. Highlighting the activism of Ken Saro-Wiwa and Wangari Maathai, Caminero-Santangelo writes that "[t]hese figures point not only to the ways that Africans have mobilized against environmental degradation, but also to the grave environmental problems faced by Africa which have become, especially in conjunction with social problems, a significant threat to its present and future well-being" (698). In his view, an ecocriticism meaningful to Africa is one that is decentered to the degree that, besides staging indigenous proenvironment efforts, it recognizes the continent's distinctive political and social features.

While Huggan and Tiffin seem to accept the importance of recognizing this distinctiveness as they examine the meeting point between ecocriticism and postcolonialism, they assert that "postcolonial ecocriticism—like several other modes of criticism—performs an *advocacy* function both in relation to the real world(s) it inhabits and to the imaginary spaces it opens up for contemplation of how the real world might be transformed" (13). In other words, to perform ecoadvocacy is to make the world more ecologically egalitarian. On these notions of difference and advocacy, I encourage my students to develop a working definition of Nigerian ecocriticism anchored in the nation's colonial and postcolonial specificities, in order to use ecocriticism (or the knowledge of it) to make Nigerian society more ecologically balanced. This ecocriticism intertwines the social and the natural, the human and the nonhuman, with specific attention to Nigeria's postcolonial condition, and it advocates a socioecological vision that, on the one hand, recognizes premodern, indigenous forms of ecological knowledge and, on the other, resists modern-day organized ecodestruction. Perhaps what is Nigerian about this definition is its attention to the nation's local postcolonial condition. And yet from this vantage point we can see the fate Nigeria shares with other African nations, which may have similar postcolonial conditions. Like Nigeria, they may also be grappling with capitalist ecodestruction and the repression of indigenous forms of ecological knowledge.

Rob Nixon's "Environmentalism and Postcolonialism" and Anthony Vital's "Toward an African Ecocriticism: Postcolonialism, Ecology, and *Life and Times of Michael K*" usually form our background readings. These essays are fundamental to the understanding of postcolonial ecocriticism. To convince students that literature, in spite of its aesthetic character and its tendency to refract, may be used to teach, to transform, I introduce them to Chinua Achebe's essay "The Novelist as Teacher." Arguing against the high modernism that overly determined the criticism of early African literature, Achebe maintains that African writers must train readers to recognize discourses built on falsehood. While the definitional stage enables us to map out the object of our study, to theorize the Nigerian experience in ecocriticism, it does not mean that we turn a blind eye to the universal connections of ecocriticism—that is, ecocriticism as a global problematic that requires what Ursula Heise calls "Sense of Planet" (3). In fact, I usually tell my students that it is more fruitful to approach the highways of global environmentalism from a local point—a sense of their indigenous nature and environment, with which they are often organically connected, which will enable them to speak meaningfully to the global advocacy to save the earth.

The definitional stage leads us to three conceptual categories: nature, environment, and activism. We structure the class around these categories, taking our in-class and out-of-class activities from nature through environment to activism. We use the concept of nature (that is, human existence in the natural world, among biotic and abiotic beings) to step back into precolonial communities, their contacts with colonial forces, and their emergence as postcolonial communities, as captured in literary works like Chinua Achebe's *Things Fall Apart* and *Arrow of God*, Wole Soyinka's *Death and the King's Horseman*, and Zaynab Alkali's *The Stillborn*. Questions that inflect our readings of these texts include: To what degree are human beings and the natural world interdependent before colonial invasion? What role does nature play in human reliance on spirits in traditional religion? Is animism a function of the relation between human beings and nature, and how relevant is it today? What are the limits of human agency before the onset of Western modernity? These questions enable us to revise colonial views, some of which still exist, about the implications of locals' being close to nature and therefore being "uncivilized." We tackle essentialisms concerning the relations between human beings and nature, such as the simple-mindedness of locals, the natural inferiority of females, and the cultural superiority of Europeans. We pay particular attention to the roles of males and females in precolonial communities and discuss how knowing more about those roles can enhance our understanding of the natural world. We focus on the entanglement of gender, spirituality, and nature—on how gods and goddesses are products of the natural world. However, we tackle these entangled forces not from a Western (logocentric) perspective, in terms of a nature-culture dialectic (Soper), but from a perspective that foregrounds their imbrication. But a far more important lesson here is what we learn from a greater concentration on other-than-human life-forms. For instance, we are interested to know why a forest in *Things Fall Apart* is branded evil, and what this act implies about human inadequacies and fears. And yet the taboo status of the forest speaks eloquently to unintended acts of conservation embedded in spiritual practices of Nigerian communities. An attention to nonhuman life-forms, captured in literary works, is something rare in African literary scholarship, and ecocritics are opening up insights in this direction. Under the rubric of nature, therefore, I draw students' attention to the roles of other life-forms, especially in communities where human beings value their closeness to nature. I consistently point them to Cajetan Iheka's argument that "the relationship between humans and other life forms in African literature has significant implications for rethinking questions of agency and resistance in African studies" (2).

Modern ecological realities, positive or negative, are what we look for in literary and cultural works, as we move from nature to environment, to the force humanity exerts on the environment. In this section of the course, we discuss negative effects of human beings' actions on their environments, subjugation of natural beings, technological colonization such as extractive capitalism, and other forms of cruelties performed on biotic and abiotic life-forms. Although the Niger Delta is usually the starting point of discussions and readings on environmental degradation in Nigeria, I encourage the students to focus on other zones of environmental hazards, putting on the reading list literary works that have emerged in response to those hazards. For instance, we read from *The Promise This Time Was Not a Flood: A SevHage Anthology of Flood Poems*, edited by Hyginus Ekwuazi, Tubal Cain, Su'eddie V. Agema, Debbie Iorliam, Servio Gbadamosi, and Maik Ortserga, and *The Rainbow Lied: A SevHage Collection of Flood Stories*, edited by Agema, two volumes that deal with the ubiquitous floods in Nigeria. Although SevHage is a publisher based in Makurdi, north-central Nigeria—a city that suffers devastating floods almost annually—these collections contain tales and poems by writers from different parts of Nigeria. The environmental crises captured in these books are created by human beings. Under the category of environment, we pursue the connection between human-created crisis and climate crisis, emphasizing how indigenous peoples create, face, and interpret ecological crisis, bearing in mind that "Indigenous peoples are likely to suffer disproportionately from climate change because marginalized populations are often among the most heavily affected but have the fewest resources to respond to rapid environmental change" (Carey et al. 86). For instance, devastating flooding in Nigeria can be caused by human actions such as blockage of drainages, by excessive rainfall, or by both, and yet it is often interpreted as a sign of God's anger.

Most of those who write about ecological crisis, such as flooding, have experienced or know people who have experienced it. To deepen their understanding of our environmental readings, students seek to experience the real event outside the text—that is, to embark on place-based studies. As Hal Crimmel argues, place-based studies have greatly enhanced the learning of environmental literature. In his words, "Students in environmental literature courses are becoming accustomed to researching, sketching, taking notes, idea collecting, writing, and discussing—all while gathered on rock outcrops, sandbars, tree stumps, or city streets" (338). There are three ways we try to connect with the realities outside the text. First, we take a trip to the location, the setting of the text, hoping that we can still see and feel the event it depicts. We can, for instance, after reading a poem about the famous Zuma Rock in Abuja, Nigeria's capital city, pay a visit to the rock because it is a couple of hours' drive from our campus. This is what Crimmel calls "the half-day excursion, often consisting of trips to locations integral to understanding a particular text, author, or concept" (340). Second, we ask students who come from or live in the place where the work is set and have probably experienced the emplotted events to share their experience with the class, thereby transporting us to the events. Most of the students I encounter have stories of floods, and they can identify their home environments in some of the stories we study. Their perspectives broaden our understanding of the situation. Third, we watch video clips of the events. Such clips could be personal or from commercially distributed material. Personal clips are made by the students, or their friends, or taken from social media, especially *Facebook* and *Instagram*.

We also read a number of works that belong to the category of activism—literary works that appear programmatic about performing advocacy and that usually reflect the authors' political stance. For instance, some of the authors of ecoliterature about the Niger Delta, most of whom are natives of the region, have themselves been victims of petrodollar ecodestruction, and some, like the poet Nnimmo Bassey, run or belong to nongovernmental organizations or pressure groups fighting environmental injustice in the region. Their writing and activism could be seen as the continuation of Saro-Wiwa's work. Rob Nixon and other ecocritics pay attention to this kind of practice, pointing out its usefulness to the emergence of a proenvironment tradition that contests multinational institutional powers in Africa (Nixon, *Slow Violence* 14–16).

The argument can be made—and we try to substantiate this in our seminars—that the judicial killing of Saro-Wiwa in the 1990s marked the environmental turn in Nigerian literature. His death prompted writers to focus their aesthetic instrumentalism, with a generous dose of militant metaphors, on the regime's system of silencing writers and activists, and on the fate of human and nonhuman beings in the Niger Delta. Tributes to Saro-Wiwa in the form of volumes of poetry, short fiction, and essays like those in *Ogoni's Agonies: Ken Saro-Wiwa and the Crisis in Nigeria*, edited by Abdul-Rasheed Na'Allah, emerged in the late 1990s, part of a flowering of Nigerian ecowritings, most of them by natives of the Niger Delta. Most of these works, such as Bassey's *We Thought It Was Oil but It Was Blood*, Ahmed Yerima's *Hard Ground*, and May Ifeoma Nwoye's *Oil Cemetery* contain aggressive jeremiads, in which the fictional characters rise up against ecological violence and environmental injustice. The phenomenon of militancy in the region (unemployed youths visiting violence on government and oil workers as a way of demanding justice) feeds into this literature. However, the writers, even if they base their stories on the incidents of youth militancy, seek to create the true militant, the genuine activist, in the image of Saro-Wiwa, who is supposedly not driven by self-aggrandizement. I often ask the students to place side by side the attributes of the real Niger Delta militant, which we read about in the news or encounter personally, and those of the fictional ecoactivist. The response generally is that the fictional activist is discursively shaped to deliver the utopian vision of the writer and as such is presented as a hero or heroine with all the standard qualities required to rescue his or her society from petrodollar capitalism. How about seeing this ecowriting, which narrates the rise of militant unrest, as literary militancy? This question unfolds a line of argument whereby we see the writers (who may themselves be activists or not) as literary militants who invest their writings with a political force characterized by an aggressive tone and tenor, rhetorical invective, caricature, and targeted demotic diction, among other things. Literary militancy, chiefly based on real ecological militancy in the Niger Delta, is therefore a form of ecoactivism that needs analyzing in any understanding of Nigerian ecocriticism.

Ecoactivism in Nigeria is not limited to the Niger Delta, as we see in novels like Aliyu Kamal's *Fire in My Backyard*, Elaigwu Ameh's *Climate of Change*, and Adamu Kyuka Usman's *The Death of Eternity*, in which we encounter an ecoactivist working to save the earth in northern Nigeria. I ask the students if they have a personal connection with the fictional setting of ecoactivism in these novels. A student from Kano, for instance, who knows, understands, or can identify with the suburban town in Kano

State used as a setting in *Fire in My Backyard*, can give us sociological or anthropological information about that town based on personal experience. I encourage my students to sharpen their sense of place all the time: having understood a local (Nigerian) form of ecoactivism, they can fruitfully connect to the notions of ecoactivism and environmentalism in other parts of the world. Another strand of Nigerian ecoactivism foregrounds women and the argument that they are doubly subjugated under the forces of ecodestruction. While nearly all the books studied under activism foreground the peculiar helplessness of women, others (Nwoye's *Oil Cemetery*, Ameh's *Climate of Change*) cast female protagonists as environmental activists fighting for their communities, especially in situations where men collude with capitalists to destroy the ecosystem.

All is not theory and literary texts, however. We often take advantage of our campus's location in a provincial town of Lapai, where, without traveling far, we can physically encounter ecology. As I often do with my creative writing class, I hold some classes in what I call the ecological zones of the campus or the town, zones characterized by thick foliage, woods, plantations, farms, streams, ponds, erosion sites, floods, and illegal mining sites. When we're lucky, the environment we encounter in the text resembles the one we are physically experiencing. Aside from the fact that "[f]ifty-minute outings are easily coordinated and are effective at institutions where students may be unwilling or unable to participate in longer trips because of jobs, finances, or family responsibilities" (Crimmel 339), which is often the case in Nigeria, students find the outdoor experience exciting and inspiring. I have two aims in exposing the students to the environment through physical contact. First, I try to prove to them that, in spite of the antimimetic arguments in the wake of poststructuralist thinking, literature, at least the kind of literature produced in Nigeria, and perhaps in other parts of Africa, does not shy away from relating, sometimes directly, to extratextual realities. All our studies through nature, environment, and activism are therefore rooted in a kind of realism that subjects literary aesthetics to the instrumental force of art. Second, I want the students to develop ecological empathy, to "slip into a biocentric groove," in the words of William Slaymaker, so that "they are inclined to sympathize or empathize with other-than-human life" (310). Physically encountering a site of erosion, for instance, and not just reading a moving story about it, could generate empathy for the nonhuman world, especially since the story about erosion is likely to focus on the fate of human beings, not of the earth. It is precisely this experience that I hope leads students to channel their feelings and passions into real-world activism, transforming them from participants in the class to advocates for the well-being of nature and the environment.

Between environmental issues as emplotment and lived experience, or reality, we recognize literary mediation as an aesthetic force. To understand this force, we study topics such as form and content, focalization, interpretation, and the ideal, implied, and actual readers. In responding to literary works concerned with the fate of the environment, my students unveil the rhetorical strategies that appeal to them more. They are interested, for instance, in hypothesizing what strategies a literary writer should use to get readers to empathize with the fate of nonhuman beings, especially in the context of African literature, in which little attention is paid to the suffering of the nonhuman. In probing rhetorical devices, we get to fully see one of the features of Nigerian ecocriticism: namely, its ecosocial vision—that is, the "imbrications of the social and the ecological" (Slovic et al. 3). I ask my students, How do we account for the pervasive use of nature and animal metaphors in Nigerian literature? When Musa Idris Okpanachi alludes in his poem "Sail" to the *Titanic* and presents Nigeria as a huge ship sinking, only to be rescued by "sharks, crocodiles / Seals, dolphins / And sea brutes" (lines 7–9), how do we interpret his deployment of these sea creatures, which he casts in a seemingly negative light? One way is to go behind these natural metaphors to understand the sociopolitical historicity that triggered this ecological imagination, with the hope that the images, relying on the natural habits of those animals, help us understand the social dynamics that inspired the poem. If we choose this interpretive process, we are, in one breath, unveiling the habits of these animals and the sociopolitical reality the poem has emplotted.

We are likely to conclude that this poem is therefore powered by an ecosocial vision whereby nature and society are aesthetically integrative, at least at the level of metaphorization, which here represents the heart of literariness or aestheticism. The conflation of nature and culture in Okpanachi's poem is common in African literature, and an ecocriticism attentive to literary aesthetics is thus not likely to prioritize culture over nature, or vice versa. Rather, it will foreground what Roman Bartosch sees as "the harmonising potential of imaginative literature—if its status as an aesthetic discourse is taken into account" (23). But our concern with the aesthetic form of literature does not in any way undermine our emphasis on its instrumental force. Here I disagree with poststructuralist ecocritics like Bartosch, who, relying on Derek Attridge's notion of the singularity of literature, claims that "ecocriticism cannot talk about the instrumental value of literature" (280). Nigerian ecocriticism is certainly built on literary instrumentalism.

Teaching ecocriticism in Nigeria, and perhaps in other parts of Africa, requires deliberately deviating from the normative pedagogy that restricts text-based studies to classroom activities. Students need to take excursions to zones of ecology in order to appreciate the fate of biodiversity in societies where poverty, misery, and other unsavory aspects of the postcolonial condition compel human beings to brutalize nonhuman beings. But much more important is the reconceptualization of ecocriticism based on the lived experience of human and nonhuman beings mapped by specific spatiality. Students must become acutely aware of their immediate locality, its ecological dynamics, and the social and political happenings that condition it.

Teaching ecocriticism in Nigeria, but also in other nations of Africa, requires notions of place-based ecopedagogy, oriented by literary and cultural texts. This is, however, not to limit the scope of ecocritical studies, because the goal here is to focus not on one place but on various places within the nation, emphasizing what makes each distinctive. In African nations, for instance, connections can be made, depending on real (not constructed) commonalities—on similar ecologies, indigenous practices, and struggles against the ecohostile character of global capitalism. From this zone of local awareness, of being fully acquainted with issues of nature, environment, and activism in their nation and in other parts of Africa like theirs, students can reach out to other ecological experiences and epistemologies at the global level. And yet a more crucial goal is to nudge students to respond with empathy to the ecoliterary works they read in connection to the ecological zones they are able to physically experience in the hope that they transform from readers into advocates.

## Works Cited

Achebe, Chinua. *Arrow of God*. Heinemann, 1964.

———. "The Novelist as Teacher." *Morning Yet on Creation Day*, by Achebe, Heinemann, 1977, pp. 42–48.

———. *Things Fall Apart*. Heinemann, 1958.

Agema, Su'eddie V., editor. *The Rainbow Lied: A SevHage Anthology of Flood Stories*. SevHage Publishing, 2014.

Alkali, Zaynab. *The Stillborn*. Longman, 1984.

Ameh, Elaigwu. *Climate of Change*. University Press PLC, 2011.

Bartosch, Roman. *EnvironMentality: Ecocriticism and the Event of Postcolonial Fiction.* Rodopi, 2013.

Bassey, Nnimmo. *We Thought It Was Oil but It Was Blood.* Kraft Books, 2002.

Buell, Lawrence. *The Environmental Imagination: Thoreau, Nature Writing, and the Formation of American Culture.* Harvard UP, 1995.

Caminero-Santangelo, Byron. "Different Shades of Green: Ecocriticism and African Literature." *African Literature: An Anthology of Criticism and Theory,* edited by Tejumola Olaniyan and Ato Quayson, Blackwell, 2007, pp. 698–706.

Carey, Mark, et al. "Teaching about Climate Change and Indigenous People: Decolonizing Research and Broadening Knowledge." *Teaching Climate Change in the Humanities,* edited by Stephen Siperstein et al., Routledge, 2017, pp. 86–93.

Crimmel, Hal. "Place-Based Courses and Teaching Literature Outdoors: An Overview." *Teaching North American Environmental Literature,* edited by Laird Christensen et al., Modern Language Association of America, 2008, pp. 335–44.

Ekwuazi, Hyginus, et al., editors. *The Promise This Time Was Not a Flood: A SevHage Anthology of Flood Poems.* SevHage Publishing, 2016.

Estok, Simon C. "A Report Card on Ecocriticism." *AUMLA: The Journal of the Australian Universities Language and Literature Association,* vol. 96, 2001, pp. 220–38.

Gabriel, Hayden, and Greg Garrard. "Reading and Writing Climate Change." *Teaching Ecocriticism and Green Cultural Studies,* edited by Garrard, Palgrave Macmillan, 2012, pp. 117–32.

Glotfelty, Cheryll. "Literary Studies in an Age of Environmental Crisis." Introduction. *The Ecocritical Reader: Landmarks in Literary Ecology,* edited by Glotfelty and Harold Fromm, U of Georgia P, 1996, pp. xv–xxxvii.

Heise, Ursula K. *Sense of Place and Sense of Planet: The Environmental Imagination of the Global.* Oxford UP, 2008.

Huggan, Graham, and Helen Tiffin. *Postcolonial Ecocriticism: Literature, Animals, Environment.* Routledge, 2010.

Iheka, Cajetan. *Naturalizing Africa: Ecological Violence, Agency, and Postcolonial Resistance in African Literature.* Cambridge UP, 2018.

Jameson, Fredric. *The Political Unconscious: Narrative as a Socially Symbolic Act.* Routledge, 1983.

Kamal, Aliyu. *Fire in My Backyard.* Informat Publishers, 2004.

Na'Allah, Abdul-Rasheed, editor. *Ogoni's Agonies: Ken Saro-Wiwa and the Crisis in Nigeria.* Africa World Press, 1998.

Nixon, Rob. "Environmentalism and Postcolonialism." *Postcolonial Studies and Beyond,* edited by Ania Loomba et al., Duke UP, 2005, pp. 233–51.

———. *Slow Violence and the Environmentalism of the Poor.* Harvard UP, 2011.

Nwoye, May Ifeoma. *Oil Cemetery.* Parresia Publishers, 2015.

Okpanachi, Musa Idris. "Sail." *The Eaters of the Living,* by Okpanachi, Kraft Books, 2007, pp. 3–4.

Slaymaker, William. "Ethnic Ecoethics: Multicultural Environmental Philosophy and Literature." *Teaching North American Environmental Literature,* edited by Laird Christensen et al., Modern Language Assocation of America, pp. 306–18.

Slovic, Scott, et al. "Ecocriticism of the Global South." Introduction. *Ecocriticism of the Global South*, edited by Slovic et al., Lexington Books, 2015, pp. 1–10.

Soper, Kate. *What Is Nature? Culture, Politics and the Non-human.* Blackwell, 1995.

Soyinka, Wole. *Death and the King's Horseman.* W. W. Norton, 2002.

Usman, Adamu Kyuka. *The Death of Eternity.* University Press PLC, 2012.

Vital, Anthony. "Toward an African Ecocriticism: Postcolonialism, Ecology, and *Life and Times of Michael K.*" *Research in African Literatures*, vol. 39, no. 1, 2008, pp. 87–106.

Yerima, Ahmed. *Three Plays.* Kraft Books, 2011.

**Shalini Nadaswaran**

# Postcolonial Environmental Justice and Ken Saro-Wiwa in Malaysia

I teach in the English department, in the faculty of arts and social sciences, at the University of Malaya, a public university in Kuala Lumpur, Malaysia. It is the oldest department of English in the country that offers an extensive coverage of not only canonical works but also postcolonial literature and theory. As an African literature scholar in Malaysia, I often look for opportunities to integrate my passion for African literature into the courses I teach. In an undergraduate core course on critical thinking and writing, I wanted to teach an intersection of various discourses to offer a more enriching and enlightening experience for my students—propaganda in advertising, critical discourse analysis, and postcolonial ecocriticism. I found the Nigerian writer Ken Saro-Wiwa's works and the Ogoni people's oil struggle a good fit to begin discussions on exploitation, political violence, and environmental justice. Like many postcolonial nations such as Nigeria, Malaysia, which received independence in 1957 from the British, has found itself scrambling for coherence and stability and struggling with notions of belonging, place, economy, political stability, and national identity.

I concur with Adrienne Cassel that "it is important to incorporate into our pedagogy ways to help students understand that many of the problems they face are not just personal or local; instead, that they are part of the larger problem . . . more importantly, that they are not powerless in the face of these situations" (27). It was vital that students saw a link between what they experienced in their local spaces and a larger picture, that while methods and tools of oppression may differ according to context, the frameworks that govern these situations are similar. I used inquiry-based learning for this class to facilitate a discussion of how power operates in the postcolony (Nigeria, Malaysia) and the systematic policies of intimidation used by the state and elites to continuously subjugate the masses. I found Frantz Fanon's *The Wretched of the Earth* most useful, because Fanon discusses the failure of the local elite during the colonial and post-colonial periods. Fanon states that "before independence, the leader generally embodies the aspirations of the people for independence, political liberty and national dignity. But as soon as independence is declared, far from embodying in concrete form the needs of the people . . . the leader will reveal his inner purpose: to become the general president of that company of profiteers" (133).

J. A. McIntyre refers to Saro-Wiwa as a "writer and agitator," and Saro-Wiwa embodies this role in his writing as he questions his country's profiteers, the complicity of Nigeria's elite with General Sani Abacha's regime, and Royal Dutch Shell's involvement in oil production in Ogoniland in the Niger Delta (McIntyre 295). Crucial to this lesson was showing students the connections between postcoloniality and environmental issues, because "postcolonial studies has come to understand environmental issues not only as central to the projects of European conquest and global domination, but also as inherent in the ideologies of imperialism and racism on which those projects historically—and persistently—depend" (Huggan and Tiffin 6). My essay explores the devastation of Ogoniland through a text-to-world-to-self sequence and demonstrates how I use Saro-Wiwa's works as an archive of environmental justice to teach my undergraduate students how to analyze violence and repression in the postcolony.

An effective way to engage students in preliminary discussions on a topic like ecology and ecocentrism is through visuals, such as Shell's advertisements. I used advertisements I found on the Internet to familiarize my students with Shell's presence in the global oil market. These advertisements not only projected Shell's performance goals but also alluded to its environmental commitment. However, Shell's advertisement taglines are troubling because though they proclaim that Shell promotes human and nonhuman thriving, in reality "for decades Shell has been extracting oil from Ogoni, a small piece of land in the Nigerian Delta, home to the ethnic minority Ogoni people . . . [reaping] massive profits from Ogoni, [while] the people live in abject poverty and extreme environmental contamination from Shell's operations" (Leonaro). This was indeed a troubling revelation for my students, not because they were unaware of environmental concerns, but because of how advertisements create false impressions of reality. There is also a pressing need to focus on "the question of 'broadened' social justice" in such classes (Westra, *Environmental Justice* [2006] xv). My students initially failed to make the connection between the advertisements and the course themes. However, when I began to lead students into a discussion on propaganda and Saro-Wiwa's final statements to the tribunal that sentenced him to death, it produced results—a clearer recognition of how injustice is an endemic repercussion of absolute power.

In "A Walk in the Prison Yard," Saro-Wiwa writes that "the environment is man's first right" and that "man and companies unholy"—Nigerian elites and multinational corporations—have abused the land (qtd. in Westra 281). In *Postcolonial Ecocriticism*, Graham Huggan and Helen Tiffin argue that alongside the colonial project of domination, "material and ideological impositions" included displacement of indigenous people, plants, and animals (8). Thus, hegemony over the colony during colonial times—over people, land, natural resources, flora and fauna—extended to the postcolony, where Saro-Wiwa tells us that the country's elites commit "treason" by allowing companies to pollute the land because of insatiable "greed." These preliminary ideas and Saro-Wiwa's ecojustice work came together for students when they read Saro-Wiwa's final statement to the tribunal, helping them build a conceptual thread that was both affective and analytical as they attuned themselves to understanding the links between broader issues such as the systematic nature of abuse and oppression; the relationship between landscape and humans; and colonialism, postcolonialism, and the environment. Since visuals illuminate ideas, I also showed my students images of oil spills in Ogoniland. These images were jarring contrasts to the advertisements, succeeding in drawing students' attention to the realities of environmental degradation and the gulf between the content of Shell's advertisements and the reality in Nigeria.

As he does in "A Walk in the Prison Yard," in *Genocide in Nigeria* Saro-Wiwa articulates the idea that the Ogoni see the land, rivers, and streams as more than simply resources: "to the Ogoni, rivers and streams do not only provide water for life—for bathing, drinking, etc.; they do not only provide fish for food, they are also sacred and are bound up intricately with the life of the community, of the entire Ogoni nation" (12–13). Cajetan Iheka in *Naturalizing Africa* posits that

> Saro-Wiwa gestures to the significance of the more-than-human world for these African communities. More pointedly, his astute observations suggest a relationship between the people and the rivers and streams that nourish them physically but also constitute a source of spiritual replenishment. In many Delta communities, people believe in the existence of water gods and goddesses that manage the affairs of humans. (89)

Despite the clear sociocultural differences between Nigeria and Malaysia, it wasn't difficult for my Malaysian students to understand the spiritual connection African communities have to nature and that nature was more than just a provider of resources. The Orang Asal (indigenous people) in Malaysia are a clear example of people who believe in the intrinsic link between nature and spirituality, indigenous spirituality born of the land and nature imbued in their very existence. Furthermore, students had also been exposed to other African literary texts and spiritual-ethereal concepts, like one's *chi* or an *abiku* child (which is the spirit-child who dies at a young age), in my other courses, which made Saro-Wiwa's anger toward the despoliation of Ogoniland more palpable. This allowed students to consider moving from an anthropocentric stance to an ecocentric position because they were now conscious of not only human subjectivities but also the concept of human-nonhuman coexistence, which clearly needed more attention.

In his final statement, Saro-Wiwa traces the haphazard practices of various entities, devoid of consideration for Ogoniland, its people, and its natural resources:

> My Lord, we all stand before history. I am a man of peace, of ideas. Appalled by the denigrating poverty of my people who live on a richly endowed land, distressed by their political marginalization and economic strangulation, angered by the devastation of their land, their ultimate heritage, anxious to preserve their right to a life and to a decent living. . . . We all stand before history. I and my colleagues are not the ones on trial. Shell oil is here on trial . . . the ecological war the company has waged in the delta. . . . On trial are also the Nigerian nation, its present rulers, and all those who assist them. ("Final Statement" 58)

Saro-Wiwa's words were a direct indictment of Abacha and his coconspirators, who schemed and found ways to siphon Nigeria's resources. While Saro-Wiwa focuses on the abject poverty experienced by the Ogoni people, he also directs our attention to the dichotomies in Ogoniland, a distinction between a richly endowed past and the devastation of the present. He also describes Ogoniland as the Ogoni people's heritage, which informs us that nature, the nonhuman, is an integral part of the human, going beyond capitalist profiteering, materialism, and ownership (Mukherjee 55). Abacha was the leader Fanon describes as corrupt, "on the side of exploiters," a leader who saw the oil in Ogoniland only as black money to fill his pockets (134). Ann Leonaro describes the "cosy relationship between" Abacha and Shell in Nigeria, where "Shell alone accounts for just over 50 per cent of Nigeria's total production."

Iheka in the introduction to his book *Naturalizing Africa* poses an intriguing question: "if human imbrication with nonhumans has always been a feature of African societies and the literary expressions that emerge from them, why then has African literary criticism not paid much attention to the interlinkages and their ecological significance?" (6). Thought of in this context, "money-making" during Abacha's dictatorship obstructs the practice of ecological interconnection in the Delta (Fanon 135). As one Shell Nigeria official, Nnaemeka Achebe, put it, "for a commercial company trying to make investments, you need a stable environment; dictatorships can give you that" (qtd. in Leonaro). People like Saro-Wiwa with "the capacity to think beyond the human . . . [and] imagine new ways in which human and non-human societies . . . [can be] ecologically connected" were silenced and executed (Huggan and Tiffin 215). Fanon describes this policy of intimidation as "a breaking-power on the awakening consciousness of the people," breaking anyone who has the courage to stand up against ecocide (135). This power was evident when Saro-Wiwa and eight other Ogoni leaders were executed on 10 November 1995, sentenced to death in a secret military trial, like many others from the region who were condemned to die for their protest against the exploitation of their land.

In *Environmental Justice and the Rights of Indigenous Peoples*, Laura Westra proposes a "biological/ecological integrity model" as "the best possible antidote against eco-footprint crime." As she argues, "If the rights of indigenous peoples are based, first, on their rights to biological integrity and natural function; and second, these rights cannot be separated from the protection of the ecological integrity of their lands; then third, entrenching such rights would limit the freedom of Western industrial operations to commit crimes" (19). It was this biological/ecological integrity that Saro-Wiwa was proposing for Ogoniland, protecting the ecosystem from oil-extraction operations. However, the Abacha military dictatorship was heavy-handed and ruthless.

Despite understanding the outcomes of a dictatorship, my students were shocked at the blatant disregard displayed by Abacha toward human and nonhuman beings. It is perhaps the cloaked nature of their previous education and knowledge (which tertiary education is expected to unmask) that caused my students' initial reactions. Saro-Wiwa's exploration of systemic ecological crises brought to the forefront the importance of human-nonhuman links. Most important, what lies at the heart of such ecocrimes is the hegemonic power held by the oligarchic leaders of the country, as well as the use of propaganda or other tactics to hide illegal activities. The neoliberal policies that were introduced by General Babangida and executed fiercely by Abacha further cemented Abacha's hold over the nation and its resources. The convergence of these ideas is explicated best in Upamanyu Pablo Mukherjee's theory of "ecomaterialism," discussing the unchecked amassing and mining of natural resources and stemming from "a long tradition of materialist thinking about the relationships between environment and culture" (80). It was necessary to engage in a class dialogue on the inseparability of the environment from hegemonic structures such as dictatorships and policies like neoliberalism, linking everyday materiality with an awareness of endemic corruption.

Certainly then, Saro-Wiwa's final statement to the tribunal attracted the interest of my students, prompting them to comment on ecological crisis, pollution, habitat, and the destruction of biodiversity. It was important that these conversations in my classroom led students to realize that the modus operandi for construction of power and hegemony in postcoloniality extends across scenarios, nations, and continents. To accomplish this, we explored different cross-cultural frameworks and thought about the context of our Malaysian experiences and their complexities. In tutorial sessions, these implications made students uneasy because they were unexpectedly confronted with thinking about environmental issues in Malaysia and complex ethical questions about the ecosystem that included affective subjectivities (human and nonhuman) and cross-cultural and translocal parallels with the Ogoni experience. Our discussions in class were initially broad and covered many issues, becoming focused only much later during tutorial sessions.

S. Robert Aiken and Colin H. Leigh explain that in Malaysia "land clearance for agriculture, selected logging, hunting and collecting, and pollution of water bodies have taken a heavy toll on the region's fauna" (15). While I did not assign any Malaysian texts for my course, I wanted students to consider ecocritical issues in Malaysia, specifically those involving land rights. My department offers a robust English program where students take a course on literature and the environment. Because students have been exposed to key Malaysian environmental literary works by Muhammad Haji Salleh, K. S. Maniam, and Shirley Lim in that course, I did not want to repeat the same lessons in my class but merely examined these works briefly as a quick reminder for my students before linking these ideas to other Malaysian concerns like land rights. I wanted to challenge students to think beyond the literary scope they were most familiar with and to look at the boundary-crossing nature of ideas—making it possible to discuss Saro-Wiwa and Malaysia using critical discourse analysis. I posed two questions to aid this exploration: How does Saro-Wiwa's work help us understand ecocriticism and environmental justice? Do we see parallels between Saro-Wiwa's fight for the Ogoni people and developments in Malaysia? As Erin James suggests in her essay on teaching postcolonial ecocriticism, by exploring these critical links in this manner, "organically, a postcolonial/ecocritical dialogue began to emerge" as some students began to see a pattern in relation to land (James 63).

My students discussed how Saro-Wiwa's fight for Ogoni rights is like the Orang Asal's experiences in Malaysia. The Orang Asal's fight for rights over their ancestral land is a continuous struggle against unchecked logging, landfills, and land clearance for development, which ultimately leads to their displacement from their home, the ancestral forest. Over the years, efforts have been made to designate their lands as heritage sites to protect their way of life, but the process remains daunting. Communicating their ideas verbally proved slightly challenging for my students. I noticed a hesitation on their part to express ideas surrounding constructs of power and discourse. This was probably due to the shocking revelations from our class discussion on power. Their responses to written assignments displayed a better sense of their abilities. In responding to the devastation faced by the Ogoni people and the death of Saro-Wiwa, my students came back to exploring the plight of the Orang Asal in Malaysia, thinking about their individual as well as collective needs. Students voiced their shock and disbelief at Saro-Wiwa's murder and the blatant disregard to people's suffering by those in power.

I was inclined to cover as much ground as possible in this course, to help students understand the intricacies and links between literature, eco-criticism, power structures, injustice, and oppression. Therefore, for their class assignment, my goal was to get students to focus on the framework that governs power. Since I assigned Saro-Wiwa's work as part of a critical thinking and writing course, I decided that a well-known literary text should be used as a means of comparison. Students were tasked with comparing Saro-Wiwa's works with George Orwell's *Animal Farm,* using the analysis of environmental justice to discuss ideas of freedom, equality, and power struggle in the texts. The results were interesting, because students were able to make connections between text (*Animal Farm*) and circumstance (Ogoniland), recognizing the oppressiveness of unchecked power. Rob Nixon in *Slow Violence and the Environmentalism of the Poor* briefly refers to Saro-Wiwa's "generic versatility," which "places him in an established tradition of African writing," yet he notes that Saro-Wiwa is the first African writer "to articulate the literature of commitment in expressively environmental terms" (109). Drawing on these generic qualities, students discussed the dangers and consequences of absolute power and analyzed the struggle of the masses against tyranny. By identifying these ideas, students were also able to recognize "the experiences of minorities who are barely visible on the global economic periphery" (Nixon 112).

I found teaching postcolonial ecocriticism by integrating it with other discourses stimulating and inspiring. It allowed me to cover a breadth of ideas, multimodal texts, and resources that would have otherwise been taught separately. Timothy Morton, in his discussion of deconstruction as vital to ecological criticism and justice, notes that "reflection is a vital part of reality and it's politically necessary to get as many people as possible to reflect on their actions in an ecological sense." Although Morton's emphasis here was on teaching through meditation, which was not something I used in my class, his assessment of reflection as "a form of ecological action" is certainly accurate, because reflecting and making transnational parallels was useful for my students, enabling them to deconstruct previous constructs of fundamental ideas (160). Indeed, contemplation is a step in the right direction of mindfulness, especially in the context of unfamiliar experiences like Malaysian students learning about Nigerian ecologies.

Students' final essays are a good gauge of the success of comparative learning, because "one judge of the course's ability to stimulate a postcolonial ecocritical dialogue lies in the range of topics presented by the end-of-term papers" (James 68). Students made intriguing and insightful comments on the similarities between the structures of power in *Animal Farm* and Saro-Wiwa's fight for the Ogoni. They also found nuanced ways to relate the aforementioned to either the Orang Asal's plight or other environmental struggles in Malaysia. From an informal feedback session I had with the students at the end of the course, I learned that they found this comparative exercise helpful "in their understanding of a potential postcolonial ecocritical dialogue" that also culminated in a recognition of the connections between larger constructs that govern power and discourse (James 68). It was clearly an illuminating exercise for students to have different approaches come together in a course as well as a syllabus designed to elicit and deconstruct ideas in a critical manner.

When I first discovered Saro-Wiwa's fight for his people and his judicial murder, as a young postgraduate student, concepts of power, hegemony, racism, ethnic hatred, and indifference that I learned about in my postcolonial literature classes made me realize that marginalization was preponderant across geographic spaces. When I became a university lecturer, I saw that the challenge in teaching this kind of material lies in helping students make a conscious move from a capitalist, materialistic mindset to perhaps a cultivation of environmental consciousness, because the human-nonhuman predicament is inextricably linked to conditions of power regardless of country.

## Works Cited

Aiken, Robert S., and Colin H. Leigh. "On the Declining Fauna of Peninsular Malaysia in the Post-colonial Period." *Ambio*, vol. 14, no. 1, 1985, pp. 15–22.

Cassel, Adrienne. "Walking in the Weathered World." Garrard, pp. 27–36.

Fanon, Frantz. *The Wretched of the Earth.* Grove Press, 1963.

Garrard, Greg, editor. *Teaching Ecocriticism and Green Cultural Studies.* Palgrave Macmillan, 2012.

Huggan, Graham, and Helen Tiffin. *Postcolonial Ecocriticism: Literature, Animals, Environments.* Routledge, 2010.

Iheka, Cajetan. *Naturalizing Africa: Ecological Violence, Agency and Postcolonial Resistance in African Literature.* Cambridge UP, 2018.

James, Erin. "Teaching the Postcolonial Ecocritical Dialogue." Garrard, pp. 60–71.

Leonaro, Ann. "Crimes of Shell." *Economic and Political Weekly*, vol. 32, no. 36, 1997, p. 2226.

McIntyre, J. A. "The Writer as Agitator: Ken Saro-Wiwa." *Africa Spectrum*, vol. 31, no. 3, 1996, pp. 295–311.

Morton, Timothy. "Practising Deconstruction in the Age of Ecological Emergency." Garrard, pp. 156–66.

Mukherjee, Upamanyu Pablo. *Postcolonial Environments: Nature, Culture and the Contemporary Indian Novel in English*. Palgrave Macmillan, 2010.

Nixon, Rob. *Slow Violence and the Environmentalism of the Poor*. Harvard UP, 2011.

Saro-Wiwa, Ken. "Final Statement to the Tribunal." 1995. *African Literatures*, edited by Frank Schulze-Engler and Geoffrey V. Davis, Wissenschaftlicher Verlag Trier, 2013, pp. 57–59.

———. *Genocide in Nigeria: The Ogoni Tragedy*. Saros International Publishers, 1992.

Westra, Laura. *Environmental Justice and the Rights of Indigenous Peoples: International and Domestic Legal Perspectives*. Earthscan, 2008.

———. *Environmental Justice and the Rights of Unborn and Future Generations: Law, Environmental Harm and the Right to Health*. Earthscan, 2006.

**Kristin Lucas and Gyllian Phillips**

# Narrative Close Reading and Land Education: "On the Wings of This Prayer" and *Medicine Walk*

This essay was written at Nipissing University in North Bay, Ontario, a small city situated on Nipissing territory, part of the traditional territory of the Anishinaabeg peoples, and within the lands protected by the Robinson Huron Treaty of 1850. It was written in early spring, though here that means late winter: lots of snow still on the ground, nights below freezing, days just above—maple syrup time. Our discussion of postcolonial pedagogy responds to the calls to action from the Truth and Reconciliation Commission (TRC)—a sweeping inquiry into the terrible harm perpetrated on Indigenous people in Canada by the Indian residential school program, in effect from 1884 to 1996. One of the central claims in the TRC's reports, which were released in 2015, is that this education system bears considerable responsibility for the trauma and violence, cultural genocide, and disenfranchisement that Indigenous people in Canada still experience today. The TRC recommends that some of the remediation for this harm begin in the education system, and as settler academics we have felt increasingly compelled to respond to these calls in our classrooms (Truth and Reconciliation Commission 1, 7).

This essay outlines some of the practical approaches we have used in our efforts to decolonize English studies at Nipissing University by bringing into our courses a sustained consideration of land in Indigenous texts. By performing close reading, studying genre, and situating the texts we read on the land we inhabit and share, we aim to engage settler students in a consideration of the daily effects of colonization and to open a more welcoming space for Indigenous students. Developing an awareness of the links among literature, land, and decolonization helps students shift their conceptions of the environment from objective to relational. These pedagogical objectives have implications beyond the academy, and that scope may seem a lot to ask of a given class. But, to a great extent, the literature we read enables these aims.

The works we address are a short story by Richard Van Camp (Dogrib-Tlcho), "On the Wings of This Prayer," and a novel by Richard Wagamese (Ojibwe), *Medicine Walk*. Although we teach these texts in separate courses—Kristin Lucas teaches "On the Wings of This Prayer" in Indigenous Literatures of North America, and Gyllian Phillips teaches *Medicine Walk* in Into the Wild—we bring them together here because they engage both with the displacement of Indigenous people and knowledges and with the need for a relationship with land that is mutual and sustainable. These stories, in other words, dwell at the nexus of postcolonial and ecological concerns—as does a great deal of contemporary Indigenous fiction. The texts themselves teach us how to be attentive to and within this space. They help us think critically about the prevailing Euro-Western approach to land and the long-accumulating ramifications—literary, personal, social, and ecological—of that approach. Our pedagogy begins with the premise that knowledge is conveyed in many forms, and we see these works and our teaching of them as one response to the disjunction between postcolonial studies and ecocriticism detailed by Greg Garrard, Graham Huggan and Helen Tiffin, and Rob Nixon as well as to the challenge to place-based pedagogy by scholars such as Kate McCoy, Eve Tuck, and Marcia McKenzie (*Land Education*).

Nothing we undertake is radically different from many close-reading practices. For instance, Jonathan Culler suggests that navigating complexity and opacity is foundational to the endeavor and that close reading "need not involve detailed interpretation of literary passages" but may attend "to how meaning is produced or conveyed" (22). And Paul Duck calls on the pedagogy of close reading "to register [language's] materiality" (18). These positions largely align with our own, but the differences, detailed below, reflect our pedagogical aims.

A point Culler makes toward the end of his essay "The Closeness of Close Reading" reveals where our scheme diverges from his: "the notion of closeness might alert us to the importance . . . of remaining close to the language of the text . . . instead of treating portions of a text that have been closely examined as markers for a reading whose interests lie altogether elsewhere" (23). Our interest is neither bound within the text nor "altogether elsewhere": it is both. We don't see a necessary incongruity between focusing on language and engaging with environmental and political concerns that exceed it. Indeed, it is through an in-depth consideration of linguistic and formal features that we begin to apprehend a narrative's conception of land and the various conflicts surrounding it.

This attention to the world within and beyond the text is not only a critical practice, it is a pedagogical one. All of us in the classroom, settler and Indigenous, have diverse lived experiences with land; these experiences are personal, cultural, and political, and they are relevant to our reading and discussion. Culler identifies close reading as a method that requires instruction, despite a widespread assumption to the contrary (22): close reading is foundational to our teaching, but we do not start from an assumption that the classroom is homogeneous, nor do we attribute an ahistorical transparency to text and practice.

## Take Time to Consider Detail and Possibility

For Culler, close reading is slow reading; it "enjoins looking at rather than through the language of the text" (23) and has a pressing significance for Indigenous literatures. There is a long history of appropriating Indigenous stories and treating them as deracinated objects to be interpreted, as if stories had nothing to do with conveying knowledge, and as if knowledge was the exclusive purview of the academy. Our first goal is to foster a disposition toward the text that is respectful and thoughtful, to receive the story being told with humility and compassion. We approach this objective through readings about appropriation, knowledge, and hierarchy (e.g., Battiste and Henderson; Coleman; Eigenbrod; Lowan-Trudeau; McKegney; Robinson), and we ask ourselves and our students to remember the history of appropriation in our discussion. Privileging listening and receiving, and thinking carefully about literary nuance and detail, are not new; we believe it is crucial to read from a place of respect, and not a presumption of mastery.

## Make Room for Experience and Affect

To Erin James's suggested mindfulness of how "a text's language and form encode a construction of and subsequent interaction with a text's environment" (66), we add a consideration of what is lost when feeling and embodiment are removed from literary studies, and what is gained when we welcome them. The Indigenous ecological fiction we read is about the relation between land and people, and our second goal is to reflect on our own relation to land and to its exploitation. We may begin with something as simple as taking a walk in the woods, or making time to talk about and acknowledge our fears about climate change. The intimate ties between these reflective experiences and the stories we read need to become a conscious part of classroom practice. As Delores Calderon suggests, "land education takes up what place-based education fails to consider: the ways in which place is fundamental to settler colonialism" (33).

## Teaching "On the Wings of This Prayer" (Kristin Lucas)

Daniel Heath Justice refers to Indigenous literature as "the storied expression . . . of the living relationship between the People and the world" ("'Go Away'" 150), and one of my pedagogical aims when I teach Richard Van Camp's short story "On the Wings of This Prayer" is for us to consider that world, and its attendant responsibilities, in the present tense. To that end, the course focuses on contemporary Indigenous literatures of North America, and it is organized around depictions of conflict between Indigenous persons and repressive mechanisms of the state. The texts we study represent conflict in three realms: government and law, school and education, and land and ecology. These are not, of course, discrete areas, and numerous texts elicit a consideration of the ways they converge and the effects of that convergence. The course concludes with a unit on land for two reasons: first, because Indigenous ecofiction reveals the profound differences between settler-colonial uses of land and Indigenous knowledges about land and, second, because the subjects of these texts—land, resource extraction, and climate change—tend to matter enormously to students. The sense of urgency we feel about the world around us helps bring into focus the scope and the immediacy of the ideological conflicts studied in the course. Van Camp's short story about widespread ecological devastation is the final work we read. Its zombies and dystopian landscape are conventions many students are familiar with, and "Wings" brings them to bear on the intersection of climate change, resource extraction, and incursions into traditional territory. The setting is largely unspecified, but the events appear to take place in Northern Alberta; the one named location is the Alberta tar sands. The tar sands are bitumen deposits that are being extracted on a scale that renders vast areas of land utterly unrecognizable. "The Alberta Tar Sands," a photographic essay published in 2014 in *The Atlantic*, conveys a sense of the scale of that destruction (Korol). In Van Camp's story, this ecocide has fittingly monstrous effects—it releases hoards of Wheetagos, or zombies (both words are used), which devour humans and animals and leave almost no creatures alive on land or in water (only winged creatures survive). Across this dystopian landscape, the narrator, Four Blankets Woman, and a boy named Thinksawhile travel "downwind, upwind and through the fog. East. Always moving east" (13). Theirs is a story of tracking and being tracked, of outmaneuvering and killing predators that are constantly "getting smarter, crueller" (13).

While the story has elements that make it accessible and fun, it also contains challenging narrative features, which are ultimately why close reading has a significant payoff. As Conrad Scott has discussed, the story's temporal cues are ambiguous, making it hard for the reader to stay oriented in time. In the first sentence, the narrator introduces two stories that his grandfather told him; the dystopian Wheetago narrative appears to take place in the future, though it is tied to these stories in the past; at the end of "Wings," the Wheetago narrative is revealed to be a dream given to the narrator so that he, and by extension we, can respond before the crisis becomes insurmountable. Because of this temporal complexity, students report finding the story disorienting and, occasionally, even a little frustrating (Scott 76). I'm okay with that, and initially my goal is not to lecture about, explain away, or minimize feelings of confusion. Indeed, I want us to remain there, experience disorientation, and do the work (Culler's slow reading) of puzzling our way into a fuller understanding of the text.

To that end, we think together about the temporal contours of "Wings." By their third year in college, literature students know that close reading involves paying attention to detail and pattern, and we draw on that skill to gather up temporal references and markers. In class, initially in small groups, and then as a whole, we work through the text to collectively develop a better understanding of the "when" of the story as well as the ways Van Camp crafts ambiguity. Students need to understand the when of the story to move forward with it, and their understanding is guided by prompts like, Identify temporal references or cues you find significant, noting the verb tenses used. What events seem to happen in the past? Which ones seem to happen in the future? What people, places, and actions connect past and future? To encourage students to examine the ways Van Camp crafts ambiguity, I ask them to reflect on specific areas in the story where time is confusing, and our discussion is guided by prompts like, Identify passages where you feel lost or where the relation between events is confusing. Suggest reasons for your confusion about a specific moment. What features of the text shape disorientation? Spending time on time aligns with Culler's suggestion, noted above, that close reading can be productively directed to understanding how meaning is produced.

Staying with the disorientation is important because whatever explanation I might give isn't going to alter the reading experience itself, and because the uncomfortable sensation of being a bit adrift is crucial to understanding the story. Here is where we get back to the story's ecological concerns. When "Wings" asks us to dwell in uncertainty and experience the feeling of temporal dislocation, it effectively swaps time and space. It is a story about crisis and loss brought about by industrial-scale resource extraction and the upheaval of the world—seen in the resurrection of the Wheetago—due to climate change. The characters in "Wings" undergo a wholesale evisceration of their land and lives, and the spatial dislocation they navigate is made palpable to the reader through temporal dislocation within the narrative. My goal is to reach the ecological concerns of the story not by quickly skirting over the experience of reading but by acknowledging it and understanding it from the inside.

Although the story's temporal markers are nebulous, it is full of physical and emotional detail. We conclude with the story's focus on emotion because it readily invites a consideration of relationality. "Wings" contains striking expressions of love, grief, and fear, and attending to them foregrounds networks of kinship and responsibility (Justice, "Go Away" 150, *Why Indigenous Literatures Matter* 33–43) that are world-making in the midst of a dystopian landscape. These networks are capacious, encompassing the natural world, linking past and future, and even reaching beyond story to the reader. In this last gesture, we are called on to examine our relation to land and petrol, and—if we wish to respond to climate crisis—to acknowledge our responsibilities. Discussion questions and prompts could include, What acts of love and care occur in the story? What acts of violence? What doesn't violence dismantle? Identify moments when the second person "you" appears in the story. What is "you" asked to do? What actions do you take in response to climate change? "Wings" is a hopeful story; do you share its optimism?

"Wings" pairs well with a wide range of Indigenous ecofiction, and four other texts in particular could make productive companions on a syllabus: Louise Erdrich's novel *Tracks*, Cherie Dimaline's novel *The Marrow Thieves*, Waubgeshig Rice's postapocalyptic novel *Moon of the Crusted Snow*, and Leanne Betasamosake Simpson's story "Big Water." Resource extraction (logging-deforestation), land rights, and storytelling are central to *Tracks*. In *The Marrow Thieves*, climate crisis has upended the world and the ability to dream is lost to everyone but Indigenous people, who are hunted for their marrow, essential for the widespread recovery of dreaming. In *Moon of the Crusted Snow*, a northern Anishinaabe community contending with lost infrastructure is visited by a disturbing stranger, reminiscent of the Wendigo, asking for shelter. These recent novels by Dimaline and Rice share with "Wings" a focus on catastrophe, settler colonialism, and rapacious consumption. Finally, in "Big Water," Chi'Niibish (Lake Ontario) is a living entity with agency and the ability to text. Simpson's story shares with Van Camp's an environment that is out of balance and the possibility that we might just be humble enough to listen and make amends.

## Teaching *Medicine Walk* (Gyllian Phillips)

If "On the Wings of This Prayer" offers an opportunity to feel and think about the disorientation and displacement caused by colonialism, capitalism, and climate change, *Medicine Walk* is an example of a story in which land becomes reinhabited through narration. In the classroom, I have students discover through close reading of genre how the novel rethinks the classic (and colonial) adventure trope to shift an ontological relation with land from one of mastery and ownership, or displacement, to one of interdependence. When I take the class outdoors, I work toward a land-based critical practice that makes space for an embodied dimension of reading that brings an affective experience of land to students' responses to the text. Whereas in studying Van Camp's story students are engaged in developing a robust critical analysis of industrial degradation, colonial occupation, and climate change, in the study of *Medicine Walk* we build a restorative reading practice and an epistemological shift in human-land relations.

I teach *Medicine Walk* in a small fourth-year seminar in the context of wilderness adventure narratives—such as Jack London's novel *Call of the Wild*, the film *Into the Wild*, and Cheryl Strayed's memoir *Wild*—written from settler perspectives. We focus on the way in which these other narratives provide an affective response to the environment while, at the same time, erasing Indigenous presence on the land. The conventional adventure story shares some rhetorical features with the pastoral, as outlined by Graham Huggan and Helen Tiffin, in which colonial "entitlement operates as a legislative mechanism for the recognition of affective ties to land" (81). In both modes, affective response by settlers to nature, wild or pastoral, is represented as originary and thus confers an implicit ownership of space. For students, close reading of narrative involves unpacking this political and textual mythmaking by discovering the "legislative" process of erasure of Indigeneity and its replacement by settler experience. This is particularly challenging for students since it entails looking for what is not said, not acknowledged, which parallels Culler's notion that the reader "needs to be willing to take seriously the difficulties of singular, unexpected turns of phrase, juxtapositions, and opacity" (22). Students, especially settler students, must deploy close reading to find the omissions and occlusions of Indigenous people and histories in settler adventure stories. This kind of defamiliarizing is an example of how close reading and Culler's notion of ideologically inflected analysis as somehow "elsewhere" are at odds.

Richard Wagamese's novel takes the adventure story and shakes it loose from its roots in individual mastery. Instead, the protagonist, Franklin Starlight, becomes powerful as he realizes his own connection with land and as he reluctantly learns to care for his dying father. In the novel, the sixteen-year-old Frank agrees to take his estranged father out on the land to die and be ceremonially buried. The narrative voice is conversational and carries the marks of an oral story, which helps generate a stylistic trope familiar in Indigenous literature, that of storytelling. As Warren Cariou has pointed out, oral storytelling "'keeps and transforms' the meaning through embodied practices" (475), and this evocation of the oral tradition is part of Wagamese's rhetorical strategy in building an adventure novel that privileges relationality and embodiment.

In the classroom, we perform close reading to find the markers and meaning of the oral, embodied traditions of storytelling, the significance of the text as a print novel, and the connections to the land experience embedded in the text. In comparing *Medicine Walk* to stories like *Call of the Wild*, *Into the Wild*, and *Wild*, our close readings of passages are guided by questions like, Is the hero identified more by mastery and acquisition of power or by relations and the acquisition of humility and compassion? Where do we find the textual and verbal markers of oral storytelling and written tradition and how do we interpret the overlaps and the tensions between them? In this course students learn how land-based knowledge can participate in a narrative and how that participation can shift the colonial assumptions of land ownership. When the text and the discussion engage "directly with settler-European ways of thought . . . , the self-replicating, self-reinforcing dominance of colonial epistemologies [can] be disturbed and interrupted" (Coleman 22). Students discover the colonial ideology in conventional adventure narrative and then unpack the way it is disrupted in the texts of Indigenous writers.

I have brought students into relation with local Indigenous expertise by inviting a Nipissing First Nations elder into the classroom to talk about land and healing philosophy in Anishinaabeg practice (McLeod-Shabogesic). As the semester goes on, I have the students engage in a number of place-based practices. For example, rather than reciting a standard land or territorial acknowledgment at the start of the course (for more on land acknowledgments, see King), I work with the students to build one together; I ask each student to tell a story about their personal relation to the land and to research some element of local colonial history. We also hold an entire class outside, during which I ask students to spend one minute in mindful contemplation of an element of nature around them, to discuss what thoughts arose during their contemplation, and to link these thoughts to a reading on the syllabus. What value do these kinds of active engagements with the land bring to the close reading of texts? The intersections between physical and affective experiences of the outside open concrete ways of thinking about "reinhabitation and decolonization" of the land under our feet (Lowan-Trudeau 512). I would argue, as well, that these activities offer a fundamental source of meaning, equal to conventional textual meaning, to draw on as we consider how land is reclaimed through experience in *Medicine Walk*, and indeed in all the books we read.

We then bring that knowledge back to the text and explore the ways in which the very architecture of space is created in the novel through the language of sensory experience in a passage such as this one: "When the kid alit he could smell the fecund bog of the meadow, the seep of it just below the grass. There were hints of cedar on the breeze. The sun splayed across his face and he closed his eyes against it and he could hear the creek jostle its way through the outcrops of rock" (Wagamese 128). Our close-reading discussion questions and activities might be something like this: Compile a list of sensory terms. How do these construct the space of the passage? What meaning does each sensation convey? How does Frank's sensory experience contribute to his building of knowledge in the narrative? How does *our* sensory experience translate into a fuller reading of the story? The aim of these discussions is to foster a deep engagement that includes "the savoring and the word-by-word nose-to-the-ground modes" of analysis favored by Culler (24). Adding to the Culler model, we also bring into the discussion more materially derived epistemologies to help us explore the language of Wagamese's novel. Indeed, a close reading *and* land-based methodology are invited by the novel itself. Frank learns from his experiences on the land where "there was no need for elevated ideas or theories or talk" (4). This mode of learning sounds similar to Simpson's idea that "land is pedagogy," where "'[t]heory' is generated and regenerated continually through embodied practice and within each family, community, and generation of people. Theory isn't just an intellectual pursuit. It is contextual and relational. It is intimate and personal with individuals themselves holding the responsibilities for finding and generating meaning within their own lives" (*As We Have Always Done* 151). Simpson's call for land as pedagogy is specific to Indigenous knowledge-keeping-and-generating traditions embedded in practice and ceremony on the land and within Indigenous communities. While certainly a challenge for the contemporary classroom and non-Indigenous faculty member, Simpson's ideas nevertheless can help make the space where experience of land can be brought into connection with embodied experiences of text. To my mind, this is the level of engagement and "savoring" required by Culler, but amplified and extended by bringing the knowledge held by the reading bodies into the classroom with the text.

Ashley Courchene, Daniel Heath Justice, and Pamela Palmater have detailed ways—from teaching to hiring practices to pension holdings—that "reconciliation" in higher education remains deeply flawed. Justice observes that the term *reconciliation* has "become the shorthand" for truth and reconciliation, and truth has been "largely dropped from the discussion." In Justice's account, without truth there is no reconciliation, because actions are "devoid of the accountability that comes from hearing, embracing, and answering to the truth" ("'Go Away'" 158). When we teach Indigenous texts about land, we don't suppose doing so produces reconciliation. But it does open up conversations about settler-colonial relationships to land, and the texts themselves offer a form of truth to which we are accountable.

Accountability begins in many ways, and to give a flavor of how our students have responded to these teaching practices we'll conclude with two anecdotes drawn from our courses. In Indigenous Literature, when the class read about appropriation, Kristin asked if anyone wondered why a white settler academic was teaching this course. To be sure, there are many reasons students might not be comfortable taking up that question, but it was striking that the student who responded first was Indigenous. Her bravery in the moment initiated a conversation about university hiring, research, and teaching that helped us reflect on our assumptions about higher education and our role within it, a reflection that carried into our study of literature.

At the start of the Into the Wild seminar, Gyllian was about to give a land acknowledgment, similar to the one at the start of this essay, but on the spur of the moment she instead asked the students to share their individual knowledge about the cultures and histories of the region where Nipissing is built and their experiences of land. As we talked, we created a collective land acknowledgment. The students were uncomfortable at first but ultimately energized by naming colonialism directly, by the shift of classroom voice and authority, and by the acknowledged value of their own knowledge and experience. Perhaps partly in response to this shift in the classroom dynamic, the two Indigenous students in the class assumed a role of intellectual and political leadership, and their guidance, experience, and wisdom throughout the semester helped the rest of us read "in a good way"—respectfully, closely, and with accountability.

## Works Cited

Battiste, Marie, and James (Sákéj) Youngblood Henderson. *Protecting Indigenous Knowledge and Heritage.* UBC Press, 2000.

Calderon, Dolores. "Speaking Back to Manifest Destinies: A Land-Based Approach to Critical Curriculum Inquiry." *Land Education,* edited by Kate McCoy et al., Routledge, 2016, pp. 24–36.

Cariou, Warren. "Who Is the Text in This Class? Story, Archive and Pedagogy in Indigenous Contexts." *Learn, Teach, Challenge: Approaching Indigenous Literatures,* edited by Deanna Reder and Linda M. Morra, Wilfrid Laurier UP, 2016, pp. 467–76.

Coleman, Daniel. "Towards an Indigenist Ecology of Knowledges for Canadian Literary Studies." *Studies in Canadian Literature*, vol. 37, no. 2, 2012, pp. 5–31.

Courchene, Ashley. "A Move toward Conciliation in Academia." *Academic Matters*, Spring 2019, academicmatters.ca/a-move-towards-conciliation-in -academia/.

Culler, Jonathan. "The Closeness of Close Reading." *ADE Bulletin*, no. 149, 2010, pp. 20–25.

Dimaline, Cherie. *The Marrow Thieves*. Cormorant Books, 2017.

Duck, Paul. "Making Sense of Close Reading." *Changing English*, vol. 25, no. 1, 2018, pp. 14–28.

Eigenbrod, Renate. *Travelling Knowledges: Positioning the Im/migrant Reader of Aboriginal Literatures in Canada*. U of Manitoba P, 2005.

Erdrich, Louise. *Tracks*. Henry Holt, 1988.

Garrard, Greg, editor. *Teaching Ecocriticism and Green Cultural Studies*. Palgrave MacMillan, 2012.

Huggan, Graham, and Helen Tiffin. *Postcolonial Ecocriticism: Literature, Animals, Environment*. Routledge, 2010.

*Into the Wild*. Directed by Sean Penn, performances by Emile Hirsch et al., Paramount, 2007.

James, Erin. "Teaching the Postcolonial/Ecocritical Dialogue." Garrard, pp. 60–71.

Justice, Daniel Heath. "'Go Away, Water!': Kinship Criticism and the Decoloni-zation Impulse." *Reasoning Together: The Native Critics Collective*, edited by Craig S. Womack et al., U of Oklahoma P, 2008, pp. 148–68.

———. *Why Indigenous Literatures Matter*. Wilfrid Laurier UP, 2018.

King, Hayden. "'I Regret It': Hayden King on Writing Ryerson University's Territorial Acknowledgement." *Unreserved*. CBC, 18 Jan 2019. cbc.ca

Korol, Todd, photographer. "The Alberta Tar Sands." *The Atlantic*, 25 Sept. 2014, www.theatlantic.com/photo/2014/09/the-alberta-tar-sands/100820.

London, Jack. *Call of the Wild*. Macmillan, 1903.

Lowan-Trudeau, Gregory. "Narrating a Critical Indigenous Pedagogy of Place: A Literary Métissage." *Educational Theory*, vol. 76, no. 4, 2017, pp. 509–25.

McCoy, Kate, et al., editors. *Land Education: Rethinking Pedagogies of Place from Indigenous, Postcolonial and Decolonizing Perspectives*. Routledge, 2016.

McKegney, Sam. "Strategies for Ethical Engagement: An Open Letter concern-ing Non-native Scholars of Native Literatures." *Studies in American Indian Literatures*, vol. 20, no. 4, 2008, pp. 56–67.

McLeod-Shabogesic, Larry. "Healing." ENGL 4547: Into the Wild, Nipissing University, North Bay, Ontario, 15 Nov. 2017. Talk with students.

Nixon, Rob. "Environmentalism and Postcolonialism." *Postcolonial Studies and Beyond*, edited by Ania Loomba et al., Duke UP, 2005, pp. 233–51.

Palmater, Pamela. "Reconciliation with Indigenous Peoples in Universities and Colleges." *Indigenous Nationhood Blog*, 17 May 2019, indigenousnationhood .blogspot.com/2019/05/reconciliation-with-indigenous-peoples.html.

Rice, Waubgeshig. *Moon of the Crusted Snow*. ECW Press, 2018.

Robinson, Jack. "Re-storying the Colonial Landscape: Richard Wagamese's *Indian Horse*." *Studies in Canadian Literature*, vol. 38, no. 2, 2013, pp. 88–105.

Scott, Conrad. "(Indigenous) Place and Time as Formal Strategy: Healing Immanent Crisis in the Dystopias of Eden Robinson and Richard Van Camp." *Extrapolation*, vol. 57, nos. 1–2, 2016, pp. 73–93.

Simpson, Leanne Betasamosake. *As We Have Always Done*. U of Minnesota P, 2017.

———. "Big Water." *This Accident of Being Lost*, by Simpson, House of Anansi Press, 2017, pp. 65–68.

Strayed, Cheryl. *Wild*. Knopf, 2012.

Truth and Reconciliation Commission of Canada. "Calls to Action." National Centre for Truth and Reconciliation, U of Manitoba, 2015, ehprnh2mwo3. exactdn.com/wp-content/uploads/2021/01/Calls_to_Action_English2.pdf.

Van Camp, Richard. "On the Wings of This Prayer." *Godless but Loyal to Heaven*, by Van Camp, Enfield and Wizenty, 2013, pp. 9–17.

Wagamese, Richard. *Medicine Walk*. Penguin Random House, 2015.

**Sarah Dimick and Cheryl Johnson**

# Working with Environmental Justice Organizations in Postcolonial Environmental Literature Classes

In January 2018, students from Voices of Environmental Justice, a postcolonial environmental literature course at Northwestern University, arrived at People for Community Recovery (PCR), a grassroots environmental justice organization located roughly thirty miles south of campus in Chicago's Lake Calumet Industrial Corridor. They viewed abandoned industrial sites—once occupied by the Sherwin Williams Paint Company and the Pullman Company (of Chicago railroad fame)—that remain saturated with volatile organic compounds and heavy metals. They sniffed the air near one of the nearby landfills and noted the pipes jutting out from its surface, releasing methane. They stood on a property in Maryland Manor that once, as a farm owned by the abolitionist Jan Ton, was a stop on the Underground Railroad. They learned about chronic health concerns in the neighborhood: cancer, lupus, cardiovascular disease, and asthma. They examined the photographs and news clippings decorating PCR's office walls, documenting the neighborhood's ongoing environmental justice campaigns. Although environmental literature courses often include a place-based component, a visit to a site that features prominently in a course text, this approach—as Erin James notes—is "difficult to replicate in the teaching of most postcolonial literatures" without international travel (61). However, the concentrated toxicity, environmental racism, and corporate negligence shaping many of the texts in this postcolonial literature course also affect Chicago's South Side. Acute environmental injustices mark pockets of the United States as well as postcolonial nations. In remembering this class visit, we—Sarah Dimick, the instructor of this literature course, and Cheryl Johnson, the executive director of PCR—argue for the pedagogical potential of partnerships between postcolonial literature courses and local environmental justice organizations.

While readers of this volume are likely familiar with many of the texts taught in this course—including Indra Sinha's novel *Animal's People*, Ken Saro-Wiwa's memoir *A Month and a Day*, and Muriel Rukeyser's long poem *The Book of the Dead*—a brief history of environmental justice organizing in Chicago's South Side may provide useful context for our discussion. PCR is located in Altgeld Gardens, a public housing project now under the purview of the Chicago Housing Authority. The neighborhood's low-rise homes were built in 1945 to provide housing for black veterans returning from World War II, and the area remains predominantly African American to this day. Hazel Johnson, who moved to Altgeld Gardens in 1962, became concerned about local toxicity when her husband died of lung cancer in 1969 and her seven children complained of rashes and shortness of breath. Johnson spurred an investigation that would reveal endemic environmental injustice: Altgeld Gardens is located on top of a toxic waste site and sewage farm, it is surrounded by 50 landfills and 250 leaky underground storage tanks, its soil is full of polychlorinated biphenyls dumped by the Chicago Housing Authority, and its first homes contained asbestos insulation in the attics. This form of environmental racism—the concentration of toxins in a black community—is not uncommon in Chicago. Almost eighty percent of illegal garbage dumping in Chicago occurs in the twenty-four wards where people of color make up at least sixty-five percent of the population, and in five of the six zip codes in Chicago with the highest toxic releases, more than seventy-nine percent of the residents are people of color (Pellow 69). To resist and repair these kinds of environmental injustices, Johnson founded PCR, which officially became a nonprofit in 1982. Since then, PCR has worked to hold corporations and the government accountable for environmental harm. Residents insisted that the Chicago Housing Authority comply with the Occupational Health and Safety Administration's standards during asbestos removal, a blockade of PCR protesters prevented fifty-seven dump trucks from entering a local landfill, and Johnson testified before Congress in

1993. Because of the work of PCR and other environmental justice organizations, President Clinton signed Executive Order 12898, known as the Environmental Justice Executive Order, in 1994, focusing attention on environmental injustice in minority populations and low-income communities. Since Hazel Johnson passed away in 2011, PCR and committed residents of Altgeld Gardens have continued the struggle for environmental justice on Chicago's South Side, often guiding university classes through the neighborhood and relating its history in order to raise awareness and lay the groundwork for potential collaborations.

In what follows, we reflect on the risks and rewards of partnerships between university literature courses and local environmental justice organizations. Sarah begins, offering a theoretical justification for including narratives from the South Side of Chicago on a postcolonial literature syllabus and reflecting on the value of introducing students to "toxic discourse" as both a literary and a rhetorical mode. We then turn our attention to the class visit to PCR, noting the easy slippage between place-based education and tourism and then providing logistical guidance for literature professors hoping to work with local environmental justice organizations. While integrating a local environmental justice organization into a postcolonial literature course is by no means a simple task—either theoretically or logistically—we hope that our reflections here inspire further collaborations between humanities courses and the communities that surround them. Ultimately, these connections can foster a more robust understanding of environmental justice, a shared aspiration of postcolonial educators and communities working toward environmental equity.

## The South Side and the Postcolonial

There are crucial connections to be made between narratives of environmental injustice in marginalized communities in the Global North and narratives of environmental injustice in the Global South, but the infrequent overlap of American literature and postcolonial literature on course syllabi can make it difficult to discern how "the call for environmental justice can be heard from Chicago's South Side to Johannesburg's Soweto" (Bullard 1). Many postcolonial literary scholars are understandably reluctant to include the United States in the geographic scope of their syllabi—especially in light of recent concerns that the category of global anglophone writing is diluting the political potency of postcolonial literary study.[1] However, to the degree that postcolonialism, as Yogita Goyal argues, "often names the uncertain, volatile place in the US academy where concerns about social justice meet the literary text," it is worth placing narratives from Chicago's South Side alongside narratives from Ogoniland and Bhopal, remembering that postcolonial studies "was always a comparative project, and releasing new possibilities of relation across time and space [will] only bolster the critical purchase of our frames of analysis." Recent approaches in environmental studies—subaltern environmentalisms or environmentalisms of the poor, for instance—may be useful modes for this kind of comparative work. Moreover, without domestic context, students from relatively unpolluted areas of the United States who enroll in a postcolonial environmental literature course may inadvertently come to associate sacrifice zones—the places where toxic waste, radiation, and other health risks are relegated, the sites Val Plumwood refers to as the "shadow places" of corporate industry—with distant geographies (139). Although sacrifice zones are frequently located in former colonies or occupied territories—as Naomi Klein argues, "there must be theories of othering to justify sacrificing an entire geography" to environmental degradation—it is crucial to remember that othering occurs both on the scale of city planning and on the scale of geopolitics. Environmental justice work is an arena in which voices from poor communities of color in the United States can amplify—and inform—postcolonial calls for clean water, uncontaminated air, and food sovereignty.

This environmental justice course was designed, therefore, not to dilute the categories of the Global South and Global North but to encourage students to understand these categories as conditions rather than as strict cartographies. Our work was premised on the assumption that neoliberal economics and the increasing wealth gap now produce a Global North and Global South divide "within national borders as well as beyond them," allowing for connections—and divergences—to be traced in environmental justice narratives emerging from postcolonial nations, indigenous peoples, and economically and racially marginalized communities in the United States (Trefzer et al. 3). For instance, when students read Rukeyser's *The Book of the Dead*, which depicts an outbreak of silicosis among African American laborers digging a tunnel without air masks in West Virginia in the early 1930s, they noted that the tunnel was financed by the Union Carbide Corporation, the same corporation responsible for the 1984 gas leak in Bhopal, India, fictionalized in Sinha's *Animal's People*. They considered the writing emerging from Standing Rock and the protests against the Dakota Access Pipeline beside Ken Saro-Wiwa's account of the Ogoni people's resistance to Royal Dutch Shell's devastating extractive practices in the Niger Delta, thinking about the ways in which nations or peoples forcibly contained in other nations articulate environmental sovereignty. While this course certainly sacrificed the geographic and historical precision of a course focused on a single nation or region, it highlighted routes of corporate harm and allowed students to ask what an activist movement located in the Dakotas might gain from the writing of an activist movement located in West Africa. The ability to connect and contrast disparate environmental injustices yields important insights not only for students of literature but also for environmental activists and nonprofits.

## Toxic Discourse in the More-than-Literary World

Hearing environmental justice organizers describe toxic conditions and their efforts to restore environmental health—particularly when these organizers live in the community they represent—allows students to track toxic discourse as not only a literary but also a rhetorical mode. Before visiting PCR, students in this course analyzed Lawrence Buell's anatomization of toxic discourse, the "expressed anxiety arising from perceived threat of environmental hazard due to chemical modification by human agency" (31). Seated in their circle of desks at Northwestern, students adeptly identified postcolonial inflections of toxic discourse in course texts, noting, for example, how the David-versus-Goliath scenario that characterizes many community fights against corporate polluters is exacerbated and amplified by colonial legacies in Saro-Wiwa's *A Month and a Day*. However, even though many of the texts assigned in this course were distinctly activist works, students tended to read these articulations of toxicity as purely literary, conceiving of toxic discourse as a reflection of rather than a contribution to efforts to secure and restore homelands. After listening to organizers at PCR discuss their neighborhood's growing awareness of corporate pollution and its toll on their health, the false barrier between the textual and the agential broke down. Hearing toxic discourse uttered by local advocates, observing the way accounts of toxicity circulate in backyard conversations, students began to recognize this environmental mode as a strategy, part of the craft of environmental justice work. Class discussions increasingly moved toward an understanding of toxic discourse as a tool that allows both authors and communities to increase the visibility of environmental injustices.

Visiting PCR also enhanced students' understanding of the literary works read in class. At PCR, students were introduced to the idea of "community science"—which, as it came to be employed in later class discussions, encompassed not only the labor of citizen scientists in Altgeld Gardens monitoring local air quality but also the community networks through which information about toxicity and health circulated. Students began using the term to signify the intimate knowledge of a place that can be gained only by living in it. As we read *Animal's People*, students argued that Animal's "jamisponding" (105)—the detailed observations he makes about his neighbors, his knowledge of daily patterns in Bhopal's slums, his awareness of resources, his work to distribute information across social divides—can be understood as a practice of community science. These sorts of feedback loops between the community organizing work of environmental justice advocates in Altgeld Gardens and the characters of a novel based in Bhopal are reminiscent of Paulo Freire and Donald Macedo's porous definition of literacy, which implies an ability to trace forms through both the world and the written word: "reading the world," Freire and Macedo argue, "always precedes reading the word, and reading the word implies continually reading the world" (35). The visit to PCR illuminated concepts already embedded in course readings, providing students with a more visceral experience of toxic loads and body burdens, but it also introduced concepts—like community science—that enriched their understanding of course texts.

## Place-Based Education and Tourism

Despite the many pedagogical benefits of incorporating a visit to PCR into this course syllabus, the risk of a class visit to southeast Chicago—the risk of walking Northwestern undergraduates through lead-saturated lots abandoned by the Sherwin Williams Paint Company and bringing them to the city dump that gives residents of Altgeld Gardens headaches when its vapors drift through their homes—was that students would categorize this experience not as place-based education but as tourism. Analyzing "toxic tours" much like the one PCR offers through Altgeld Gardens, Giovanna Di Chiro frames these guided trips "as a species of ecotourism," but toxic tours may increasingly be mistaken for disaster tourism, particularly the kind of for-profit disaster tours commemorating events like the Chernobyl nuclear meltdown or the Union Carbide gas leak in Bhopal (295).[2] Moreover, since Northwestern's student body is exceedingly wealthy and most students in this course were white, there was a risk that visiting brown-fields and sacrifice zones—which are overwhelmingly located in poor communities of color—would be experienced as a form of slum tourism, a domestic variation of South Africa's township tourism or Brazil's favela tourism.[3] As Kennedy Odede argues in his critique of international tourism in Nairobi's Kibera neighborhood, "slum tourism turns poverty into entertainment, something that can be momentarily experienced and then escaped from." While the localness of this class visit altered these dynamics slightly—the students were, during their undergraduate years, residents of the same metropolitan area as PCR—the vast gap in environmental conditions between Northwestern's campus and Altgeld Gardens heightens the risk of seeing the latter through a touristic lens. Ultimately, place-based education of this kind must navigate the narrow path between—or around—what Andrew Mahlstedt calls "the twin features of marginalization" at work in ongoing environmental injustices: "invisibility—for when we cannot see something, we cannot even begin to ensure social or political recognition" and "spectacle, something to marvel at, to pity or romanticize" (61). Not traversing the thirty miles between Northwestern and Altgeld Gardens would have left our own region's shadow places invisible, but in guiding students through Altgeld Gardens, we had to avoid framing injustice as spectacle by foregrounding the knowledge generated by—and the ongoing inquiries and protest work of—neighborhood residents.

Literary narratives can be powerful tools in alerting students to the risks of spectacle. Our class visit to Altgeld Gardens was deliberately scheduled during a unit on tourist narratives. By the time they visited PCR, students had read multiple accounts of postcolonial tourist economies and gained familiarity with critiques of ecotourism. We had watched and reflected on the film *Angel Azul*, which depicts an underwater sculpture museum off the coast of Cancun, and we had analyzed Njabulo Ndebele's essay "Game Lodges and Leisure Colonialists," which narrates a black South African's overnight stay in a game lodge laden with the spatial trappings of white leisure under apartheid.[4] However, the scene that students returned to again and again during our conversations is from *Animal's People*, a moment in which the main character, Animal, overhears the American doctor Elli Barber describing his neighborhood as a place that "looks like it was flung up by an earthquake." The students were preoccupied with this scene because it exemplifies the way privilege and distance become lenses through which a place is seen. "On hearing Elli speak this one word, *earthquake*, something weird and painful happens in my head," Animal explains. "Up to that moment this was Paradise Alley, the heart of the Nutcracker, a place I'd known all my life. When Elli says *earthquake*, suddenly I'm seeing it as she does. . . . Everywhere's covered in shit and plastic" (Sinha 106). Viewing and describing the homes of others can be a violent act, particularly when those homes are in sacrifice zones. As we drove back to Northwestern, students grappled with feelings of complicity in their roles as people who consume products by corporate polluters, as transient visitors able to avoid daily exposure to heavy toxins, and as residents of the Chicago metropolitan region that sacrificed Altgeld Gardens. This discomfort and unease with their environmental privilege and power is evidence of student learning. Postcolonial literary texts are in many ways uniquely suited to prepare students to reflect on their own positionalities and actively confront their environmental privilege.

## Logistics and Further Considerations

Despite their pedagogical potential, collaborations between university literature courses and local environmental justice organizations present logistical challenges. PCR became such a frequent topic of subsequent course discussions that students unable to attend because of sickness or family obligations may occasionally have felt isolated. Additionally, collaborations between universities and nonprofits require significant legwork. We met in PCR's office months before the course began to discuss the objectives of the course and PCR's expectations for undergraduate visitors. Cheryl pointed Sarah toward articles on PCR's past and ongoing efforts that students could read before the class visit, and Sarah outlined the concepts and terms students would be familiar with by the time they arrived at PCR so Cheryl could pitch her narration at the level of student comprehension. These conversations would surely have been more extensive if PCR did not regularly host undergraduate visitors, and the sheer amount of preparatory work involved may render class visits a burden for local environmental justice organizations during times of heightened advocacy. However, if a local organization welcomes the prospect of undergraduate visitors, conversations can continue over many iterations of a course, leading to refinements that strengthen the relationship between the university and nonprofit. For instance, as a final project, one of the students in Voices of Environmental Justice designed an informational brochure for people fishing in Flatfoot Lake or the Little Calumet River, providing the history of water contamination in the neighborhood and outlining the Environmental Protection Agency's and the Illinois Department of Health's recommendations for anglers. If this course were to be taught at Northwestern again, we would like to see more reciprocity of this kind, particularly through assignments that publicize the remediation priorities of local residents or inform community activists about analogous situations in other areas of the world.[5]

We want to conclude by noting the ways in which engagement with local environmental justice activists can alter the emotional arc of a course. Postcolonial environmental literature courses—much like courses on the literature of climate change—can easily acquire a declensional arc, leaving students adrift in helplessness or distress by the end of the semester. As Robert Wilson notes, environmental humanities courses addressing vast environmental crises and systemic injustices "commonly generate profoundly unempowering emotions" (57). Rather than glibly tacking on an optimistic text or film at the end of the course to boost class morale, integrating a local environmental justice organization into the curriculum can provide students with a model of the persistent care and labor required in the face of widespread toxicity and accelerating change. Observing—or contributing to—local environmental justice work allows students to conceptualize hope not as a naive response to the environmental calamities of the twenty-first century but rather, in Teresa Shewry's words, as "an attentive attunement to individuals' and communities' hard-fought struggles across decades and even centuries for a viable environmental life" (179). One student noted in an anonymous course evaluation that "hearing of Cheryl Johnson's work to defend her community was one of the most eye-opening experiences of my life." It was not the dramatic toxicity that astounded this student but rather the committed work of community organizers. Moreover, highlighting local activist commitments and campaigns early in a course can preempt the emotional shutdown and self-protective apathy that students often retreat into after repeated exposure to environmental crisis. Partnering with a local environmental justice organization is one possible route toward a pedagogy responsive to the affective repercussions of expanding knowledge of environmental injustice. It also offers students introductory training in how pain and vibrant activism commingle in environmental justice work, an affective phenomenon they will continue to experience if they decide to actively join local struggles.

**Notes**

1. See the 2019 forum "Forms of the Global Anglophone" on the website *Post45* (post45.research.yale.edu/sections/contemporaries/global-anglophone/).

2. Through a course enhancement grant that Sarah wrote, Northwestern donated five hundred dollars to PCR, roughly twenty dollars per student. This donation offset the organizational labor surrounding the visit and compensated the nonprofit for its staff's knowledge and expertise. Crucially, however, PCR uses toxic tours as an advocacy tool, not as an entrepreneurial endeavor.

3. Matthew Choi, writing for *The Daily Northwestern* in 2017, reports that approximately two thirds of Northwestern students come from families in the top twenty percent of household income and fourteen percent of students come from families in the top one percent.

4. Ndebele's essay was particularly useful for reflecting on the way a place is understood through the lenses of our own identities. Students of color, students from poor neighborhoods, and students who grew up in Chicago experienced the visit to Altgeld Gardens very differently than did other students in the class.

5. Faculty turnover inhibits these kinds of ongoing relationships. Sarah taught this course as a postdoctoral fellow in environmental humanities at Northwestern, and she has since left Chicago for a job on the East Coast.

**Works Cited**

Buell, Lawrence. *Writing for an Endangered World: Literature, Culture, and Environment in the U.S. and Beyond.* Belknap Press, 2001.

Bullard, Robert D. Introduction. *The Quest for Environmental Justice: Human Rights and the Politics of Pollution*, edited by Bullard, Sierra Club Books, 2005, pp. 1–16.

Choi, Matthew. "New York Times Report Reveals Income Imbalance among Northwestern Students." *The Daily Northwestern*, 19 Jan. 2017, dailynorthwestern.com/2017/01/19/campus/195843/.

Di Chiro, Giovanna. "Bearing Witness or Taking Action? Toxic Tourism and Environmental Justice." *Reclaiming the Environmental Debate: The Politics of Health in a Toxic Culture*, edited by Richard Hofrichter, MIT Press, 2000, pp. 275–99.

Freire, Paulo, and Donald Macedo. *Literacy: Reading the Word and the World.* Bergin and Garvey Publishers, 1987.

Goyal, Yogita. "Postcolonial, Still." *Post45*, 22 Feb. 2019, post45.research.yale .edu/2019/02/postcolonial-still.

James, Erin. "Teaching the Postcolonial / Ecocritical Dialogue." *Teaching Ecocriticism and Green Cultural Studies*, edited by Greg Garrard, Palgrave Macmillan, 2012, pp. 60–71.

Klein, Naomi. "Let Them Drown: The Violence of Othering in a Warming World." *London Review of Books*, vol. 38, no. 11, June 2016, www.lrb.co.uk /v38/n11/naomi-klein/let-them-drown.

Mahlstedt, Andrew. "Animal's Eyes: Spectacular Invisibility and the Terms of Recognition in Indra Sinha's *Animal's People*." *Mosaic*, vol. 46, no. 3, Sept. 2013, pp. 59–74.

Odede, Kennedy. "Slumdog Tourism." *The New York Times*, 9 Aug. 2010, www.nytimes.com/2010/08/10/opinion/10odede.html.

Pellow, David Naguib. *Garbage Wars: The Struggle for Environmental Justice in Chicago*. MIT Press, 2002.

Plumwood, Val. "Shadow Places and the Politics of Dwelling." *Australian Humanities Review*, vol. 44, Mar. 2008, pp. 139–50.

Rukeyser, Muriel. *The Book of the Dead*. West Virginia UP, 2018.

Saro-Wiwa, Ken. *A Month and a Day: A Detention Diary*. Penguin Books, 1995.

Shewry, Teresa. *Hope at Sea: Possible Ecologies in Oceanic Literature*. U of Minnesota P, 2015.

Sinha, Indra. *Animal's People*. Simon and Schuster, 2007.

Trefzer, Annette, et al. "Introduction: The Global South and/in the Global North: Interdisciplinary Investigations." *The Global South*, vol. 8, no. 2, Fall 2014, pp. 1–15.

Wilson, Robert. "Will the End of the World Be on the Final Exam? Emotions, Climate Change, and Teaching an Introductory Environmental Studies Course." *Teaching Climate Change in the Humanities*, edited by Stephen Siperstein et al., Routledge, 2017, pp. 53–58.

# Web Resources

### *Antennae: The Journal of Nature in Visual Culture*

antennae.org.uk

This journal's website includes images of animal and environmental art alongside critical articles, book reviews, and links to essential readings on related topics.

### *Arithmetic of Compassion*

arithmeticofcompassion.org

This website offers important psychological and environmental humanities paradigms for responding to environmental crises, many of them relevant to the conditions of postcoloniality. It contains a dedicated environmental humanities page worth examining in detail.

### *ASLE Teaching Resources Database*

www.asle.org/teach/teaching-resources-database

A project of the Association for the Study of Literature and Environment (ASLE), the *Teaching Resources Database* is designed as a hub for sharing teaching materials related to the environmental humanities and learning from the teaching of others. The database is searchable, open-access, and crowdsourced. It is designed to collect and make available syllabi, lesson plans, assignments, and exercises for a range of disciplines, on a variety of themes, and in a number of languages.

### *Covering Climate Now*

coveringclimatenow.org/

This is a useful website led by two journalists based in the United States, but it has three hundred partners from around the globe. It gathers print media, radio, podcasts, websites, television, and multimedia, locating climate stories under one banner.

### *Edge Effects*

edgeeffects.net

The digital magazine of the Center for Culture, History, and Environment at the University of Wisconsin, Madison, *Edge Effects* is a useful pedagogical resource. The posts are short enough that they are easy to assign alongside a more substantial work, infusing secondary material into a course without overloading students with critical reading. Their series on the Plantationocene might be of particular interest for postcolonial environmental literature courses.

### Environmental Justice Atlas

ejatlas.org

*Environmental Justice Atlas* is an interactive world map that allows activists and other invested parties to pin environmental justice issues by region. The issues are coded by type (climate justice, mineral extraction, water management, etc.) but also by their secondary implications, which helps students unpack how climate catastrophes are almost always interconnected.

### Environmental Protection Agency (EPA)

epa.gov/students/lesson-plans-teacher-guides-and-online-environmental-resources-educators

The EPA provides resources like lesson plans and other online materials for teaching environmental topics.

### H-Animal Syllabus Exchange

networks.h-net.org/node/16560/pages/27594/h-animal-syllabus-exchange

This web page offers a place to share and download syllabi for teaching animal studies. This H-Net site also offers a collection of book reviews, calls for papers, and discussions dedicated to thinking about animals in literature and culture.

### Humane Education Coalition

hecoalition.org/toolkit.html

The Humane Education Coalition's "Resource Toolkit" provides reading lists, classroom projects, and other resources in the areas of human rights, animal protection, and environmental ethics. The recommended reading list on the page "Outdoor Classrooms" is particularly useful for instructors teaching environmental themes.

### I Am From Project

iamfromproject.com/

This website offers a template for creating awareness of diversity and representation in the literature classroom. The poet George Ella Lyon created this during her time as Kentucky poet laureate (2015–16). The resource provides a powerful way to begin conversations about postcolonial ecofiction, offering a vehicle for fostering connections among students otherwise separated by race, gender, sexuality, class, and other categories of difference.

### *Learning to Read through Other Eyes*

developmenteducation.ie/resource/learning-to-read-the-wor d-through-other-eyes

This is a downloadable study program focusing on engagements with Indigenous perceptions of global issues. It offers excellent strategies for thinking about inclusive global citizenship.

## National Association of Biology Teachers

nabt.org/Resource-Links-Ecology-Environment

This website includes useful materials relating biology to ecology and environment.

## National Oceanic and Atmospheric Administration (NOAA) *Sea Level Rise Viewer*

coast.noaa.gov/digitalcoast/tools/slr.html

NOAA's *Sea Level Rise Viewer* allows users to sleuth out the effects of sea level rise on a specific location. Students can be encouraged to plug in two locations: one that returns results and one that does not. The locations that are not included are typically in postcolonial nations, which do not have the resources to document sea level rise. This discovery usually segues into a productive conversation about climate justice and economic inequality between nations and within nations.

### *Postcolonial Studies at Emory*

scholarblogs.emory.edu/postcolonialstudies/databases

This blog contains entries written by students introducing concepts, issues, theorists, and writers in postcolonial studies.

## Science and Education Resource Center at Carleton College

serc.carleton.edu/integrate/teaching_materials/climate_fact/index.html

This resource was developed by a collaborative team composed of humanists and scientists. The teaching module helps instructors in the sciences use climate change fiction (cli-fi) in their classes and helps literature professors use science.

### *Seeing the Woods*

seeingthewoods.org

*Seeing the Woods* is a blog by the Rachel Carson Center with posts about women and energy.

### TED Ed

ed.ted.com/lessons?category=environmental-science

This site contains a compilation of TED Talks, videos, and animations on environmental science.

### 350.org

350.org/resources

350.org is an international movement whose goal is to replace the use of fossil fuels with renewable energy sources. Their website includes guides on using the arts—especially visual arts, music, and performance—for climate activism. A sample featured work is "Rise" (350.org/rise-from-one-island-to-another/), a 2018 collaborative poem by the Marshallese poet Kathy Jetñil-Kijiner and the Inuk poet Aka Niviâna, from Kalaalit, Greenland, on the enduring environmental legacies of colonialism and military occupations of the islands. These legacies include melting glaciers and rising sea levels.

### University of Illinois

guides.library.illinois.edu/c.php?g=347015&p=2349036

This site contains useful guides for environmental education with strategies for bringing environmental issues into the classroom.

### Vanderbilt University Center for Teaching

cft.vanderbilt.edu/guides-sub-pages/teaching-sustainability/

This website includes resources useful for teaching sustainability.

### Yale Climate Connections

www.yaleclimateconnections.org

This website includes syllabi and other resources relevant for understanding climate change and other environmental topics.

# Notes on Contributors

**Sofia Ahlberg** is associate professor of English and pedagogy and vice dean of the Faculty of Languages at Uppsala University, Sweden. Her first book, *Atlantic Afterlives in Contemporary Fiction* (2016), empowers readers to imagine a future for narrative in the Information Age. Her most recent book, *Teaching Literature in Times of Crisis* (2021), provides teachers with resources for using literary form and content to respond to global crises.

**Amit R. Baishya** is associate professor of English at the University of Oklahoma and the author of *Contemporary Literature from Northeast India* (2018). He coedited *Northeast India: A Place of Relations* (2017) and *Postcolonial Animalities* (2019) and is coediting a special issue of *Postcolonial Studies* titled *Planetary Solidarities: Postcolonial Theory in the Era of the Anthropocene and the Nonhuman.*

**Byron Caminero-Santangelo** is professor of English at Indiana University. He is the author of *Different Shades of Green: African Literature, Environmental Justice, and Political Ecology* (2014) and of *African Fiction and Joseph Conrad: Reading Postcolonial Intertextuality* (2005) and is coeditor of *Environment at the Margins: Literary and Environmental Studies in Africa* (2011).

**Nicole Cesare** received her PhD from Temple University and is a lecturer in writing arts at Rowan University. Her research on cartography and the contemporary African novel has appeared in *Research in African Literatures*, *Ariel*, and the *Journal of Commonwealth and Postcolonial Studies*.

**Tjawangwa Dema** is a poet, playwright, and honorary senior research associate at the University of Bristol. Author of *The Careless Seamstress* (2019), which won the Sillerman First Book Prize, Dema has given readings in over twenty countries and taught workshops in detention centers and universities. She is an alumna of the University of Iowa's International Writing Program and coproduces the Africa Writes festival in Bristol.

**Sarah Dimick** is assistant professor of English at Harvard University. She received her PhD from the University of Wisconsin, Madison, and spent two years as the Andrew Mellon Postdoctoral Fellow in Environmental Humanities at Northwestern University. Her research focuses on environmental writing of the twentieth and twenty-first centuries, concentrating on literary representations of climate change and environmental justice.

**Sule Emmanuel Egya** is professor of African literature and cultural studies and director of the Centre for Arts and Indigenous Studies at Ibrahim

Badamasi Babangida University, Lapai, Nigeria. His latest monograph is *Nature, Environment and Activism in Nigerian Literature* (2020).

**Simon C. Estok** is professor and senior research fellow at Sungkyunkwan University. He teaches literary theory, ecocriticism, and Shakespearean literature. His award-winning *Ecocriticism and Shakespeare* appeared in 2011; *The Ecophobia Hypothesis*, in 2018. Estok has coedited several collections and has published extensively in such journals as *PMLA*, *Mosaic*, *Configurations*, and *English Studies in Canada*.

**Christina Gerhardt** is associate professor and founding director of the environmental humanities initiative at the University of Hawai'i, Mānoa, and a senior fellow at the University of California, Berkeley. She is the author of *Atlas of Islands and Sea Level Rise* (forthcoming) and coeditor of *ISLE: Interdisciplinary Studies in Literature and the Environment*.

**Stacy Hoult-Saros** is professor of Spanish at Valparaiso University. She holds a PhD in Romance languages from the University of Chicago and a graduate certificate in humane education from Valparaiso University. She has published on Latin American poetry and narrative and on Latinx children's texts, and she serves on the board of directors of the Institute for Humane Education.

**Graham Huggan** teaches in the School of English at the University of Leeds. His research straddles three fields: postcolonial studies, tourism studies, and environmental humanities. His latest book is *Colonialism, Culture, Whales: The Cetacean Quartet* (2018); other published work includes *Postcolonial Ecocriticism: Literature, Animals, Environment* (2010, coauthored with Helen Tiffin) and *The Postcolonial Exotic: Marketing the Margins* (2001).

**Cajetan Iheka** is associate professor of English at Yale University. He is the author of *Naturalizing Africa: Ecological Violence, Agency, and Postcolonial Resistance in African Literature* (2018) and of *African Ecomedia: Network Forms, Planetary Politics* (2021). He coedited *African Migration Narratives: Politics, Race, and Space* (2018) and *Environmental Transformations*, a special issue of *African Literature Today* (2020).

**Cheryl Johnson** is the executive director of People for Community Recovery (PCR). She is the daughter of the late Hazel Johnson, the "mother of environmental justice," who founded PCR to fight for environmental justice and equality in Chicago. Cheryl Johnson is a member of the Illinois Environmental Justice Commission and the National Environmental Justice Advisory Council of the United States Environmental Protection Agency.

**Roanne L. Kantor** is assistant professor of English at Stanford University. Her research focuses on literatures and media forms of the Global South as they circulate globally. She is completing her first book, *South Asian Writers, Latin American Literature, and the Unexpected Journey to Global English.*

**Rhonda Knight**, professor of English at Coker University, has published articles on a wide variety of subjects, from *Sir Gawain and the Green Knight* to *Doctor Who*. She has published a coedited collection, *Stage Matters: Props, Bodies and Space in Shakespearean Performance* (2018), and is currently co-editing a collection that explores fandoms and franchise storytelling.

**Mary Laffidy** is a graduate student studying communication at Northern Arizona University. Her research interests include the role of linguistics in public outreach and creating health equity through improved literacy and accessibility. As an undergraduate, Laffidy studied English at Coker University and specialized in professional writing as an advisee of Rhonda Knight.

**Kristin Lucas** is associate professor in the English Studies Department at Nipissing University. She has published on early modern and contemporary drama and contemporary short fiction.

**Juan Meneses** is associate professor of English at the University of North Carolina, Charlotte, where he teaches anglophone and global literatures, theory, and visual studies. He has published essays in the *Journal of Modern Literature, Afropolitan Literature as World Literature, European Review,* and elsewhere. He is the author of *Resisting Dialogue: Modern Fiction and the Future of Dissent* (2019).

**Salma Monani** is associate professor in Gettysburg College's environmental studies department, which she also chairs. She has published extensively on explorations of film and environmental justice, and on Indigenous ecomedia, and is coeditor of three anthologies. She is currently working on a monograph, *Indigenous Ecocinema: Decolonizing Media Environments.*

**Hanna Musiol** is associate professor of English and a member of the Art and Technology Task Force at the Norwegian University of Science and Technology. She publishes on American literature, transmedia storytelling, and pedagogy, with emphasis on migration, human rights, and political ecology, and she frequently organizes public humanities, curatorial, and global classroom initiatives across Europe and the United States.

**Shalini Nadaswaran** is a senior lecturer in the English department, in the Faculty of Arts and Social Sciences, at the University of Malaya. She received her PhD in English from the University of New South Wales. Her research examines the intersecting and evolving trends in African literature in local and global spaces, modern-day slavery, and postcolonial women's literature.

**Supriya M. Nair** is professor in English language and literature at the University of Michigan, Ann Arbor. She is the author of *Caliban's Curse: George Lamming and the Revisioning of History* (1996) and of *Pathologies of Paradise: Caribbean Detours* (2013). She is coeditor of *Postcolonialisms: An Anthology of Cultural Theory and Criticism* (2005) and editor of *Teaching Anglophone Caribbean Literature* (2012).

**Brendon Nicholls** is associate professor of postcolonial African studies in the School of English, University of Leeds, and acting director of the Leeds University Centre for African Studies. He is the author of *Ngũgĩ wa Thiong'o, Gender, and the Ethics of Postcolonial Reading* (2010) and of articles in *Modern Fiction Studies*, *Journal of Commonwealth Literature*, *English in Africa*, and *African Identities*, and he has research forthcoming in *Cultural Critique*.

**Gyllian Phillips** is associate professor in the English Studies Department of Nipissing University. Her articles on British modernism and postcolonial literature have appeared in *Caribbean Literature*, *Twentieth-Century Literature*, *Postcolonial Studies*, *Journal of Modern Literature*, and (forthcoming) *Studies in the Novel*.

**Jason Price** is assistant professor of English at the University of North Alabama. His research interests include southern African literature, postcolonial studies, animal studies, and ecocriticism. He has published in *Ariel*, *Configurations*, and *Humanimalia*; his book, *Animals and Desire in South African Fiction*, was published in 2017.

**Rachel Rochester** is an instructor at the University of Oregon. Her current book project, grounded in anticolonial theory and the digital and environmental humanities, considers which rhetorical strategies most effectively inspire real-world action in response to climate change. She has published on the rhetoric of interplanetary colonization, postcolonial cli-fi, and how podcasting technology can drive meaningful climate action.

**Elaine Savory** is professor emeritus at the New School. She has published widely on Caribbean and African literatures, including *Out of the Kumbla: Caribbean Women and Literature*, coedited with Carole Boyce Davies (1990), and *The Cambridge Introduction to Jean Rhys* (2009). She coedited, with Erica Johnson, *Wide Sargasso Sea at Fifty* (2020), and her book in progress is an ecocritical reading of Caribbean literature.

**Kirk B. Sides** is assistant professor in world literatures at the University of Bristol and a specialist in African environmental literatures. His current book project explores environmental and decolonial thinking in African literatures. He is a recipient of the Rachel Carson Center for the Environment and Society Fellowship in Munich.

**Brady Smith** explores the intersections of experimental pedagogy, environmental humanities, and African literary studies. His work has appeared in *Research in African Literatures, Comparative Literature Studies, Cambridge Journal of Postcolonial Literary Inquiry,* and *Safundi.* He teaches English at Park City Day School in Park City, Utah.

**Margaret Anne Smith** is president and professor of English literature at St. Stephen's University, a small liberal arts university in St. Stephen, New Brunswick, Canada. She holds a PhD from Queen's University at Kingston, Ontario, and teaches and writes on American and environmental literature and arts education.

**Jonathan Steinwand** is professor of English and codirector of the environmental and sustainability program at Concordia College in Moorhead, Minnesota, where he teaches courses on global literature and environmental justice, mentors Fulbright candidates, and serves on the President's Sustainability Council.

**Charly Verstraet** is assistant professor of French at the University of Alabama at Birmingham. His research and teaching focus on Caribbean studies, ecocriticism, postcolonial studies, and translation studies. His articles, translations, and interviews on Caribbean literature and culture have appeared in publications and series such as *Nouvelles Études Francophones, Francosphères, Small Axe Salon, SITES: Contemporary French and Francophone Studies,* Penguin Classics, and the Presses Universitaires des Antilles.

**Laura Wright** is professor of English at Western Carolina University, where she specializes in postcolonial literatures, ecocriticism, and animal studies. She is the author of *Writing "Out of All the Camps": J. M. Coetzee's Narratives of Displacement* (2006), *Wilderness into Civilized Shapes: Reading the Postcolonial Environment* (2010), and *The Vegan Studies Project: Food, Animals, and Gender in the Age of Terror* (2015). With Jane Poyner and Elleke Boehmer, she coedited *Approaches to Teaching Coetzee's* Disgrace *and Other Works* (2014).